Mastering™

IIS 7 Implementation and Administration

John Paul Mueller

BICENTENNIAL
1807
WILEY
2007
BICENTENNIAL

Wiley Publishing, Inc.

Acquisitions Editor: Tom Cirtin

Development Editor: Dick Margulis

Technical Editor: Russ Mullen

Production Editor: Elizabeth Britten

Copy Editor: Cheryl Hauser

Production Manager: Tim Tate

Vice President and Executive Group Publisher: Richard Swadley

Vice President and Executive Publisher: Joseph B. Wikert

Vice President and Publisher: Neil Edde

Book Designer: Maureen Forys

Compositor: Craig Woods, Happenstance Type-O-Rama

Proofreader: Nancy Riddiough

Indexer: Jack Lewis

Anniversary Logo Design: Richard Pacifico

Cover Designer: Ryan Sneed

Cover Image: © Ryan McVay/Digital Vision/GettyImages .

Copyright © 2007 by Wiley Publishing, Inc., Indianapolis, Indiana

Published simultaneously in Canada

ISBN: 978-0-470-17893-5

For general information on our other products and services or to obtain technical support, please contact our Customer Care Department within the U.S. at (800) 762-2974, outside the U.S. at (317) 572-3993 or fax (317) 572-4002.

Wiley also publishes its books in a variety of electronic formats. Some content that appears in print may not be available in electronic books.

Library of Congress Cataloging-in-Publication Data is available from the publisher.

10 9 8 7 6 5 4 3 2 1

Dear Reader

Thank you for choosing *Mastering IIS 7 Implementation and Administration*. This book is part of a family of premium quality Sybex books, all written by outstanding authors who combine practical experience with a gift for teaching.

Sybex was founded in 1976. More than thirty years later, we're still committed to producing consistently exceptional books. With each of our titles we're working hard to set a new standard for the industry. From the paper we print on, to the authors we work with, our goal is to bring you the best books available.

I hope you see all that reflected in these pages. I'd be very interested to hear your comments and get your feedback on how we're doing. Feel free to let me know what you think about this or any other Sybex book by sending me an email at nedde@wiley.com, or if you think you've found a technical error in this book, please visit http://sybex.custhelp.com. Customer feedback is critical to our efforts at Sybex.

Best regards,

Neil Edde
Vice President and Publisher
Sybex, an Imprint of Wiley

This is my 75th book and I thought about a dedication for it for a long time. Writing 75 books has taken 19 years and it wasn't always easy, so I thought this dedication should be special. I have so many people to thank that it would be impossible to thank everyone. Finding a particular person to thank or even a group to thank would be difficult task too, so I decided to dedicate this book to all of the readers who have supported me these many years. Thank you so much for your help!

Acknowledgments

Thanks to my wife, Rebecca, for working with me to get this book completed. I really don't know what I would have done without her help in researching and compiling some of the information that appears in this book. She also did a fine job of proofreading my rough draft and page proofing the result. Rebecca also helps a great deal with the glossary and keeps the house running while I'm buried in work.

Russ Mullen deserves thanks for his technical edit of this book. He greatly added to the accuracy and depth of the material you see here. Russ is always providing me with great URLs for new products and ideas. However, it's the testing Russ does that helps most. He's the sanity check for my work. Russ also has different computer equipment from mine, so he's able to point out flaws that I might not otherwise notice.

Matt Wagner, my agent, deserves credit for helping me get the contract in the first place and taking care of all the details that most authors don't really consider. I always appreciate his assistance. It's good to know that someone wants to help.

A number of people read all or part of this book to help me refine the approach, test the coding examples, and generally provide input that all readers wish they could have. These unpaid volunteers helped in ways too numerous to mention here. I especially appreciate the efforts of Eva Beattie, who read the entire book and selflessly devoted herself to this project.

Finally, I would like to thank Tom Cirtin, Dick Margulis, Liz Britten, Cheryl Hauser, and the rest of the editorial and production staff at Sybex for their assistance in bringing this book to print. It's always nice to work with such a great group of professionals and I very much appreciate the friendship we've built over the last few years.

About the Author

John Mueller is a freelance author and technical editor. He has writing in his blood, having produced 75 books and over 300 articles to date. The topics range from networking to artificial intelligence and from database management to heads down programming. Some of his current books include a Windows command line reference book, books on VBA and Visio 2007, and programmer's guides for Web development with Visual Studio 2005 and Visual Web Developer. His technical editing skills have helped over 52 authors refine the content of their manuscripts. John has provided technical editing services to both *Data Based Advisor* and *Coast Compute* magazines. He's also contributed articles to magazines like *DevSource, InformIT, SQL Server Professional, Visual C++ Developer, Hard Core Visual Basic, asp.netPRO, Software Test and Performance,* and *Visual Basic Developer*. Be sure to read John's blog at `http://www.amazon.com/gp/blog/id/AQOA2QP4X1YWP`.

When John isn't working at the computer, you can find him in his workshop. He's an avid woodworker and candle maker. On any given afternoon, you can find him working at a lathe or putting the finishing touches on a bookcase. He also likes making glycerin soap and candles, which comes in handy for gift baskets. You can reach John on the Internet at `JMueller@mwt.net`. John is also setting up a Web site at `http://www.mwt.net/~jmueller/`. Feel free to look and make suggestions on how he can improve it. One of his current projects is creating book FAQ sheets that should help you find the book information you need much faster.

Contents at a Glance

Contents

Introduction

Internet Information Server (IIS) has steadily collected a bigger share of the Internet server market as Microsoft has changed IIS and added new features. In past versions, the changes were incremental—Microsoft added a feature here, changed a setting there. IIS 7 is an entirely different story. Everything has changed this time. You won't believe your eyes! Fortunately, you have a light in the darkness. *Mastering IS 7 Implementation and Administration* provides the information you need to get up and running quickly. More important, you'll gain insights into how to work with the new IIS.

IIS 7, a Significant Departure from the Past

From the moment you open the new Internet Information Services (IIS) Manager console until the time you start your first application, you can't help but see changes. It's no small claim that Microsoft has literally changed everything. The interface is certainly different and you'll find that it's significantly easier to use once you get used to it. Of course, there's the problem of getting used to it and that's where *Mastering IIS 7 Implementation and Administration* can help. The opening chapters of this book discuss every new icon in detail. You won't have to guess about how something works because every feature appears in the book.

Using the interface isn't the only thing that concerns someone who works with IIS. Microsoft has set a goal of getting administrators and developers to work together in IIS 7 and it certainly shows in how the features are arranged. Unfortunately, they forgot to tell anyone precisely how this new cooperation is supposed to work. *Mastering IIS 7 Implementation and Administration* won't leave you in the dark. Throughout the book you'll find tips to help administrators and developers to work together to attain specific goals.

Microsoft changed more than just the interface. The entire IIS 7 architecture differs from what you used in the past—no more binary storage of settings. Every feature relies on XML now for settings information, which means that you have an easier time of changing features. Chapter 12 of this book describes many of the low-level details and you'll find other details throughout the book. In some cases, this book presents up to three completely different ways to change a setting so that you have the flexibility to change settings using a technique that fits your style.

One of the reasons that *Mastering IIS 7 Implementation and Administration* will help you so much is that it provides tips for developers and administrators alike. For example, if you've had trouble getting settings to change in ASP.NET applications in the past, this book provides some new techniques for ensuring that the administrator and developer can work together to perform changes that make sense. You'll find code snippets throughout the book that demonstrate how new IIS 7 features are incorporated in custom application code so that the developer and administrator can now speak the same language.

Goals for Writing This Book

The moment I laid eyes on IIS 7, I knew that it wasn't only a good change—it was a great change! The only problem is that everything has changed so much that I knew many people would have problems making the transition. There isn't any way to use your existing skills in IIS 7 because none of those old techniques exist any longer. Therefore, the first goal for this book is to help people make the changeover from the old interface. If you looked at the interface and threw up your hands, try this book. You'll be up and running again quite quickly.

However, the IIS goal that intrigued me the most was how Microsoft planned to get developers and administrators to work together as a team. The whole idea of administrators and developers cooperating in a large Web site environment is amazing and, yet, IIS 7 really does make it possible. The theme throughout this book is cooperation—working together to achieve goals. If your goal is to find a better way of doing things, then you'll find the techniques you need in *Mastering IIS 7 Implementation and Administration*.

It was only after I began writing the book that I realized how broken all of the old utilities are. I tried techniques I used in the past to make changes to IIS and found that they no longer work very well, or sometimes at all. That's why this book contains so many details. After experimenting with all of the tricks I tried in the past and finding they failed, I had to throw out that old IIS administration book (the skills I had used in the past) and come up with something new. The results appear in this book, especially in Chapter 12.

The final goal for this book was to demonstrate that you can create a secure IIS 7 setup. It's true; you'll find that IIS 7 provides significantly more security and fewer holes than previous versions of IIS. You can still shoot yourself in the foot though, so the book contains numerous caveats on things you should avoid, as well as things you'll want to try to enhance the security on your own server.

Who Should Read This Book?

This book is designed to meet the needs of administrators and developers. No, you won't find extensive coding details, but you will find a lot of usage and low-level configuration details. This book contains the kind of details that administrators and developers commonly need, but often don't find anywhere else.

I'm assuming that you already know how to use Windows quite well and that you've performed administration tasks in the past. Although I go though every icon in the Internet Information Services (IIS) Manager and Information Services (IIS) 6.0 Manager consoles, you'll still need to know how to work with administration programs before you begin this book. The complete novice won't be able to keep up with the pace of this book.

What You Need to Use this Book

You'll very likely want to set up a test server using either Vista or Windows 2008 Server—the only two versions of Windows that support IIS 7 at the time of writing. Don't use your production server for experimentation because IIS 7 is just about as unforgiving of incorrect changes as previous versions of IIS. Fortunately, wrong changes are easier to fix in IIS 7—I know; I made plenty of mistakes while writing the book so you wouldn't have to. Even so, as a minimum, you'll want to test the techniques in this book using a test copy of IIS 7 on either Vista or Windows 2008 Server.

If you want to work with ASP.NET applications, you'll probably want to obtain a copy of Visual Studio 2005 or Visual Web Developer (http://msdn.microsoft.com/vstudio/express/downloads/). The interesting part about Visual Web Developer is that you can download it free and begin writing applications immediately. It even includes a sample application (a complex application at that) so you can test IIS 7 features without writing any code.

The book contains descriptions of numerous utilities that you can download and use free for the most part. You may prefer other utilities, but I used these utilities to create the content for the book. If you find a technique useful, trying downloading the utility that goes with it and try it too. I'm always on the lookout for new utilities, so please be sure to tell me about your IIS 7 utilities at `JMueller@mwt.net`.

Conventions Used in This Book

It always helps to know what the special text means in a book. The following table provides a list of standard usage conventions. These conventions make it easier for you to understand what a particular text element means.

TABLE I.1: Standard Usage Conventions

CONVENTION	EXPLANATION
`Inline Code`	Some code will appear in the text of the book to help explain application functionality. The code appears in a special font that makes it easy to see. This monospaced font also makes the code easier to read.
Inline Variable	As with source code, variable source code information that appears inline will also appear in a special font that makes it stand out from the rest of the text. When you see monospaced text in an italic typeface, you can be sure it's a variable of some type. Replace this variable with a specific value. The text will always provide examples of specific values that you might use.
User Input	Sometimes I'll ask you to type something. For example, you might need to type a particular value into the field of a dialog box. This special font helps you see what you need to type.
Filename	A variable name is a value that you need to replace with something else. For example, you might need to provide the name of your server as part of a command line argument. Because I don't know the name of your server, I'll provide a variable name instead. The variable name you'll see usually provides a clue as to what kind of information you need to supply. In this case, you'll need to provide a filename. Although the book doesn't provide examples of every variable that you might encounter, it does provide enough so that you know how to use them with a particular command.
[*Filename*]	When you see square brackets around a value, switch, or command, it means that this is an optional component. You don't have to include it as part of the command line or dialog field unless you want the additional functionality that the value, switch, or command provides.
File ➢ Open	Menus and the selections on them appear with a special menu arrow symbol. "File ➢ Open" means "Access the File menu and choose Open."

TABLE I.1:   Standard Usage Conventions *(CONTINUED)*

CONVENTION	EXPLANATION
italic	You'll normally see words in italic if they have special meaning or if this is the first use of the term and the text provides a definition for it. Always pay special attention to words in italic because they're unique in some way. When you see a term that you don't understand, make sure you check the glossary for the meaning of the term as well. The glossary also includes definitions for every nonstandard acronym in the book.
`Monospace`	Some words appear in a monospaced font because they're easier to see or require emphasis of some type. For example, all filenames in the book appear in a monospaced font to make them easier to read.
`URLs`	URLs will normally appear in a monospaced font so that you can see them with greater ease. The URLs in this book provide sources of additional information designed to improve your development experience. URLs often provide sources of interesting information as well.
➡	This is the code continuation arrow. It tells you when a single line of code in a file actually appears on multiple lines in the book. You don't type the code continuation arrow when you use the code from the book in your own code. Rather, you continue typing the code in the book on a single line in your code. For example, you would type the following code on a single line, even though it appears on multiple lines here.

```
<add connectionString=
    ➡"Server=MAINVISTA\SQLEXPRESS;
    ➡Database=ReportServer$SQLExpress;
    ➡Integrated Security=true"
    ➡name="MySQLConnection" />
```

Part 1

Using IIS 7

- ◆ Chapter 1: Working with the New Interface
- ◆ Chapter 2: Configuring IIS 7 Features
- ◆ Chapter 3: Working with Files

Chapter 1

Working with the New Interface

To say that the new Internet Information Services (IIS) 7 interface is different from the IIS 6 interface is akin to saying that a plane is different from a boat. Anyone who looks at the new IIS will instantly see that Microsoft has made significant changes. Some people may be mystified as to why anyone would call the new product IIS, because it doesn't look anything like the previous version of the product.

Microsoft has specific goals for IIS 7 that will help developers and administrators alike to work together. In addition, they've added features to make IIS more reliable and to help it perform better. All of these changes (and many more) define an IIS that looks nothing like its predecessor and, for once, almost all of the changes are for the best. After you read this chapter, you'll agree that Microsoft has made some good decisions this time around.

Of course, the fact that the changes are good doesn't mean you'll like all of them. Some of them will affect your applications and will mean doing a little rework. All of the changes will definitely affect any scripts you have for working with IIS and you'll generally find yourself starting again at the basics. You'll find yourself asking why Microsoft didn't produce this IIS in the first place because it really is so much better.

In this chapter, you will learn how to do the following:

◆ Define a new way to manage IIS

◆ Apply the drill-down approach to management

◆ Understand the features view versus the contents view

◆ Sort features and contents in a specific order

◆ Perform specific actions with objects

Defining Microsoft's New Approach to IIS Management

One of the problems with the older versions of IIS is that Microsoft didn't encourage the parties responsible for maintaining a Web site to work together. The new IIS fixes that problem by placing a focus on the application and on the tasks administrators and developers must perform together. In addition, IIS 7 places a major emphasis on ASP.NET. Instead of being a mere add-on, ASP.NET is now a major part of IIS, which means that your ASP.NET applications will run better and with fewer errors. No longer will you need to rely on command line utilities such as ASPNet_RegIIS.EXE to fix registration problems with your IIS setup. The following sections provide an overview of Microsoft's new approach. Chapter 2 provides a detailed view of individual IIS features.

This book assumes that you've already installed IIS 7. You'll find the IIS setup features in the Windows Features dialog box shown in Figure 1.1. To access this dialog box, click the Turn Windows Features On or Off link in the Control Panel\Programs and Features folder. Installing some features automatically installs other features as needed by IIS. For example, if you install File

Transfer Protocol (FTP) support, IIS also installs some of the IIS 6 Management Compatibility features because you manage FTP using the Internet Information Services (IIS) 6.0 Manager (see Chapter 7 for details).

FIGURE 1.1
Install the IIS features you want to use by selecting them in this dialog box.

TIP   I strongly suggest that you install the full IIS 7 suite when working with this book. You can always remove features you don't want to use later. If you really want to see what IIS 7 can do, you need to install everything and test it out. Never use a production machine for an initial installation.

Administrators and Developers Work Together

In the past, you needed several different tools, along with command line utilities, to manage IIS completely. With IIS 7, you use a single tool to perform all of your work. As shown in Figure 1.1, this one tool helps you manage Web sites and all of the ASP.NET functionality in one location. You can sort the icons in a number of ways (feature name and description), group them (category and area), and show them in a number of forms (details, icons, tiles, and list). Figure 1.2 shows the default setup, which relies on a feature name sort, area group, and icon display.

TIP   Older versions of IIS placed restrictions on a client setup—in part, to force you to buy a server for some needs. IIS 7 lets you create as many Web sites as needed and it no longer has the 10-connection limit. These changes mean that you can perform real-world application testing and use a client setup in ways that may have required a server in the past.

The changes to IIS also affect Web site hosting. You can use the delegated administration feature to let a customer administer their Web site. The customer can only see their Web site and not any of the other Web sites on the server. To go along with this new setup, IIS 7 uses HTTP-based Web services for the administration tool, rather than the Distributed Component Object Model (DCOM) connectivity used in the past. The difference in communication technique means that someone can administer IIS through a firewall—firewalls often blocked the DCOM connection.

Of course, this new connectivity also makes it possible for a developer to make tweaks needed to an application from a remote location, rather than making them on site. A developer can fix any application errors faster because it's easier to get to them quickly.

FIGURE 1.2
The new interface places a definite focus on working with applications.

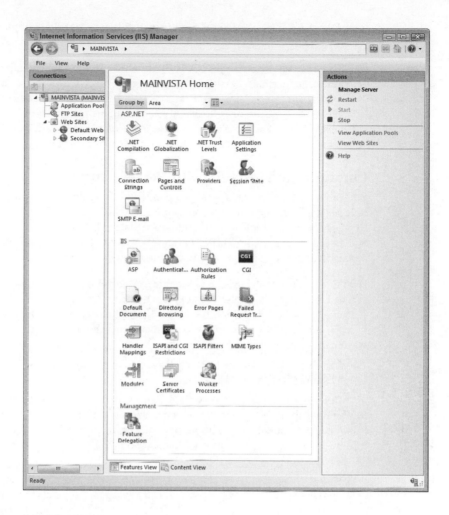

An Emphasis on ASP.NET

You'll find that ASP.NET appears everywhere in IIS 7. Some of the changes aren't immediately obviously by looking at Figure 1.1. IIS 7 doesn't rely on a single metabase configuration store any longer. Instead, it uses the same Web.CONFIG file setup that ASP.NET uses to store configuration settings. This change means that you can copy the settings for a Web site from the test server to the production server without having to rely on scripts or other messy solutions. You can also copy settings from your system to a client system as needed to support applications as a third-party resource.

The Internet Information Services (IIS) Manager has more than just a new look. Microsoft wrote this administration tool using .NET technology. What you're seeing in Figure 1.1 is Windows form technology. You can use this feature to extend the administration tool. For example, you could write your own HyperText Transport Protocol (HTTP) runtime modules and configuration settings.

Security is a significant problem on any Web site. In the past, there was a difference between IIS and ASP.NET when it came to security. You always had to write workarounds and kludges to use .NET security within your applications. IIS 7 places the .NET role-based security at the forefront. For example, when you open the .NET Roles icon, you can set the roles for .NET applications executing on the server. No longer do you need to go through some odd configuration procedure before the security on your application works.

NOTE   You must have a copy of SQL Server installed on your system to employ many of the IIS security features. For example, even though you can select the AspNetWindowsTokenRoleProvider as a provider, this choice limits you to the roles defined as part of Windows security, which means you can't configure custom roles. In short, if you want to obtain the full benefits of IIS 7, you must have SQL Server installed. Fortunately, you can use SQL Server Express, a free product, for a local setup. See "Obtaining and Installing SQL Server Express" for more details.

Obtaining and Installing SQL Server Express

You can use SQL Server Express to implement the advanced IIS 7 features on a client machine if you only need a limited number of connections or you're performing development tasks. SQL Server Express doesn't provide the robust interface that the full version of SQL Server does, but if you obtain SQL Server Express from http://msdn.microsoft.com/vstudio/express/sql/register/default.aspx, you should have everything you need.

NOTE   You'll actually see two versions of SQL Server Express on the Web site. The only time you need to obtain SQL Server 2005 Express Edition with Advanced Services SP2 or Microsoft SQL Server 2005 Express Edition Toolkit is when you need the functionality these two products provide, such as reporting services. Developers also need the advanced version to obtain full functionality with Visual Studio. Even though you don't need them to use IIS, you'll likely want to download the SQL Server 2005 Books Online so that you can obtain answers you have about configuration and SQL Server errors when they occur.

After you download a copy of SQL Server Express, either version, you'll need to install it. The following steps help you set up your hard drive and perform the required installation. You can skip this section if you haven't compressed your hard drive. SQL Server requires an uncompressed folder for installation, so you need to create one manually or the setup program complains.

1. Create a folder for SQL Server. Right-click the new folder and choose Properties from the context menu. You'll see a folder Properties dialog box.

TIP   If you have two hard drives on your system, install IIS on one of them and SQL Server on the other to gain better performance. If you have three hard drives, install the SQL Server log files on the third drive to obtain even better performance. Using a three-drive setup provides optimal performance for an IIS configuration. Three partitions on a single drive aren't the same as three physical drives. The goal is to use different hardware for each activity so the system doesn't spend as much time waiting for actions to complete.

2. Click Advanced. You'll see the Advanced Attributes dialog box shown in Figure 1.3.

3. Clear the Compress Contents to Save Disk Space option and click OK twice. The folder is now ready for use by SQL Server.

Now that your hard drive is prepared, you can begin the SQL Server installation. The following steps tell how to perform this task.

1. Double-click the icon for the version of SQL Server that you downloaded. You'll see the End User License Agreement dialog box.

FIGURE 1.3
SQL Server won't use
a compressed folder,
so you must create
an uncompressed
folder for it.

2. Read and accept the licensing terms. Click Next. You'll see an Installing Prerequisites dialog box if you haven't installed SQL Server on the system in the past.

3. Click Install. SQL Server installs the Microsoft SQL Native Client and the Microsoft SQL Server 2005 Setup Support Files.

NOTE If you choose to remove SQL Server from your system, you need to uninstall the prerequisite features separately. Make sure you uninstall the SQL Native Client as the next-to-last feature and the Microsoft SQL Server 2005 Setup Support Files as the last feature or you'll experience problems uninstalling SQL Server and its support features.

4. Click Next. You'll see the Welcome dialog box.

5. Click Next. SQL Server performs a system configuration check. When this check is complete, you'll see a System Configuration Check dialog box like the one shown in Figure 1.4. All of the checks should have success indicators. If you see a warning, check the message and try to fix the problem before you proceed. If you see an error, you must fix the problem before you proceed or SQL Server Express won't work well. In most cases, if your system runs Vista well, it will also run SQL Server Express well.

NOTE The help files provided with SQL Server Express work well with Windows XP or Windows 2000 but not with Vista. For example, the instructions tell you to open the Add/Remove Programs applet, even though this applet appears as Programs and Features in Vista. You'll need to perform some conversions for the help instructions until Microsoft fixes this problem.

6. Click Next. SQL Server performs a few installation steps and then asks you to enter your name and company name.

NOTE Clear the Hide Advanced Configuration Options dialog box if you want to configure all of the advanced SQL Server features, such as how it performs sorting. In most cases, you won't need to configure these options when installing SQL Server Express for IIS.

7. Type your name as a minimum and then click Next. You'll see a Feature Selection dialog box similar to the one shown in Figure 1.5. (Figure 1.5 shows the advanced version—the standard version contains fewer features.)

FIGURE 1.4
Verify that SQL Server Express will work on your system.

FIGURE 1.5
Choose the features you want to use with SQL Server Express.

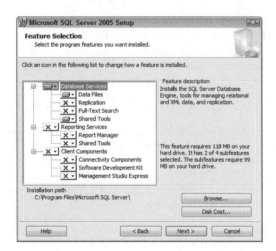

8. Choose the features you want to use. As a minimum, choose the Management Studio Express entry so that you can manage your SQL Server Express installation. Developers should choose all of the Client Components group entries. The only time you need Reporting Services is if you plan to report on IIS database entries (security and advanced features). Normally, you won't need this feature on a local machine. If you've set up special folders for your SQL Server installation, perform these additional steps as well.

A. Highlight the Database Service entry and click Browse. Choose the folder you have set up for the SQL Server database files.

B. Highlight the Shared Tools entry and click Browser. Choose the folder you have set up for the shared tools files.

9. Click Next. You'll see an Authentication Mode dialog box. For security reasons, you always want to choose Windows Authentication Mode unless you have existing code that requires Mixed Mode.

10. Choose an authentication mode and click Next. You'll see a Configuration Options dialog box.

11. Check the Add User to the SQL Server Administrator Role option to ensure you can manage SQL Server Express. Click Next. At this point, you can see one of two dialog boxes, depending on the options you selected: Report Server Installation Options or Error and Report Usage Settings. If you see the Error and Report Usage Settings dialog box, skip to step 13.

12. If you selected the Report Server option, SQL Server asks if you want to use the default configuration. Normally, you'll want to use the default configuration, so click Next to get past this dialog box. If you want to see the default settings, click Details instead and follow the prompts. At this point, you'll see the Error and Report Usage Settings dialog box.

13. Choose the error and report usage settings that you want to use and then click Next. You'll see a Ready to Install dialog box.

14. Click Install. SQL Server performs the required installation. When the installation completes, you should see a success dialog box like the one shown in Figure 1.6.

FIGURE 1.6
Verify that the SQL Server Express installation completed successfully.

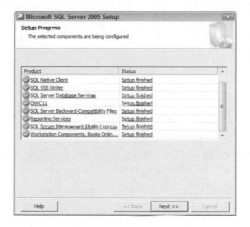

15. Verify that all of the SQL Server Express elements installed correctly. If a feature didn't install correctly, click the Setup Finished link for that feature to see the log entries. In most cases, you'll need to fix any installation errors as a separate action before you can use SQL Server Express.

16. Click Next. You'll see a Completing Microsoft SQL Server 2005 Setup dialog box.

17. Click Finish.

SQL Server Express is installed but not ready for use yet.

1. Open Start ➤ Programs ➤ Microsoft SQL Server 2005 ➤ Configuration Tools ➤ SQL Server Configuration Manager. You'll see the SQL Server Configuration Manager console.

2. Open the SQL Server Configuration Manager\SQL Server 2005 Network Configuration\ Protocols for SQLEXPRESS folder shown in Figure 1.7.

3. Right-click the TCP/IP entry and choose Enabled from the context menu. You'll see a Warning dialog box. Click OK to accept it.

FIGURE 1.7
Configure the TCP/IP protocol so that IIS can use it.

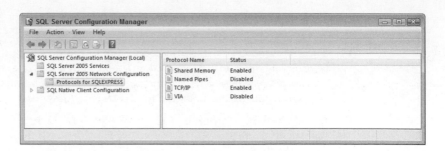

4. Open the SQL Server Configuration Manager\SQL Server 2005 Services folder. You'll see a list of services like those shown in Figure 1.8.

FIGURE 1.8
Make sure the services are set up and restarted as needed.

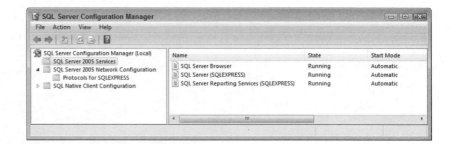

5. Right-click the SQL Server (SQLEXPRESS) entry and choose Restart from the context menu. Windows restarts the database engine service for you.

6. Right-click any other services that start automatically and choose Restart from the context menu. Windows restarts the service for you.

7. If you plan to use SQL Server Express for development, you need to activate the SQL Server Browser so Visual Studio can locate your server. Follow these configuration steps to activate the service.

   A. Double-click the SQL Server Browser entry. You'll see a SQL Server Browser Properties dialog box.

   B. Select the Service tab.

   C. Choose Automatic in the Start Mode field.

   D. Click Apply. SQL Server sets the service to start automatically.

   E. Select the Log On tab.

   F. Click Start. SQL Server starts the SQL Server Browser service.

   G. Click OK.

8. Close the SQL Server Configuration Manager. The SQL Server Express setup is now ready for use with IIS.

Using the Drill-Down Approach

Previous versions of IIS used an interface that relied heavily on Properties dialog boxes. The tabs on these Properties dialog boxes could vary a great deal depending on the features you installed. For example, adding FrontPage Extensions to your setup added another tab to some, but not all, dialog boxes. ASP.NET also added tabs in some cases. The problem is that it was possible to become quite confused as to where to find something because you never really saw an overview of anything. Everything was in its own little tab pocket. IIS 7 uses a drill-down approach to overcome this problem. You begin with an overview and then drill down to the functionality you actually require. At no time do you have to worry about becoming overwhelmed with details that you don't actually need. The following sections describe this drill-down approach in more detail.

As shown in Figure 1.2, IIS 7 uses an Explorer-like display. Choosing an entry in the Connections (left) pane defines icons you see in the Features (middle) pane and the actions available in the Actions (right) pane. Consequently, when you choose a Web site, the icons change, as shown in Figure 1.9.

FIGURE 1.9
Selecting a different element in the Connections pane changes the icons in the Features pane.

NOTE The name of the middle pane can vary according to activity. You'll find several activity-based names for it in this chapter alone.

IIS provides specific functionality at different levels. For example, when you set the .NET Compilation values for the entire site, they become the default values for all Web sites you create. However, you can set these same values for an individual Web site and it affects everything on that Web site. It's possible to go down another level and change the .NET Compilation setting for a folder or an application. In this case, the settings affect only that folder or application. Table 1.1 describes the various icons and the levels where you can use them.

TABLE 1.1: Icon Summary for IIS 7

Icon Name	Entire Site	Individual Web Site	Folder	Application	Description
.NET Compilation	X	X	X	X	Defines the settings for compiling a .NET application.
.NET Globalization	X	X	X	X	Determines how IIS handles globalization issues for .NET applications. You also use these settings to determine the encoding used for text.
.NET Profile		X	X	X	Configures the per user settings. This configuration information affects everything from the features the user can access to how the Web site behaves.
.NET Roles		X		X	Defines groups of users by the roles that they fill within an organization. For example, you might have roles for administrators, developers, managers, and standard users.
.NET Trust Levels	X	X	X	X	Defines the trust level for management modules. This feature is part of code-based security. You use it to restrict the actions that code can perform.
.NET Users		X		X	Defines a list of users for access purposes. You can use this list for authorization and as a means of determining user access to site features.

TABLE 1.1:   Icon Summary for IIS 7 *(CONTINUED)*

Icon Name	Entire Site	Individual Web Site	Folder	Application	Description
Application Settings	X	X	X	X	Lets you create custom settings for your applications. You can use these settings to control application behavior.
ASP	X	X	X	X	Defines the settings used to host Active Server Pages (ASP) applications. You can control everything from the default scripting language to the use of COM+.
Authentication	X	X	X	X	Determines which forms of authentication that IIS accepts. The default setting provides anonymous access. You can also choose to enable ASP.NET, basic, digest, forms, and Windows authentication.
Authorization Rules	X	X	X	X	Provides rules for allowing access to a Web site or Web site element (such as an application). The default setting allows all users access to the Web site as a whole.
CGI	X	X	X	X	Defines basic rules for working with Common Gateway Interface (CGI) applications.
Connection Strings	X	X	X	X	Provides connections to database managers.

TABLE 1.1:   Icon Summary for IIS 7 *(CONTINUED)*

ICON NAME	ENTIRE SITE	INDIVIDUAL WEB SITE	FOLDER	APPLICATION	DESCRIPTION
Default Document	X	X	X	X	Sets the default document—the one that the user sees when typing just the Uniform Resource Locator (URL) without a document name. The default settings include `Default.htm`, `Default.asp`, `index.htm`, `index.html`, `iisstart.htm`, and `default.aspx` as the default documents.
Directory Browsing	X	X	X	X	Determines what data the user sees when using directory browsing. IIS disables directory browsing by default.
Error Pages	X	X	X	X	Defines the pages that IIS uses to handle specific HTTP error responses.
Failed Request Tracing Rules	X	X	X	X	Creates a set of rules for tracing failed requests. IIS doesn't provide any default failed request tracing. The trace can affect a specific technology, such as ASP.NET, and a specific HTTP error. You can also set the level of output information.
Feature Delegation	X				Helps you control the delegation state of IIS features. For example, you might want someone to know the CGI settings for the server, but not be able to change them when they only have access to a single Web site.
Handler Mappings	X	X	X	X	Tells IIS how to handle specific file types.

TABLE 1.1:   Icon Summary for IIS 7 *(CONTINUED)*

ICON NAME	ENTIRE SITE	INDIVIDUAL WEB SITE	FOLDER	APPLICATION	DESCRIPTION
ISAPI and CGI Restrictions	X				Determines how IIS handles Internet Server Application Programming Interface (ISAPI) and CGI modules. IIS provides default ASP and ASP.NET ISAPI modules. It doesn't provide any default CGI modules.
ISAPI Filters	X	X			Provides a means of configuring ISAPI filters on IIS.
MIME Types	X	X	X	X	Defines the Multipurpose Internet Mail Extensions (MIME) types for certain file extensions. The MIME type determines how an email program handles the file and which helpers it uses to interact with the file.
Modules	X	X	X	X	Configures and administers managed code modules used with IIS to provide services.
Pages and Controls	X	X	X	X	Defines application level settings for pages and controls, such as the namespaces that they rely on for support code.
Providers	X	X	X	X	Determines which security features that IIS uses in managing user access. The providers affect users, roles, and profiles.

TABLE 1.1: Icon Summary for IIS 7 *(CONTINUED)*

Icon Name	Entire Site	Individual Web Site	Folder	Application	Description
Server Certificates	X				Provides a means of adding certificates to the server. You can install third-party certificates or create a self-signed certificate for local (personal) use.
Session State	X	X	X	X	Controls how IIS manages the client session data. These settings include timeout values and the use of cookies.
SMTP Email	X	X	X	X	Determines the Simple Mail Transfer Protocol (SMTP) settings that IIS uses when sending email from an application.
SSL Settings		X	X	X	Determines the Secure Sockets Layer (SSL) settings. You use SSL to encrypt documents. IIS supports 128-bit encryption. It's also possible for require a client certificate for mutual authentication.
Worker Processes	X				Displays the state of worker processes running on the server.

Using Features View versus Contents View

The fact that you see a hierarchical Explorer-like display in the new IIS naturally prompts the question of how you can see the content of each of the entities. The answer lies in the tabs at the bottom of Figure 1.2. Whenever you select an entry in the Connections pane, the contents of the middle pane vary. Up to this point in the chapter, you've seen the Features pane, which contains all of the icons that help you configure IIS. Click the Contents tab at the bottom of the screen and you'll see the Contents pane, as shown in Figure 1.10.

As with the Features pane, the Contents pane reflects the element you select in the Connections pane. The Actions pane reflects the major tasks you can perform with the selected element in the Contents pane. You can also right-click the element to choose actions from the context menu.

FIGURE 1.10
Use the Contents pane to work with the content of a particular IIS connection.

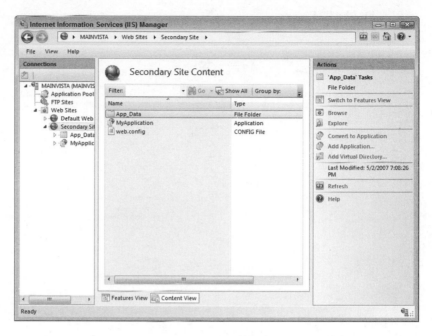

TIP   Notice in Figure 1.10 that one of the actions is Convert to Application. Microsoft made this feature more accessible in IIS 7 so that you can easily set up a folder as an application. Whenever you move an application from one machine to another, there's a chance that the new machine will see an application as a folder. This feature makes it very easy to configure the folder as an application so that IIS will work with it correctly. You must configure ASP.NET folders as applications before IIS will use them to serve the desired content.

Displaying Features and Content in Order

Figure 1.2 shows the Features pane in the default configuration, while Figure 1.10 shows the default setup for the Contents pane. In most cases, these views will work fine, but they may not always meet your needs. For example, you might want to group features in a particular way or you might want to see a detailed view of them. Features let you display the content based on:

♦ Group (Area and Category)

♦ Sort (Feature Name and Description)

♦ View (Details, Icons, Tiles, and List)

Figure 1.11 shows the Features pane using the Category grouping, sorted by Description, and with a Details view. As you can see, the display is significantly smaller than the one shown in Figure 1.2 and provides more information, but the icons are harder to see, so you might actually spend more time looking for what you need. You can select the grouping using the Group By field, the view by choosing an option from the View split button, and a sort by choosing a column in the Details view. If you aren't using the Details view, choose an option from the View ➢ Sort By menu instead.

FIGURE 1.11
Choose a display that helps you work faster and more efficiently in IIS.

When working in the Contents view, you can choose not to use a grouping at all or group the content by type. In addition, you can choose some level of filtering or no filtering at all. When you filter content, you can choose to filter it by:

◆ Name

◆ Type

When you filter by name, the filter applies to the entire entity name. For example, if you type App, then everything with the word App in it appears in the Contents pane, as shown in Figure 1.12. If you want to remove the filtering, click Show All. You can change the kind of filtering that IIS uses by clicking the down arrow next to Go and choosing a different option from the list. All of the grouping and filtering options also appear on the View menu. This figure also shows the effects of grouping the display by type.

Working with the Actions Pane

The Actions pane shows the most common activities that you can perform with a particular selection. If you select an entry in the Connections pane, the Actions pane will reflect the tasks you can perform with that entry. However, the moment you select an entry in either the Features or Contents pane, the Actions pane entries reflect the activities you can perform with that entry. Consequently, it's possible to see different Actions pane views even when the other panes haven't changed. The Actions pane always reflects the tasks you can perform with the highlighted element.

The Actions pane may not show advanced tasks. Consequently, if you want to see everything you can do with a particular entry, right-click the entry and choose an option from the context menu. That said, the Actions pane contains most of the tasks you'll perform and you may never need to rely on the context menu.

Don't confuse the Actions pane with a properties pane. The Actions pane never displays settings changes you can make to a feature. When you need to make a settings change, always double-click the icon for the feature to view its settings. For example, Figure 1.13 shows the settings for the Pages and Controls feature. The Actions pane will always include only the activities you can perform with a given feature or content.

FIGURE 1.12
Use filtering and grouping in the Contents pane to make the information more usable.

FIGURE 1.13
Double-click the icon for the feature you want to change to view its settings.

Understanding Friendly Names and Configuration Names

IIS 7 uses a Web.CONFIG file to hold the settings you provide. So you can modify the Web.CONFIG file by hand or using a custom application—you don't even need to use the Internet Information Services (IIS) Manager to perform most configuration tasks. Of course, it helps to know what the settings are so that you have a better idea of how to modify them. IIS helps you discover the entry names. Figure 1.13 shows the friendly name of the entries for the Pages and Controls feature. However, if you select Configuration Names from the Display field, the names change, as shown in Figure 1.14.

Some of the names are quite similar. For example, Buffer in Figure 1.13 appears as buffer in Figure 1.14. Other names are different. For example, Enable Authenticated View State in Figure 1.13 appears as enableViewState in Figure 1.14. Let's say you make a change to the enableViewState option and then click Apply in the Actions pane. The change will appear in the Web.CONFIG file for the entry, as shown in Figure 1.15.

The enableViewState option appears as an attribute of the <pages> element. You could just as easily make the change directly to the Web.CONFIG file, as shown here. Of course, it's much easier using the Internet Information Services (IIS) Manager to make the change.

FIGURE 1.14
Use the Configuration Names option to see how the settings appear in the Web.CONFIG file.

FIGURE 1.15
The Web.CONFIG file contains any changes you make using the Internet Information Services (IIS) Manager.

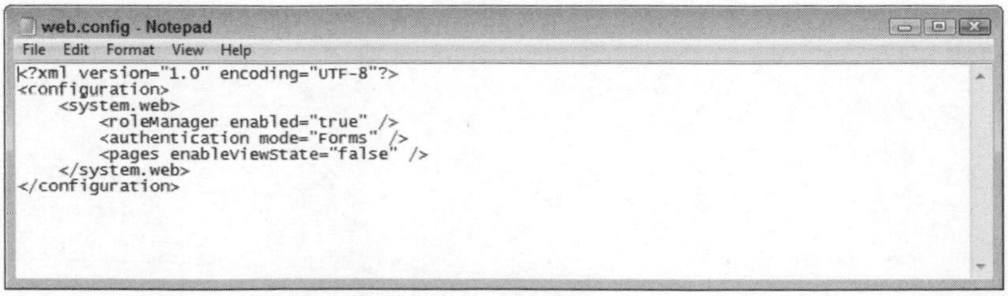

Let's Start Building

This book is about building—building Web sites, building applications, building a good user experience, and building a secure environment. Most of all, it's about building a team. Instead of using separate tools to perform tasks separately, all of the members of the Web site team now work together using a single tool. Although IIS 7 involves a lot of change, it also provides many new features that help you create and manage Web sites with greater ease. This chapter helps you build these skills:

- Define how administrators and developers work together
- Understand the use of ASP.NET in IIS 7
- Use the user interface to locate features
- Modify the basic IIS 7 setup
- Define the difference between features and content
- Order the information on screen
- Perform common actions
- Define the difference between friendly and configuration names

Now that you have these new skills, it's time to put them into action. IIS 7 uses a drill-down approach that requires you click things to explore. Consequently, one of the tasks you should perform first is to open a copy of Internet Information Services (IIS) Manager and start clicking icons to see how things work. Because the interface is so different, you'll want to spend some time exploring it before you do any real work with it.

In addition to exploring the interface, take the time now to install a copy of SQL Server if you want to use some of the advanced features that IIS 7 provides. Remember that you don't need to purchase a copy of the full SQL Server product; all you really need is the free version of SQL Server Express to get the job done. Download and install the product as mentioned in the "Obtaining and Installing SQL Server Express" section of the chapter.

Chapter 2 provides details about using the new interface. Make note of the features you don't understand as you click around the user interface. You'll find information about using them in Chapter 2. In addition to more information about the new interface, Chapter 2 shows how to perform some additional management tasks. Many of these tasks are generic—you'll perform them with most of the applications you create, no matter what kind of application it is. For application-specific tasks, make sure you review Part 2 for older applications and Part 3 for ASP.NET applications.

Chapter 2

Configuring IIS 7 Features

Despite the seeming overabundance of icons and the massive changes to the interface, Microsoft has actually made IIS easier to configure than with past versions of the product. No longer will you spend hours looking for just the right setting on the properties page that seems to elude the most desperate search during a system meltdown. The icons that Microsoft uses make the settings significantly clearer and can reduce the chance that you'll miss the setting completely during an emergency.

The use of levels is also much clearer in IIS 7. Making a good choice about the level for a setting is easier because you can better see how the level works with the Web server as a whole. The use of levels makes delegation easier too—you needn't give someone more access to the server than they actually require. This chapter helps you configure the Web server in a general way. Later chapters will help you perform application-specific configuration tasks.

In this chapter, you will learn how to do the following:

- ◆ Understand the new icons
- ◆ Manage the ASP.NET setup
- ◆ Manage the IIS setup
- ◆ Redefine the management features
- ◆ Choose the IIS configuration level

Understanding the New Icons

Chapter 1 provided a brief overview of the new icons that IIS uses to expose features in the interface. Of course, each of these icons provides access to some type of configuration functionality. In all cases, you double-click an icon to see its configuration parameters. The following sections describe the major icon categories and the individual icons.

ASP.NET

The features exposed by the ASP.NET icons work together to define the functionality, security, and management of ASP.NET applications. As mentioned in Chapter 1, Microsoft has placed considerable emphasis on ASP.NET in IIS 7. Even though you can continue to build other application types, IIS 7 makes it quite easy to perform any level of configuration your ASP.NET application might require. The following sections describe each of the ASP.NET icons in detail.

.NET COMPILATION

When a developer creates a .NET application, the application itself remains in code form unless the developer precompiles it. When the first person requests the application from the Web site, the system compiles the code into an executable form. Subsequent requests use the executable rather than recompiling it. Using this approach means that the user always sees an application compiled for the host machine instead of the developer's machine. Unfortunately, using this approach also presents a delay for the first user to make a request. To combat this problem, many administrators have used an approach called touching, where they make the first request and incur the delay themselves rather than cause a delay for the user.

Opening the .NET Compilation icon presents a list of configuration options for .NET applications as shown in Figure 2.1. Some of these options control the application output, such as the Maximum File Size setting that determines the maximum executable size (1 MB for the default setup). Developers will use some of the settings, such as Debug, to correct application errors. It's also possible to control the assemblies that the application uses for resources, the default application programming language (Visual Basic), and the location of the temporary directory used for the compile process. Chapter 8 describes the .NET compilation features in detail.

FIGURE 2.1
Set the compilation settings to provide the best application performance.

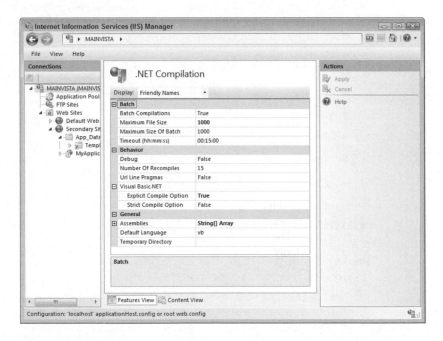

TIP   If you set the Temporary Directory field to use a different hard drive, the system can usually compile the application faster because it's using two different channels for the information it needs. However, you need to make sure that the second drive is physically different from the first drive. Using a different partition on the same hard drive won't yield any gain in compilation speed.

.NET GLOBALIZATION

The .NET Globalization icon helps you configure the use of languages for the .NET application. The settings control how the server reacts to incoming requests and cues the application about the user's language so it can provide the appropriate text strings. All of the language-specific features appear in the Culture group as shown in Figure 2.2. If you set the Culture group settings as shown, IIS passes the user's culture information to the ASP.NET application and lets it determine how best to handle the user's language.

FIGURE 2.2
Configure globaliza-
tion for your server
to match the needs of
the users.

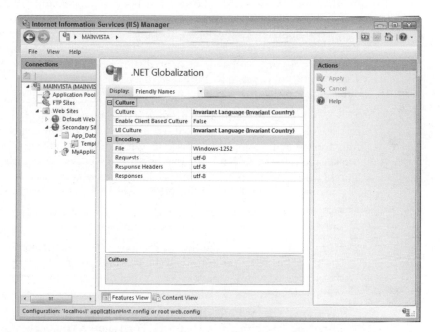

As shown in Figure 2.2, globalization affects more than just the user's language and method of presenting information, such as numbers. Globalization also affects how the system encodes data for transmission. The most common encoding method is the Unicode Transformation Format (UTF), which commonly comes in two forms, UTF-8 and UTF-16. The Unicode Transformation Formats: UTF-8 & Co. Web site at `http://www.czyborra.com/utf/` tells you more about the UTF. Encoding comes in a vast array of forms including Windows, International Business Machines (IBM), Code Page (CP), and International Standards Organization (ISO) forms. You can find an excellent tutorial on character sets and encoding at `http://www.cs.tut.fi/~jkorpela/chars.html`. You can discover more about working with .NET globalization in Chapter 14.

.NET PROFILE

The .NET Profile icon provides access to per user settings. A per user setting is a configuration option that affects one user but not another. You can set the configuration options by groups as well. For example, you might give all administrators a special setting that lets them control the debug feature of an application. A global setting, one that applies to everyone, might record the last person who made a change to the application configuration from within the application.

Settings rely on specific data types. For example, an application can't store a number in a date property. In addition, the settings are normally only usable by users who are logged into the system, but you can make them available to anonymous users as well. Finally, you can make settings read/ write or read only. The read-only settings provide configuration, while the read/write settings provide the means to record state or other information. The "Storing User Settings with the .NET Profile" section of Chapter 10 describes this feature in detail.

.NET ROLES

The .NET Roles icon displays a list of roles. A role describes a task that the user performs or a position that requires special application functionality. For example, a developer role might describe any number of positions within a company, but all of these positions perform some type of application development task. An administrator role might describe anyone who manages the Web server in some way, even though the actual titles for these people will differ. The "Understanding Role-Based Security" section of Chapter 9 describes role-based security in detail.

.NET TRUST LEVELS

The .NET Framework introduces the idea of code trust. Instead of placing the full burden of security on the user, the .NET Framework also examines the code running on the system. When the code is fully trusted, it has complete access to the server and all of its resources. Unfortunately, this level of trust is about the same as turning the code-based security completely off. In fact, the only time you should use the default setting of Full is when you're working with IIS on a development machine that has no outside access. Here are the .NET trust levels that IIS supports.

Full   Use this setting only for development and local Web services needs. This setting doesn't provide any security for connected scenarios.

High   You should use this setting for connected scenarios within a firewall. For example, you could use this setting within an intranet to serve content for people within your company. Using this setting provides minimal security, but does prevent some actions that would compromise your system.

Medium   The medium setting works well when you have applications that require good resource access on a private network. For example, you might use this setting on a network that only provides connectivity to trusted third parties. This setting provides moderate network protection but doesn't provide enough for a public setting. Someone with talent could probably bypass your security measures and gain access to your network, given enough time.

Low   Use the Low setting when working in a public access scenario. This setting does provide good network protection. However, using this setting could also choke your application because it won't be able to gain access to all of the resources it needs unless the developer and administrator both work to configure the application correctly.

Minimal   You could also call this the paranoid setting. Use it when you can't trust anyone or anything. It's so strict that you'll find that most applications won't run at all. However, it does ensure your server remains safe.

It's important to understand that code-based security doesn't end with the setting in the .NET Trust Levels icon—it only begins there. The administrator can also use the Microsoft .NET Framework 2.0 Configuration console to configure modules. You can read more about this console in the "Using the Microsoft .NET Framework 2.0 Configuration Console" section of Chapter 9. In addition, the developer can add security features to the code itself. Consequently, code-based security is multi-tiered and very flexible. See "Understanding Code-Based Security" in Chapter 9 for more detail.

.NET USERS

Don't confuse the settings in the .NET Users icon with those used for standard Windows security. You use the options in this icon to configure .NET users, those that can access .NET applications. The user entries work with the .NET Framework's role-based security in that you assign users a role after you configure them. "Understanding Role-Based Security" describes role-based security in detail and "Considering Operating System Security" (both in Chapter 9) explains how Windows security will affect your application.

APPLICATION SETTINGS

Developers can create custom code that reacts to settings the administrator provides as part of an Application Settings icon entry. The entries for this icon consist of a name and value pair. The code reads the setting value by name and performs tasks based on the value provided. Even though this setup may seem simple, you can actually perform complex tasks with it given the right environment. The "Controlling Application Settings" section of Chapter 8 provides detailed information on how to make application settings work for you.

CONNECTION STRINGS

One of the problems with older applications is that they commonly use databases in ways that make it impossible to move things around when the need arises. Over the years, developers have come up with all kinds of ways to make connectivity easier, including the use of Open Database Connectivity (ODBC) scenarios, but nothing seems to work very well. The Connection Strings icon is another in a long series of methods to tell applications how to connect to a database. IIS uses a considerably easier method to create connection strings.

When you open the Connection Strings icon, you'll probably see a LocalSqlServer entry that IIS uses for authentication and other purposes. Don't change this connection. You'll also see options to add, remove, and edit database connections. When you add a new connection, you specify arguments to tell IIS where to find the database, as shown in Figure 2.3.

IIS also provides the means to define the credentials used to access the database, or you can choose to use Windows integrated security. Using custom strings lets you define complex database connectivity. You can learn more about using connection strings and database connectivity in general in Chapter 11.

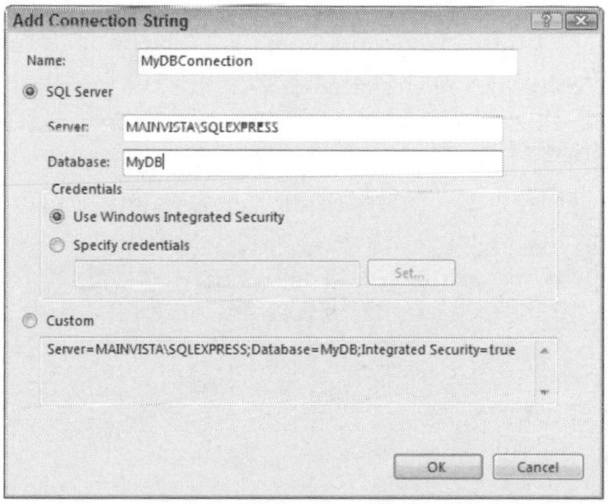

FIGURE 2.3
Add database connections as needed to serve your applications.

PAGES AND CONTROLS

The Pages and Controls icon works with new ASP.NET 2.0 features to provide your ASP.NET applications with a robust appearance. You can use this feature to define the master page and theme used for an application as shown in Figure 2.4. In fact, you can use this feature to control many aspects of the ASP.NET 2.0 user interface.

FIGURE 2.4
Configure the
ASP.NET 2.0 features
using this dialog box.

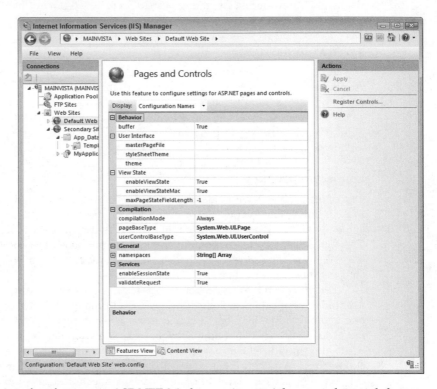

The new user interface features in ASP.NET 2.0 also require special page and control classes. These classes contain the code used to draw the elements in the user's browser. The developer can supply an administrator with special versions of the default classes to provide complex behaviors. The "Defining Application Behavior Using Pages and Controls" section of Chapter 13 describes these complex user interface scenarios in detail.

PROVIDERS

A provider is a means of connecting a database to an application or other IIS feature. You begin with a connection string and then couple the connection to the application. Figure 2.5 shows a typical example of a provider setup. The Providers icon contains a number of these entries by default, including those used for the .NET users, .NET roles, and .NET profiles.

The connection you create won't provide database connectivity of the usual sort—you won't use it for storing data. Instead, this provider helps you create a connection to a source of users, roles, and profiles for your application. The "Managing Database Providers" section of Chapter 11 provides details on working with providers.

FIGURE 2.5
Define a connection between an application and a database using a provider.

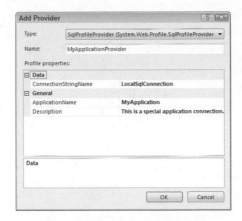

SESSION STATE

HTTP doesn't maintain any session information. When a user makes a request, the connection begins and ends with the request. The response is an entirely different communication and any follow-on requests are individual communications as well. Consequently, developers have created a number of different ways to maintain information about the conversation between the user and the server. Otherwise, you couldn't have applications such as shopping carts that require a means of tracking the individual purchases. The information that defines the communication is called state and the server maintains it for one communication stream called a session. The Session State icon shown in Figure 2.6 provides access to the means of maintaining the session state on IIS.

TIP   Some administrators miss an opportunity to improve the performance of their server. If the Web site is only serving static data, then the user doesn't need to maintain any type of session state. You can obtain a performance boost by setting the Session State Mode Settings option to Not Enabled.

Notice that you can modify features such as the means to maintain the state. For example, you can choose to use cookies to maintain the information. It's also possible to define how the server manages session state. For example, you could place the data within a database, but the default setting uses local memory for the task. Using memory does increase consumption of this resource but makes the application run faster. The "Managing Session State" section of Chapter 8 provides details on all of the configuration features of this icon.

TIP   Choose the server state settings with care. For example, you can only use cookies when you know the client will have cookies enabled. A safer option for public Web sites is to detect the browser's ability to store cookies automatically or simply place the information within the Uniform Resource Identifier (URI).

SMTP E-MAIL

The SMTP E-mail icon helps you create connectivity between the server and the people administering it. The setup uses email to send messages to the administrator as shown in Figure 2.7.

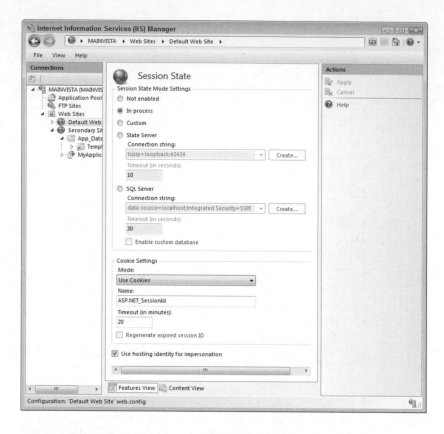

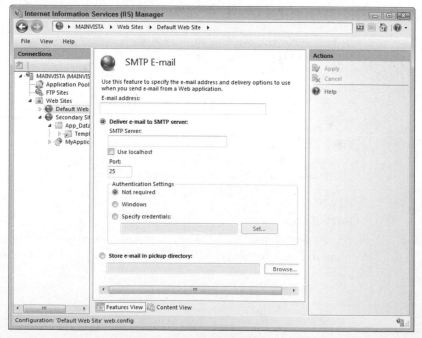

The E-mail Address field contains the "from" portion of the email message. The address tells the administrator that the message is authentic and not to reply to it since the server won't pick up the email. You can also choose from several delivery methods including:

◆ External server

◆ Local server

◆ Email folder on the server

Make sure you provide the proper credentials when using either an internal or an external Simple Mail Transfer Protocol (SMTP) server. Otherwise, the system generates error messages saying it couldn't deliver the emails telling the administrator that something is wrong with the system. The "Configuring SMTP E-mail" section of Chapter 6 provides additional details about using email with applications.

IIS

The IIS icons control overall IIS functionality and provide support for non-ASP.NET applications. You'll use these icons much as you used the configuration features of previous versions of IIS. Although the positions of many of these configuration items have changed, you'll definitely notice some similarities, as well, in the following sections.

ASP

Active Server Pages is a scripting language that lets you create moderately complex Web pages that include a level of intelligence. Even though ASP seems like it should be the predecessor to ASP.NET, the two technologies have little to do with each other. ASP.NET does use a few holdovers from ASP, but you really wouldn't recognize the similarities in most cases.

The ASP icon helps you configure ASP applications. Don't confuse these settings with those used for ASP.NET because the two are completely different, as shown in Figure 2.8.

FIGURE 2.8
Define the appropriate settings for your ASP applications.

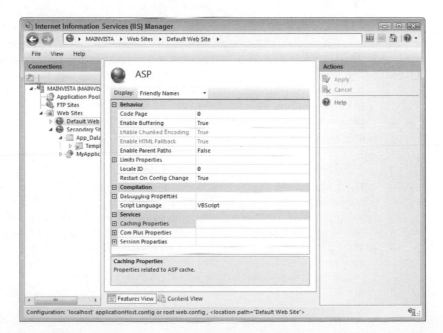

You do need to define how ASP presents information to the user. The Code Page (CP) defines the character set that ASP uses, which in turn affects the display of special characters used by many languages. A list of code pages that Windows provides appears at `http://www.microsoft.com/globaldev/reference/WinCP.mspx`. The Locale Identifier (LCID) identifies the user's location and controls the presentation of information, such as monetary amounts and dates. You can find a complete list of the LCIDs for Windows at `http://krafft.com/scripts/deluxe-calendar/lcid_chart.htm`.

ASP provides extensive debugging configuration. This is because unlike ASP.NET, you won't have the Visual Studio .NET debugger to help you locate errors. Many of the debugging features for ASP are on by default because you don't know when an error will occur.

Besides behavior and debugging issues, you can configure the services that ASP relies on to present information to the user. The default services include caching (to improve performance), COM+ (to provide business logic and database connectivity), and session (to control how the server interacts with the user). You can learn more about how to work with ASP application in Chapter 5.

AUTHENTICATION

The Authentication icon controls how IIS performs security checks. The default setting of anonymous doesn't perform any security checks—the server never knows who is accessing it. Users of older versions of IIS will recognize the basic, digest, and Windows authentication methods as three techniques that do determine who is accessing the system, but at varying levels of safety. The basic security level sends the username and password in cleartext, which is almost like having no security at all since anyone can determine the required credentials using a simple sniffer (an application to read network packets). The Windows security method is most secure because it encrypts the user information and provides other checks to ensure that no one is spoofing the server.

WARNING IIS 7 defaults to using Anonymous Authentication mode. This mode doesn't perform any authentication of the user at all and leaves your server wide open to attack. A good first step in configuring IIS is to disable the Anonymous Authentication and enable Windows Authentication (at least until you have everything set up).

IIS 7 adds ASP.NET impersonation and forms authentication. These two authentication methods can provide you with good alternatives to the old standbys when it comes to determining who is at the other end of the line. ASP.NET impersonation provides the same functionality as an ASP.NET application would provide, which means a combination of role- and code-based security. The forms authentication method relies on multiple Web pages and redirection to perform its task. Forms authentication also sends the user information in cleartext, but you can encrypt it using Secure Sockets Layer (SSL). You can learn more about authentication setup and requirements in the "Setting Authentication Requirements" section of Chapter 10.

AUTHORIZATION RULES

The Authorization Rules icon determines who can access what on the server. You can make the rules very specific by setting the authorization rules at the correct level. For example, you can enable access to one application or folder, but disable access to another. The use of verbs helps you control precisely what kind of access the user can request, such as the ability to post data to the Web site but not get any data from it. It's important that you consider the level of configuration, as well as the use of verbs when working with authorization rules. You can learn more about authorization in the "Modifying the Authorization Rules" section of Chapter 10.

WARNING   IIS 7 defaults to letting anyone do anything anywhere they want. One of the first configuration tasks you should perform is to restrict access by removing All Users from the list and providing a list of trusted users who have the proper levels of access to the various Web server connections.

CGI

The Common Gateway Interface (CGI) is one of the oldest methods available for running applications on a Web server. To use this feature, you write scripts that perform actions on the user's behalf on the server. The CGI icon provides the few configuration options that IIS supports for CGI, including the ability to time out when the script fails and a setting that controls CGI security. You can learn more about this feature in the "Working with CGI Applications" section of Chapter 6. Make sure you also read about restrictions you can place on CGI applications in the "Managing ISAPI Extensions and CGI Restrictions" section of Chapter 6 because your CGI application can't run until you configure the server to allow it to run.

DEFAULT DOCUMENT

The Default Document icon provides a means of specifying the default document the user sees after providing just the domain and possibly a folder as the URL. You can also disable the use of default documents, in which case the user must enter the specific document name before seeing it on screen. Default documents can open security holes, in some cases, because they present information to others that may help them discover more about your Web setup. However, most public and private Web sites do provide a default document to make it easier for the user to select content. You can learn more about working with default documents in the "Setting a Default Document" section of Chapter 3.

DIRECTORY BROWSING

The Directory Browsing icon lets you control directory browsing on the Web server. Normally, IIS 7 disables this feature because of the security risks. Anyone who can browse the directory structure of your server might find a way to circumvent your security. However, the feature does provide benefits when you want to provide a download directory or other functionality where directory browsing is a requirement. The directory-browsing feature also lets you control what the user sees. The display elements include:

- Time
- Size
- Extension
- Date
- Long date (when available)

The user will always see filenames and an icon for each of the files. The icon identifies the file type and therefore the file extension. Most administrators frown on the use of directory browsing and your Web server gains a security benefit when you don't enable it. You can learn more about directory browsing in the "Controlling the Use of Directory Browsing" section of Chapter 3.

ERROR PAGES

Whenever the server or an application encounters an error, the error generates an error code. The error code, in turn, triggers a specific response page on the server so that the user can see the error and react to it. The Error Pages icon shown in Figure 2.9 lets you control the error pages that IIS uses to present information.

FIGURE 2.9

Special error Web pages tell the user about an error in an application or the server.

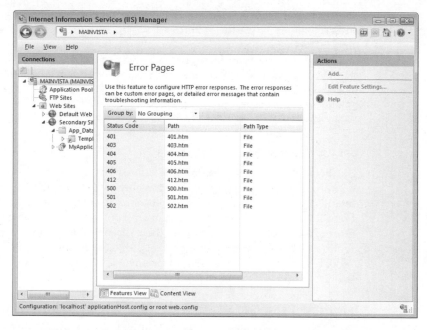

As shown in Figure 2.9, IIS hasn't changed its method of handling errors because the static Web page system seems to work fine. However, you don't have to continue using this method. You can also perform an action based on an error or redirect the user to a new URL. Because IIS provides great support for ASP.NET, you can now use ASP.NET applications to provide intelligent handling of errors. You can learn more about working with error pages in the "Managing Error Pages" section of Chapter 4.

NOTE The Error Pages icon only provides support for responses based on an error code. Applications often create their own error page or use error codes the IIS doesn't understand natively. Make sure you configure the server to handle unknown error codes, but don't defeat applications in their attempt to provide custom error responses.

FAILED REQUEST TRACING RULES

A failed request signifies that the server couldn't respond to a user request. In fact, the server generally provides an error page to signal the event. This particular error can happen for any reason, including a typo made by the user. In sum, a failed request need not signal a security failure (however, it can signal such an event). Most administrators don't track failed requests unless a user makes a complaint about not finding a particular resource or the administrator suspects something is happening with the server.

IIS 7 doesn't come with any failed request tracing rules in place, so you need to add them using the Failed Request Tracing Rules icon. When you click Add in the Actions pane, you launch a wizard that takes you through the steps of configuring a failed request tracing rule. You can use these rules to track all content, ASP.NET, ASP, or custom content. The rule can check for a particular error code or even a request that takes too much time to complete (making it possible to use this technique to look for performance problems as well). Finally, you can configure the providers used to track the request and how much information they provide. The "Setting Failed Request Tracing Rules" section of Chapter 4 provides more information on this feature.

HANDLER MAPPINGS

A Web server doesn't know by instinct how to handle user requests—you must provide this information as a handler mapping. The mapping tells the server to use a particular application to answer a request based on the request's file extension. The Handler Mappings icon provides a way to support any file type as long as you have an application to support it as shown in Figure 2.10.

FIGURE 2.10
Supply the name of a handler to process a request based on file extension.

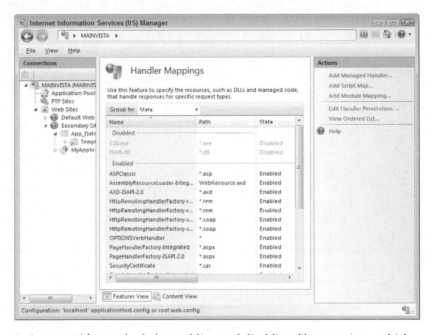

Notice that the window provides methods for enabling and disabling file extensions, which means that you can tell the server about a particular file extension and then insist the server not handle it. Disabling extensions can provide a security benefit for your server by blocking requests that you never intended the server to support. An outsider could use known vulnerabilities to get your server to perform tasks that it normally wouldn't simply by making the right request. You can learn more about working with handlers in the "Working with Handlers" section of Chapter 3.

ISAPI AND CGI RESTRICTIONS

IIS 7 requires you to enable both Internet Server Application Programming Interface (ISAPI) and CGI applications before you use them using the ISAPI and CGI Restrictions icon. In short, because these technologies are old and untrusted, you must specifically tell IIS 7 to use them, which means you must know about the application before anyone can use it. This restriction makes IIS significantly safer than ever before, even while it lets you continue using older ISAPI and CGI applications when needed. The "Managing ISAPI and CGI Restrictions" section of Chapter 6 provides additional information on working with ISAPI and CGI applications.

ISAPI FILTERS

ISAPI applications come in two forms: ISAPI extensions and ISAPI filters. An ISAPI extension handles requests, much like an ASP script, CGI script, or ASP.NET application does. All it provides is another method of performing the task. An ISAPI filter performs a different service for the server—one that isn't easy to replace with other technologies. Instead of answering requests, the ISAPI filter actually filters the content. For example, you could tell an ISAPI filter to review logon requests for certain criteria and reject those that look like they might be from unreliable sources. Interestingly enough, the .NET Framework uses an ISAPI filter to look for ASP.NET requests. This is the only filter that you'll find configured in IIS 7 by default.

In order to use any ISAPI filter, you must configure it using the ISAPI Filters icon. Click add and you'll see a simple dialog that asks for the filter name and executable name. When you click OK and restart the Web site, the filter becomes active and silently performs its task in the background. Generally, you won't have to configure ISAPI filters by hand because vendors who use them configure them for you as part of the installation routine. You can learn more about ISAPI filter configuration in the "Managing ISAPI Filters" section of Chapter 6.

MIME TYPES

A Multipurpose Internet Mail Extension (MIME) entry defines how the Web server tells the client to handle a particular file type. The technology was originally used in email to help the email reader know what to do with a particular file type that the user received as an attachment. The technology spread to Web servers as part of the response to a client request. The browser on the client machine can use the MIME type to launch a helper application to handle the file. Microsoft is even using MIME in Windows to help handle file extensions consistently—you'll find the entries with the file definitions in the registry. Figure 2.11 shows the default MIME configuration for IIS 7. As you can see, the number of file types is extensive.

Adding a new MIME type isn't always easy and it's not something you'll need to do very often. When you click Add in the Actions pane, IIS asks you to provide the file extension (which isn't hard to discover) and the MIME type (which can be quite hard to discover. Fortunately, IIS comes with a number of common MIME types predefined. In addition, when you install an application that requires a special type, the installation routine normally adds the required information for you. The Web site at `http://www.webmaster-toolkit.com/mime-types.shtml` provides an extensive list of MIME types that you'll find helpful. The "Setting the MIME Type" section of Chapter 3 provides additional information on working with MIME types.

MODULES

IIS needs to know where to find the code it requires to perform tasks. Because IIS 7 is based on the .NET Framework, you'll find that it needs a combination of .NET (managed) and native code modules to function. A managed code module is one that relies on the .NET Framework and contains tokens. The Common Language Runtime (CLR) compiles these files into a native executable and then runs them. A native code module is already in machine code form—the form that your processor can understand natively.

The Modules icon contains a whole list of native and managed code modules when you install IIS. You can see a partial list of these modules in Figure 2.12.

FIGURE 2.11
Define MIME types to handle specific file extensions.

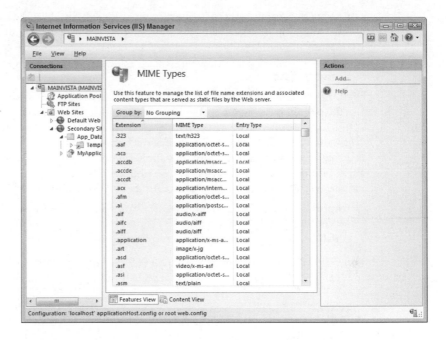

FIGURE 2.12
Create module entries to make IIS aware of where to locate code it needs.

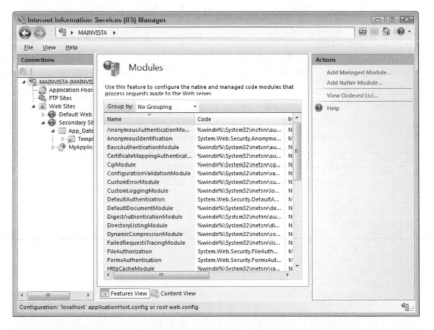

IIS requires two different procedures to install a module. When you click Add Managed Module to add a new managed code module to IIS, you see an Add Managed Module dialog box where you must supply a module name and type. You can also choose to load the module only when an application or handler requests the services of the module. When you click the Add Native Module, you'll see an Add Native Module dialog box where you'll choose one or more native module types.

To change the specifics of the native module, click Edit. IIS lets you change the name and the path to the executable. You can learn more about modules in the "Working with Response Modules" section of Chapter 4.

SERVER CERTIFICATES

Digital certificates answer the question of how someone can know whether your Web site is actually the one that they want. A digital certificate added to SSL ensures that your communication with a user remains secure. In order to implement the security features that digital certificates provide, you must create an entry in the Server Certificates icon.

Past versions of IIS were definitely limited in how they'd work with digital certificates—your only option was to install one. IIS 7 makes things considerably easier by offering other options. You can use any of these techniques for creating a certificate on your system.

Import This is the old standby option. You obtain a certificate from a third-party source, such as VeriSign, and then import it into your server. All you need to do is supply the location of the certificate and the password required to open it.

Create Certificate Request This is a two-part process where you begin by creating a request and sending it to a third party, such as VeriSign. The third party eventually responds and you use the Complete Certificate Request action to install the certificate. It's a bit like the Import option, except you don't have to go through the work of creating the request on a Web site and, then, extract and install the certificate manually.

Create a Domain Certificate Using a domain certificate server was a messy and error-prone process in the past. You ended up spending time using a Web interface to contact the server and hopefully obtain a digital certificate that you installed manually into IIS. Now you can use this option to create a certificate that works great for an intranet or in a private Web site where trusted third parties participate. Using this approach saves the time, money, and effort of using a third party and provides a perfectly acceptable means of identification.

Create Self-Signed Certificate Developers often require server certificates for test purposes. This option provides a certificate that works fine for testing and probably for a small network, but may not be a very good choice even for a private network because anyone can generate this certificate if they have access to IIS. Previous versions of IIS didn't even consider this need, which often left developers looking for a digital certificate to use. Since a company would be ill advised to install their public certificate on a test server, the developer often had to resort to odd testing strategies and command line tools to accomplish the task.

All of these certificate options mean that there isn't a good reason not to have one installed on your server any longer. After you install the certificate, you can begin working with SSL and securing your setup to make it harder for outsiders to gain unauthorized access. You can learn more about working with server certificates in the "Working with Server Certificates" section of Chapter 10.

SSL SETTINGS

Anyone who's used the HyperText Transfer Protocol Secure sockets (HTTPS) protocol knows something about SSL. You can see the SSL settings for IIS 7 in Figure 2.13. Using SSL means that you can encode the communication between client and server so that no one can eavesdrop on your conversations. SSL sees use for a number of tasks, including public uses such as shopping cart applications and password entry screens. You can use SSL exclusively on a private Web site to ensure the integrity of any communications you perform.

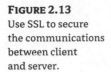

FIGURE 2.13
Use SSL to secure
the communications
between client
and server.

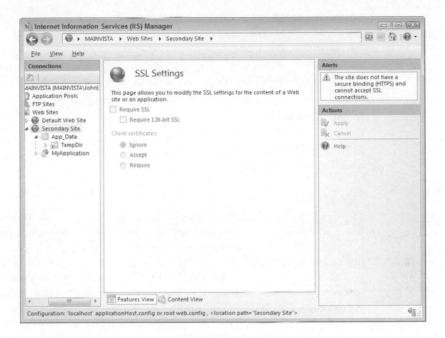

NOTE Microsoft sets the SSL Settings feature delegation to Read Only in the default configuration. This setting means that you can't change the SSL Setting at any level because this setting isn't available at the Web server level and none of the other levels can access it. Since SSL security is a mandatory feature for secure transactions today, make sure you use the Feature Delegation setting to change the SSL security setting to Read/Write.

Before you can begin working with SSL, you need to create a server certificate (see the "Server Certificates" section of the chapter for details). Once you have a server certificate, you can create a Web site that's bound to the SSL protocol. It's even possible to add this binding to a current Web site by clicking Bindings in the Action pane (see the "Creating an HTTPS Binding" section of Chapter 10 for details).

TIP Use 128-bit SSL security whenever possible to improve Web site security. Although SSL is relatively secure at any level of encryption, doubts have recently surfaced about the 40-bit encryption level. Someone with the proper equipment can probably break the 40-bit level in a day, assuming you have something valuable enough to use an entire day to break. Most browsers also support the 56-bit level, which is considerably more secure. When you reach the 128-bit level, you can be sure that no one is going to break the encryption unless they have thousands of years to do it. However, you also give up some compatibility with older browsers. See the VeriSign PDF at http://www.verisign.com.br/static/032932.pdf for additional insights into using SSL.

After you create a Web site that uses the SSL protocol, you can redirect the user to it using the HTTPS protocol. You can learn more about working with SSL in the "Configuring an Application to Use SSL" section of Chapter 10.

WORKER PROCESSES

The Worker Processes icon answers the question of what is currently running on your server. You can determine whether it's currently running, discover the amount of memory it's using, and see the amount of processor time it requires. It's also possible to view the current requests for this process. You can learn more about worker processes in the "Managing Worker Processes" section of Chapter 8.

Management

IIS only provides one Management area icon, Feature Delegation. It appears that Microsoft is planning to add to this area in the future. In the mean time, the following section discusses the one Management area icon in detail.

FEATURE DELEGATION

IIS places strict control over the use of features in your hands. You can choose to delegate the feature and determine how the delegation occurs. When the Web server administrator decides to remove delegation, a Web site administrator can't even see the feature. You control all of this functionality using the Feature Delegation icon shown in Figure 2.14.

The trick is to provide the right level of delegation. If you provide too much access to Web server features, you might endanger the Web server integrity. However, when you provide too little delegation, the Web site administrator can be hindered in efforts to protect the individual Web site. As with many issues, you must provide a good balance of access for your particular setup. The "Considering Feature Delegation" section of Chapter 13 provides more information about feature delegation.

FIGURE 2.14
Use feature delegation to define how others can manage the server.

Choosing the Configuration Level

The configuration level you choose for a particular setting is important because changes at higher levels affect more of the Web server than changes at lower levels. In addition, the configuration level also determines required access, which ultimately affects security. You might find it quite reasonable to give someone remote access to a particular Web site, but giving them access to the entire Web server is reckless. Leaving your Web server open to outside access is almost certainly going to result in security breaches, which your company can ill afford. Consequently, choosing the right configuration level, even if that means making the same change in multiple locations, is paramount to providing accurate and efficient Web server configuration.

Web Server

The Web server acts as a container. It holds the Web site, which in turn holds content in folders. Because the Web server is the container that holds everything else, it also acts as a gatekeeper and is your first line of defense against intruders. The following sections describe the Web server configuration level and how it affects your system as a whole.

CONFIGURING THE WEB SERVER SETTINGS

The Web server level is the most dangerous place to make settings changes because it affects everything. You should provide only local access to your Web server to ensure that the Web server remains firmly under your control. If someone requires access to multiple Web sites, give them access to each of the Web sites individually, rather than taking the easy way out and granting them access to the Web server as a whole. The effect of giving them individual access is the same, but the security ramifications aren't. In addition, if the Web site administrator later requires a reduction in privilege, you can make the change without affecting every other Web site the administrator can access.

Any settings you modify at the Web server level will affect every Web site the Web server hosts, unless that Web server has a custom configuration for that setting. For example, if you enable forms authentication at the Web server level, a Web site administrator can disable this feature. However, the fact that you've enabled forms authentication means that the Web site administrator must manually disable the feature if forms authentication is one of the items the Web site administrator doesn't want to support.

TIP Always provide notification when you make a change to the Web server settings. Otherwise, Web site administrators can receive a nasty surprise when they discover a particular feature is changed. For example, disabling a particular form of authentication can result in lost logons at the Web site if the Web site administrator doesn't enable the authentication.

Not all settings have a direct correlation at lower levels. Table 1.1 in Chapter 1 lists all of the IIS icons and tells where you can access them. Consequently, you must make some settings, such as Feature Delegation, at the Web site level. The use of levels in this way makes sense. You want to determine whether someone can change the Authentication – Forms setting at a lower level from the Web site level. It doesn't make sense to let the Web site administrator make this decision. You can configure the following features only at the Web site level:

◆ Feature Delegation

◆ ISAPI and CGI Restrictions

◆ Server Certificates

◆ Worker Processes

You also have to exercise care with some settings because they flow down to the next level unimpeded in most cases. For example, if you set a role at the Web site level, then that role also appears at every other level. A Web site administrator could gain unauthorized access to a Web site feature through a configuration error that flows from a higher level to a lower level. The flow-down effect is one of the reasons that you can't set roles at the Web server level. Microsoft was smart in making this decision because you shouldn't set roles any higher than the Web site. However, you can set application settings globally and this potentially powerful feature can backfire when you make the change at the Web server level, rather than using the Web site or application level (use the application level whenever possible for application settings).

WARNING   Always make a configuration change at the lowest level possible. If possible, grant access to the Web server through individual applications or folders, rather than at the Web site level to reduce the risk of unauthorized access. Likewise, whenever possible, use the Web site level rather the Web server level to make changes. Using the lowest possible level reduces risk. Everyone makes mistakes at one time or another; using the lowest level reduces the risk the error presents. Failure to use the lowest level approach can result in nasty surprises when an unauthorized person gains access to critical features of your Web server and uses them against you.

RESTARTING THE SERVER

It's important to consider the actions you perform at this level. When working with the Web server, the Restart action also restarts all of the Web sites. If you have someone connected to any of the Web sites, the server disconnects them as part of the restart process. When a setting change you make requires a restart to implement, you must consider the effect of that restart on all of the Web sites hosted by the server. In many cases, a restart is a less than optimal action and you'll want to make the settings change at a lower level. IIS also provides you with the option of stopping and starting the Web server as a whole.

The Web server level also provides the option of viewing the status of the Web sites. To see the current Web site status, click View Web Sites in the Actions pane. Figure 2.15 shows a typical example of the information you'll see. The entries show you the currently configured Web sites, their status, their binding, and the path to their data directory. You can use this information as part of the basis to determine whether it's safe to restart the server.

FIGURE 2.15
Verify the state of the individual Web sites before you restart the server.

ADDING A WEB SITE

Individual Web sites use different folders, in most cases, and you'll want to perform any required setup before you create one. Select the Web Sites entry in the Connections pane. You must be in the Features View to add a new Web site as shown in Figure 2.15. Click Add Web Site in the Actions pane and you'll see the Add Web Site dialog box shown in Figure 2.16.

FIGURE 2.16
Create a new Web site by providing the Web site name and binding.

TIP You can also access the settings for an individual Web site by clicking Basic Settings in the Actions pane when you select a particular Web site. The resulting dialog box shows the name, application pool, and physical path for the selected Web site.

To begin the configuration process, provide a Web site name and a physical path to the folder that holds the Web site data. IIS lets you use either standard paths or Universal Naming Convention (UNC) paths in the form of \\server\share. After you have assigned a Web site name and physical path, you can configure an application pool for it. An application pool is a location in memory that hosts the Web site. The "Working with Application Pools" section of Chapter 13 describes this feature in detail.

Binding is the second part of the configuration process. The default Web site on the server accepts all inputs for port 80, the default HTTP port. You can't configure another Web site to use port 80. If you attempt to bind a second Web site to port 80, IIS will only let you run one of them at a time.

TIP You can change the binding for a particular Web site by choosing the Web site in the Connections pane and clicking Bindings in the Actions pane. The resulting dialog box shows the current bindings for the Web site. You can add or remove bindings for the Web site as needed.

The second default Web site relies on SSL. You select HTTPS in the type field to activate it. In this case, you must provide and SSL certificate for the Web site. The default port for this Web site is 443. IIS doesn't create a default SSL site, so you can configure this site if desired.

When you create a default Web site, it binds to all unassigned IP addresses, which means that the Web site responds to any request that isn't assigned to another Web site on the server. You can also bind a Web site to a specific IP address. In this case, the Web site only answers requests for the specified IP address.

The Host Header field provides a special means of configuring the Web site to match a domain name. Normally, the user will reach the Web site using `http://servername` as the URL. However, by using this feature and setting up your DNS server to recognize the name, you can give the Web site a different host name. You also use this option when your Web site already appears on the Internet. IIS lets you configure as many Web sites as necessary to address all of the domain names used to reach your Web server.

SETTING THE DEFAULT WEB SITE CONFIGURATION

Every Web site you create uses default settings as a starting point. Consequently, changing the default settings to match the most common setup will save time and effort. To change the default Web site configuration, click Set Web Site Defaults in the Actions pane of the `Web Sites` folder as shown in Figure 2.15 (you must be in Features View). You'll see the Web Sites Defaults dialog box shown in Figure 2.17.

FIGURE 2.17
Modify the default Web site configuration to match your most common configuration.

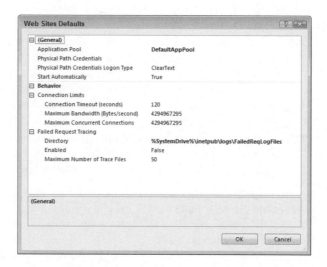

TIP Sometimes you need to adjust the settings shown in Figure 2.17 for a particular Web site. In this case, select the Web site in the Connections pane and click Advanced Settings in the Actions pane. You'll see a dialog box that looks like the one in Figure 2.17 where you can change the settings for a specific Web site.

The General area contains settings for the application pool and determines whether you want the Web site to start automatically when you finish configuring it. The credentials in this area determine how the request (user or otherwise) accesses the physical folder. The default settings uses pass-through authentication, where the user sees a dialog box requesting name and password. IIS accepts the name and password in clear text. You can also set up the system to use a specific user's credentials, which is a standard in public Web sites, but makes your IIS setup less secure. The setup also requires a logon type, which can be any of the following values.

Interactive Lets the user log on interactively using a terminal server, remote shell, or similar process. This logon type allows for disconnected sessions and could affect overall Web site performance. You don't want to use this logon type for public Web sites, but it can work well with Web sites where the user is accessing a specific application or data folder.

Batch   Allows the system to log on in the user's behalf using a batch server. Processing occurs in the background without the user's intervention. This logon type doesn't work well for public Web sites or in situations where you want the user to work with the Web site interactively. However, it does work well for Web site applications and Web services where the user might not even be aware that the host application is accessing the Web site. This logon type doesn't provide cached passwords and therefore doesn't support disconnected sessions.

Network   Relies on an authentication server to validate the user's credentials. This setup works well in decentralized scenarios where the user could use a single set of credentials to access multiple Web sites (think of a setup similar to Microsoft's Passport). This logon type doesn't cache passwords.

ClearText   Provides basic user authentication and is the most common authentication method used on the Internet. The user's credentials arrive at the server in one of many forms and an authentication package validates the user's access. The server can then use the credentials to impersonate the user and perform tasks on the user's behalf. This is the typical Windows authentication technology and the most common authentication package is the Local Security Authority (LSA). IIS uses this setting as the default.

The Connection Limits group contains the settings that determine how the Web site manages connections. You can use the settings to limit the time a session can remain connected when the system detects a lack of activity. The settings also determine the maximum number of connections for a Web site and the bandwidth available to transmit data. This final setting, Maximum Bandwidth (Bytes/second), is especially important because you can use it to perform bandwidth throttling, where each Web site receives an appropriate share of the available bandwidth. Otherwise, one Web site could use up all of the available bandwidth for a communication-intensive task.

The Failed Request Tracing group can help you perform a number of tasks. Most people will associate this setting with troubleshooting a Web site, but you can also use it to detect various security issues. For example, every time someone attempts to access a secure Web site without providing the proper credentials, the system generates a failed request that you can track. Using this feature can consume a lot of hard drive space and drive up resource usage for a particular Web site. Consequently, you should only use request tracing when needed. The default setting disables this feature.

TIP   You can access the Failed Request Tracing settings for an individual Web site by choosing the Web site in the Connections pane and clicking Failed Request Tracing in the Actions pane. Likewise, you can access the bandwidth settings by clicking Limits in the Actions pane. However, it's often easier simply to click Advanced Settings in the Actions pane so you can see all of the settings in one dialog box.

Web Site

The Web site is actually the focus of IIS, even if you only have one of them set up on your machine. The Web site is where you work for the most part because it contains the content you want to serve to users. The following sections describe the Web site as it relates to configuration level management.

CONFIGURING THE WEB SITE SETTINGS

In most cases, you'll configure the Web server to provide administrator access at the Web site level. For example, when you host several Web sites on the same server, each administrator will have Web site level access to their individual Web site. In some cases, you'll also provide user access at the Web site level. For example, when the Web site provides general content, you'll normally configure general access at the Web site level. Often, you'll make the access anonymous when the access is for a public Web site. Obviously, you only provide read-only anonymous access for public Web sites and don't allow browsing to keep your Web site setup less visible.

WARNING Try to configure users to use the lowest possible level of a Web site. If you can limit a user's access to individual folders or applications, it reduces the surface area of the Web site that the user (or someone using the user's account) can attack. Make sure you update user accounts as needed to ensure accurate accessibility. Don't leave a user's access in place when a user no longer requires access to a particular folder or application.

As with the Web server, you perform some configuration tasks at this level, even if the settings affect a lower level. You can configure the following features only at the Web site, or at the Web site and application levels.

◆ .NET Roles

◆ .NET Users

It's important to consider how flow-down will work with a Web site. Generally, you want to set up the Web site to provide the most restricted access possible. This act ensures that any new entries start out as very restricted and someone can't gain entry to them until you have finished configuring them. After you've finished configuring the element, you can relax the settings for it to provide the required level of user access. Unless you are hosting a public access Web site with anonymous authorization, you should always keep the Web site itself locked down tight. It's best to view the Web site in the same light as the root directory of a hard drive, in that you want it to remain secure to prevent unwanted access to child folders.

NOTE Unlike the Web server level, changing to the Content View provides other configuration opportunities at the Web site level. The most important configuration issues are for application folders. Chapter 8 provides a wealth of information about working with applications. You'll need to know this information to configure ASP.NET applications effectively and to move them from one location to another.

RESTARTING THE WEB SITE

Sometimes you'll need to restart a Web site. Unlike the Web server, restarting a Web site only affects the users of that site, not every other Web site on the server. Consequently, performing this task is a little less risky than restarting the Web server. Of course, you'll still disconnect the users who are currently working with the Web site, but even so, if the user doesn't make any requests that time out during the restart; it's possible that they won't even notice the fact that you've done anything. Administrators typically perform a restart for the following reasons.

◆ Configuration changes

◆ A failed application

◆ An application update

◆ Resource issues such as lack of memory

◆ A server update

◆ To prevent an unwarranted outside intrusion

NOTE   Some users will always notice a Web site reset. Although a restart may not affect someone who is browsing static data or working with a scripted application where the state information resides on the client machine, some tasks will fail during a restart. Depending on how you create ASP.NET applications, the user may find that the application suddenly forgets things because the state information that was on the server is now gone. Always restart the Web site with care and consider how the restart will potentially affect users.

It's essential to perform a Web site restart correctly because an incorrect selection can cause another Web site to restart or you could restart the entire server. Choose the Web site you want to restart in the Connections pane. Click Restart in the Actions pane. You can also stop or start a Web site using the appropriate options in the Actions pane.

Folder

The folder level provides access to static data. You use it to store information of various kinds. For example, you'll use folders to organize basic HyperText Markup Language (HTML) pages or database files. Folders store graphics and other kinds of resources. In short, folders are containers within containers that store both files and other folders. Because folders are such good organizational aids, you'll want to set security for them using the standard Windows security as well as both .NET user- and code-based security.

Unlike a Web site, the folder entry in IIS doesn't provide many configuration options. You can convert the folder to an application using the techniques described in Chapter 8. You can also use the techniques in Chapter 8 to add an application to an existing folder.

Both applications and folders can contain virtual directories. A virtual directory is a pointer to another location. It appears as a subfolder of the current folder to the user, but in reality, the user is looking in a completely different physical location of the server. Because virtual directories hide their physical location, they can help in securing your server. Outsiders often rely on a knowledge of the Web site structure to aid in performing nefarious acts. Using a virtual directory structure can thwart their efforts by making the structure less apparent. The "Adding Virtual Directories to the Web Site" section of Chapter 3 tells how to work with virtual directories.

Application

Think of applications as specialized folders. In many respects, they have the same attributes. For example, both act as containers for files and folders. In addition, you secure them using a combination of Windows and .NET security. The application level provides access to an application. The application may provide an interactive environment or work in the background as something like a Web service. Normally, you'll create applications using a product such as Visual Studio .NET. The important issue to remember is that applications rely on executable code to perform a specific task and you need to consider the task orientation of these entities during the configuration process.

Let's Start Building

This chapter provides most of the essentials you need to configure your IIS setup in a generic way. You'll still need to configure IIS for specific application types, but after reading this chapter, you should know how to perform the basic setup for any application. Management includes several areas: ASP.NET, IIS, and Management. You can also configure IIS at the Web server, Web site, folder, and application levels. In addition, you can always perform configuration on individual files. This chapter helps you build these skills:

◆ Working with each of the icons to perform configuration tasks

◆ Defining a generic IIS setup that works with all application types

◆ Performing configuration tasks at the appropriate level (Web server, Web site, folder, or application)

Now that you have these new skills, you'll want to spend some time configuring your IIS setup. Experiment with the various configuration techniques described in this chapter on a test server. Once you're satisfied with the setup, move the configuration to your production server. Remember that IIS relies on the Web.CONFIG file to provide setup information, so all you need to do is move the file you created to the appropriate folder on your production machine to perform the setup. After you move the setup to your production system, you must restart your server to ensure that the Web server uses all of the configuration information.

Chapter 3 goes beyond basic configuration by exploring individual files and begins the journey of learning to work with specific files when you want to perform certain tasks. You'll also begin considering how IIS handles files. For example, you'll discover how to use MIME types to change the way IIS views particular file types. Chapter 3 also examines the use of handlers and virtual directories in IIS.

Chapter 3

Working with Files

Web sites depend on files. Even if you generate your Web site content using databases or other virtual means, the database itself is a file. You'll also use files for configuration settings, applications, and resources. Consequently, even if you never add one page of static content to your Web site, you'll work with files at some point.

This chapter describes how to work with documents (individual pieces of content such as a Web page or graphic image) of various types. Documents are a subset of files because files can include content, data storage, executables, and so on. In some cases, the documents represent common Web site data, such as the default document that most Web sites provide. In other cases, the files provide configuration information or resources.

You'll also find explanations of how to work with uncommon file types. For example, you might include PDF files on your Web site. While PDF files are commonly known, they aren't commonly associated with Web pages and aren't understood by your browser, yet they commonly appear on Web sites. With the correct MIME entry, you can tell the browser which helper to use to display the PDF to the user. In many cases, the helper will display the file directly within the browser, rather than opening it as a separate file. In either case, the user sees the PDF content. The same holds true for graphics, sound, and other media—you must often provide the correct helper for the job through MIME to obtain the proper result.

In this chapter, you will learn how to do the following:

◆ Locate files as you need them

◆ Define a default document

◆ Use directory browsing effectively

◆ Define MIME types for files

◆ Manage content handlers

◆ Manage virtual directories

Browsing and Exploring

Web sites use files for a variety of tasks. It's important to realize that Web sites perform valuable services based partly on the content of the files you create. You can group files into the following categories.

◆ Configuration

◆ Application

◆ Resource

◆ Log

◆ Data

Notice that only one category has anything to do with data. Many Web sites don't use static Web content any longer, so the data files are actually limited to one or more database files. Even so, you couldn't have a Web site without data of some sort. All IIS 7 Web sites have configuration files. The IIS-specific data files use eXtensible Markup Language (XML) to store the configuration information, but you can find configuration files in other forms too, such as INI files. Application files come from developers and provide a nice user interface for your Web site. Resource files contain graphics, sound, video, and other multimedia, as well as specialized content, such as strings to handle multiple languages. Log files tell what's happened on the Web site and you use them to perform tasks such as locating application errors and noting the presence of unwanted visitors.

Now that you have a better idea of what kind of files you're looking for, the following sections tell you how to look. You can view a Web site as a whole, or you can choose to work with individual files. It's also possible to browse for files, which means simply looking for them, or explore files, which means working with the file in some way. Exploring opens a copy of Windows Explorer where you can add, delete, copy, or modify files.

Working with Web Sites

When you select the Features View for a Web site, you see two options for working with the Web site content as shown in Figure 3.1: Browse and Explore. The term *browse* means something special when it comes to a Web site. Instead of simply looking at the content, as you would by clicking the Content View tab, you see the content as the user sees it. On the other hand, when you explore a Web site, you see the content in Windows Explorer.

FIGURE 3.1
Web sites provide a means for browsing and exploring content.

To browse any Web site, select the Web site as shown in Figure 3.1. Choose the Features View. Click the Browse link and you'll see the Web site content. Figure 3.2 shows the default page that IIS7 supplies when you install it. The links on this page take you to a Web site that contains additional IIS 7 information in your particular language. For example, the current English language link is `http://go.microsoft.com/fwlink/?linkid=66138&clcid=0x409`, which redirects you to `http://www.iis.net/default.aspx?tabid=7`. The resulting page contains the help pages you need to work with IIS. You'll eventually want to remove this default page from view, so it's important to add the URLs to your browser.

Clicking Explore in the Actions pane opens a copy of Windows Explorer. You'll see the root directory for the Web site you want to manage, which may not even appear on your local system. Figure 3.3 shows the Windows Explorer view for the default Web site. You can interact with the files that you see just as you normally do in Windows Explorer, which means you can copy, delete, add, or edit the file.

FIGURE 3.2
The default page supplied by IIS 7 during installation provides many helpful links.

FIGURE 3.3
Exploring a Web site means opening a copy of Windows Explorer to the Web site's root directory.

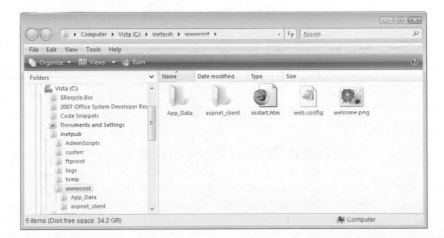

Figure 3.3 also shows the default files for an IIS setup. The default Web site includes the `iisstart.htm` and `welcome.png` files that form the default Web page shown in Figure 3.1. The `aspnet_client` folder contains special files for your applications—it's empty when you first start using IIS 7. These two files and special folder only appear as part of the default Web site.

The `web.config` file contains configuration information for the Web site. The `App_Data` folder contains SQL Server database files that hold data for the Web site. For example, this database holds the per user configuration information. Your .NET applications also use this database unless you provide an alternative. IIS supplies this file and folder with every Web site you configure.

Working with Files

You can only browse files in IIS 7. If you want to explore a file, then you must explore the Web site using the techniques described in the "Working with Web Sites" section of the chapter. Browsing tells you some additional information about the file, such as the last time someone modified it, as shown in Figure 3.4.

FIGURE 3.4
Browse files to learn more about them, such as the last time someone modified them.

The information you see depends on the entry you select. Figure 3.4 shows typical file information, which includes the filename, date of last access, and the size. When you select a folder, you can perform tasks such as creating an application or adding a virtual directory. You can learn more about virtual directories in the "Adding Virtual Directories to the Web Site" section of this chapter (see also "Creating New Applications" in Chapter 8).

Setting a Default Document

Most public Web sites provide a default document. For example, when you type `http://www`
`.microsoft.com` in your browser's address bar and press Enter, the Web site actually takes you to `http://www.microsoft.com/en/us/default.aspx` and shows you the `default.aspx` Web page.

Even though you didn't type the whole URL, the Microsoft Web site was able to complete it for you and display the proper Web page. Designing a Web site to use a default document makes it considerably easier for a user to find and work with the Web site.

NOTE   The /en/us portion of the Microsoft URL is an example of globalization. In this case, the server showed the United States English version of the default.aspx Web page. Many Web sites are coming up with similar schemes for providing global support for different languages. The use of globalization doesn't affect the default document setting except to choose a default document based on a particular language. Chapter 14 considers the issue of globalization in detail.

Unfortunately, creating a default document also opens potential security holes on your Web site. If you have a private Web site, you might not want people to find you simply by typing the domain for your Web site. The Web site could use an unusually named file as the entry point and typing the entire URL, including the filename, could provide one method for securing your Web site.

Whether or not you offer a default document depends on the security setup for your Web site. However, even if you do offer a default document, you still need to perform some configuration with IIS 7 because the default setup offers several default documents.

As a minimum, you should disable the default document at the Web server level because the Web server should provide the additional security of not having a default document. In addition, when you host several Web sites, you can't know whether the Web site administrator will use a particular default document and a Web server setting could conflict with that choice. To disable the server's default document, select the server entry in the Connections pane and double-click the Default Document icon in the Features View. You'll see a display like the one shown in Figure 3.5. Click Disable in the Actions pane and IIS will disable default documents at the server level. If you need to enable them again later, simply click Enable in the Actions pane.

FIGURE 3.5
Disable the default document at the server level to provide a modicum of protection to Web sites that won't need a default document.

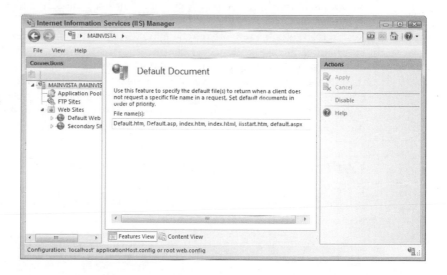

NOTE   When you disable the default document at the server level, you must enable it at the Web site level. The default IIS configuration sets the default document at the server level—disabling the server level automatically disables the Web site too.

IIS 7 also offers a whole host of default documents, none of which reflects your actual default document. For example, many Web sites use a query page, rather than a default document or index page. Here are the default documents that IIS offers.

- `Default.htm`
- `Default.asp`
- `index.htm`
- `index.html`
- `iisstart.htm`
- `default.aspx`

IIS uses these documents in the order in which you list them. The default order looks for `Default.htm` first, followed by `Default.asp,` and so on. When IIS finds a default file, it displays it and doesn't continue looking through the list. Someone with ill intent could place a document that's higher in the list into the directory. Everyone will see the new document when they go to your Web site, rather than the one you had planned for them to see. Interestingly enough, since no one has modified your default Web page, you may not notice the change until someone tells you about it. That's because most developer tools only load the pages you're working with, not those that someone else has added.

Because IIS may not offer the default page you want to use and due to the security risk of keeping all of those other pages in place, you'll want to reconfigure IIS to use just the default page you want to use. To change the default document for a Web site, select the Web site in the Connections pane and double-click the Default Document icon in the Features View. You'll see the same information, as shown in Figure 3.5, except that it will reflect the Web site, rather than the server. Type the name of the default document you want to use in the File Names field. Click Apply in the Actions pane. Restart the Web site to ensure the change takes place. If you make an error in entering the Web page information, the user will see an error message like the one shown in Figure 3.6

The reason you need to know about this error page is that it says very little about a typo in the default document name. Instead, it tries to tell the user that the Web site isn't configured for directory browsing. Only when you get near the bottom of the page does IIS mention anything about configuring the default document and, even then, it doesn't provide helpful information. Typos can cause interesting effects in IIS 7 that you need to consider during troubleshooting.

Controlling the Use of Directory Browsing

Directory browsing is a feature that you don't see used much on public Web sites that serve typical content. You'll normally see this feature offered in places where someone needs to download a particular file. Here are some examples of places you might see directory browsing.

- A vendor uses directory browsing to help people find a particular version of a driver to download.

- A research group or standards organization uses directory browsing to make it easier to locate standards documents.

- A company uses directory browsing to make it easier to find forms by number.

- An organization could use directory browsing to promote a document-sharing scheme.

FIGURE 3.6
A bad default page
entry will cause
the user to see this
error message.

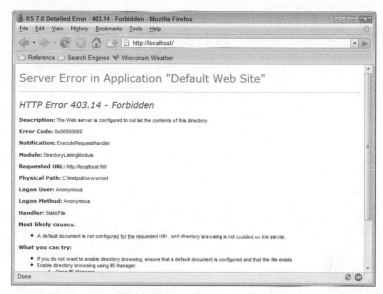

In fact, there are many uses for directory browsing, but not in the typical organization setup. Enabling directory browsing opens a huge hole in your security because it lets people see the structure of your Web site. You can partially fix this problem by using virtual directories (see the "Adding Virtual Directories to the Web Site" section of the chapter for details), but you can't overcome the problems completely. Of course, if you're a standards organization serving up the documents needed to implement a standards-based technology, the likelihood of significant damage is diminished.

From a security perspective, enabling directory browsing at the server level is almost certainly going to cause problems. In fact, enabling it at the Web site level is ill advised unless you plan to keep the Web site private or serve up information that everyone already knows about. Fortunately, with IIS, you can also enable directory browsing at the directory level. All you need to do is choose the directory you want to work with, and then double-click the Directory Browsing icon in Features View. You'll see a display similar to the one shown in Figure 3.7. Click Enable and IIS will enable directory browsing for the directory, but not for anything else.

At this point, you need to choose the items that the user sees when browsing the directory. Make sure you enable long dates when you want the user to see the full date information for a file (sometimes the time is important). Whenever you make a change, click Apply in the Actions pane. After you finish the configuration, restart the Web site to ensure the changes take effect. Figure 3.8 shows a user view of a directory with directory browsing enabled.

Setting the MIME Type

The MIME type for a document originally started as a way for email programs to handle files that they didn't natively support (read the history at `http://www.tcpipguide.com/free/ t_MIMEMessageFormatOverviewMotivationHistoryandStand.htm`). However, since MIME was originally introduced as a means of overcoming the limitations of text-based email, it's found its way into a variety of applications including the browser and even Windows. In short, setting the MIME type correctly is critical if you want IIS to provide the right support to the client. If you want to read about the internal workings of MIME, you can find the standard at `http://www.faqs.org/rfcs/rfc2049.html`. The following sections describe working with MIME in detail.

FIGURE 3.7
Enable directory browsing at the lowest level possible.

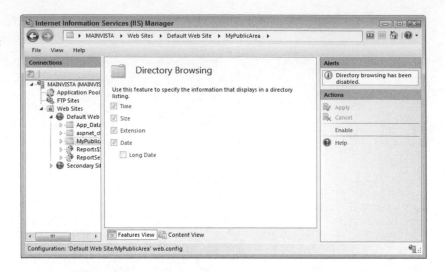

FIGURE 3.8
The user sees the complete directory structure for the areas where you enable directory browsing.

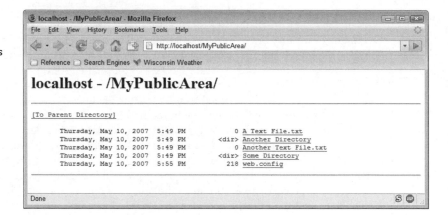

Understanding the Basic MIME Types

From the administrator's perspective, MIME types include a file extension and a string that tells what kind of application to use to handle the file. For example, the PDF file extension has a MIME type of application/pdf. The first part of the MIME type tells you that the system uses an application to handle the file and the second part tells you that the application is the type assigned to the PDF file extension. As another example, a WAV file, which contains a sound bite in most cases, uses a MIME type audio/wav. The first part specifies this is an audio file and that the system should use the application responsible for WAV files to handle it. There's a very definite pattern to creating a MIME type—the file type comes first, followed by the handler type. The file types normally fall into the following categories:

- Application
- Audio

- ◆ Example

- ◆ Image

- ◆ Message

- ◆ Model

- ◆ Multipart

- ◆ Text

- ◆ Video

NOTE   Even though you define the MIME type within IIS, the user never actually sees it because the MIME type appears as part of the Web page header. A Web page always uses a complex header that includes multiple MIME types because Web pages contain more than one kind of information. You can read more about how these headers work at `http://www.tcpipguide.com/ free/t_MIMEBasicStructuresandHeaders.htm`.

As previously mentioned, IIS does define a considerable number of common MIME types for you. To see the list of existing MIME types, select the connection you want to work with in the Connections pane and then double-click the MIME Types icons. You'll see a list of MIME types as shown in Figure 3.9.

However, you might have to work with some uncommon MIME types. In this case, you can rely on a number of alternatives sources to determine the MIME type to add to IIS. The first source you should consider is the vendor responsible for creating the file extension. Often, a vendor provides the information as part of the application documentation.

FIGURE 3.9
Locate the MIME type for your file extension by reviewing the list in IIS.

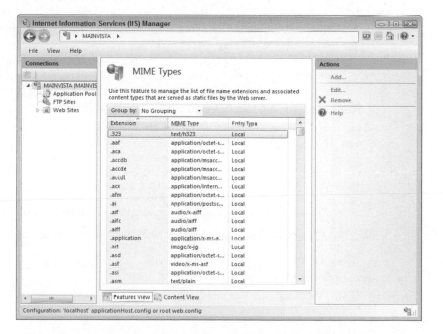

When a vendor source doesn't exist, you can always check the registry. Choose Start ➤ Run, type **RegEdit** in the Open field, and then click OK. Locate the file extension you want to add in the HKEY_ CLASSES_ROOT hive. Figure 3.10 shows the .wav file extension. Notice the Content Type value in the right pane contains the MIME types for WAV files.

FIGURE 3.10
In many cases, you can find the MIME information you need in the registry.

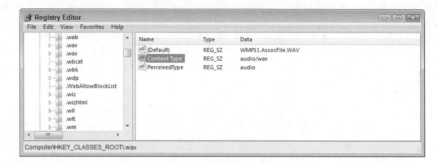

TIP If you find that the MIME type in the registry is incorrect, double-click the Content Type value and change the MIME information it contains. Likewise, if the registry lacks a MIME type, you can add a Content Type value as shown in Figure 3.10.

In some cases, you won't have a local resource you can use. If the vendor who created the file extension has a Web site, you might be able to find the information there. You could also find the MIME type defined on one of many Web sites that provide a list of standardized MIME types such as Internet Assigned Numbers Authority (IANA) at http://www.iana.org/assignments/ media-types/ and LANTech at http://www.ltsw.se/knbase/internet/mime.htp.

TIP If you truly can't find a MIME type for a particular file extension, then you should register it with IANA at http://www.iana.org/cgi-bin/mediatypes.pl. This group will verify that the MIME type doesn't exist and add it to their list if necessary. In no case should you ever make up a MIME type of your own and attempt to use it with a Web application. If everyone used this approach, then chaos would result because each file could have multiple MIME types associated with it.

Associating a MIME Type with an Application

Despite all of the help IIS provides, you may eventually need to add a MIME type to the list. Make sure you use a valid MIME type for the file extension, or users of your Web site will experience problems. (The user also has to have the correct association on their machine and have an application that supports that MIME type installed.) Use these steps to add a new MIME type.

1. Select the connection you want to use in the Connections pane and then double-click the MIME Types icon. You'll see the display shown in Figure 3.9.

2. Click Add. You'll see the Add Mime Type dialog box shown in Figure 3.11.

FIGURE 3.11
Adding a new MIME type requires you provide a file extension and registered MIME type.

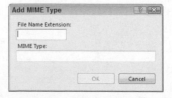

3. Type the file extension you want to use, complete with initial period, in the File Name Extension field.

4. Type the registered MIME type in the MIME Type field.

NOTE   Make sure you include the file type (or category, depending on which resource you use), followed by a slash, followed by the file handler type. For example, application/wav is valid, wav alone is not. MIME types don't typically include any spaces—application / wav isn't valid either.

5. Click OK. IIS adds the new MIME type to the list in alphabetical order by file extension.

Setting the MIME type in IIS doesn't assure that there's a program to handle the file type. The registry contains a number of file extensions that lack a corresponding application. Consequently, when an application sees the file extension, it won't know what to do with the file even though it has an associated MIME type. Theoretically, Windows will ask the user to look for an application to handle the file either locally or online. However, you can also help the user to set the correct handler. Use these steps to associate an application with a file type in Windows 2003, Windows XP, and earlier versions of Windows:

1. Choose the Tools ➢ Folder options command in Windows Explorer.

2. Select the File Types tab in the Folder Options dialog box shown in Figure 3.12.

FIGURE 3.12
The file associations appear in the File Types tab in earlier versions of Windows.

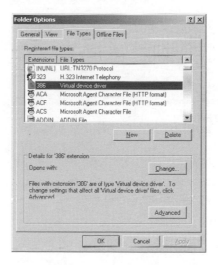

3. Locate the file extension you want to associate with an application.

4. Click Change. You'll see an Opens With dialog box.

5. Choose the application you want to associate with the file and then click OK. Windows will create the file association and use the application to handle files of that MIME type.

Windows Vista and future versions of Windows use a different technique to set the file association. Use the following steps to work with these newer versions of Windows.

1. Open the Default Programs applet of the Control Panel. You'll see a list of defaults options, as shown in Figure 3.13.

FIGURE 3.13
Vista and newer versions of Windows provide a different method of setting file associations.

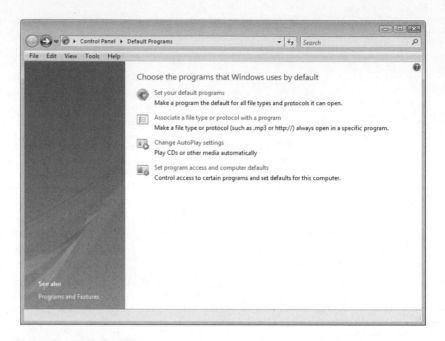

2. Click Associate File Type or Protocol with a Program. You'll see a list of file extensions, such as those shown in Figure 3.14.

FIGURE 3.14
The Vista interface makes a direct correlation between the file extension and the application.

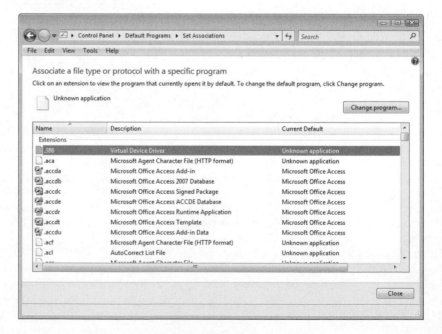

3. Click Change Program. You'll see an Open With dialog box.

NOTE   If you try to change a system file extension, such as .386, Vista warns you that the file is an executable and encourages you not to associate an application with it. If you still want to associate an application with the file extension, click Open With and you'll see the normal Open With dialog box.

4. Choose the application you want to associate with the file and then click OK. Windows creates the file association and uses the application to handle files of that MIME type.

Editing and Deleting MIME Types

You may run into a situation where you have to modify a MIME type. In very rare cases, you might have to edit one to correct it for mistakes. The MIME types that you obtain with IIS should be correct, as are those from IANA. However, you might obtain a bad MIME type from the registry (rare, but it could happen during an application installation), the vendor, or a third-party Web site. The steps for editing a MIME type are similar to those used to add one. The only difference is that you click Edit, instead of Add. See the "Associating a MIME Type with an Application" section of the chapter for details.

You may decide that you don't want the server to support a particular MIME type. For example, the MIME type may not exist on your server and shouldn't exist under normal circumstances. Removing the MIME type could alert you to problems with content that others are placing on the Web site or to the changes an outsider is making to your files. Normally, you won't want to remove standard MIME entries that someone could legitimately use to ensure the output from the Web site is correct. When you want to remove a MIME type, highlight the entry and click Remove.

Working with Handlers

A handler is a DLL or other executable that responds to a particular request from a client. IIS receives the request, locates the appropriate handler for the request, and then passes request information to that handler. You can view the handlers for IIS by choosing the connection you want to work with in the Connections pane and then double-clicking the Handler Mappings icon. The following sections describe handlers in detail.

Understanding Handler Functionality

The request is always in the form of a file. You define the request in the form of a path. If you include only the file specification, then the handler applies to all requests of that type at the level you specify. A file specification can include wildcards, so you could provide a handler for all ASP files by using the *.asp file specification. If you want the handler to apply to all requests, then you simply provide the * (asterisk) wildcard character. IIS also lets you specify a folder as a path when you specify a folder, without providing a file specification.

A request can include more than one handler. For example, Figure 3.15 shows that the *.ashx path requires two handlers. In fact, you'll notice several paths require two or more handlers to complete the response. IIS passes the request to each of the enabled handlers in turn. IIS skips any disabled handlers, so you never have to uninstall a handler when you simply want to keep it from working with the requests for testing or other reasons.

IIS does let you set the order of the handlers on the system. However, because this functionality is open to anyone, you can't always assume that the handlers will appear in a certain order. To change the handler order, click View Ordered List in the Actions pane. The list changes as shown in Figure 3.16. Click Move Up or Move Down to change the handler's order in the list. IIS calls handlers at the top of the list first and then moves down. Consequently, when you have two handlers for the same path, the first handler will work with the request first, and then the second. When you've placed the handlers in the order that you want, click View Unordered List to return to the view shown in Figure 3.15.

FIGURE 3.15
Each path can have one or more handlers that IIS calls in turn.

FIGURE 3.16
Set the order of the handlers by using the ordered view shown here.

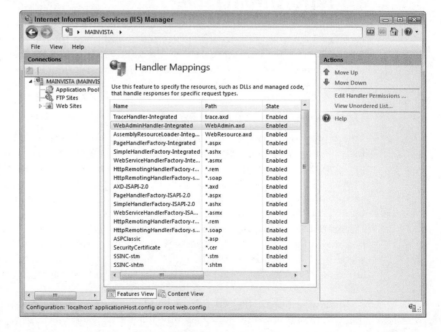

WARNING   You can't assume anything about the calling order of the handlers. Consequently, you can't create handlers that require pre- or post-processing by another handler. Each handler must provide stand-alone services to IIS. In addition, you can't assume that a particular handler is even present because another administrator could disable or uninstall one handler and leave another handler in place. Always assume a single, isolated handler scenario for testing purposes on your server to ensure that the handlers work as required. Obviously, you must also ensure that handlers will work in the presence of other handlers because the administrator could install more than one.

You can modify handler functionality using several techniques. It's possible to enable and disable handlers as needed (see the "Enabling and Disabling Handlers" section of the chapter for details). IIS also lets you change handler permissions so the handler will work in some situations, but not in others. For example, you can set a handler to perform tasks when the user requests a folder, but not a file. In addition, you can set restrictions on the verbs that the handler affects, such as GET, HEAD, POST, and others. The "Changing Handler Restrictions" section of the chapter describes handler restrictions in detail.

Enabling and Disabling Handlers

A handler is only functional when you enable it. IIS provides the means for enabling and disabling handlers as needed. You can install a handler, but decide not to use it for requests until needed. A handler could provide special functionality, such as debugging, or it might represent a security risk in certain circumstances.

IIS disables two handlers by default: CGI-exe and ISAPI-dll. In both cases, modern Web sites don't commonly use the functionality they provide and they both have security issues. You must enable the CGI-exe handler if you want to use CGI scripts on your server. Likewise, you need the ISAPI-dll if you want to use ISAPI extensions (as contrasted to ISAPI filters) on your Web site. IIS doesn't offer a choice of which handlers to enable. You enable both of these handlers by enabling one of them.

WARNING   The risks posed by both CGI and ISAPI extensions are real. CGI resides on just about every Web server, not just IIS. Consequently, the security issues for CGI don't just affect IIS, but affect many other servers such as Apache. You can find a wealth of information about CGI security risks online including the FAQs at http://www.w3.org/Security/Faq/ and http://www.irt.org/articles/js184/index.htm. To learn more about possible ISAPI extension risks, read the articles at http://msdn2.microsoft.com/en us/library/ms525338.aspx, http://www.microsoft.com/technet/security/Bulletin/MS01-004.mspx, and http://www.microsoft.com/technet/security/Bulletin/MS01-023.mspx. In fact, you'll find a considerable number of articles online about security risks for both technologies—you should only use these technologies in a safe environment and only when necessary for backward compatibility.

IIS enables and disables handlers based on the permissions you provide to a specific level of the hierarchy. In fact, IIS provides three levels of permissions for handlers:

Read   Only a few handlers require just read permission. In fact, in a default IIS configuration, you can only rely on three handlers: OPTIONSVerbHandler, TRACEVerbHandler, and StaticFile to work with just the read permission. The read permission simply gives the handler permission to read data. The important handler at this level is the StaticFile handler because it lets the Web server provide a default document, allows the user to perform browsing, and provides the means to serve static content. Even though you can separately enable the scripts permission and make many handlers active, the loss of the StaticFile handler will almost certainly affect the user's ability to interact with your Web site.

Scripts   The scripts permission lets script files, but not executables, run at the designated level. Consequently, allowing this permission enables the ASPClassic handler, along with a host of others, but not the StaticFile handler. The interesting issue, here, is that you could set up the Web site such that the user can only access the scriptable items, such as ASP files. The user would need to know the precise URL for accessing the entry point, but then you could provide links in the Web pages to move from page to page. The user wouldn't even know that you had all of the features provided by the StaticFile handler unless they tried to access the Web site without using a precise URL.

Execute   Some handlers, such as CGI-exe and ISAPI-dll, require permission to execute code. In order to set this permission, you must also enable the scripts permission. However, you don't need to enable the read permission. Consequently, you can still obtain a little added security when using the CGI-exe and ISAPI-dll handlers by disabling the read permission.

NOTE   Besides opening security holes in your Web site, enabling the execute permission also places a performance penalty on your Web site. Use the execute permission only when absolutely required.

To change the permission for a particular level (and therefore enable or disable handlers), select the level you want to change in the Connections pane. Double-click Handler Mappings and you'll see a display like the one shown in Figure 3.15. Click Edit Handler Permissions in the Actions pane. You'll see an Edit Handler Permission dialog box like the one shown in Figure 3.17. By default, IIS enables the read and scripts permissions. Change the permissions as needed and click OK. IIS changes the permission for the selected level. Since the server, Web sites, and every folder can have different permissions, you should set the permissions as needed at the lowest possible level.

FIGURE 3.17
Modify the handler permissions to enable or disable handlers.

Adding a Managed Handler

A managed handler relies on managed code developed using the .NET Framework. CLR compiles and runs the code. A managed handler relies on a specific .NET Framework class as a base class—the class that defines the initial or starting characteristics of the managed handler. IIS comes with all of the default-managed handlers configured. Normally, the only time you need to add a managed handler is when a developer creates one based on one of the other .NET Framework classes. You may also need to add a managed handler when you want to configure an existing handler to work with a new path.

To add a managed handler, select the level you want to use as a starting point for the handler in the Connections pane. Double-click Handler Mappings and you'll see a display like the one shown in Figure 3.15. Click Add Managed Handler in the Actions pane and you'll see the Add Managed Handler dialog box shown in Figure 3.18. Type the new path Request Path field. Choose one of the handler classes from the Type field. Provide a human-readable name for the handler in the Name field. Optionally, click Request Restrictions to configure the handler restrictions (see the "Changing Handler Restrictions" section of the chapter for details). Click OK. IIS adds the new handler to the list.

FIGURE 3.18
Provide a path, executable file type, and common name for the managed handler.

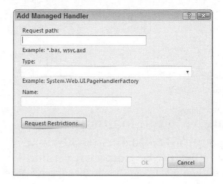

TIP Microsoft is still working on the documentation for writing a managed handler at the time of this writing. However, you can find one example at http://msdn2.microsoft.com/en-us/library/bb332050.aspx. This article also shows how to add the custom handler directly to the ApplicationHost.CONFIG file located in the \Windows\System32\inetsrv\config folder. The ApplicationHost.CONFIG file holds all of the configuration information normally added using the Add Managed Handler dialog box. If the handler doesn't appear to work, make sure the managed module is registered in the Global Assembly Cache (GAC) using the GACUtil. You can find directions for using this utility at http://msdn2.microsoft.com/en-us/library/ex0ss12c(VS.80).aspx. You may also want to purchase a copy of my book, *Windows Administration at the Command Line* (Sybex, 2007) to receive full instructions in human-readable form.

Adding a Script Map

A script map is a connection to an unmanaged handler of some type. In most cases, the handler is an EXE or DLL file. You use a script map to provide support for older native code handlers. For example, you'll use a script map to create a handler entry for your ISAPI extension.

NOTE IIS requires that any EXE files you enter using a script map conform to the CGI specification. You can find this specification at http://www.w3.org/CGI/. Any DLL files you enter using a script map must conform to the requirements for ISAPI extensions. See the ISAPI extension overview at http://msdn2.microsoft.com/en-us/library/ms525172.aspx.

To add a script map, select the level you want to use as a starting point for the handler in the Connections pane. Double-click Handler Mappings and you'll see a display like the one shown in Figure 3.15. Click Add Script Map in the Actions pane and you'll see the Add Script Map dialog box shown in Figure 3.19. Type the new path Request Path field. Type the name and location of the executable file in the Executable field (you can also use the browse button to locate the file). Provide a human-readable name for the handler in the Name field. Optionally, click Request Restrictions to configure the handler restrictions (see the "Changing Handler Restrictions" section of the chapter for details). Click OK. IIS adds the new handler to the list.

FIGURE 3.19
Use script maps to create a connection between a path and an unmanaged handler.

Adding a Module Mapping

It's important to know the difference between modules and handlers. A module processes every request, no matter what the user is requesting. A handler works with specific files. For example, you can add an authentication module to the server, Web site, or folder that authenticates all incoming requests. The type of request doesn't matter—the module always performs the authentication. A module mapping performs the additional task of mapping specific files to a module. Before you can use this feature, you must first create the module entry. The "Working with Response Modules" section of Chapter 4 describes how to work with modules in detail.

Module mappings tend to refine how a module works, rather than determine the handling of a particular file. For example, select the OPTIONSVerbHandler entry in the list and click Edit. You'll see that the module mapping uses the * path to check all requests. The module type is a Protocol-SupportModule. If you don't go any further, you'll never see why this mapping is necessary. Click Request Restrictions and choose the Verbs tab. The reason for the mapping becomes clear at this point. The only verb that this mapping reacts to is the OPTIONS verb. The selection of verb refines how the module works in this case, rather than determining which file the module handles.

To add a module mapping, select the level you want to use as a starting point for the handler in the Connections pane. Double-click Handler Mappings and you'll see a display like the one shown in Figure 3.15. Click Add Module Mapping in the Actions pane and you'll see the Add Module Mapping dialog box shown in Figure 3.20. Type the new path Request Path field. Choose the module you want to use from the list in the Module field. Provide a human-readable name for the handler in the Name field. Optionally, click Request Restrictions to configure the handler restrictions (see the "Changing Handler Restrictions" section of the chapter for details). Click OK. IIS adds the new module mapping to the list.

FIGURE 3.20
Provide a path, executable file type, and common name for the managed handler.

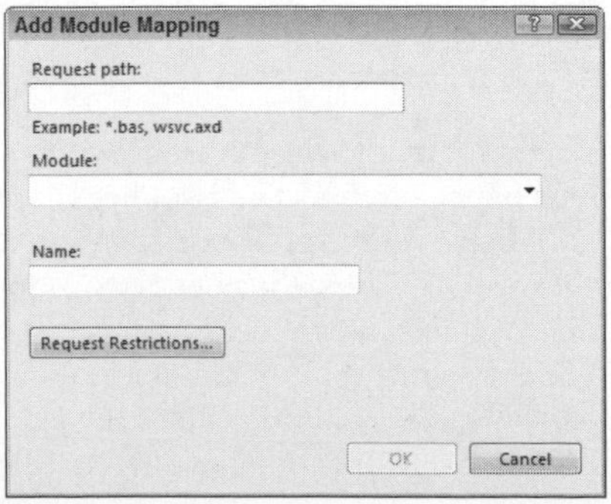

Editing Handler Settings

Whenever you need to modify the settings for a handler, choose the handler from the list and click Edit. IIS automatically opens the correct editor (managed handler, script map, or module mapping) to edit the handler settings. After you complete the changes, click OK and IIS automatically implements them.

Renaming Handlers

IIS only allows you to rename handlers that you add. The default handler names are permanent. To rename a handler, highlight the handler you want to change and click Rename. IIS turns the handler name into an edit box where you can type a new name. Press enter when you finish changing the name to make the name permanent.

Removing Handlers

In most cases, you'll only remove handlers that you added to IIS. Removing default handlers can cause problems for the server. When you need to remove a handler, choose the handler from the list and click Remove. IIS asks if you're sure that you want to remove the handle. Click Yes. The handler becomes unavailable for use immediately.

Changing Handler Restrictions

No matter what type of managed handler, script map, or module mapping you create, you can restrict how the entry works by adding a restriction to it. A restriction affects the entry in two ways.

Mapping Determines the request level of the entry. You can choose files, folders, or both. The unselected, or default, setting is both. When the user requests a file, the entry must have the file mapping level selected in order to react to the request and provide a response. Some entries react only to files, such as the ASPClassic script map.

Verb Determines the action the request is making. A verb defines some type of action, such as getting a Web page or deleting a file. Limiting the number of verbs that an entry supports can have security and performance implications. The more verbs that an entry supports, the greater the performance hit and the more likely it is that someone will break into the system using a flaw in the entry code.

IIS supports a number of verbs. These verbs describe the kind of request that the client is making. For example, the client may want to GET the specified resource, which is normally a file. The number of verbs available to you depends on the applications you have installed and the capabilities of the handlers that you provide. The most common verbs include:

◆ GET

◆ HEAD

◆ POST

◆ DEBUG

◆ TRACE

◆ PUT

◆ DELETE

◆ CONNECT

◆ OPTIONS

These nine verbs appear as part of the HTTP 1.1 standard found in RFC 2616 (`http://www.faqs`
`.org/rfcs/rfc2616.html`). However, this is just the tip of the verb iceberg. For example, if you're
working with Web Document Authoring and Versioning (WebDAV), then you also have WebDAV
verbs such as PROPFIND and MOVE available to you. The article titled "Distributed Authoring
and Versioning Extensions for HTTP Enable Team Authoring" at `http://www.microsoft.com/`
`msj/0699/dav/dav.aspx` provides a better description of the WebDAV verbs.

WARNING   Many verbs have known security issues. In fact, these issues have been around since
IIS 4.0. Limit the verbs you use to just those that the user actually requires. For example, instead
of providing all of the verbs when a user only needs to see a static page, support GET alone
instead. As another example, when a user needs to upload a form to your Web site, allow only the
PUT verb, not the other verbs that IIS supports. Only support the DELETE verb when you truly
want the user to delete files on your server.

To change the restrictions for an entry, click the Request Restrictions button shown in Figures 3.18,
3.19, and 3.20. You'll see the Request Restrictions dialog box shown in Figure 3.21. You can select the
Mapping and Verbs tab as needed to add restrictions to the handler. Click OK twice and IIS makes
the required changes to the entry's restrictions.

FIGURE 3.21
Define restrictions
for the entry so that
it only processes the
requests that you
want it to process.

Adding Virtual Directories to the Web Site

Virtual directories let you add information stored in another location to the current Web site. The
directory appears as if it belongs within the Web site, but it physically resides somewhere else.
The most important issue is that the user sees the virtual directory as a local directory. The physical location of the directory remains hidden from view. Unless you give someone access to your
server, they won't know that the directory isn't where the Web server says it's located. Consequently, using virtual directories can provide a security boost to your system. Someone outside
of your organization will have a significantly harder time trying to figure out the organization of
your Web server and won't be able to use that organization against you.

Of course, virtual directories have a number of other benefits too. You may not have room on
a single hard drive to store all of the data for your Web site. Using virtual directories lets you put
multiple hard drives together in order to form one large Web site.

Even when you do have room for the entire Web site on one system, using virtual directories lets you split up the Web site into functional areas. Each group that works on the Web site can modify their data locally. They won't see the data provided by other groups. The user sees a final cohesive result, but each group only sees the data that they need to modify in order to maintain the Web site. For these reasons, and others, you should always use virtual directories whenever possible when designing a Web site. The following sections describe how to create virtual directories and manage their settings.

Creating a Virtual Directory

You can add virtual directories to Web sites, folders, and applications. You can't add virtual directories to the Web server. The options for adding virtual directories to Web sites and applications appear in both the Contents View and Features View. When you want to add a virtual directory to a folder, you must select Contents View and choose the folder from within Contents View, rather than in the Connection Pane.

To add the virtual directory, select the entry that will receive the virtual directory in either the Connections pane or Content View as needed. Click Add Virtual Directory in the Actions pane. You'll see the Add Virtual Directory dialog box shown in Figure 3.22. Type the name of the virtual directory as you want it to appear on the Web site in the Alias field. Type the physical location of the virtual directory in the Physical Path field (you can also click the browse button to locate the physical directory). Click OK. IIS adds the virtual directory for you.

Viewing Virtual Directories

IIS allows viewing of virtual directory information at the Web site and application levels. To view a virtual directory, select the entry in the Connections pane and choose View Virtual Directories in the Actions pane. You'll see a display similar to the one shown in Figure 3.23. Notice that the Actions pane includes the Add Virtual Directory option. The "Creating a Virtual Directory" section of the chapter shows how to perform this task. Even if you don't have a virtual directory selected, you can change the overall defaults for all virtual directories. The "Defining Default Virtual Directory Settings" section of the chapter shows how to modify the default settings.

When you select a particular virtual directory, as shown in Figure 3.23, IIS makes additional options available in the Actions pane. Click Explore to open a copy of Windows Explorer with the physical location of the virtual directory selected. You can use this feature to make changes to the content of the virtual directory. Likewise, click Browse to see how the virtual directory appears in your browser. You can remove an existing virtual directory by selecting its entry and clicking Remove.

FIGURE 3.22
Add virtual directories as needed to provide data connectivity to your Web site.

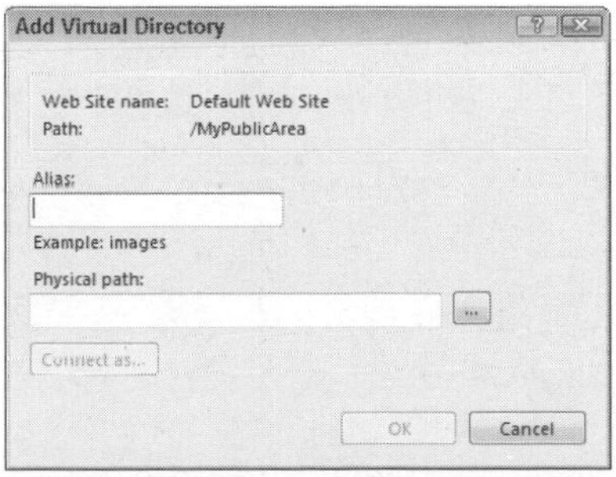

FIGURE 3.23
IIS makes it easy to view all of the virtual directories for a Web site or application.

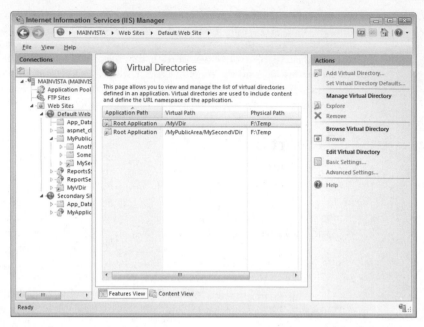

The remaining two entries let you configure an individual virtual directory. Click Basic Settings and you'll see a dialog box similar to the one shown in Figure 3.22. This dialog box lets you change the virtual directory alias and physical location. When you click Advanced Settings, you see the Advanced Settings dialog box shown in Figure 3.24 where you can change the virtual directory's physical location and provide the credentials used to access the directory. The "Setting the Default Web Site Configuration" section of Chapter 2 describes the Physical Path Credentials Logon Type field entries.

Defining Default Virtual Directory Settings

It's important to set the default settings for the virtual directories you create to reflect the minimum security setup. In other words, you should restrict access as much as possible within the guidelines for your company. It's easy enough to relax the restrictions for a virtual directory later. If you create the virtual directory with the minimum access, then relaxing the restrictions later will pose less risk to your organization.

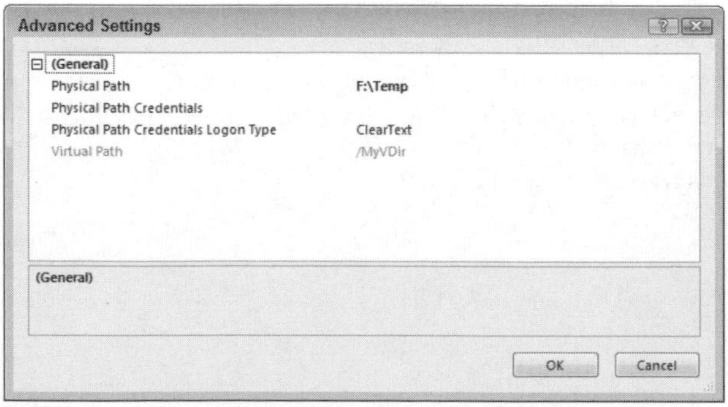

FIGURE 3.24
Modify the physical location and credentials for a virtual directory.

When you click Set Virtual Directory Defaults in the Actions pane, you see a Virtual Directory Defaults dialog box that's similar to the one shown for a specific virtual directory in Figure 3.24. Obviously, you won't see any physical path information or alias. However, you'll see the credentials and logon type information shown in Figure 3.24. You configure the settings just as you would for an individual virtual directory except that the new settings affect all new virtual directories you create (existing virtual directories continue to use the defaults in place at the time you created them or any special settings you provided).

Let's Start Building

This chapter introduces you to files. Every Web site uses files for some purpose, even if all of the content resides on virtual pages. At some point, you use configuration, application, resource, log, or data files. Working with files also means adding MIME information and providing handlers for them. In some cases, for security reasons or simply for convenience, you have to place files in locations other than the directory that the user sees. This chapter helps you build these skills:

- Locate files as you need them using both browsing and exploring techniques

- Define a default document, which may mean removing documents you don't need

- Use directory browsing to provide a directory-like interface for visitors who need to find content based on type or other means

- Define MIME types for files

- Manage content handlers

- Manage virtual directories for both convenience and security

Now that you have these new skills, you'll want to practice them on a test server. Begin by simply browsing and exploring. It's important to know how to perform both tasks. Make sure you define a default document for your Web site. IIS comes with a default document that probably doesn't meet your needs. Now that you're aware of the files on your system, you'll want to replace that default with a specific document for your Web site. Decide whether to use directory browsing to help users find complex data. You'll also want to make a list of MIME types for special files on your Web server. Add new MIME types as needed. Work with the content handlers on your system to ensure applications work correctly. Finally, try creating a virtual directory or two to see how they work and understand how they can protect your Web server from prying eyes.

Chapter 4 addresses a topic that may almost seem outdated—basic HTML files. In actuality, IIS 7 comes with some HTML files in place. You'll want to either replace those files with new ones or learn how to work with them. HTML isn't actually dead. Many people still use it in situations where content is static and likely to remain so. Because HTML is so reliable and understood by so many browsers, it also provides a fallback when newer technologies fail to address a particular need or simply don't work right. In other words, you have a lot of reasons to read Chapter 4, even though the topic might seem outdated.

Part 2

Configuring Older Applications

- ◆ **Chapter 4: Working with Basic HTML**
- ◆ **Chapter 5: Working with ASP**
- ◆ **Chapter 6: Working with Other Application Types**
- ◆ **Chapter 7: Using the Internet Information Services 6.0 Manager**

Chapter 4

Working with Basic HTML

You may think that the basic HyperText Markup Language (HTML) file has gone completely away, never to make an appearance again. After all, the basic HTML file is a technology from the early days of the Internet that doesn't make sense anymore with ASP.NET applications, data served from databases, and content created from multiple sources—even Web services. A standard IIS 7 setup still contains basic HTML pages. You can remove these pages and substitute your own, but most people won't replace the standard error message pages that are part of an IIS 7. Therefore, you'll at least need to consider those pages.

Basic HTML pages aren't as useless as you might think. The fastest page you can serve from IIS 7 is the basic HTML page. Consequently, if you have a piece of static content you need to present that seldom, if ever, changes, using a basic HTML page might be the best method of providing a quick, reliable method of accessing the data online. This chapter considers a number of valid uses for the aging HTML technology so you shouldn't count it as dead yet.

Even though HTML pages provide solid performance and reliability that's often missing from other solutions, you still might encounter broken links and other problems with them. Just because you use an HTML page for some content, doesn't mean that everyone should be able to view it as well. All these scenarios end in one way—a failed request. This chapter discusses techniques you can use to trace and handle failed requests quickly.

Part of working with HTML files (and most other file types) is configuring a request module. The request module provides a means of evaluating and serving the content that the caller needs. The request module itself is some type of executable file with which IIS interacts. After the request module receives the input from IIS, it evaluates the request and formulates a response. Even though request modules deal with many file types, you'll find them discussed in this chapter as part of the first file type they service, the basic HTML file.

In this chapter, you will learn how to do the following:

◆ Configure a basic HTML page

◆ Move existing HTML to IIS 7

◆ Develop an error page strategy

◆ Trace and handle failed requests

◆ Implement and maintain request modules

Working with Basic HTML Pages in IIS 7

Some readers are almost certainly wondering why any discussion of basic HTML even appears in this book. This technology is definitely old, but you really do want to know about it for a number of reasons. Here are the most common reasons to know about HTML today.

◆ Your company has older content that you don't want to update but still need to support.

◆ Web sites require a reliable means of displaying error pages when problems occur and HTML is about as reliable as you can get.

◆ The server is hosting a number of smaller personal Web sites where using HTML is probably the easiest way of presenting information.

◆ All request modules provide output that's a combination of basic HTML and script, so knowing how HTML works is still important, and experimenting with HTML pages is often the best way to gain the required knowledge.

◆ It's important to provide some static content that rarely changes in a form that the user can always request, such as company contact pages.

◆ Your company wants to provide a default document with a common name that users might request directly.

◆ The Web page must appear on multiple servers and the servers rely on multiple platforms such as Apache and Tomcat, in addition to IIS.

◆ Users that have personal Web sites on your server will normally use an application that generates only HTML to provide content for their personal Web site.

IIS 7 hasn't changed support for basic HTML pages. You still create, manage, and manipulate HTML pages as you always have when working with IIS. Like Windows 2003, the default Web page that IIS creates for you is IISStart.HTM. In earlier versions of IIS, the default page worked with ASP technology, which has fallen out of favor with Microsoft (but not administrators in general). Consequently, you'll see a basic HTML page on your first use of IIS. In addition, IIS still uses error pages with an .HTM extension.

NOTE   Don't get the idea from this section that you should use HTML for any kind of new development. Although HTML does work well and it's reliable, most companies use other technologies today for creating Web pages that are dynamic, full featured, and responsive to the viewer's needs. View this section as the exceptions to the rule. Yes, if you own a personal Web site with only a few pages on it, HTML is probably a good choice, but most corporations won't use HTML for anything new.

HTML pages have a number of benefits, especially for novice users, so you shouldn't rule them out on smaller Web sites. In fact, it's surprising that Microsoft uses HTML at all in IIS 7 since IIS 7 has ASP.NET support built in. Because Microsoft is so adamant about ASP.NET, you'd think they would have made all of the Web pages ASP.NET pages. The inclusion of so many HTML pages prompts the question of why Microsoft is using them. Obviously, no one at Microsoft will comment on such a question, but there are some good reasons when you think about them, and they appear in the following list.

Simplicity   Learning to use HTML isn't too hard and most people understand it after only a few sessions. You'll find many tutorials for creating HTML online and many third-party products create the HTML for you as you draw the Web page you want to see.

Portable   You can use HTML on any Web server. Although there are ways to port other technologies to multiple platforms, HTML is possibly the only solution that's compatible on everything. (For an example of how you can port ASP.NET applications to Java and use it with Tomcat, see the article at http://www.devsource.com/article2/0,1759,1738159,00.asp.)

Standardized   HTML and its associated technologies, such as Cascading Style Sheets (CSS), enjoy a significant level of standardization. The standards ensure that everyone knows how significant features should work and make it easier for browser vendors to provide full compliance. When you use basic HTML, you can assume the fullest browser support, which translates into reliability when it comes to application use. Of course, you give up a whole bunch of flexibility and dynamic features for this support, so standardization can spell rigid and boring.

Tool Support   Because HTML appears on every Web server and every browser, you'll find more tools to work with HTML than any other form of Web presentation. In fact, it's likely that so many tools are available that you couldn't possibly use them all in a lifetime. In addition, because HTML is relatively simple and standardized, the tools usually work flawlessly (and have no reason to do otherwise).

No matter what you might think about basic HTML, you can see that it still has a small, but important, role to fulfill in IIS 7. Of course, you can always choose to ignore it completely and build all those error pages out of ASP.NET—a task that Microsoft chose not to perform.

Moving Existing HTML Pages to IIS 7

One of the best reasons to work with HTML is that it's extremely simple to move the files. You can use a utility such as XCopy to move the entire application in a matter of minutes, while preserving the entire application structure. In fact, if you use XCopy with the /O command line switch, you can copy security information along with the application. The XCopy utility is actually very handy for Web site administrators, especially when you host personal Web sites. For example, you can use it to create a default directory structure and provide one or two default files for the new Web site owner.

No matter how you move the HTML files, security is a concern. If you decide not to set security based on the existing files, then you need to set security manually, which means working in Windows Explorer. It's important to remember that .NET security won't affect your HTML files, which is one more reason to set them aside at some point.

Finally, you need to consider the configuration settings that IIS does provide for HTML files. For example, you need to consider the default document and determine whether you'll allow directory browsing. The following sections discuss all of these issues.

NOTE   Newer versions of Windows also provide the RoboCopy utility, which provides significantly more flexibility than XCopy. Because XCopy is the most common utility and provides everything that most people are going to need, I chose to use it in this chapter. However, you can read about the RoboCopy utility at http://www.ss64.com/nt/robocopy.html. You may also want to review the Knowledge Base articles at http://support.microsoft.com/kb/323275 and http://support.microsoft.com/kb/250267.

Moving Your Files with XCopy

The XCopy utility is one of the few that even Microsoft mentions regularly because it's so handy to have. You use the XCopy utility to perform bulk file transfers from anywhere on a local network to anywhere else on a local network. In addition to copying single files, XCopy can copy entire directory structures. It also has a wealth of command line switches so you have precise control over the copying process. This utility uses the following syntax:

```
XCOPY source [destination] [/A | /M] [/D[:date]] [/P] [/S [/E]] [/V]
      [/W] [/C] [/I] [/Q] [/F] [/L] [/G] [/H] [/R] [/T] [/U] [/K] [/N]
      [/O] [/X] [/Y] [/-Y] [/Z] [/B] [/EXCLUDE:file1[+file2][+file3]...]
```

The following list describes each of the command line arguments.

source   Specifies which files to copy. You can use wildcard characters to define the file specification. The file specification can also include a drive and absolute or relative path.

destination   Specifies the destination for the files. When working with a single file, you can also specify a new filename for the file.

/A   Copies only the files with the archive attribute set. Copying the files doesn't change the attribute status, so you need to use the Attrib utility to change the archive bit. Some people use this particular feature to create a simple, but effective, backup utility. They send any changed files to a hard drive on another machine and then clear the archive attribute. As an alternative, if you know the copying methodology works without flaw, you can use the /M command line switch.

/M   Copies only the files with the archive attribute set. However, unlike the /A command line switch, this command line switch does reset the archive bit.

TIP   Some people use the XCopy utility as an inexpensive way to back up their Web site data to another location. You can use the /A or /M command line switches to create a backup of the Web site in another location, just in case the primary location fails. By using the archive bit as an indicator of change, you can reduce the time required to create the backup.

/D[:Month-Day-Year]   Copies files changed on or after the specified date. When you leave out the date, then XCopy only copies the file when the date of an existing file in the destination is older than the source file. If the dates are the same or newer, then XCopy doesn't copy the file.

/P   Prompts the user before creating each destination file. You definitely don't want to use this command line switch when moving a Web site from one location to another.

/S   Copies all files in the current directory, plus all subdirectories and their files except empty subdirectories. You can't use this command line switch to create an empty directory structure for a user or application; use the /E command line switch instead.

/E   Copies all files in the current directory, plus all subdirectories and their files including empty subdirectories. You must use this command line switch with the /S command line switch.

/V   Verifies each new file as the system writes it. This command line switch overrides the system verify setting.

/W   Waits for the user to insert a floppy disk or other removable media before beginning the copy process. Generally, you'd use this option as part of a batch file where the copying process requires more than one disk.

/C   Forces XCopy to continue copying files even when an error occurs. Normally, XCopy stops when it encounters the first copy error.

/I   Forces XCopy to assume the destination is a directory when the destination doesn't exist and you're copying more than one file. Otherwise, XCopy displays a message asking the user whether the destination is a file or a directory. This will cause a batch file to halt to wait for user participation.

/Q   Copies the files without displaying the filenames. You can use this option in a batch file where you don't necessarily want the user bothered or aware of everything that's happening in the background.

/F   Displays full source and destination filenames while copying, including both the drive and the path. Normally, XCopy displays only the filenames. This feature often comes in handy when diagnosing problems with complex batch files because it shows precisely where XCopy copies each file.

/L   Displays a list of files that XCopy would copy, without actually copying them. This is a diagnostic mode where you can log the files and verify the command line syntax produces the desired result.

/G   Copies encrypted files to a destination that doesn't support encryption. This is a Windows-specific command line switch. The resulting destination files are unencrypted when you complete the copy, so using this command line switch can result in a security hole in your system.

/H   Copies any files marked hidden or system. Normally, XCopy only copies the files without these attributes since hidden and system files are normally associated with operating system requirements (they aren't data files).

/R   Forces XCopy to overwrite read-only files. Normally, XCopy won't overwrite read-only files to preserve their content.

/T   Creates the directory structure, but doesn't copy any of the files. You can use this feature to create an empty directory structure for a new user or application without compromising data that might appear in an existing pattern directory structure. This command line switch won't include empty directories and subdirectories in the source. To include the complete directory structure in the destination, combine the /T and /E command line switches.

/U   Copies only the source files that already exist in the destination. You could use this feature to perform updates on another system without compromising any unique files in the source system.

/K   Copies all of the file and directory attributes. XCopy normally resets some of the attributes, such as read-only.

/N   Creates a destination file with an 8-character filename and a 3-character file extension. Use this command line switch when you must create destination files for older systems that rely on the DOS 8.3 naming convention. Avoid using this command line switch on files with long filenames unless you really do want to create a compatible file.

/O   Copies the file ownership and Access Control List (ACL) information. The ACL provides security for the file. If you don't use this command line switch, the destination system will use the default security settings for that system, which might not provide sufficient security for sensitive data. Using this particular command line switch is especially important with IIS because you want to ensure that Windows protects the files fully. If you choose not to use this command line switch, secure the files using the information in the "Considering Security Issues" section of the chapter.

/X   Copies the file audit settings in addition to the file ownership and ACL information. File auditing monitors each file as Windows opens, closes, or modifies it. Using file auditing helps you track user and system activities, but does cause a performance hit. Normally, it's not a good idea to use this command line switch when you make a copy of a Web site because you won't want Windows to audit all of the Web sites on a server.

/Y and /-Y Suppresses or enforces the prompt for overwriting destination files with the same name as the destination file provided as input to the XCopy utility. Use the /Y command line switch in batch files where you know the batch file will overwrite an existing destination file. The /-Y command line switch is the default, so you never need to use it.

/Z Copies networked files in restartable mode. If the copy process stops for any reason, XCopy will attempt to restart the file copy. You should always use this command line switch when moving IIS files from one server to another.

/B Copies a symbolic link to the target instead of the actual file pointed to by the symbolic link when the source is a symbolic link. This command line switch is only available in Vista.

/EXCLUDE:Definition1[+Definition2][+ Definition3]... Excludes files or directories based on the strings you provide. For example, specifying .TXT as a string will exclude all text files from the copy. On the other hand, specifying a string such as \MyDir will exclude the entire \MyDir subdirectory from the copy. You can make strings ambiguous to describe a number of conditions. For example, including the string My would include files or directories with the word *My* in them as any part of the name, including the extension. You can create multiple excludes by separating each exclude string with a plus sign (+).

TIP The command line is one of the more powerful, yet less appreciated, parts of Windows. XCopy is just one of many utilities at your disposal for making quick work of moving applications. Obviously, I can't discuss every command line feature in this chapter. You can obtain a new view of the command line through my book *Windows Administration at the Command Line for Windows Vista, Windows 2003, Windows XP, and Windows 2000* (Sybex, 2007).

Considering Security Issues

HTML is possibly the least secure means of providing information to users, from many perspectives—at least if you're using it to provide two-way communication. You don't obtain all of the code- and rule-based security provided with ASP.NET when working with HTML. In addition, many known security problems exist within HTML. For example, unless you specifically define the maxlength attribute for an <input> tag, the user can inject a script into your server with ease. However, even when you provide the maxlength attribute, some injection techniques still work, such as those used to circumvent security in older versions of SQL Server. Even so, you can overcome some HTML issues by ensuring you follow the HTML 4.01 specification (see http://www.w3.org/TR/REC-html40/ for details) and validate your code using a product such as the HTML validator (http://validator.w3.org/).

TIP If you find that your HTML coding techniques are a bit rusty or you haven't developed good techniques in the first place, check out the tutorials at http://www.w3schools.com/html/. Microsoft also provides some great tutorials and overviews at http://msdn2.microsoft.com/en-us/library/aa155093.aspx.

One of the best methods for securing HTML files is to ensure you set up the Windows security for them correctly. Unfortunately, IIS 7 doesn't provide a very secure environment. Use these steps to check your configuration.

1. Open the Internet Information Services (IIS) Manager console.

2. Select the Web site you want to configure.

3. Click Content View and locate the folder that contains your HTML files.

4. Click Explore in the Actions pane. IIS will open a copy of Windows Explorer with the HTML folder selected, as shown in Figure 4.1.

FIGURE 4.1
IIS automatically opens the correct folder no matter where the Web site base folder is located.

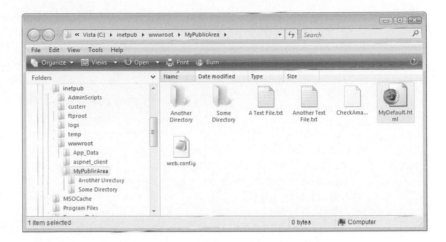

5. Right-click the selected folder and choose Properties from the context menu. Select the Security tab. Locate the IIS_IUSRS entry. You'll likely find it configured as shown in Figure 4.2.

FIGURE 4.2
Configure the HTML security to provide only what the user actually needs.

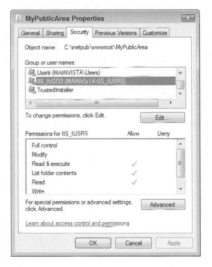

   The problem with this IIS_IUSRS configuration is that it represents the Internet Information Server Internet Users (IIS_IUSRS) account, better known as the anonymous access account. Anyone accessing this folder can read the files, list the directory content, and execute applications. This sounds like an innocuous list of rights, but really, it could backfire. When working with an HTML folder that contains static data, all that the user really needs is the right to read the files—nothing more. If you plan to use forms with HTML, then place the forms in their own special directory and allow only the forms to perform any additional acts that the application may require. In general, when configuring HTML security, fewer rights are better.

   Windows security isn't always easy to configure—it can become confusing. The user inherits rights at this level from a higher level. Consequently, if you click Edit and attempt to clear the Read & Execute right, you'll also clear the Read right. You must remove the inherited permissions first, and then set the rights at this level to match the rights the user actually requires. The following steps show how to change the rights or any user or group.

1. Click Advanced. Select the Permissions tab. You'll see the Advanced Security Settings dialog box shown in Figure 4.3.

FIGURE 4.3
Use the advanced security features provided by Windows to access HTML security.

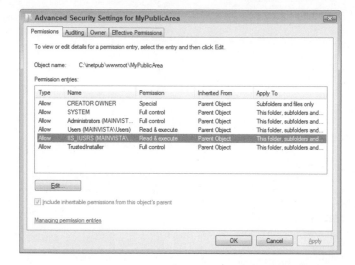

2. Click Edit. You'll see a new Advanced Security Settings dialog box like the one shown in Figure 4.4. Notice that this dialog box has options that control inheritance. In addition, you can Add, Edit, or Remove entries. At this point, you can proceed in two ways.

   ◆ Clear the Include Inheritable Permissions from this Object's Parent option. When you clear this option, Windows asks how you want to work with the security attributes. You can copy the security options from the parent and modify them as needed or you can remove the security completely, which means you'll have to set the security options for all users. In most cases, you'll want to copy the existing options so that you can modify them as needed.

   ◆ Select the individual user and perform a detailed change of rights for just that user. This option is a better choice when you have only a few users and most of them won't require any changes to their privileges. Instead of creating new rights, you simply deny access to the existing rights at a level far more detailed than allowed in other dialog boxes.

3. Highlight the user entry you want to modify and click Edit. You'll see a Permission Entry dialog box like the one shown in Figure 4.5. This dialog box requires that you use one of two techniques to set permission, based on the action you performed in the previous step.

   ◆ If you chose to clear the Include Inheritable Permissions from this Object's Parent option, check or clear options in the Allow column to modify user security. When you choose this option, you may see additional Allow entries in the dialog box shown in Figure 4.4.

   ◆ If you chose to retain the current privileges, check or clear options in the Deny column to remove rights allowed at higher levels in the directory hierarchy. When you choose this option, you'll see additional Deny entries in the dialog box shown in Figure 4.4.

FIGURE 4.4
Modify the advanced
security settings as
needed to create a
secure environment.

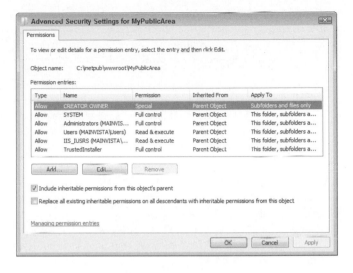

FIGURE 4.5
Change the security
settings for individual
users to meet security
requirements.

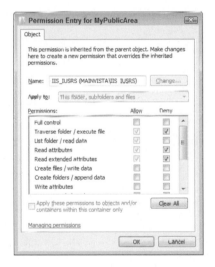

4. Click OK. When you set Deny permissions, Windows warns you that these settings take precedence over the Allow permissions. Click Yes to proceed. Windows applies the changes you requested to the folder.

TIP If you set the rights for a directory too strictly, you'll see a 500.19 – Internal Server Error message. Add the privileges back in slowly to determine which privilege has caused problems. The user is normally going to require the List Folder/Read Data right as a minimum, and may require the Read Attributes, Read Extended Attributes, and Read Permissions rights. You can usually remove the Traverse Folder/Execute File without any problem.

5. Test your application with the new settings to ensure it continues to work.

You can also control security using other IIS features. For example, you might want to remove the default page or disable features such as directory browsing (see the "Setting a Default Document" and the "Controlling the Use of Directory Browsing" in Chapter 3 for details). A good security plan controls security at multiple levels to reduce risk.

WARNING   A great security plan and setup can't overcome poor programming practices. If your Web site does use HTML content, you need to ensure that you protect yourself by using all of the appropriate attributes on Web pages, such as the maximumlength attribute. Verify any data you request from the user. In general, provide only what the user actually needs, keep security tight, and use good programming practices to limit the exposure of your Web site.

Defining the IIS Setup for HTML

Before you can support basic HTML in IIS, you need to install the required support. IIS normally includes this support by default. However, you can modify the support by choosing Start ➢ Settings ➢ Control Panel ➢ Programs and Features (in Vista and Windows Server 2008). Click the Turn Windows Features On or Off link to display the Windows Features dialog box. Open the Internet Information Services\World Wide Web Services\Common Http Features entry, as shown in Figure 4.6.

FIGURE 4.6
Select the HTML features you want to use with your Web server.

IIS 7 gives you considerable control over the HTML setup for your Web server and you can choose not to support HTML at all (closing a potentially large security hole). Notice that you can individually install features such as:

- Default Document
- Directory Browsing
- HTTP Errors
- HTTP Redirection
- Static Content

Each of these features helps you work with HTML in some way. If you really do want to support error pages, but you don't want to support other forms of HTML pages, all you need to do is clear the Static Content option. Removing static content will also remove your ability to serve static images, but won't interfere with serving graphics as part of an application. Any changes you make may require that you restart the server, so don't make these changes when someone else needs the server.

NOTE   Most application development platforms now include custom error pages of their own. For example, when you create an ASP.NET application, the application provides the error pages it requires. Consequently, if you only intend to offer applications written in ASP.NET and never allow static access to Web pages, you can probably remove HyperText Transfer Protocol (HTTP) error page support as a feature.

Managing Error Pages

Whenever the server experiences an error, it displays an error page (when one is available) instead of the content that the user expected to see. IIS always displays an error message of some type, even if the error message only tells the user that IIS doesn't know how to respond to the error. The more precise you can make error information, the easier it is for the user to provide you with usable information about it and the faster you can fix it. Consequently, having good error pages is a requirement on most Web sites. The following sections detail the use of error pages in IIS.

Understanding Status Codes in IIS

Error pages are distinct between servers and a smart user can often determine which server you're running based solely on the error pages it presents. However, most servers follow specific guidelines in providing error pages and all servers provide certain standardized pages. Error pages are always the result of a server status code. A *status code* is a numeric value that indicates the server's reaction to a request; it doesn't necessarily signify that an error has occurred. In fact, you can group error pages into the following three categories.

Standardized   The World Wide Web Consortium (W3C) specifies that Web servers support certain error messages. The W3C has defined the standard loosely and the standard doesn't address all server needs, but it's a starting point. Servers must implement these features or most browsers won't work. For example, every browser looks for the 200 status code (OK) that signifies the response is what the user expected. The standards document at http://www.w3.org/Protocols/rfc2616/rfc2616-sec10.html provides more information on these defaults.

IIS Specific   The W3C status codes provide only so much information to end users—usually not enough to understand errors precisely. Consequently, Microsoft has defined a number of status codes for IIS. You'll find some of these status codes in use by other servers, but others are only familiar to IIS users. The Microsoft Knowledge Base article at http://support.microsoft.com/kb/318380 provides a complete list of the IIS specific status codes. It's important to remember that not all of these status codes represent an error. For example, a 307 status code simply signifies that the Web site has temporarily redirected some content and that the user will find it in another location. In fact, the user probably won't ever see this code because the Web server automatically redirects the user to the new content location.

Custom   Custom error pages represent specifics about your application. You can use them for any need, not just errors. For example, you could create a custom error page that tells the user to enter more information to gain entry to the server (beyond the normal name and password, which standard or IIS-specific status codes already cover). Normally, however, you'll create these special status codes to indicate an error. In fact, your language platform may create many of them for you. For example, ASP.NET generates error pages to display information about application exceptions.

Now that you know a little more about error pages, it's time to work with them. To display the error pages for a Web site, select the Web site in the Connections pane and double-click the Error Pages icon in the Features View. You'll see the standard list of error pages shown in Figure 4.7, along with any special error pages you've defined.

FIGURE 4.7
Use the Error Pages pane to work with the error pages on your server.

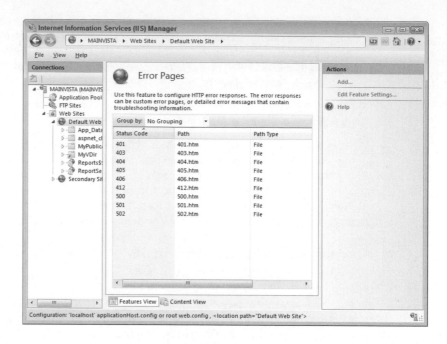

Adding a New Error Page

It's important to remember that the times you'll need to add a new error page are rare. Most new applications generate their own error pages in response to error-specific conditions. When you install a third-party product, it will more than likely install custom error pages (when required) as well. You can't simply add a new error page without a corresponding status code. Consequently, the only time you might have to add a new error page is if someone introduces a new status code that IIS can handle or you create an application that doesn't support error pages internally. For example, you might create a scripted application that falls into this category.

There are always exceptions to the rule. For every standard error page scenario, you'll run into some exceptions. You may find a situation where you want to redirect users to a location based on request when the server can't find a resource. It's possible to call on an executable to handle this sort of error and provide intelligent redirection. As an alternative, you could redirect a user to the site map or other location, rather than to the error page.

To add a new error page, click Add in the Actions pane. You'll see the Add Custom Error Page dialog box shown in Figure 4.8. Type the status code that triggers the custom error page and the location of the custom error page. Use the browse button when you need to locate the file on your server.

FIGURE 4.8
Create a new custom error page to handle specific status codes.

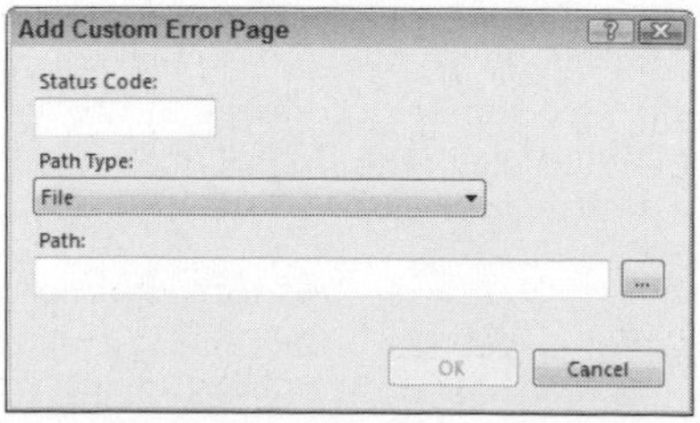

WARNING You can only create one error page entry for each status code. For example, it's not possible to create a file and redirection entry for the same status code. However, you can also create an error page entry for each subcode. For example, if you want to answer most 500 status codes with one error page but answer the 500.19 status code with a special error page, then you'd need two entries, one for 500 status codes in general and one for the 500.19 status code in specific.

An error page entry can actually perform three different tasks. The default is to honor a request with a specific file. However, you need to consider the other options at times because a static file may not do the job. Here are the three kinds of error page entries (all of which work the same from a configuration perspective).

File The default error page entry simply sends an error page in response to the client's request. The error page can be any resource that IIS supports in your configuration—it need not be an HTML file (the default). For example, you could output a graphic image if desired. IIS lets you use any static content for this option.

TIP You won't see the custom error pages when working locally with your Web server using the default IIS settings. To see the custom error pages, select the Custom Error Pages option in the Edit Error Pages Settings dialog box that you access using the Edit Feature Settings option. The "Editing the Feature Settings" section of the chapter provides additional details on this topic.

Execute URL Use the Execute URL option when you want to provide dynamic content to the client. For example, you use this option when you want to rely on ASP or ASP.NET applications, in place of static content.

Redirect Sometimes you don't want to display an error page; you want to send the user to a non-error location on the Web site. For example, when the user requests a Web site resource that doesn't exist, you can redirect them to the search page. The user can access the search page using other means, but it also works as a way to let the user locate information that doesn't appear at the specified location on the Web site. Redirection is also useful when you've moved content or changed the Web site location.

EDITING THE DEFAULT PAGES

Microsoft provides generic error pages that almost, but not quite, work for your Web site. In this case, you might want to edit the default error pages to make them match your needs better. The default error pages appear in the \inetpub\custerr\en-US folder of your hard drive. The last part of the folder is actually language dependent. In this case, the contents would contain United States English files. You'll need to locate the files in the folder for your language.

Remember that these files contain the content for the remote user—the custom error page. IIS also supports a detailed error page that these changes won't affect for the local user. See the "Editing the Feature Settings" section of the chapter for more information about detailed error pages.

When you open the files, you'll notice that they all contain style information. Microsoft chose to include this information within each file, instead of using a centralized CSS file. One of the changes you might want to make is to include the CSS information in the file and create your own CSS file. You can find a tutorial for CSS at http://www.w3schools.com/css/.

Make sure you edit the correct file. Many of the subcodes have their own Web page in the \inetpub\ custerr\en-US folder. If you change the wrong file, the changes will appear for the wrong status code and the user won't see the information you want to provide.

Editing an Existing Error Page

Sometimes you'll want to change the information for a particular status code. You may decide not to use the standard Microsoft page for errors that affect security on a Web site, but may choose to use an application to create a complete summary of the problem for the administrator instead. For the most part, editing an existing error page entry is similar to creating a new one. You still have the same options. The only difference is that you select the entry you want to change and then click Edit in the Actions pane. You'll see an Edit Custom Error Page dialog box similar to the one shown in Figure 4.8.

NOTE Your browser might hide error information you need to diagnose and fix problems on the server. For example, Internet Explorer has a feature where it displays friendly messages, rather than the actual error text from the server. Although the friendly messages are indeed more readable, they also hide valuable information you need. The Microsoft Knowledge Base article at http://support.microsoft.com/kb/294807 describes how to turn off friendly messages at both the client and the server. Even though the information is a little outdated, the techniques do work for the most part. In fact, Internet Explorer 7 includes the Show Friendly HTTP Error Messages option described in the article.

You can't use the Edit Custom Error Page dialog box to change the status code. In fact, it's not a very good idea to change the status code unless you're working with a subcode such as 500.19. Changing the status code could leave some status codes without a handler, which means the user would see a generic error page that tells them nothing about the issues surrounding the problem. If you must change the status code, use the information in the "Changing a Status Code" section of the chapter to do it.

Removing an Error Page

You should never remove one of the main error page entries such as 401 because doing so will keep your server from responding to errors properly in even a generic way. However, you might need to remove custom error pages you create. To remove an existing error page, highlight its entry and click Remove in the Actions pane. IIS will present a Confirm Remove dialog box that asks if you're sure you want to remove the entry. Click Yes to complete the task.

Changing a Status Code

Sometimes you'll make an error in entering the status code for an error page entry you create. In this case, select the entry with the error and click Change Status Code in the Actions pane. IIS will change the status code entry to an edit box, rather than a label. Type the new status code and press enter. You should never change the status code of a main error page entry such as 401. Changing the status code means that the server won't provide a generic message for all subcodes associated with that status code.

It's important to note that most status codes have one or more subcodes associated with them. For example, the 500 status code has at least 19 subcodes associated with it (IIS provides pages for 7 of them). The convention for using subcodes is to separate the subcode from the main code with a period. For example, 500.19 is the 19th subcode of the main 500 status code. You'll find that IIS has a few nonstandard subcodes, such as 500.100, which displays a "The page cannot be displayed" error message. In this case, the subcode services ASP pages and it appears when the ASP page experiences an error condition.

Editing the Feature Settings

IIS can serve up two different kinds of error pages. The first is the detailed error page that you normally only use locally. It contains a lot of additional information about an error and you can use it to troubleshoot your setup and applications. Figure 4.9 shows a detailed error page for the 404 status code. The second page is the custom error page that contains less information and you normally use it for remote connections. Figure 4.10 shows the custom page for the 404 status code. Notice how much less information a custom error page provides. Of course, you can always modify the custom error pages to provide more information.

FIGURE 4.9
Detailed error pages provide a lot of information about an error.

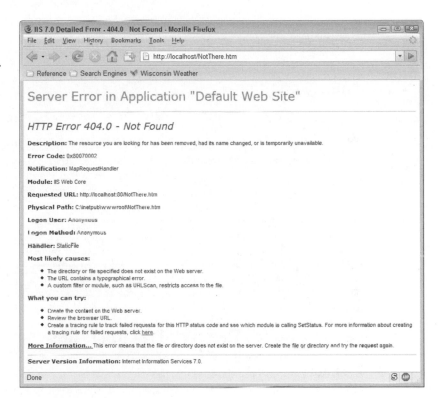

FIGURE 4.10
Custom error pages only provide a brief overview of the error information.

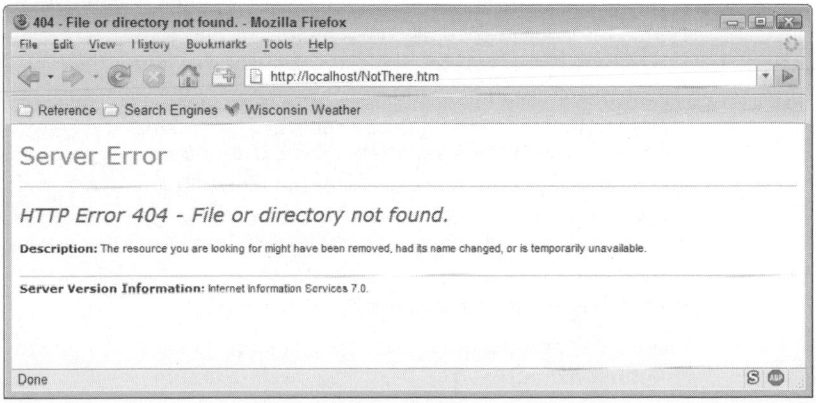

The IIS feature that controls how much information you receive appears as part of the Error Pages pane. To change this setup, click Edit Feature Settings in the Actions pane. You'll see an Edit Error Pages Settings dialog box like the one shown in Figure 4.11.

FIGURE 4.11
Modify the error pages settings to determine the level of detail people see.

The default setting sends detail pages to local clients (your machine) and custom pages to everyone else. You can choose to send the custom error pages to everyone if you're not performing development work or other tasks that require detailed error information. It's also possible to send everyone the detail error pages. This setting comes in handy when you're working with a group of developers and everyone needs to see the detailed error messages. Of course, you won't want to send the details to just anyone—doing so can open a large hole in your security.

Notice the Default Page group at the bottom of the Edit Error Pages Settings dialog box shown in Figure 4.11. This setting lets you define a default error page that IIS can use when none of the custom settings apply. As with the custom error page entries, you can choose from File, Execute URL, or Redirect as sources for the default page. See the "Adding a New Error Page" section of the chapter for details.

Setting Failed Request Tracing Rules

Failed requests can happen for many reasons. A user typo can result in a failed request because the server can't guess about the resource the user wants. Someone with less than honorable intentions can experience failed requests as they probe your defenses. An application can fail, resulting in failed requests for the application. It's also possible to experience failed requests when someone moves files on the Web site. In fact, you can probably come up with many more reasons than you care to think about for failed requests.

In many cases, you can repair an application error or help a user find a Web site without using failed request tracing. In addition, you'll find many ways to spot and track individuals who would love to grab your Web server for their own use. Sometimes, however, failed request tracing is the only way to see trends and discover the true source of a problem. Every failed request of the type you define appears on the hard drive as a log entry. Consequently, you have to exercise care when using this feature because the hard drive can quickly fill with those failed request entries if you're not careful. The following sections describe failed request tracing.

Enabling and Disabling Tracing Rules

IIS disables failed request tracing by default. Tracing failed requests uses a number of resources including memory, processor cycles, and most important, hard drive space. To display the Failed

Request Tracing Rules pane for a Web site, select the Web site in the Connections pane and double-click the Failed Request Tracing Rules icon in the Features View.

To enable failed request tracing, click Edit Site Tracing in the Actions pane. You'll see the Edit Web Site Failed Request Tracing Settings dialog box shown in Figure 4.12. Check Enable and click OK to enable request tracing. Of course, IIS doesn't start a log at this point. You still need to add tracing rules that IIS can use to determine when to make an entry in the tracing log.

FIGURE 4.12

Enable failed request tracing to track why users are experiencing difficulty in finding resources.

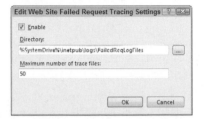

The Edit Web Site Failed Request Tracing Settings dialog box also contains entries for the location of the tracing logs and the number of logs you want to keep. It's always a good idea to place the log on a different hard drive (or even better, a different machine) to ensure you can read the log in the event of a hard drive failure.

The second entry determines the number of logs that IIS maintains. The only problem is that Microsoft doesn't document what this means. Every time someone makes a request that the system can't honor, IIS creates a new log. Consequently, if you set this value to 50, then IIS will maintain the last 50 failed requests of all types for that Web site. A verbose log entry can consume 110 KB or more. Consequently, the 50 logs will take up a little over 5.3 MB. The number of logs you create depends entirely on the amount of traffic on your Web site. You need to have enough logs set aside to record enough data to make it possible to track the failed requests accurately.

The logs contain a significant amount of information. Opening one of the logs in Internet Explorer provides a lot of detail about each failed request, as shown in Figure 4.13.

FIGURE 4.13

Failed request tracing produces incredible amounts of information about each error.

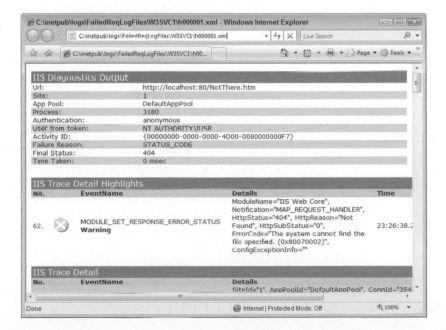

The report begins with the information you'd expect—a summary of all of the particulars of the request. The next section tells you what went wrong in brief. In this case, the file doesn't exist, so IIS can't serve it to the caller. The IIS Trace Detail section provides a moment-by-moment report on everything IIS did to serve the information. Even a simple request can produce a considerable amount of activity.

Creating a Tracing Rule

Even if you enable the failed request–tracing feature, you won't see any log entries until you define at least one tracing rule. A tracing rule tells IIS what to trace. It's usually a good idea to define your tracing rules carefully. Otherwise, you'll end up with many log entries that you can't use and will only make it harder to detect the information you need. IIS provides a wizard to create the tracing rules. The following steps describe this process.

1. Click Add in the Actions pane. You'll see the Specify Content to Trace dialog box shown in Figure 4.14. Notice that Microsoft assumes you'll want to trace a new technology. However, you can trace any kind of request. For example, if you're only interested in tracking Portable Network Graphics (PNG) files on your server, you can choose Custom and then type ***.PNG**. Make the request specification as accurate as possible, even if it means creating multiple tracing rules. You want to reduce the number of unusable log entries to a minimum.

FIGURE 4.14
Provide a description of what kind of request you want to trace.

2. Provide a request specification and click Next. You'll see the Define Trace Conditions dialog box shown in Figure 4.15. IIS lets you provide both a status code and the time the request requires to fulfill (timeout) in seconds. Separate multiple status codes using commas. Again, it pays to provide accurate information. Instead of using 500 as the status code and collecting all 500 series values, use the specific status code you want, such as 500.19 instead. Using a timeout value helps you locate applications that are running slowly or might be experiencing some other difficulty even if they eventually provide the required response. By looking for a specific time of day in the log entries, you can detect overload and other conditions on your Web server.

FIGURE 4.15
Define the conditions under which IIS should create a failed request trace log.

3. Enter a status code and/or a timeout value. You don't have to enter both, but you do have to enter at least one. Click Next. You'll see the Select Trace Providers dialog box shown in Figure 4.16.

FIGURE 4.16
Choose a provider and level of information for the log entries.

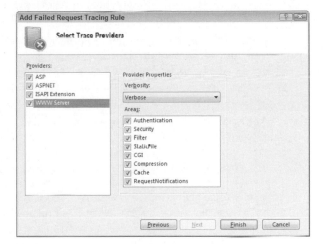

4. Check one or more of the providers in the list. To improve performance select just the provider you actually need to make the log entries. Adding or removing a provider won't change the size of the log unless you actually need that provider to create the log entry. When working with static resources, all you need is the WWW Server provider.

5. Select a verbosity level in the Verbosity field. The verbosity levels range from General to Verbose. As you increase the verbosity level, IIS provides more information in the logs and the log size increases. Selecting the Warnings level will produce more information than the Errors level. It's important to set the verbosity level correctly. If you set it too high, you'll waste hard drive space. If you set it too low, you won't obtain the information you need.

6. Choose the areas you want to see included in the log entry. Every area you include increases the size of the log, provided there's information to add in that area. For example, selecting CGI for an ASP.NET application won't generate any information. The areas work independently from the verbosity level. While the verbosity level tells how much information to include, the areas setting determines what to include. The available areas depend on the provider you choose. Here's a summary of the various areas.

NOTE Microsoft supplies the ASP and ISAPI extension providers, but neither provider has any areas associated with it. The ASP and ISAPI extension providers apparently provide only information about the specific files used for a request. Consequently, you still get a log, but you can't choose which areas to monitor within the log. You can choose a verbosity level for the ASP and ISAPI extension providers. Couple these providers with the WWW Server provider to obtain additional information.

Infrastructure   This area is only available to ASP.NET applications. It helps you monitor events related to entering and leaving ASP.NET components.

Module   This area is only available to ASP.NET applications. Requests generally rely on the use of multiple modules to create a response. This area monitors the flow of information from module to module. It helps you treat the ASP.NET application as a black box, where you look at the inputs and outputs, but don't really care about the inner workings of the module. This area works with both the HTTP pipeline and the managed modules within an ASP.NET application.

Page   This area is only available to ASP.NET applications. ASP.NET applications use a significant number of events to signal application processing requirements. For example, when the page loads, the application fires a `Page_Load()` event. You use this area to monitor all of the standard ASP.NET events during the processing of a request. In addition, you can use this area to monitor the debugging output of `Trace.Write()` and `Trace.Warn()` events.

AppServices   This area is only available to ASP.NET applications. Use this area to log events associated with the new application services functionality found in ASP.NET 2.0. This feature makes it easier to create robust applications. For example, using application services, you don't need to write common code for managing users or application personalization (see the overview at `http://msdn2.microsoft.com/en-us/library/ms164596.aspx`). Application services also helps you work with Web services (see the Web service usage information at `http://msdn2.microsoft.com/en-us/library/ms379597(VS.80).aspx`). This feature requires that you configure SQL Server (see the details at `http://msdn2.microsoft.com/en-us/library/2fx93s7w.aspx`).

Authentication   This area is associated with the WWW Server provider, but you can use it for any request type. You use it to trace authentication attempts that rely on standard IIS authentication, rather than the special features of ASP.NET. The log file contains the authenticated username, the authentication scheme (such as Anonymous or Basic), and the results of the authentication attempt.

Security   This area is associated with the WWW Server provider, but you can use it for any request type. You use it to trace all security events. For example, if a user requests a resource and lacks rights to it, IIS would make a log entry describing the security event.

Filter This area is associated with the WWW Server provider and you use it only for ISAPI filters. When a user makes a request that requires ISAPI filter support, this area monitors the time required to perform the processing. You can use it to determine when an ISAPI filter causes unacceptable processing delays.

StaticFile This area is associated with the WWW Server provider and you use it only for static files, such as HTML files or graphics. Use this area to monitor requests for static resources. It also helps you monitor the ways in which ISAPI filters modify the flow of processing.

CGI This area is associated with the WWW Server provider and you use it only for Common Gateway Interface (CGI) executables. The log file contains all request information for CGI files.

Compression This area is associated with the WWW Server provider, but you can use it for any request type. Use this area to determine the effects of compression on server responses.

Cache This area is associated with the WWW Server provider, but you can use it for any request type. Use this area to determine the effects of the server cache on server responses.

RequestNotifications This area is associated with the WWW Server provider, but you can use it for any request type. Use this area to monitor all client requests on both entrance to and exit from the HTTP pipe.

7. Click Finish. IIS creates the new tracing rule.

Editing a Tracing Rule

Editing a tracing rule is much like creating one. You use the same wizard to perform the task, so perform all of the steps in the "Creating a Tracing Rule" section of the chapter to edit a tracing rule. To begin the process, you highlight the tracing rule you want to change and click Edit in the Actions pane. The wizard won't let you change some of the information. For example, you can't change the content you want to trace. However, you can add more status codes, change or add a timeout value, and modify the trace provider information.

Removing a Tracing Rule

At some point, you'll want to remove tracing rules you no longer need. To remove a tracing rule, highlight the rule you want to remove and click Remove in the Actions pane. IIS will ask if you're sure that you want to remove the tracing rule. Click Yes to complete the process.

Working with Response Modules

For some people, IIS is a black box. The requests come in, the server locates the desired resource, and the response goes back to the caller—nothing could be simpler. Of course, it isn't actually that simple. Various requests have differing needs. In order to service each of these requests, the server must have software that understands the request and provide the desired response. That's the purpose of response modules. IIS calls a response module based on the user's request. The response module handles the details.

To display the response modules for a Web site, select the Web site in the Connections pane and double-click the Modules icon in the Features View. You'll see the standard list of response modules shown in Figure 4.17, along with any special response modules you've installed. The following sections describe how to perform various response module management tasks.

FIGURE 4.17
Response modules provide the answers to incoming requests.

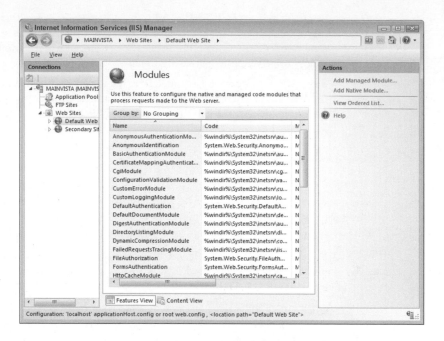

Adding a Native Module

Native code modules use older languages that produce an executable that IIS can read directly. You'll use the technique in this chapter to add one of those older executables to your IIS setup. To add a registered native module, click Add Native Module. You'll see the Add Native Module dialog box shown in Figure 4.18. The modules shown in the screenshot are the additional modules that come with IIS. You can add any of these modules as needed to assist in processing data on your server. Simply check the module you want to use and click OK to install it.

Of course, you might need to use a native module someone else wrote. In this case, click Register in the Add Native Module dialog box. You'll see the Register Native Module dialog box shown in Figure 4.19. To register a module, type a name for it in the Name field and provide a path to the executable file (DLL or EXE file). Use the browse button to locate the executable file quickly. Click OK and the new module appears in the list in the Add Native Module dialog box.

FIGURE 4.18
Native modules are executables that IIS understands without any additional interpretation.

If you provide incorrect information for a module, highlight the module in the Add Native Module dialog box and click Edit. You'll see an Edit Native Module Registration dialog box that looks the same as the one shown in Figure 4.19 (the only difference is the title bar). Never edit a native module supplied with IIS unless you actually encounter a problem with it.

Eventually, you'll need to remove modules from the list. Only remove modules that you add—leave the modules that come with IIS in place so you can work with them later. To remove a module from the list, highlight the entry in the Add Native Module dialog box and click Remove. IIS will ask you to verify that you want to remove the module. Click OK to complete the action.

Adding a Managed Module

Managed modules rely on code that a developer creates using the .NET Framework. Whenever a caller requests a resource that this module can provide, IIS transmits the request through CLR, which in turn compiles the module and starts it. After this initial communication, the managed module works much like the native code version. Consequently, you can obtain all of the benefits of working with a managed module without incurring a significant performance penalty.

To add a managed module to IIS, you click Add Managed Module in the Actions pane. You'll see the Add Managed Module dialog box shown in Figure 4.20. Type a name for the managed module in the Name field and choose a managed module type from the Type field. IIS provides a number of type entries that don't already appear in the modules list. For example, you can add additional support for mobile devices by adding the appropriate managed module. You can also choose to let the module service only ASP.NET applications. This choice makes sense when your server runs mostly ASP.NET applications and the module won't work with other content. Checking this option can save system resources and improve performance slightly. Click OK to add the new module to the list.

Unlike native code modules, you can't easily add your own managed modules to the Type field. In order to add a new module, you must create a managed application with the required interfaces and then register it with CLR through the GAC. Normally, the installation program for any third-party product will perform all of the required registration for you, so the entry will appear in the Type field automatically. You can see some of the requirements for creating a new managed module at `http://msdn2.microsoft.com/en-us/library/aa480180.aspx` and `http://msdn2.microsoft.com/en-us/library/aa480181.aspx`.

Editing Module Settings

You may eventually need to edit one of the module entries you created. To perform this task, highlight the entry in the list and click Edit in the Actions pane. IIS will display the appropriate native code or managed module dialog box. Make any required changes and click OK. The "Adding a Native Module" and "Adding a Managed Module" sections of the chapter provide details about the dialog boxes.

WARNING   Never edit a module entry that Microsoft provides with IIS unless told to do so by product support. Changing a module entry can have unexpected results and may even cause a server crash (or worse). Always record edits you perform so you can return the module information to its original state should the edit fail.

Removing a Module

When you no longer need a module, you can remove it from the list. IIS will no longer use the module for processing incoming requests. IIS doesn't actually delete the module from the machine. It reappears in the appropriate list for native code or managed modules on the machine. You can add the module back in by re-creating the entry.

WARNING   Never remove a module entry that Microsoft provides with IIS unless told to do so by product support. Removing a module entry can have unexpected results and may even cause a server crash (or worse). Fortunately, you can overcome this particular problem by adding the module back in using the techniques described in the "Adding a Native Module" and "Adding a Managed Module" sections of the chapter.

Changing a Module Priority

IIS calls the modules in a particular order. Modules earlier in the list receive the first opportunity to satisfy the request and send a response. On the other hand, modules later in the list may not see the request at all when an earlier module satisfies the need. Therefore, the order in which your server processes requests is very important and you should order the modules by the probability that they'll satisfy the request. You can see the module priority by clicking View Ordered List in the Actions pane. IIS displays the ordered list, as shown in Figure 4.21.

To change the order of a particular item, highlight its entry in the list and click Move Up or Move Down as needed. When you complete the required changes, click View Unordered List in the Actions pane to return to the standard view.

Let's Start Building

This chapter has demonstrated a number of techniques for using and managing basic HTML pages. Admittedly, the technology is outdated for many purposes—new strategies often provide better results because Web site developers don't need to learn the vagaries of HTML. Even so, you'll find basic HTML used for content that rarely, if ever, changes, such as error pages. You probably won't want to remove this tool from your toolbox completely. This chapter helps you build these skills:

◆ Configure a basic HTML page

◆ Move existing HTML to IIS 7

◆ Develop an error page strategy

◆ Trace and handle failed requests

◆ Implement and maintain request modules

FIGURE 4.21

IIS calls on the modules as they appear in the ordered list.

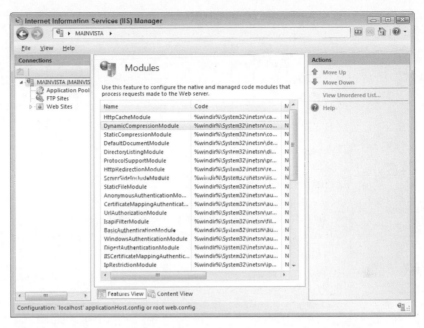

Because basic HTML is outdated, you don't want to spend a lot of time figuring out how to use it. Basic HTML has certain reliability and performance characteristics that could make it attractive on your Web site. For example, you want users to find error pages whenever they need them and these pages rarely change, so using HTML makes sense in this case. You'll want to spend a few minutes deciding on where (or even if) you want to use basic HTML on your Web site and then provide the required resources for them.

Chapter 5 discusses another older technology, ASP. The ASP technology isn't as outdated as basic HTML and you might find many uses for it on your Web site. It has the advantage of using a scripting language that combines script with HTML to provide a response that's dynamic, rather than static. Some administrators prefer to work with ASP because it's simple and can be easily store in a database. Chapter 5 considers the ins and outs of working with the older, but viable, technology.

Chapter 5

Working with ASP

Active Server Pages (ASP) is an older technology, but many Web sites still use it for a number of reasons. For example, ASP relies on a simple scripting technology that most administrators can modify quickly and easily. You don't have to worry about complex application code, using Visual Studio, installing the .NET Framework (even though you have to anyway for IIS 7), or going through complex configuration procedures. That said, ASP also has a considerable number of limitations that you can read about in the "Considering ASP Limitations" section of the chapter. Even with these limitations, some administrators won't switch. Features such as Server Side Includes (SSIs) make it exceptionally easy to include a lot of information in ASP applications. Fortunately, IIS 7 doesn't force anyone to make a decision about ASP today.

This chapter guides you through the requirements for working with ASP on IIS 7. You'll find that most of the features you worked with in the past still work today, but that you'll need to tighten up your code because IIS 7 isn't as forgiving about small errors. Some third-party products may refuse to work, especially if the vendor flouted the rules in the past to achieve some special purpose. You'll also find that configuration differs, but this chapter takes the curve out of learning the new process.

In this chapter, you will learn how to do the following:

◆ Define the requirements for moving the ASP application

◆ Configure an ASP page

◆ Move existing ASP application to IIS 7

Working with ASP Pages in IIS 7

ASP works in IIS 7 as it has for every previous version of IIS from an administrator perspective. Because IIS 7 relies on the .NET Framework as a basis for creating the infrastructure, there are many differences under the cover. Also, the addition of application pools means that applications can be separated from each other, making the entire installation more reliable. However, changes do create problems. The sections that follow describe issues you should consider before you make your move from a previous version of IIS to IIS 7.

Considering ASP Limitations

Before you begin moving your ASP application to IIS 7, you need to consider some ASP limitations seriously. It isn't that ASP isn't a useful language or that you can't create robust applications with it, but the fact remains that ASP wasn't well considered by Microsoft and that lack of planning can cause problems for you. In fact, most people who've used ASP for a long time agree on limitations (all of which will affect your move to IIS 7).

WORKING WITH OTHER LANGUAGES IN ASP

It's possible to work with a number of scripting languages in ASP. Even though many people think about VBScript first, you can also use languages such as JavaScript and interestingly enough, Perlscript. Perlscript is actually a form of the Practical Extraction and Report Language (PERL) that you can use in an ASP application. The comparison of IIS development technologies Web page at `http://msdn2.microsoft.com/en-us/library/ms525913.aspx` provides some interesting information about Perlscript.

Unfortunately, one chapter of a book can't adequately tell you about using Perlscript. If you want more details about working with Perlscript, consider these Web sites.

Using PerlScript to Create ASP Pages `http://www.4guysfromrolla.com/webtech/021100-1.shtml`

ActiveState Perlscript FAQ `http://www.xav.com/perl/Components/Windows/PerlScript.html`

Introduction to PerlScript `http://cpan.org/authors/id/M/MS/MSERGEANT/PSIntro.html`

Apache::ASP Perlscript `http://www.apache-asp.org/perlscript.html`

Perl Tutorials `http://www.taxpolicy.com/tutorial/pltutor.htm`

◆ ASP only runs on Windows systems.

◆ The resulting applications don't scale well (they can't accept additional load easily and don't fail gracefully when overwhelmed).

◆ You need to purchase a lot of third-party support to obtain some basic functionality and these components may not run on IIS 7.

◆ The source code isn't available so you can't examine how features are supposed to work.

◆ Microsoft regularly breaks previous implementations when it makes upgrades to IIS.

Microsoft has documented a number of the component limitations for ASP. For example, the Knowledge Base article at `http://support.microsoft.com/kb/243826` describes performance and concurrency problems for some ASP add-ons. When you add these limitations to the increased security and modularization of IIS 7, you may find that your application won't work because the modules it uses no longer work. Of course, testing will tell you whether this issue affects your application, but you must perform the required testing to know for certain.

Considering Security Issues

Many of the security issues for ASP applications are the same as for HTML configurations. For example, your application will rely on Windows security to protect resources and code modules alike. You can read about these common security issues in the "Considering Security Issues" section of Chapter 4.

ASP applications do have some other security issues to consider. Some administrators are in the habit of setting the ASP environment globally, which can lead to unauthorized access of resources.

Real World Scenario

USING THE RIGHT CODING TECHNIQUES WITH ASP

One of the biggest problems that administrators encounter when moving an ASP application to IIS 7 is that the code that used to work yesterday doesn't today. Previous versions of IIS didn't enforce some coding rules very well, or sometimes at all. Because of the security problems on the Internet, Microsoft has tightened all of the code-checking features of IIS considerably, including those used for ASP. Some marginal coding techniques of the past won't work at all today.

VBScript is a relatively easy-to-use language and many administrators learn it quite quickly. However, there are traps for the unwary when it comes to using VBScript for your ASP applications. The first is that some VBScript features are disabled on the server because the application executes on the server, rather than on the client. You can't use either the InputBox or MsgBox statements on the server. Most developers realize that these statements pose a problem from the outset anyway, but it's good to review the lack of support for some features before you make the move to IIS 7.

Another issue is that the ASP developer can't use the CreateObject() and GetObject() methods for server-side scripts. Because of the way that IIS creates application pools, you can't access server objects using these methods. Instead of these methods, use the Server.CreateObject() method instead. This alternative method lets the ASP application participate in transactions and the server can track the tasks the application performs with greater ease. As with many programming principles, there's an exception to the Server.CreateObject() method rule—when working with Admin Objects or Java monikers, you still need to use the CreateObject() method.

The "Setting the ASP Configuration" section of the chapter describes how to configure the ASP environment for your application. Some settings, such as the code page, are innocuous and you don't have to worry too much about them. However, you can't easily dismiss some other settings, such as the debugging properties, as a source of potential problems. Always follow the principle of least privilege. Configure the upper levels of the ASP environment in a way that doesn't provide any information to those who want to break into your Web site. Add privileges at lower levels, preferably at the folder level, so that users can run the applications without problem.

SSIs are an exceptionally useful feature of ASP because they let you include server information and perform a variety of tasks from within the ASP application. However, some of these features aren't as safe as others are. In fact, Microsoft recommends disabling the #exec SSI. The Knowledge Base article at http://support.microsoft.com/kb/195291 describes how to disable the #exec SSI. Unfortunately, the folder provided in the article is incorrect. You'll find the ADSUtil.VBS script in the \inetpub\AdminScripts folder. To determine the status of the #exec SSI in any folder, use the get command like this:

```
CScript ADSUtil.VBS Get W3Svc/SSIExecDisable
```

TIP The ADSUtil.VBS script is an exceptionally useful utility. You can use this utility to perform many common configuration tasks, some of which you can't perform using the GUI. See the "Performing Configuration with the *ADSUtil.VBS Script*" section of Chapter 12 for details on working with this script. The "Performing Configuration Tasks without the GUI" section of Chapter 12 contains a number of ways to work outside the graphical environment described throughout most of this book.

You can extend the path information using the Web site and virtual directory name as described in the Knowledge Base article to determine the #exec SSI status at a given level. The output of the get command provides a simple Boolean value, as shown in Figure 5.1.

FIGURE 5.1
Determine the status of the #exec command using the ADSUtil.VBS script.

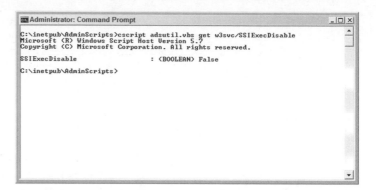

Because ASP can present a problem with security, you want to make the scripts hard to find. Fortunately, you can use the information found in the "Editing Handler Settings" section of Chapter 3 to change the default .ASP file extension to something else. Now you can give all of your ASP files a different extension, something unexpected by the person searching your drive for clues. It may seem like a very flimsy security measure, but it works because someone accessing your system will look for ASP files, not for MyAlternative files. When you use this technique, you'll want to be sure to use an extension that isn't in use for something else—your extension must be unique.

TIP   As a security measure, many administrators try to remap or disable certain extensions because they've gained a bad reputation in the security community. These extensions include: .ASA, .ASP, .BAT, .CDX, .CER, .HTR, .HTW, .IDA, .IDC, .IDQ, .PRINTER, .SHTM, .SHTML, and .STM. If you must enable these extensions and can't map them to something else, make sure you set the security for the folders containing the scripts to read-only to help prevent script tampering.

Defining the IIS Setup for ASP

Windows may not automatically install ASP support when you set up IIS. If you find that you need ASP support, but don't have it, you can add it later. Modify the support by choosing Start ➢ Settings ➢ Control Panel ➢ Programs and Features (in Vista and Windows Server 2008). Click the Turn Windows Features On or Off link to display the Windows Features dialog box. Open the Internet Information Services\World Wide Web Services\Application Development Features entry, as shown in Figure 5.2. Notice that you can choose ASP without installing SSI. Keeping SSI out of the picture is always a good idea when you can achieve it because SSI does increase the risk of a security breach.

Many of the same issues that affect HTML pages also affect ASP. For example, you still need to consider the use of a default document, directory browsing, and error pages. In many cases, you'll couple static content in the form of graphics and sound with your ASP application, so you must consider this requirement as well. All of these common requirements appear as part of the "Defining the IIS Setup for HTML" section of Chapter 4.

Working with Server Side Includes (SSI)

Administrators who've used ASP for a while know the benefits of using SSI. Yes, you can create good ASP applications without using SSI, but the addition of SSI lets ASP create flexible applications that really make ASP a significant application platform.

FIGURE 5.2

Install support for
ASP and SSI to create
robust applications.

Like other parts of IIS, SSI requires special processing in the form of a handler that you'll find the in the Handler Mappings pane (see the "Working with Handlers" section of Chapter 3 for details). SSI normally uses the .SHTML, .SHTM, and .STM extensions, but as with ASP, you can use any other extension you wish as long as you provide the correct handler mapping. In fact, for security reasons, you may want to use an alternative mapping. Unlike previous versions of IIS, IIS 7 uses a managed module named ServerSideIncludeModule to handle the request (contrast this with ASP, which still uses the native code \Windows\system32\inetsrv\ASP.DLL executable).

The SSI files you create rely on ASP script. Consequently, anything you do with ASP, you can also do with SSI. An SSI file can contain a number of directives that tell the server what to do, in addition to displaying information or performing other tasks contained within the file. These directives include:

#config Determines how IIS displays data that it outputs as part of the response. For example, when the response includes a date, you can configure it to appear in a certain way.

#echo Inserts the content of a CGI or server variable into the response. For example, if you wanted to display the name of the server in the response, you'd use the SERVER_NAME variable. You can see a list of all of the common variables at http://msdn2.microsoft.com/en-us/library/ms525581.aspx.

#exec Executes the specified command, CGI executable, or ISAPI DLL and inserts the output in the response. (See the Knowledge Base article at http://support.microsoft.com/kb/169996/ for information on running ISAPI DLLs as part of a #exec directive.) This directive is so dangerous that Microsoft disables it by default. A disabled setup displays the simple message, "The CMD option is not enabled for #EXEC calls."

#flastmod Determines the last modification date of the specified file and injects it into the response. This directive doesn't work with folders (directories).

#fsize Determines the size of the specified file and injects it into the response. This directive doesn't work with folders (directories).

#include Includes the content of one file within another file. The included content begins at the directive. IIS replaces the #include directive with the file content so the included file appears as part of the main file.

You can find a number of resources for SSI on the Internet and even a few add-ons for it. None of these other SSI directives appear to work—although it's hard to test every one of them. You can find complete explanations and sample code for the acceptable SSI directives at http://support.microsoft.com/kb/203064.

Setting the ASP Configuration

Configuring your ASP application environment in IIS 7 differs from the process used in previous versions of IIS. Microsoft has centralized the settings and made them easier to maintain. As previously mentioned, it's important to set the ASP configuration at the proper level, rather than try to set the configuration globally and risk a security breach. To display the ASP settings for any level, select the level you want to use (Web server, Web site, or folder) in the Connections pane and double-click the ASP icon in the Features View. You'll see the standard list of ASP configuration settings shown in Figure 5.3.

FIGURE 5.3
Define the ASP environment for your application at the appropriate level.

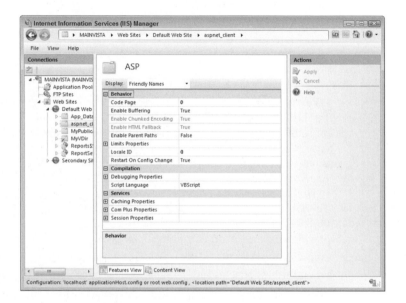

You can divide the ASP settings into three functional areas: Behavior, Compilation, and Services. The settings you make at an upper level affect all lower levels unless you make a specific change at the lower level. For example, if you set code page 0 as the default at the Web server level, then all Web sites and their folders will also use code page 0 until you set another value at one of these levels. The following sections describe each of the three functional areas and tell how you can modify the associated settings to meet specific needs.

Changing the Application Behavior

The Behavior area modifies how the application interacts with the user. Changing a property here will modify the way the application performs its task. The following list describes each of the properties in this area and describes how you can work with them (the configuration name appears in parentheses behind the friendly name).

Code Page (codePage)   A code page is the set of characters that IIS uses to represent different languages and identities. English uses one code page, Greek another. Setting the code page to a specific value helps your application support the language of the caller. You can find a wealth of information, along with all of the standard code page numbers, at `http://www.i18nguy.com/unicode/codepages.html`. IIS only understands the Windows code pages defined at `http://www.i18nguy.com/unicode/codepages.html#msftwindows`. The default setting of 0 requests the code page from the client, which may or may not be a good idea depending on the structure of your application. If you plan to support specific languages using different parts of your Web site, always set the code page to obtain better results.

Enable Buffering (bufferingOn)   Buffering is the process of using a little memory to smooth the transfer of data from the ASP application to the caller. Using this technique makes the application run more efficiently, but does cost some additional memory to gain the benefit. Generally, you'll find that buffering is a good investment on any machine that can support it and should keep this setting set to True (the default state).

Enable Chunked Encoding (enableChunkedEncoding)   Chunked transfers convert the body of a Web page into small pieces that the server can send to the caller more efficiently than sending the entire Web page. In addition, the caller receives a little of the Web page at a time so it's easier to see progress as the Web page loads. You can learn more about this HTTP 1.1 technology at http://www.w3.org/Protocols/rfc2616/rfc2616-sec3.html. Look at Section 3.6.1 of the specification to get the details. This value defaults to True.

Enable HTML Fallback (enableAspHtmlFallback)   Sometimes your server will get busy. If the server gets too busy to serve your ASP application, you can create an alternative HTML file that contains a static version of the ASP application. The name of the HTML file must contain _asp in it. For example, if you create an ASP application named Hello.ASP, then the HTML equivalent is Hello_asp.HTML. This value defaults to True.

Enable Parent Paths (enableParentPaths)   Depending on the setup of your Web server, you might want an ASP application to reference a parent directory instead of the current directory using the relative path nomenclature of ..\MyResource, where MyResource is a resource you want to access. For example, the ASP application may reside as a subfolder of a main Web site folder. You may want to access resources in that main folder. Keeping the ASP application in a subfolder has security advantages because you can secure the ASP application folder at a stricter level than the main folder. In most cases, however, the resources for the ASP application reside at lower levels in the directory hierarchy. Consequently, this value defaults to False.

Locale ID (lcid)   The Locale Identifier (LCID) indicates the country in which an application is used (contrasted to the language of the person using the application, which you set using the Code Page property). The LCID helps your application define formatting, such as date, and units of measure, such as currency. The default setting is 1033, which equates to United States English. You can find a complete list of LCIDs at http://krafft.com/scripts/deluxe-calendar/lcid_chart.htm.

Restart on Config Change (enableApplicationRestart)   Normally, when you make a change to your ASP application, IIS recompiles it immediately. The change is available to new callers immediately, which means that your changes take effect almost as soon as you make them. Since most people want this behavior, Microsoft normally sets this property to True. However, if you have an exceptionally large application or you need to make changes to other parts of the server before implementing these changes, you might want to set this value to False. When you set this value to False, you must restart the server to see the changes you made, but you also have better control over when the changes take effect.

There's a subgroup in the Behavior area named Limits Properties. You can see a list of these entries in Figure 5.4. The basic reason to change this setting is to determine how ASP applications perform the tasks they're designed to do. For example, you might have to change a timeout value to ensure the request has enough time to complete. The following list describes the Limits Properties subgroup in detail (the configuration name appears in parentheses behind the friendly name).

Client Connection Test Interval (`queueConnectionTestTime`)　Your server might experience heavy loads where the caller gets tired of waiting and disconnects. If the server still processes the client request, the time is wasted because there isn't anyone to receive the response. By verifying the caller is still waiting after a long wait interval, the server can cut out some of this wasted time. If the caller has disconnected, the server simply deletes the request from the queue. The default setting for this property is 3 seconds. However, you can tune the setting to better balance caller expectations and server performance. Checking the caller too often wastes time too, so you don't want to check too often.

Maximum Requesting Entity Body Limit (`maxRequestEntityAllowed`)　Most initial ASP application requests for information won't have an entity body as defined by the RFC 2616 standard (see `http://www.w3.org/Protocols/rfc2616/rfc2616.html` for details). However, when the user fills out a form and posts the data to the server, the form could have an entity body that contains the data from the form. Use this setting to control the maximum size of the entity body. The default setting of 200,000 bytes might be too large, depending on your application. For example, if your application requires authentication, then the application must receive up to 200,000 bytes before it can send a response that requests a name and password from the caller, resulting in wasted time and network bandwidth. In addition, a large entity body gives potential intruders a lot of space for scripts or other nasty input. This setting doesn't affect the size of the entity body for any response you send to the caller. Try to maintain a reasonable entity body size limit to promote better server performance and reduce the risk of infection. The discussion at `http://msdn2.microsoft.com/en-us/library/aa364621.aspx` provides additional information about the inner workings of the server.

NOTE　IIS 7 fixes the authentication issue found in IIS 6 with the .NET Framework 1.0 installed as described in the Knowledge Base article at `http://support.microsoft.com/kb/328863`. However, using keep-alive processing still makes sense from a performance perspective because using the keep-alive technique ensures that you don't have to re-authenticate the caller for every request. IIS 7 uses keep-alive processing by default.

Queue Length (`requestQueueMax`)　This property determines the maximum number of requests that the server can place in the queue. It's important to remember that each request consumes resources such as memory and processing time. In addition, allowing too many requests in the queue could result in a lot of wasted processing time determining whether the caller is still connected. Consequently, you must maintain a balance between allowing enough queue entries to handle peak server requests and allowing for server request handling capacity and resources.

Request Queue Timeout (`queueTimeout`)　You can somewhat mitigate the need to contact a caller about a request by defining a limit on the amount of time that a request can wait in the queue. The default setting of 00:00:00 means that the request can wait forever, which isn't a very efficient way to handle the requests. Tuning this value to allow a certain number of client connection tests and then terminating the request even if it hasn't been fulfilled usually guarantees that the server won't become completely bogged down by requests it can't satisfy. The time limit you place depends on your server's activity level and the probability it will catch up with old requests during less busy times. A value three or four times the Client Connection Test Interval usually works well.

Response Buffering Limit (`bufferingLimit`)   Response buffering, controlled by the Enable Buffering setting, makes data transfers more efficient. However, it also uses memory and you don't want to use too much memory to gain this advantage. This setting controls how much memory IIS sets aside for buffering; IIS flushes (sends) the data when the buffer is full. The default setting uses 4,194,304 bytes (4 MB) of memory for buffering.

Script Timeout (`scriptTimeout`)   A script, even one that's debugged and usually runs fine, can experience an error and continue running despite the failure. This setting determines the length of time that a script can run before IIS terminates it. The default setting of 1 minute and 30 seconds is usually enough for any moderately complex script. However, if your application works with databases and performs complex processing, you may need to increase the timeout value or IIS may terminate the application too early. Likewise, if you have a script that's short and should finish quickly, you might want to set the interval shorter to release resources earlier for a script that fails.

Threads Per Processor Limit (`processorThreadMax`)   This setting determines the number of worker threads that IIS can create to handle ASP requests. It's important to remember that this setting defines the number of threads per processor. Consequently, if your server contains two dual core processors, what IIS sees is four processors. The default setting of 25 means that IIS can create up to 100 worker processes to handle ASP requests. Normally, an ASP script and the Visual Basic objects it creates run on the same thread. So, theoretically, having up to 100 worker processes means that IIS can handle up to 100 requests simultaneously. However, it's important to remember that every out-of-process Component Object Model (COM) object requires another thread, so the actual number of requests that the server can handle will vary based on the complexity of your application. You can learn more about threading by viewing the article at `http://www.microsoft.com/mind/0299/basics/basics0299.asp`.

FIGURE 5.4
Modify the conditions under which ASP applications operate using these settings.

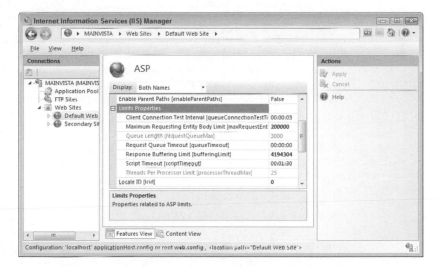

Compiling the Application

Even though you're using scripts to create your ASP application, the system compiles the application at some point to run it. Compiling the application makes it run faster and lets you add features related to debugging. The way in which you compile the application affects performance. You'll normally find the compiled applications in the \inetpub\temp\ASP Compiled Templates folder on your hard drive. Each application appears in a folder that has the Program Identifier (PID) as part of the code such as PID3164.TMP. When you shut down IIS or the application changes, IIS cleans up the folder.

Adding debugging code slows the application down, but helps you locate problems. You can see the debugging features for ASP in Figure 5.5. Obviously, you'll use a debugging mode until you're sure the application runs properly and then remove the debugging features. The following list describes each of the debugging properties in this area and describes how you can work with them (the configuration name appears in parentheses behind the friendly name).

Calculate Line Numbers (calcLineNumber)   It's normally a good idea to know the line number of the piece of code that causes an error so that you can find it more quickly within the source file. This setting does use a small number of processing cycles and memory, but hardly enough to make any difference in the processing capability of your server. This value defaults to True.

Catch COM Component Exceptions (exceptionCatchEnable)   If your application uses COM components, those components can generate errors. This setting tells IIS to trap those errors so your application can handle them. In some cases, such as providing an incorrect input value, your application can recover and continue processing. When you set this value to False, IIS doesn't trap the error and another level of the application will handle it (such as the VBScript processor or the worker process). In most cases, setting this value to False means that the application will terminate whenever it encounters a COM error. This value defaults to True.

Enable Client-side Debugging (appAllowClientDebug)   Debugging can occur in two locations: the client and the server. The client sends requests to the server and the server generates a response. This setting enables debugging on the client so that you can check issues such as input processing. It doesn't let you see how the application runs on the server, so you can't check to determine how the server handles the input data. Because debugging consumes a considerable number of processing cycles and other resources, this setting is set to False by default.

Enable Log Error Requests (logErrorRequests)   Normally, IIS writes any ASP errors to both the client browser and the Application event log on the server. This information can help you diagnose problems without spending as much time debugging the application. In fact, good error information can help you find the location of an error without any debugging at all, especially if you've encountered the error previously. This value defaults to True.

Enable Server-side Debugging (appAllowDebugging)   This setting enables you see how the server processes input data. You can step through each processing task to determine the source of errors. This setting doesn't enable client-side processing, which helps you discover input and output processing errors (see the Enable Client-side Debugging setting for details). Because debugging consumes a considerable number of processing cycles and other resources, this setting is set to False by default.

Log Errors to NT Log (errorsToNTLog)   This setting tells IIS to write detailed error information to the Application event log on the server. The detailed information includes the filename, error, line number, and description. Normally, the log entry tells you simply that an error of a specific type occurred. This value defaults to False to preserve hard drive space.

Run On End Functions Anonymously (runOnEndAnonymously)   ASP provides for some default processing of scripts. These functions appear as part of the global functions on the server. This setting determines whether the server runs the SessionOnEnd() and ApplicationOnEnd() global ASP functions anonymously. If you set this value to False, then IIS won't run the functions at all.

Script Error Message (`scriptErrorMessage`)   One of the biggest problems with getting error information is that users don't know where to send it. Even if your company policies provide this information, it's unlikely the user will take time to look it up. Consequently, you should customize this message to tell the reader what to do when an error occurs and especially where to send the error information. The default message isn't very helpful because it tells the user what they already know—an error has occurred.

Send Errors To Browser (`scriptErrorSentToBrowser`)   This setting tells IIS to write detailed error information to the client browser. The detailed information includes the filename, error, line number, and description. This value defaults to True to ensure the client receives complete error information.

FIGURE 5.5
Use the debugging features to locate and squash bugs in your application.

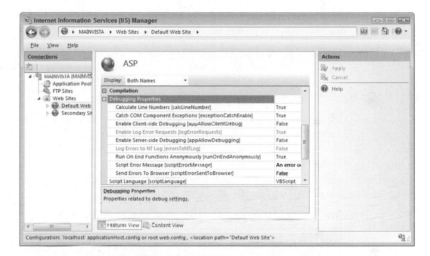

The language you use is important too because you have to tell IIS how to interpret the script. The default language is VBScript. However, you can use a number of other scripting languages including JScript, which is very close to JavaScript in features and structure. You can find the Microsoft VBScript language reference at `http://msdn2.microsoft.com/en-us/library/d1wf56tt.aspx` and the JScript language reference at `http://msdn2.microsoft.com/en-us/library/yek4tbz0.aspx`.

TIP   If you haven't worked with a scripting language before or you're just a bit rusty, using a tutorial is a fast way to learn. You can find the VBScript tutorial at `http://www.w3schools.com/vbscript/default.asp`. Because JavaScript and JScript are similar, you can use the JavaScript tutorial at `http://www.w3schools.com/js/default.asp`. You can also find a JScript specific tutorial at `http://csu.colstate.edu/webdevelop/javascript/jscript/jstutor.htm`.

Configuring Application Services

As you might imagine, the services area contains settings that affect how the application uses services that IIS offers. IIS divides these services into three areas: Caching, COM+, and Session. The following sections describe each of these service areas and how you use them.

CACHING PROPERTIES

Caching makes it possible to access resources faster. The resource is in a ready-to-use form that the server can access quickly. Consequently, even though the first person to request the resource waits the full time to access it, subsequent requests require far less time. Some administrators speed the process even faster by making the first request themselves using a process known as touching (an automated application requests each resource one at a time). Figure 5.6 shows the caching options that IIS provides for ASP. The following list describes each of the properties in this area and describes how you can work with them (the configuration name appears in parentheses behind the friendly name).

Cache Directory Path (`diskTemplateCacheDirectory`)   Use this setting to change the default location for storing the compiled ASP templates. As previously mentioned, the default cache directory is `\inetpub\temp\ASP Compiled Templates`. You can improve server performance by placing the cache on a different physical hard drive (rather than a different partition on the same hard drive) from the Web server.

Enable Type Library Caching (`enableTypeLibCache`)   Type libraries describe the content of COM components. Caching the type library makes accessing and using the component faster. Of course, caching always exacts a price in processing power and memory, but normally the performance benefit far outweighs any cost. This value defaults to True.

Maximum Disk Cached Files (`maxDiskTemplateCacheFiles`)   Every time you cache an ASP template, it consumes some amount of hard drive space. The actual amount of space used depends on the complexity of the ASP application. Unfortunately, Microsoft doesn't provide a means of specifying the maximum cache size based on memory, rather it relies on the number of templates. The default setting is 2,000. You may have to tune this number depending on the size and complexity of your application and the number of incoming requests.

Maximum Memory Cached Files (`scriptFileCacheFiles`)   IIS allows you to set the number of precompiled ASP script files to cache. A single ASP application may contain multiple script files, so this number doesn't necessarily reflect the number of applications that IIS caches. Set this value to 0 when you don't want to cache any script files. Likewise, set this value to 4,291,967,295 when you want to cache all of the script files. Use this property to tune the performance of your server. The actual results depend on the amount of memory installed on the server. The default setting is 500.

Maximum Script Engines Cached (`scriptEngineCacheMax`)   Every time someone makes a request that opens an ASP script file, the server must start an instance of the script engine to process that file. If a file uses an include to add a number of external files, then those files are treated as part of the original script file and IIS doesn't start a new script engine. However, when the file isn't part of an include, then IIS does start a new script engine. This setting determines the number of script engines that IIS can cache. The default setting is 250.

COM+ PROPERTIES

COM+ (shown in the interface as Com Plus) is a server-side COM technology that provides access to business logic, databases, and other server resources. The essential technology is COM, but it runs within a special environment. You'll also find a number of special applications in this environment, such as Queuing Services. It's even possible to turn COM+ applications into Web services (see the article at `http://www.devsource.ziffdavis.com/article2/0,1759,1627474,00.asp` for details). You can gain a better understanding of COM+ at `http://msdn2.microsoft.com/en-us/library/ms685978.aspx`.

FIGURE 5.6
Caching improves overall application performance by making some resources readily available.

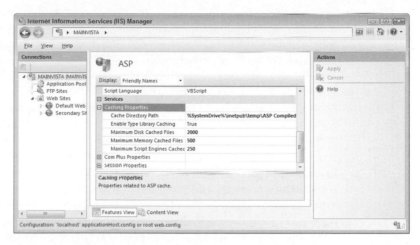

Windows XP and earlier versions of Windows make all of the COM+ configuration features available through the Component Services console in the Administrative Tools folder of the Control Panel. If you're using Vista or Windows 2008 Server (formerly known as Longhorn), you need to know the secret handshake to find the Component Services console. The following steps tell you how to open it.

1. Select Start ≻ Run to open the Run dialog box.

2. Type **COMExp.MSC** in the Open field and click OK. You'll see the Component Services console shown in Figure 5.7 where you can work with COM+ applications on your system.

FIGURE 5.7
Windows runs COM+ applications in a special environment that makes them accessible globally.

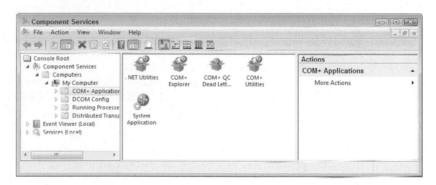

A complete description of the inner workings of COM+ is outside the scope of this book. However, it's a very powerful technology that can make your applications perform tasks that you never thought possible. The settings in the Com Plus properties subgroup determine how your applications interact with COM+, as shown in Figure 5.8. The following list describes each of the properties in this area and describes how you can work with them (the configuration name appears in parentheses behind the friendly name).

Enable Side by Side Component (appServiceFlags) ASP applications can suffer from a problem known as DLL hell where two applications require two different versions of the same

DLL or COM component (read the article at `http://msdn2.microsoft.com/en-us/library/ms811694.aspx` if you want more information about DLL hell). This setting enables the COM+ side-by-side component feature with an ASP application and defines which version of a DLL or COM component it wants to use. Since most applications don't have these entries defined, Microsoft sets this value to False by default. You shouldn't set this value to True unless you plan to include versioning information in all of your ASP applications.

Enable Tracker (`appServiceFlags`) The COM+ Tracker gives the administrator the ability to perform advanced debugging of ASP applications. However, as with all debugging, this feature uses a considerable number of resources. Consequently, you shouldn't enable this feature until you actually need it to debug an application. The default setting is False.

Execute In MTA (`executeInMta`) ASP applications normally run in a Single-Threaded Apartment (STA) where each thread has its own execution space. An STA application has performance penalties and uses more resources, but it's inherently safer from an execution (reliability) perspective than using a Multi-Threaded Apartment (MTA) because there aren't any concurrency requirements. This setting lets you set IIS to execute your ASP applications in an MTA to gain the performance benefits that an MTA can provide. You can learn more about the COM+ MTA model at `http://msdn2.microsoft.com/en-us/library/ms686448.aspx`. You'll also want to read the detailed Knowledge Base article at `http://support.microsoft.com/kb/q150777/`. The default setting is False.

Honor Component Threading Model (`trackThreadingModel`) Components normally contain information about the threading model that the developer intended for them to use. However, MTA components can run quite successfully in the default STA model used by ASP, so IIS normally won't check the component to determine whether it can use some other model. This setting lets you change the default behavior so that IIS will examine the component and run it in the threading model that the developer originally intended. Using this approach doesn't always result in a performance benefit because the system encounters performance penalties when switching threading models. The default setting is False.

Partition ID (`partitionId`) This property defines the Globally Unique Identifier (GUID) for COM+. You must use a tool such as GUIDGen (`http://www.microsoft.com/downloads/details.aspx?familyid=94551f58-484f-4a8c-bb39-adb270833afc`) to create the GUID and ensure that it's unique. Set the Use Partition property to True to enable the GUID. You can learn more about COM+ partitions at `http://msdn2.microsoft.com/en-us/library/ms686110.aspx`.

Side By Side Component (`sxsName`) This property defines the name of a COM+ application to use as a side-by-side component. To use this feature, you must set the Enable Side by Side Component property to True. This feature assumes that you have a single COM+ application that interacts with your ASP application. Normally, you'll set this option only at the folder level because it's unlikely that other ASP applications will all require the same COM+ application interaction (and you can set them individually when they do).

Use Partition (`appServiceFlags`) Application isolation, the act of placing each application in a separate container so the applications won't interact, provides an increased level of reliability for your applications, but does incur a performance penalty. When you enable this feature, the ASP applications all execute in their own COM+ partition. To use this feature, you must define a GUID using the Partition ID property. The default setting is False.

FIGURE 5.8
COM+ applications can provide access to business logic and back-end databases.

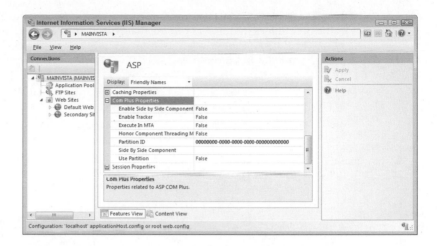

SESSION PROPERTIES

The session is the unique communication between one caller and one ASP application instance. The caller may maintain multiple sessions with multiple instances of the same ASP application, but IIS treats each instance as a unique session. The session properties define how IIS treats each ASP session. For example, the caller may choose to end a session prematurely, so IIS has to terminate the session locally so it can recover the resources used by the session. Figure 5.9 shows the properties used to start, maintain, and end a session for ASP callers. The following list describes each of the properties in this area and describes how you can work with them (the configuration name appears in parentheses behind the friendly name).

Enable Session State (allowSessionState)   HTTP is a stateless protocol, which means that every request made by the caller is a new request. Maintaining state information is necessary for most applications because the user will want to move from one step in a process to another (such as filling a shopping cart with items). IIS uses session state to maintain the caller information. Maintaining state information does incur a performance penalty, but most modern applications won't work without it. The default setting is True.

Maximum Sessions (max)   This setting determines the maximum number of sessions that your Web server can maintain. Most Web servers will fail long before they reach the default value of 2,147,483,647 sessions. You'll want to set this value to a more reasonable number to help avoid potential security issues such as a distributed denial of service (DDOS) attack. Even if no one attacks you, you'll want to set this number to a value your Web server can handle to maintain the Quality of Service (QoS) for your application. Verifying this setting means monitoring system performance—see the "Implementing Performance Monitoring" section of Chapter 13 for details.

New ID On Secure Connection (keepSessionIdSecure)   It's important to maintain the confidentiality of your connection to the user to avoid man in the middle (http://en.wikipedia.org/wiki/Man_in_the_middle_attack) and other forms of online attack. This setting tells IIS to issue a new cookie (the form of identification for the caller) every time the server switches from a nonsecure to a secure mode. The default setting is True.

Timeout (timeout) A caller can make a number of requests during a particular session. This value determines the amount of time that IIS holds onto the state information for a session. When the timeout expires, IIS frees the resources that the session information required. The default value for this property is 00:20:00.

FIGURE 5.9
Each session uses resources, so you must ensure the session settings reflect server capabilities.

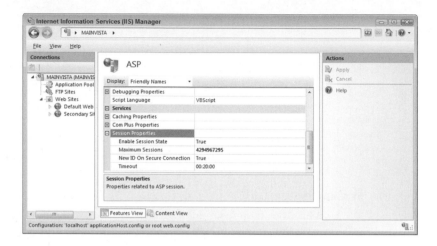

Moving an ASP Application to IIS 7

Moving an ASP application to II7 isn't very hard. You can use the XCopy utility technique described in the "Moving Your Files with XCopy" section of Chapter 4 to perform the task. Make sure you use the /0 switch with XCopy to ensure the new setup includes all of the required rights.

TIP If your application requires third-party handlers on older versions of IIS, try to reconfigure the application to use only the IIS 7 functionality. When you find that the application doesn't work without the older handlers, try to register the handler using the techniques described in the "Working with Handlers" section of Chapter 3. It's when you can't register the old handler or reconfigure the application not to use the handler that you run into problems moving your ASP application. At this point, you may need to consider rewriting the parts of the application that won't work without the handler.

After you move the files, make sure you perform any required security setup. The "Considering Security Issues" section of Chapter 4 describes all of the security considerations for the static content. Use the "Considering Security Issues" section of this chapter to continue the security setup once you have the initial security in place.

Now that your application is secure, use the information in the "Setting the ASP Configuration" section of this chapter to perform the required ASP environment configuration. Perform this configuration on the folder that holds your application and not at the Web site or Web server levels. Otherwise, you may open a security hole. It's important that your setup let the user get work done, but you don't want to make things too easy for individuals who don't have your best interests in mind.

At this point, you'll need to begin testing your application. It might fail because IIS 7 places greater restrictions on precisely what you can do within the code. You also have to remember that IIS 7 uses a managed handler for SSI, but not for ASP. The combination of the two technologies could produce odd effects in your application and make it necessary to rewrite some portions.

It's important to remember that Microsoft has also placed a strong emphasis on security in IIS 7, which means you may have to perform some reconfiguration at the command line to get your application running. The "Performing Configuration Tasks without the GUI" section of Chapter 12 contains a number of techniques for configuring IIS 7 at the command line. Unfortunately, you can't perform some of the tasks listed in this section of Chapter 12 using the GUI. Microsoft has formulated the GUI features to meet common tasks that you'll perform multiple times—some of the command line features will see just one or two uses during the life of your server.

Let's Start Building

ASP may be an old technology with lots of warts, but it's still the preferred method of displaying content for some administrators. The most important consideration, if you choose to use this technology, is the issues you might encounter during usage under IIS 7. Previous versions of IIS provided more leeway in what you could expect to make work, despite being not quite correct in ASP. This new environment places tighter restrictions on what it'll accept, so you need to configure the setup carefully and make appropriate changes to the application when necessary. This chapter helps you build these skills:

◆ Define the requirements for moving the ASP application

◆ Configure an ASP page

◆ Move existing ASP application to IIS 7

The only way to see how well ASP works on IIS 7 is to try one of your own applications. Use the techniques described in this chapter to move your application to IIS 7. Try a simple application at first. Test every feature of the application so that you can begin building the skills required to work with ASP under IIS 7 successfully. It's important to remember that you won't have success on the first time with every ASP application and that patience is a requirement if you want to get the application to work. Check the easy things first, such as the ASP environment configuration and the security settings for the application. Once you exhaust the simple fixes, try some of the common errors, such as those described in the "Using the Right Coding Techniques with ASP" sidebar. Finally, begin troubleshooting your application using standard debugging techniques. Keep a log of what you do each step of the way so you don't have to repeat this process with every application. Fix the issues you find before you move the application to increase the odds it'll work the first time.

While Chapter 4 discussed HTML and this chapter discussed ASP, Chapter 6 exposes you to a wealth of other language options. The other application types described in Chapter 6 form the basis for a broad range of languages that you never thought you could use with IIS 7. Certainly, the product itself doesn't make most of these alternatives obvious. Besides non-Microsoft choices such as PHP and PERL, Chapter 6 also discusses some Microsoft options, such as ISAPI, and ancient options such as CGI. Even if you don't use these options, Chapter 6 can be a lot of fun to read simply because it exposes you to so many new ways of doing things.

Chapter 6

Working with Other Application Types

Chapters 4 and 5 focus on traditional application types: HTML and ASP, while Part 3 of this book focuses exclusively on ASP.NET. Between these two extremes lie an incredible number of other application types. Some of these application types, such as CGI, appear on more than just IIS. In fact, CGI has been around for a very long time. Other application types are old favorites, such as the ISAPI extensions. IIS 7 provides direct support for these application types.

Another application type is SMTP, which is the basis for email. This chapter also discusses what you need to do in order to configure and support SMTP on your system. Besides providing the obvious functionality, IIS uses SMTP for notification purposes. When something goes wrong on your server, IIS can send you an email about it when you have SMTP configured.

The final section of this chapter considers a number of other language options that IIS doesn't support directly. These non-Microsoft options see a lot of use today because they're inexpensive and easy to learn. Some of these options aren't managed languages. For example, you can find PHP Hypertext Preprocessor (PHP) on most Web server platforms today. In other cases, the product is a managed language, but you need to install some functionality to gain support for it. For example, PERL.NET is a managed language, but it doesn't come with IIS.

In this chapter, you will learn how to do the following:

◆ Develop a strategy for working with CGI

◆ Develop a strategy for working with ISAPI extensions

◆ Configure and manage ISAPI filters

◆ Define ISAPI extension and CGI restrictions

◆ Manage SMTP email

◆ Develop a strategy for working with non-Microsoft language solutions

Working with CGI Applications

CGI applications were once the cornerstone of Web applications. You could count on seeing them used with most of the older servers to perform a significant number of tasks. Some people confuse CGI with a language or a special technology. A CGI application is actually one that conforms to a particular communication protocol, rather than using a specific language or technology. You can create CGI applications on IIS using a broad range of languages including:

◆ C/C++

◆ Visual Basic

◆ Practical Extraction and Report Language (PERL)

In fact, any thought that language plays a part in CGI at all limits the protocol. It's possible to implement a CGI solution using nearly any language as long as you can find a handler to support the language and create the application so that it meets CGI requirements. In addition, CGI isn't even a Microsoft technology—it exists on many platforms. Consequently, if you create a CGI solution for Apache running on Linux, it may be possible to move that solution to IIS on Windows. You can use the following resources to learn about CGI as a technology:

The Common Gateway Interface (Overview) `http://hoohoo.ncsa.uiuc.edu/cgi/overview.html`

The CGI Resource Index `http://cgi.resourceindex.com/`

CGI Made Really Easy `http://www.jmarshall.com/easy/cgi/`

CGIexpo.com `http://www.cgiexpo.com/`

TIP Developers in your organization need to know that Microsoft has provided .NET configuration classes for IIS 7. The overview for these classes appears at `https://msdn2.microsoft.com/en-us/library/ms691259.aspx`. If you're developing configuration applications specifically for CGI, you'll want to review the `CgiSection` class information located at `https://msdn2.microsoft.com/en-us/library/ms691417.aspx`. You'll also want to review the `IsapiCgiRestrictionElement` class at `https://msdn2.microsoft.com/en-us/library/ms690611.aspx` for security purposes.

CGI does suffer from a number of problems in IIS 7. The problem that you're likely to notice first is that most of the CGI resources on the Internet rely on scripting languages, such as PERL, rather than the language you're likely to use with IIS 7. You can partially overcome this problem by looking for script examples on Web sites such as ScriptSearch (`http://www.scriptsearch.com/`). You'll also want to view the "Working with Non-Microsoft Alternatives" section of the chapter to see language-specific solutions to various IIS 7 issues.

You'll also experience a performance hit using CGI. The standard technique for working with CGI is to create a new process for every call. Creating new processes costs the server a lot of time, making your CGI application slower than other solutions such as ISAPI and ASP.NET. In fact, Microsoft optimized IIS 7 to provide the best performance when you create ASP.NET applications. That said, CGI still offers the best language support and greatest flexibility of any solution you might try on a Web server.

Securing CGI applications follows the same guidelines as HTML application, except you're working with an executable now. Consequently, you must give the caller execute rights to the folder holding the CGI scripts. It's still possible to secure static resources using the techniques described in the "Considering Security Issues" section of Chapter 4, but CGI does require that you open yourself to potential intrusions. To reduce your security exposure, make sure you follow the techniques described in the "Managing ISAPI Extension and CGI Restrictions" section of the chapter.

As with HTML applications, you can rely on XCopy to move CGI applications for the most part. The "Moving Your Files with XCopy" section of Chapter 4 tells you how to use this utility effectively with IIS 7. CGI applications can throw a curve when they rely on the registry.

Working with ISAPI Extensions

Developers originally created ISAPI extensions using C and then C++. The technology was supposed to replace CGI, and it did in many ways. ISAPI extensions offer many features not found in

CGI applications. One of the most important considerations for using ISAPI with IIS 7 is that it's more efficient—you don't have to create a new process for every caller. The article at http:// msdn2.microsoft.com/en-us/library/ms525913.aspx provides a good comparison of various IIS development technologies, including a comparison of both ISAPI and CGI.

Microsoft also relied heavily on ISAPI extensions at one point. Most applications in IIS 6 rely on ISAPI extensions to perform tasks. The technology has changed for IIS 7. Now many of the applications that run in IIS use the .NET Framework instead, which provides a significant number of security, reliability, and performance benefits. You can read an excellent comparison of how Microsoft has changed from ISAPI to the .NET Framework in the article at http://weblogs.asp.net/scottgu/ archive/2007/04/02/iis-7-0.aspx. The bottom line is that even though you can continue to use ISAPI extensions, the mainstream of IIS 7 development is headed toward use of the .NET Framework for server extensions.

Security is considerably pickier when working with IIS 7 than it was for previous versions of IIS. You must make certain that the user has access to the executable and all configuration files to make the ISAPI extension work as intended. Unlike a script-based solution, however, you can often get by with giving the user access to the executable and not the entire folder. In some respects, the less intensive access requirements actually make ISAPI a little more secure than script-based solutions such as ASP. Of course, ISAPI extensions don't share the security features of managed executables, so you'll still make some trade-offs to use them.

You use ISAPI extensions differently from script-based solutions. In most cases, you won't move the ISAPI extension to a new folder on the system; you'll simply redirect the pointer to the ISAPI extension as needed. For example, when a user accesses your ISAPI extension for a particular resource, you'll create a handler mapping using the technique found in the "Adding a Script Map" section of Chapter 3. In some cases, the ISAPI extension setup can become quite complex. To see an example of a complex setup, look at the "Working with JSP" section of this chapter. The point is that you'll move the executable as needed to other servers, but you won't often need to move the executable to a different location on the current server.

Managing ISAPI Filters

ISAPI filters work very much like their name implies—they monitor the data stream between the client and the server and filter it as necessary. Unlike ISAPI extensions, you can't call an ISAPI filter directly, but must configure it to monitor the data stream in particular ways. To display the ISAPI filters for a Web server or Web site, select the Web server or Web site in the Connections pane and double-click the ISAPI filters icon in the Features View. You'll see the standard list of ISAPI filters shown in Figure 6.1, along with any additional ISAPI filters you've installed. The following sections provide an overview of ISAPI filtering and discuss how you configure it on IIS 7.

Understanding ISAPI Filters

As previously mentioned, ISAPI filters provide a monitoring function. Filtering can take on many different forms, but in all cases the ISAPI filter provides a form of monitoring and data manipulation. The basic form of ISAPI filter functionality is the event. IIS calls on all of the ISAPI filters that can handle an event when that event occurs on the system. Here's a list of the ISAPI filter events (you can find a detailed view of these events at http://msdn2.microsoft.com/en-us/library/ms524610.aspx).

NOTE   Even though these events can happen in any order and the ISAPI filter must not rely on a particular order, the events generally occur in the order shown in the list. The system follows a particular processing order to satisfy a caller request unless the request requires special processing or a special event occurs.

FIGURE 6.1

IIS 7 always comes with an ISAPI filter for ASP.NET 2.0 installed.

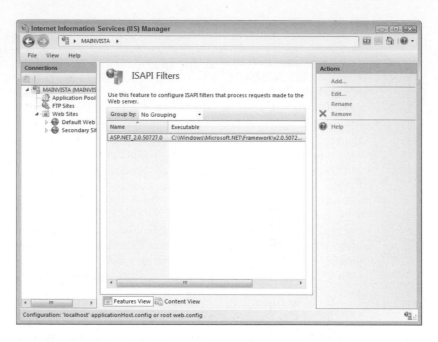

SF_NOTIFY_READ_RAW_DATA This event occurs every time a caller makes a request. In fact, the ISAPI filter generally sees one event for each of the HTTP headers sent by the caller. An ISAPI filter can use this event to monitor the incoming requests for specific headers and then act on values in those headers. The ISAPI filter could also look for missing headers or interact with the headers in other ways.

SF_NOTIFY_PREPROC_HEADERS When the server finishes reviewing the HTTP headers, but before it begins processing the information in those headers, the ISAPI filter can review the header data for errors, special contents, omissions, or other forms of content. This event only occurs once during the processing cycle.

SF_NOTIFY_URL_MAP Once the server has processed the HTTP headers and knows what the caller needs, it turns the request URL into a physical path on the system. An ISAPI filter can examine this information and perform tasks such as redirecting the output from another location.

SF_NOTIFY_AUTHENTICATION The server performs an authentication process when one of two situations occurs: the caller has requested anonymous access or the request contains an authorization header for basic authentication. In either case, the ISAPI filter can examine the request and perform additional authentication steps.

SF_NOTIFY_AUTH_COMPLETE When the server can successfully identify the caller, it fires this event. At this point, the ISAPI filter can examine the method, URL, version, and headers for the request. In addition, the ISAPI filter can act on the identity of the user since the server has negotiated this information.

WARNING Just because the server identifies the caller doesn't mean that you're actually working with that caller. The caller could have stolen the credentials or might have spoofed the server in some way. Some ISAPI filters perform additional checks to verify the caller's identity in other ways.

NOTE Additional SF_NOTIFY_READ_RAW_DATA events can occur at this point in the processing cycle. The ISAPI filter may provide additional data monitoring. From an administrative perspective, you could notice errors that appear out of place when viewing a failed request trace log.

SF_NOTIFY_SEND_RESPONSE Now that the server has identified the caller and knows which resources the caller wants, it begins formulating a response. The ISAPI filter receives this event before the server actually creates the response. This is the last chance that the ISAPI filter has to perform request processing or to modify the way the server will create the response.

SF_NOTIFY_SEND_RAW_DATA This event signals that the server is about to send data to the caller. The event occurs once for each response block. The ISAPI filter can use this event to verify that the response is correct and meets caller expectations. The server also fires a SF_NOTIFY_END_OF_REQUEST event at the end of each response block.

SF_NOTIFY_END_OF_REQUEST The server fires this event whenever it finishes sending a response block to the caller.

SF_NOTIFY_LOG This event occurs after the server has sent the data, but before it writes information about the transfer to the log. The ISAPI filter can examine and modify the potential log entry. You may need such processing to perform automated log processing or simply to pull sensitive entries out of the log.

SF_NOTIFY_END_OF_NET_SESSION It's important to tell ISAPI filters when the session is ending so that they can clear any session specific data. IIS only fires this event at the end of the session. When the server negotiates keep-alives with the caller, the ISAPI filter can receive multiple request cycles before it sees this event. This event only occurs once during each session.

ISAPI filters can also work globally or with a specific Web site. The scope of an ISAPI filter depends on where you install it: either at the Web server (global) or Web site levels. Some filters require a global orientation because they affect every Web site. ASP.NET 2.0 runs as an ISAPI filter in IIS 7, so it has a global impact. Every Web site has access to ASP.NET 2.0 functionality.

If you haven't worked with ISAPI filters before and need a good overview on this technology, the article at http://msdn2.microsoft.com/en-us/library/ms524610.aspx isn't too detailed, but provides good information on getting started.

Adding ISAPI Filters

Normally, any third-party product you install will also install any required ISAPI filters for you. However, you might need to install a custom ISAPI filter or a special ISAPI filter that you obtained from a third-party source, rather than as part of an application. The following steps tell how to install an ISAPI filter.

1. Click Add in the Actions pane. You'll see the Add ISAPI filter dialog box shown in Figure 6.2.

FIGURE 6.2
Adding a new
ISAPI filter is a
quick process.

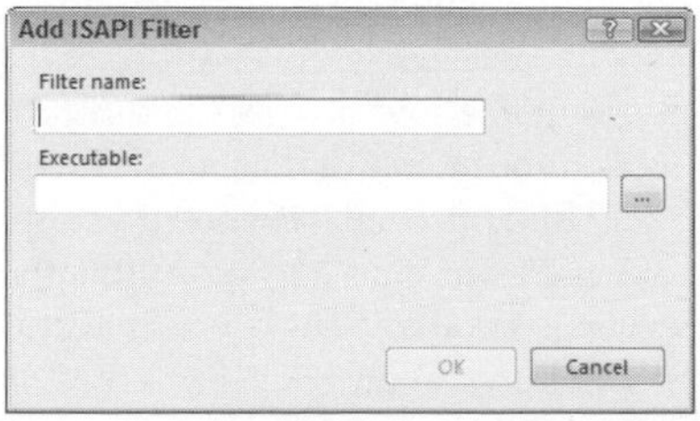

2. Type the name of the ISAPI filter in the Filter Name field.

3. Provide a location for the executable (either a DLL or EXE file) in the Executable field. You can also use the browse button to locate the executable file on disk.

WARNING   Make sure that you choose the correct ISAPI filter executable. IIS doesn't perform any checking on the ISAPI filter when you install it. The executable you choose could literally contain any information.

4. Click OK to complete the process.

5. Restart the Web server or Web site to ensure the new ISAPI filter is in the processing loop.

Editing ISAPI Filter Settings

If you choose the wrong ISAPI filter executable or have an updated version of the ISAPI filter you want to use, you can easily modify the entry as needed to correct it. Modifying an existing ISAPI filter is similar to adding one. Highlight the ISAPI filter you want to change, click Edit in the Actions pane, and you'll see a dialog box similar to the one shown in Figure 6.2. Make the required changes, and click OK to complete the process. You can't change the name of the ISAPI filter using the Edit option.

Removing an ISAPI Filter

At some point, you'll probably need to remove an ISAPI filter that you added previously. Only remove ISAPI filters that you add manually. Your setup requires the default IIS ISAPI filters in most cases. In addition, third-party products normally remove ISAPI filters as part of the uninstall process.

To remove an existing ISAPI filter, highlight the ISAPI filter in the list and click Remove. IIS will ask you to confirm that you want to remove the ISAPI filter. Click Yes to complete the process. Restart the Web server or Web site to ensure IIS removes the ISAPI filter from the processing loop.

Renaming an ISAPI Filter Entry

You may decide to rename an ISAPI filter entry so that it better reflects the purpose of the ISAPI filter. To perform this task, highlight the ISAPI filter entry you want to change and click Rename in the Actions pane. IIS will turn the ISAPI filter name entry into an edit box. Type the new name and press Enter to complete the process.

Managing ISAPI Extension and CGI Restrictions

Not every ISAPI extension or CGI application has to run on your system. In fact, you'll find that they can't run unless you enable them in some way. The first method of enabling an ISAPI extension or CGI application is to create a handler and enable the handler. Using handlers restricts the executable somewhat in that it only works for a specific resource. You can learn more about handlers in the "Working with Handlers" section of Chapter 3.

The sections that follow discuss the second method of enabling an ISAPI extension or CGI application. In this case, you enable or disable the executable on a global basis—for all of the Web sites on a particular server. This approach lets you add support for alternative scripting languages or other features that could affect the server as a whole, rather than an individual Web site. To display the restrictions for the Web Server, select the Web Server in the Connections pane and double-click the ISAPI and CGI Restrictions icon in the Features View. You'll see the standard list of restrictions shown in Figure 6.3, along with any additional ISAPI filters you've installed (the Jakarta ISAPI entry in this case).

FIGURE 6.3
Use restrictions to
specifically enable
or disable ISAPI
extensions or CGI
applications.

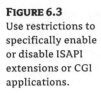

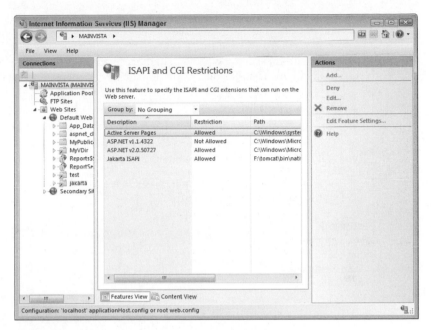

FIGURE 6.3
Use restrictions to
specifically enable
or disable ISAPI
extensions or CGI
applications.

Unlike other executable setups, it's very likely that you'll add ISAPI extensions manually to IIS 7 to accommodate a special need, such as language support. However, any third-party application you purchase should make the required entries for you as part of the installation process. Most CGI applications will also make the required entries for you when they come with Windows-friendly installation programs. The following sections provide an overview of using restrictions and discuss how you configure them on IIS 7.

Changing the Feature Settings

You can simply open up your server to any and every ISAPI extension or CGI application anyone installs. Microsoft should never have added this feature to IIS 7 because there's absolutely no reason to include it. When you use this feature, you open your server to all kinds of potential problems of such a dire nature that your only recourse might include formatting the drive and starting from scratch. In fact, you should probably stop reading now and go on to one of the other sections.

If you insist on letting anyone install any ISAPI extension or CGI application on your server, click Edit Feature Settings in the Actions pane. You'll see the Edit ISAPI and CGI Restrictions Settings dialog box shown in Figure 6.4. Check the Allow Unspecified CGI Modules option if you want unfettered access to CGI applications and the Allow Unspecified ISAPI Modules option if you want unfettered access to ISAPI. Click OK.

FIGURE 6.4
Checking these
options opens your
server to known forms
of attack.

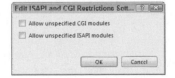

It's possible to mitigate the potential for attack slightly by making specific entries in the restriction list and not allowing that executable to run. The only problem with this approach is that you have to know about the executable and it's almost certain that persons of ill intent aren't going to send you an email with the name and location of that executable. Security by exception isn't going to work, especially in this case. It truly is better to add individual restrictions to keep your server secure.

Adding a Restriction

The term *restriction* is misleading. You can use a restriction to enable or disable an ISAPI extension or CGI application. The restriction is more of an entry in a database with an on/off switch that lets you tell IIS 7 how to treat the executable. Follow these steps to add a new restriction.

1. Click Add in the Actions pane. You'll see an Add ISAPI or CGI Restriction dialog box like the one shown in Figure 6.5.

FIGURE 6.5
Add a restriction to either enable or disable an executable on your system.

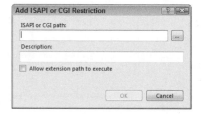

2. Type the name and location of the executable in the ISAPI or CGI Path field. Click the browse button if necessary to locate the file. The entry should include the full executable path.

3. Type a human-readable name for the executable in the Description field. Make sure you choose a name that won't conflict with other executables.

4. Check the Allow Execution Path to Execute option if you want to enable the executable.

5. Click OK. IIS adds the new restriction to the list.

Denying or Allowing a Restriction

You may need to temporarily enable or disable an ISAPI extension or CGI application. For example, you might use a particular executable only for maintenance purposes and might not want to allow access to it normally. Alternatively, an application could experience an error and you may want to disable it temporarily to allow time for repairs. In either case, IIS 7 makes it easy to enable or disable the executable. All you need to do is choose the executable you want to change and then click either Allow or Deny in the Actions pane. This setting is actually a toggle, so you'll only see the option that you need to change the status of the executable.

Editing a Restriction

Sometimes you'll need to change a restriction. For example, an updated ISAPI extension or CGI application might have a slightly different name than the original or you might encounter a conflict with the human-readable name you chose. In either case, highlight the entry you want to change and click Edit in the Actions pane. You'll see an Edit ISAPI or CGI Restriction dialog box like the one shown in Figure 6.4. IIS 7 provides full access to all of the fields, so you can make any change required.

Removing a Restriction

When you no longer need a particular restriction, it's better to remove it than simply disable it. Otherwise, you'll end up with a number of disabled entries in your restriction list and have no idea of where they came from. To remove a restriction, highlight the entry you want to remove and click Remove in the Actions pane. IIS 7 will ask you whether you're sure that you want to remove the restriction. Click Yes to complete the process.

Configuring SMTP Email

Your application might require use of the Simple Mail Transfer Protocol (SMTP) to send confirmation or status information. IIS 7 provides an option to configure an SMTP email address for use by your application. The configuration identifies the application, not the recipient. You must still provide recipient information just as you always do as part of your application. The purpose of identifying the application is to help you identify the sender.

WARNING Creating identification for your applications doesn't necessarily guarantee the safety of the information you send. Someone can spoof your sender information, making it appear their information is coming from your application, even though it isn't. However, having the information in place does add a little extra security, so it's worth having. In addition, at least the administrator will know where a message is from, rather than seeing a blank sender in an email. The sender information also helps the email make it through firewalls and virus detectors, so it does have a purpose, but you shouldn't rely on it heavily.

It's easy to configure an email address for the Web server as a whole, individual Web sites, applications, or even folders. The level at which a user makes a request determines the email address that IIS 7 chooses. When the user is in an application, IIS 7 will choose the email address for that application when you've configured one. Otherwise, IIS 7 will look one level at a time until it finds an email address to use. To display the email information for any level, select the level you want to change in the Connections pane and double-click the SMTP E-mail icon in the Features View. You'll see the SMTP E-mail pane shown in Figure 6.6.

FIGURE 6.6
Configure SMTP email settings for applications that need it.

IIS 7 provides two methods to send an email: using an SMTP server or storing the email locally. When you use the SMTP server, IIS sends the email immediately. On the other hand, storing the email locally lets an application pick it up later. You can use this second approach with a custom application to make it easier to perform custom processing on the data. In both cases, you begin the process by providing an email address in the E-mail Address field. The following sections describe both approaches.

Configuring an SMTP Server

The upper half of the SMTP E-mail window shown in Figure 6.6 contains the SMTP server settings. The following steps describe how to configure this option.

1. Select the Deliver E-mail to SMTP Server option.

2. Type the URI for the SMTP server you want to use or check the Use Localhost option. IIS automatically provides the URI for the SMTP server when you choose the Use Localhost option.

3. Provide a port number to use in the Port field. IIS provides the default setting of 25 for you. Only configure this option when your SMTP server has a special setup.

4. Choose an authentication type in the Authentication Settings area. When you choose Not Required, IIS doesn't send any authentication information. About the only time this setting works is when you use localhost. The Windows option sends you Windows credentials to the SMTP server and normally only works with an SMTP server on your network. For all other servers, you must use the Specify Credentials option. When you choose this third option, click Set and you'll see the Set Credentials dialog box shown in Figure 6.7. Type your name and password as needed.

FIGURE 6.7
Provide the credentials required to access an SMTP server outside your network.

5. Click Apply to make the settings active.

Configuring a Pickup Directory

You'll normally use a pickup directory for local distribution of email with a custom application. It's possible that you could encounter other situations where this option is helpful, but most administrators won't ever use it. The following steps describe how to configure this option.

1. Select the Store E-mail in Pickup Directory option.

2. Type the location of the pickup directory. Click Browse if you need to search for the pickup directory on your hard drive.

3. Click Apply to make the settings active.

NOTE   Make sure that everyone who requires access to the email can access the pickup directory. In addition, some administrators make the mistake of not giving IIS proper access to the pickup directory, which can prove fatal to your application.

Working with Non-Microsoft Alternatives

Although Microsoft behaves like the entire world revolves around them, most administrators know better and need solutions for working with products other than those that Microsoft provides. Fortunately, IIS 7 provides robust support for other languages through third-party products. Many of these products rely on ISAPI extensions to do their work, but third-party developers are constantly working to create new products. In fact, you can find the latest IIS 7 products at IIS Download Center (`http://www.iis.net/downloads/default.aspx?tabid=3`). The following sections describe techniques you can use to overcome issues with non-Microsoft alternative languages.

USING A NONSTANDARD INTERFACE

Some people have probably decided, by this point in the book, that they really don't like the new IIS 7 interface. Moving to a new interface can be difficult. Some of the new features really are incredible, but the interface is so different that learning to use it is difficult at best. In addition, Microsoft has apparently decided to hide some features to make the graphical interface easier to use. Consequently, the new interface also means learning to use the command line for advanced users. The changes are significant.

Fortunately, some third parties are coming up with interesting alternatives to the new user interface and you can count on more appearing on the scene as administrators and developers move to IIS 7. One such interface is the new Web site administration tool described at `http://aspnet.4guysfromrolla.com/articles/052307-1.aspx` (this product includes downloadable source code so you can customize the tool to fit your needs). The author based the custom tool described in this article on a Microsoft product, the ASP.NET Web Site Administration Tool (WSAT) that you can download from `http://msdn2.microsoft.com/en-us/library/ms228053.aspx`.

Besides WSAT and its knockoffs, you can also find distinct IIS 7 management offerings such as the one located at `http://peterkellner.net/?p=1`. In this case, the tool relies on Asynchronous JavaScript and XML (AJAX) to get the job done. Some people may find this product interesting for just the technology it provides, rather than the administration tool. As with other third-party products, you can download the source code for this tool and customize it to meet your needs.

Working with PHP

Forget everything you know about installing PHP support on IIS. There's a new way to support PHP on IIS 7 that's faster and easier than anything you've used in the past. FastCGI is a collaborative project between Zend (`http://www.zend.com`) and Microsoft designed to make PHP significantly easier under Windows. You can obtain this product at `http://www.iis.net/default.aspx?tabid=1000051`.

You don't even have to go it alone when it comes to learning how to use this product. ScottGu's Blog at `http://weblogs.asp.net/scottgu/archive/2006/10/31/PHP-and-the-FastCGI-Module-for-IIS-7.0.aspx` contains a comprehensive overview of the product. BillS' IIS Blog at `http://blogs.iis.net/bills/archive/2006/10/31/PHP-on-IIS.aspx` contains a comprehensive tutorial for using the product as well. The download site contains a list of other good places to check for additional information.

Working with PERL

Many PERL implementations won't run under IIS 7. However, ActiveState ActivePerl (http://www.activestate.com/store/productdetail.aspx?prdGuid=81fbce82-6bd5-49bc-a915-08d58c2648ca) works just fine and you only need to perform a little work to make it completely functional. You can even download a free version of this product and try it out. After you install the product, open the ISAPI and CGI Restrictions pane (see the "Managing ISAPI Extension and CGI Restrictions" section of the chapter for details). You'll see two new ActivePerl entries, as shown in Figure 6.8. The entries appear as [No Description] (you can add one if desired). ActivePerl automatically enables the ISAPI extension version of the product for you. If you choose, you can also enable the PERL.EXE version. However, there's little reason to enable both.

FIGURE 6.8

Verify the installation program made the appropriate entries for you.

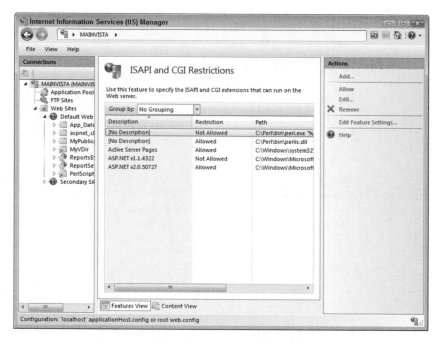

NOTE Some people have experienced difficulty getting the PERL.EXE application to work. If this problem occurs, you'll see a 502.2 error. In this case, try the ISAPI extension implementation to determine whether it works for your application.

The ActivePerl implementation is almost, but not quite, ready to use. If your application relies on Perlscript, then all you need to do is create a virtual directory pointing to your code. Because IIS 7 already has an ASP extension handler, you don't have to do anything else. However, if your application relies on PL files, you must select the virtual directory in the Connections pane and add a handler for the .PL file extension using the technique found in the "Adding a Script Map" section of Chapter 3. The best option to use is the ISAPI extension, so you'd provide the PERLIS.DLL handler in the Executable field (this file normally appears in the \Perl\bin folder).

ActivePerl provides a considerable number of examples you can try to tune your IIS 7 setup. Check the ReadMe.TXT file in the \Perl\eg folder for a list of examples. Try the example in the \Perl\eg\cgi folder if you want to see how the PL extension mapping works. You'll find a complete ActivePerl user's guide in the \Perl\html folder. Open Index.html to begin viewing the content.

As far as security and application movement are concerned, PERL developers need only follow the same restrictions as ASP developers. See the "Considering Security Issues" and "Moving an ASP Application to IIS 7" sections of Chapter 5 for details.

Working with Python

When working with Python, you have a number of good choices for an IIS 7 installation. You can choose ActiveState ActivePython (http://www.activestate.com/Products/ActivePython/), which works very much like ActivePerl described in the "Working with PERL" section of the chapter. ActiveState actually provides a significant number of Python tools, such as the Komodo Edit editor. As an alternative, you can download an open source version of Python from http://www.python.org/download/releases/.

The open source installer provides many automated features that appear to work fine with IIS 7. The setup program automatically adds the required Python restrictions for you, but you should still check them. Your display should look similar to the one shown in Figure 6.8. The only difference is that you'll see Python executables in place of the PERL executables.

After you ensure that you have the correct restrictions in place, you'll need to add the virtual directory to your applications. Select the virtual directory in the Connections pane and then create a new Python handler using the techniques described in the "Adding a Script Map" section of Chapter 3. Make sure you type the Executable field entry correctly. The entry must include two %s entries such as C:\Python25\python.exe %s %s.

As far as security and application movement are concerned, Python developers need only follow the same restrictions as ASP developers. See the "Considering Security Issues" and "Moving an ASP Application to IIS 7" sections of Chapter 5 for details. If you don't set security properly, you'll see the dreaded 502.2 error when viewing the Web page. In some cases, even setting the security correctly won't fix the problem. You'll need to use the ActiveState ActivePython product in this scenario because it includes ISAPI extension support not found in the open source version.

CONSIDERING SILVERLIGHT FOR CROSS-PLATFORM AND CROSS-BROWSER SUPPORT

Microsoft is working on a new plug-in for your browser called Silverlight (http://www .microsoft .com/silverlight/default01.aspx) that will hopefully make IIS 7 more language friendly. According to the current documentation, you can use Silverlight to support PHP, JavaScript, Ruby, Python, C#, and Visual Basic.NET. Microsoft is saying that it will eventually support other languages as well, but hasn't provided any information on these languages. Even so, with a single plug-in you can avoid using myriad products from other vendors. No one's tested to determine whether Silverlight provides complete and standardized support for all of these languages—you could encounter incompatibilities. You can find Silverlight specific information from Microsoft at http://silverlight.net/ and even a streaming media site at http://silverlight.live.com/.

The Silverlight product is .NET Framework based, which means that you gain all of the security and performance features that the .NET Framework can provide. The output from Silverlight appears to work fine with both Internet Explorer and Firefox as long as you don't use any Microsoft-specific technologies such as ActiveX. The output options include all of the latest technologies including eXtensible Application Markup Language (XAML) and AJAX. You can even use it to display vector-based graphics on screen, assuming the browser in question supports the Microsoft technologies. Unfortunately, none of Microsoft's documentation mentions whether Silverlight will follow the Scalable Vector Graphics (SVG) standard (see http://www.w3.org/TR/SVG/ for details).

If media is part of your application, you may have concerns about using Silverlight as a solution. Silverlight uses the Windows Media Video (WMV) standard instead of the VC-1 standard created by the Society of Motion Picture and Television Engineers (SMPTE) or the currently popular Motion Pictures Experts Group 2 (MPEG-2) standard. Because WMV is an alternative standard, you may experience compatibility problems. You also get both Windows Media Audio (WMA) and Media Player 3 (MP3) support with Silverlight, so audio is less of a problem.

Silverlight helps you serve applications from IIS 7 by improving the browser using a plug-in. It works on either Macintosh or Windows systems. The product is in beta at the time of this writing, so anything in this sidebar is subject to change. You can gain additional information about Silverlight in the overview presented at `http://blogs.msdn.com/tims/archive/2007/04/15/introducing-microsoft-silverlight.aspx`.

Working with JSP

Administrators have needed to support Java servlets and Java Server Pages (JSPs) for quite a while. In fact, some of the tools for working with JSP come from IIS 4 (less popular) and some from IIS 5 (more popular). Unfortunately, some of your older ISAPI extension techniques won't work in IIS 7. You can still use the ISAPI extension, but the process for making it work differs from IIS 6. If you don't need this functionality in IIS, you can still access Tomcat directly using the standard setup and testing it by accessing `http://localhost:8080/` as you always have.

The procedure for incorporating Java servlet and JSPs into IIS was straightforward in IIS 6. You could even find some applications to automate the entire process for you. Unfortunately, those techniques don't work in IIS 7, but you can still add the required support. The new process follows these steps:

1. Download and install both Java (`http://java.sun.com/j2se/1.4.2/download.html`) and Tomcat (`http://tomcat.apache.org/`) support as you normally would. Make sure you set the JRE_HOME environment variable and not the JAVA_HOME environment variable if you download and install the Java Runtime Environment (JRE). The Tomcat installation instructions appear in the `Running.TXT` file found in the top-level folder.

2. Install both products, just as you did in the past, using the vendor instructions.

3. Create a virtual directory named jakarta in the Default Web Site using the instructions found in the "Adding Virtual Directories to the Web Site" section of Chapter 3. Don't make the virtual directory into an application, as you would have in the past. The jakarta virtual directory points to the Tomcat `bin\native` folder.

4. Select the jakarta virtual directory in the Connections pane. Enable the ISAPI-dll handler using the procedure in the "Enabling and Disabling Handlers" section of Chapter 3.

5. Obtain a copy of the `isapi_redirect.dll` file. This file can prove a little difficult to find. The Web site at `http://tomcat.apache.org/download-connectors.cgi` contains the links you need. Choose one of the mirrors and then click the JK 1.2 Binary Releases link. Follow the links to the appropriate version of Windows, the newest version of the library. Download the copy of `isapi_redirect.dll` file and place it in the Tomcat `bin\native` folder.

6. Select the Web server entry in the Connections pane.

7. Create a new entry in the ISAPI and CGI Restrictions pane using the instructions in the "Managing ISAPI Extension and CGI Restrictions" section of the chapter. Give the new

restriction the name Jakarta ISAPI and enter the location of the `isapi_redirect.dll` file in the ISAPI or CGI Path field. Check the Allow Extension Path to Execute option. Click OK to complete the entry.

8. Create the required configuration files. Tomcat normally requires two configuration files (`worker.properties` and `uriworkermap.properties`) with the appropriate entries as described at `http://tomcat.apache.org/connectors-doc/webserver_howto/iis.html`.

9. Set security in the Tomcat folders so that the user can access the `isapi_redirect.dll` file. In addition, the user must have access to the `worker.properties` and `uriworkermap.properties` files in the Tomcat `conf` folder. If you set the security or configuration information incorrectly, you'll likely see a 500.0 error with very little descriptive information when you try to access the server.

Working with Ruby

Ruby developers can use the same product that PHP developers use to make their applications work on IIS 7 (see the "Working with PHP" section of the chapter for details). However, the FastCGI product doesn't support Ruby right out of the package—you need to modify it a bit first. That's where the information on the Ruby On Rails For IIS Fast-CGI Web site (`http://www.codeplex.com/RORIIS`) comes into play. You'll find complete instructions and tools for using the FastCGI product with Ruby on this Web site. Unfortunately, this product is in beta as of this writing, so I can't provide full details on using it.

Working with ColdFusion

Getting ColdFusion to run on your IIS 7 installation can prove troublesome. It almost, but not quite, installs when you use the default installation process. Some problems occur during the mapping processing that prevents ColdFusion from working and you have to add the usual IIS 7 extras for mapping the requests. The following steps tell you how to configure ColdFusion 7.0.2 for IIS 7 (this procedure should work for other versions of ColdFusion too, but I only tested it with version 7.0.2).

NOTE The procedure in this section should work fine. However, you might also want to try the alternative procedure found at `http://www.communitymx.com/content/article.cfm?cid=224AA`.

1. Install ColdFusion as you normally would on the host system. The ColdFusion installation will appear to work, but it won't create the required mappings for IIS 7.

2. Copy the `wsconfig` folder contents from an existing ColdFusion installation to the new installation. Overwrite any existing files with the new content.

3. Open the Internet Information Services (IIS) Manager and select the Web server entry in the Connections pane.

4. Create a new entry in the ISAPI and CGI Restrictions pane using the instructions in the "Managing ISAPI Extension and CGI Restrictions" section of the chapter. Give the new restriction the name ColdFusion and enter the location of the `jrun.dll` file normally found in the `\CFusionMX7\runtime\lib\wsconfig\1` folder in the ISAPI or CGI Path field. Check the Allow Extension Path to Execute option. Click OK to complete the entry.

5. Choose the Web site that will host the ColdFusion applications in the Connections Pane.

6. Open the ISAPI Filters icon and create a new entry for ColdFusion using the technique found in the "Managing ISAPI Filters" section of the chapter. Add the `jrun.dll` file location to the Executable field.

7. Create a virtual directory for your application.

8. Select the virtual directory in the Connections pane and then create a new ColdFusion (CF file) handler using the techniques described in the "Adding a Script Map" section of Chapter 3. Add the `jrun.dll` file location to the Executable field.

9. Repeat step 8 for the `.CFC` and `.CFML` extensions as a minimum.

10. Open the Default Document icon for the virtual directory you created.

11. Add entries for `index.cfm` and `index.cfml` using the techniques found in the "Setting a Default Document" section of Chapter 3.

12. Set security for the ColdFusion installation. The user must have the required access to your application as well as the ColdFusion `wsconfig` folder as a minimum.

Working with PERL.NET and IronPython

It's important to remember that there are .NET alternatives for languages other than C++, C#, and VB.NET. In fact, more alternatives appear on the market all the time. The alternative languages that IIS 7 administrators will most likely want to know about are PERL.NET (`http://download .activestate.com/PerlNET/`) and IronPython (`http://www.codeplex.com/Wiki/View .aspx?ProjectName=IronPython`).

As with all other .NET languages, you obtain extensions to Visual Studio for using these products. However, because the .NET languages actually appear as part of the .NET Framework and not as part of Visual Studio, you can use any third-party editor that you like to create applications. Needless to say, you gain all of the functionality of the .NET Framework when you use one of these alternatives and you won't have to worry quite so much about installation problems on IIS 7.

Of course, whenever you use one of these alternatives, you'll run into a few compatibility issues. That's because the .NET Framework places restrictions on the language and adds a few things to it as well. When choosing one of these alternatives, you'll have to consider the effect of these compatibility issues on your existing code. It may be that you'll want to perform the required IIS configuration and continue using your existing product when the number of code changes becomes overwhelming.

Let's Start Building

The one piece of essential information you should take away from this chapter is that any perception of IIS as a closed product that doesn't provide very much functionality is false. IIS is actually quite open and you have myriad options to choose from for creating applications. In fact, this chapter hasn't begun to explore the possibilities—it really discusses only a few of the more popular options. This chapter also demonstrates the configuration techniques you need for the languages that IIS does support directly. This chapter helps you build these skills:

◆ Develop a strategy for working with CGI

◆ Develop a strategy for working with ISAPI extensions

◆ Configure and manage ISAPI filters

- ◆ Define ISAPI extension and CGI restrictions

- ◆ Manage SMTP email

- ◆ Develop a strategy for working with non-Microsoft language solutions

Working with other products can be a lot of fun. It's often nice to install something new just to see what it can do. If you have an experimental Web server setup to work with, try installing few products that appear in this chapter. Locate a tutorial online and teach yourself a new language if you have the time. Having more than one language skill in your toolbox is often a big plus when you get a new job. Even if you don't really want to learn a new language, you might at least try out a product such as PHP because it's no harder to learn than ASP and it does run on multiple platforms.

You might think that Microsoft has moved everything over to IIS 7, but they made the odd decision to leave one element behind, File Transfer Protocol (FTP) support. If your Web site provides FTP support, then you'll want to read up on how it works in Chapter 7. This coverage should be familiar to anyone who has worked with IIS 6 because you're using the Internet Information Services 6.0 Manager to perform all of the FTP configuration tasks. In fact, if you already know how to work with FTP under IIS 6, you can probably skip Chapter 7.

Chapter 7

Using the Internet Information Services 6.0 Manager

When you install File Transfer Protocol (FTP) support for IIS 7, something odd happens. Windows installs the Internet Information Services (IIS) 6.0 Manager, which looks nothing like the new Internet Information Services (IIS) Manager used so far in the book. In fact, with a few small differences, the Internet Information Services (IIS) 6.0 Manager looks and acts very much like the one used for IIS 6. If you're already familiar with the older Internet Information Services (IIS) Manager used with IIS 6, you could probably skip this chapter and figure out most of the differences yourself. There are, however, some minor differences between the two, so you might want to at least scan this chapter, even if you're an old hand at working with IIS.

Microsoft hasn't really provided a reason for using Internet Information Services (IIS) 6.0 Manager to manage FTP sites except that it was already available. You can download the same console for Windows XP machines at `http://www.microsoft.com/downloads/details.aspx?familyid =f9c1fb79-c903-4842-9f6c-9db93643fdb7`. Besides managing your IIS 7 FTP sites, you can also use the Internet Information Services (IIS) 6.0 Manager to work with older IIS 6 Web sites. Since Microsoft doesn't intend to provide an Admin Pack for Vista, having the Internet Information Services (IIS) 6.0 Manager is a big deal because otherwise you'd have to use Terminal Server to remote into the server that holds the IIS setup (see `http://msmvps.com/blogs/ad/archive/2007/05/ 28/adminpak-for-windows-vista.aspx` for details). This chapter discusses how to accomplish both tasks, along with the information you need to create a connection to another server.

Because this chapter discusses older technology, it provides only an overview of most features. I'm assuming you have at least some knowledge of the older IIS technologies or will obtain a book (or other material) to understand specifics. The focus of this chapter is how to perform basic management tasks not supported by the new IIS 7 version of Internet Information Services (IIS) Manager.

NOTE　You can find many good books about IIS 6 on the Internet. If you want maximum depth of coverage, try the *Microsoft Internet Information Services (IIS) 6.0 Resource Kit*, Microsoft Press, 2004. Another good book for administrators (but probably not developers) is *IIS 6 Administration* by Mitch Tulloch, McGraw-Hill Osborne Media, 2003. A good quick reference book is *Microsoft IIS 6.0 Administrator's Pocket Consultant* by William R. Stanek, Microsoft Press, 2003.

In this chapter, you will learn how to do the following:

◆　Configure and manage FTP sites

◆　Connect to other FTP and Web servers

◆　Use Internet Information Services (IIS) 6.0 Manager to manage older Web sites

Working with FTP Sites

FTP provides a basic means of transferring files that most companies still support today, yet FTP has changed very little from the time the Internet began. The principle is one of providing secure access to storage on the server so that individuals can upload or download files. The idea is so simple, and yet so necessary, that many vendors have created applications to make using FTP easier, such as FTP Explorer (`http://www.ftpx.com/`). You'll find FTP used for a variety of purposes as well—everything from collaboration to a means of providing device driver downloads. The following sections describe two methods of working with an FTP server: using the graphical interface; and working with the FTP utility. You'll also find sections on the FTP site setup prerequisites, security, and use of virtual directories.

Understanding FTP Site Prerequisites

The FTP installation features appear in the FTP Publishing Service portion of the Internet Information Services installation, as shown in Figure 7.1. Notice that you can install just the FTP Management Console or the FTP Management Console and the FTP Server. When you install the FTP functionality, Windows also automatically installs the IIS 6 Management Console functionality highlighted in Figure 7.1. If you don't need FTP functionality, you can simply install the IIS 6 Management Console feature separately.

You may have noticed the FTP Sites entry in the Internet Information Services (IIS) Manager. This entry is actually a placeholder, as you can see in Figure 7.2. Click the Click Here to Launch link and you'll open up the Internet Information Services (IIS) 6.0 Manager. Microsoft will probably change this functionality in the future, but for now, you can simply use the link to open the Internet Information Services (IIS) 6.0 Manager. It's also possible to open the Internet Information Services (IIS) 6.0 Manager Console directly from the Administrative Tools folder of the Control Panel.

You won't see much when you initially open the Internet Information Services (IIS) 6.0 Manager, as shown in Figure 7.3. Instead of the setup you might have seen in earlier versions of IIS, the only feature that appears in the default configuration is the FTP site. In fact, the default setup won't even start the FTP site for you and the service itself is in manual. This change from previous versions of Windows is a security feature designed to let you set security for your FTP site before you allow anyone to visit. To start the FTP site for a short use, select the FTP site in the left pane and click Start Item on the toolbar.

FIGURE 7.1
Install the FTP server support required for your system or just the IIS 6 Management Console.

FIGURE 7.2
The FTP Sites entry is simply a placeholder for now; Microsoft may add to it later.

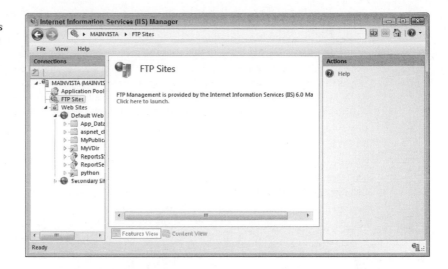

FIGURE 7.3
IIS doesn't start the FTP site by default; you must configure IIS to start it.

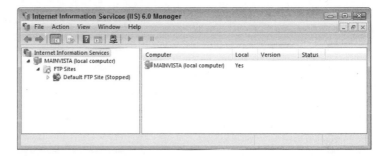

If you want to set the FTP site to start automatically, you'll need to configure the service manually. Use the following steps to perform the task.

1. Open the Services console in the Administrative Tools folder of the Control Panel. You'll see a list of services, as shown in Figure 7.4.

FIGURE 7.4
Locate the FTP Publishing Service and set it to start automatically.

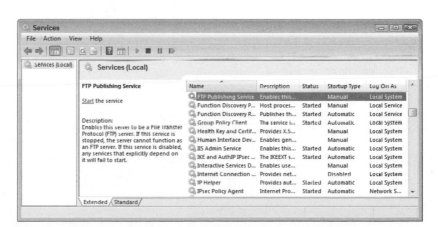

2. Locate the FTP Publishing Service in the list, as shown in Figure 7.4.

3. Right-click the entry and choose Properties from the context menu. You'll see the FTP Publishing Service Properties dialog box.

4. Click Start to start the service.

5. Choose Automatic in the Startup Type field and click OK to complete the process. The FTP Publishing Service will start automatically every time you start Windows.

Managing an FTP Server with the Graphical Interface

Whether or not you have the FTP site running, you can perform configuration tasks on it. One of the first changes you'll notice from previous versions of IIS is the server settings. Right-click the server entry in the left pane and choose Properties from the context menu. You'll notice that you can still change the Enable Direct Metabase Edit and Encode Web Logs in UTF-8 settings as you did before, but IIS disabled the MIME Types options, as shown in Figure 7.5.

Generally, you'll work with FTP sites, rather than the server or the IIS configuration as a whole. Right-click the FTP site entry and choose Properties. You'll see the Default FTP Site Properties dialog box shown in Figure 7.6. You'll use this dialog box for local FTP settings.

FIGURE 7.5
You can't set the MIME types using this console in IIS 7.

FIGURE 7.6
The Default FTP Site Properties dialog box contains settings for your local FTP site.

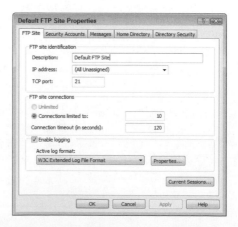

As with all hierarchical setups in Windows, you can also set properties for all FTP sites on a particular server by right-clicking the FTP Sites folder in the left pane and choosing Properties from the context menu. The FTP Sites Properties dialog box (the one used for global settings) doesn't include the FTP Site tab. In addition, you'll find a few features missing on the Home Directory tab.

The Directory Security tab doesn't work for IIS 7. Instead of using the Directory Security tab, your system must rely on a combination of account settings and permissions. The "Setting Security for Your FTP Site" section of the chapter describes how to set the permissions for your FTP site.

MODIFYING THE FTP SITE TAB

As you can see from Figure 7.6, the FTP Site tab contains the FTP site description, IP address, and TCP port. The default setting is port 21. If this is a private FTP site, using a different port can reduce the chance of attack (or, at least, slow it down a little). Setting the security for your FTP site is essential (see the "Setting Security for Your FTP Site" section for details).

The Connection properties are a little optimistic for Vista and probably not high enough for a server. In most cases, you'll want to set the number of connections to 2 or 3 for Vista or up to the number that you think your server can support. The Connection Timeout value will probably work, but you may want to set it lower in order to avoid holding resources for failed connections.

TIP It's often helpful to see how others organize an FTP site for specific purposes (and get a few download items you need while you're at it). FTP Search (http://www.ftpsearch.net/) is a great place to look for resources of all types, no matter what tasks you might need to perform. You might not need to search for files very often, but when you do, it's usually an emergency. FTP Search is the best engine around for finding files because of the number of filters it supports for narrowing your search. If you need an array of FTP search engines to find what you need, try FTP Search Engines (http://www.ftpsearchengines.com/).

The FTP Site tab also contains an option for logging all user access. The standard format is a W3C Extended Log File Format. You can also choose the Microsoft IIS Log File Format or ODBC Logging (for any database that supports ODBC). FTP for IIS 7 doesn't support all six of the log file formats found in IIS 6. You can see these logging formats at http://www.microsoft.com/technet/prodtechnol/WindowsServer2003/Library/IIS/bea506fd-38bc-4850-a4fb-e3a0379d321f.mspx.

Click Properties and you'll see a Logging Properties dialog box like the one shown in Figure 7.7. The General tab has settings that determine the interval that IIS uses the same log and the location of that log. The default settings change the log daily and place it in the \WINDOWS\System32\LogFiles folder. You can increase security by changing the default log location to another secure area of your system.

The Advanced tab shown in Figure 7.8 contains a list of standard log entries. The standard settings don't tell you much about the person using your site. If this were a public site, you'd want to save log space by using the spartan entries shown in the figure. However, if this is a private site and log size won't be a problem, you should log as much information about the individual as possible.

Click Current Sessions at the bottom of the FTP Site tab and you'll see a FTP User Sessions dialog box. This dialog box lists the names of the individuals using the FTP site, the IP addresses of the remote connections, and the amount of time they have been connected to the FTP site. You can use the Disconnect and Disconnect All buttons to remove users from the site as needed.

FIGURE 7.7
Use extended log
entry information to
help identify anyone
using the FTP site.

FIGURE 7.8
Store enough user
information to ensure
you know who has
accessed your
FTP site.

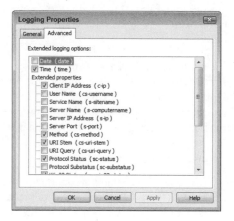

MODIFYING THE SECURITY ACCOUNTS TAB

The Security Accounts tab controls access to your FTP site, as shown in Figure 7.9. Clear the Allow Anonymous Accounts option if you want to restrict someone from logging into the site anonymously. Unfortunately, this also causes problems because FTP passes the username and password in cleartext, which means someone with a network sniffer could gain access to the user's connection information. This tab also contains options that force IIS to use anonymous connections alone.

MODIFYING THE MESSAGES TAB

FTP sites normally require the use of four messages for connecting users, as shown in Figure 7.10. The Messages tab contains Banner, Welcome, Exit, and Maximum Connections fields to handle all four messages. IIS doesn't include any default messages, so visitors to your site will see a blank screen until you define a message.

FIGURE 7.9
Set the security for
your FTP site to ensure
proper access levels.

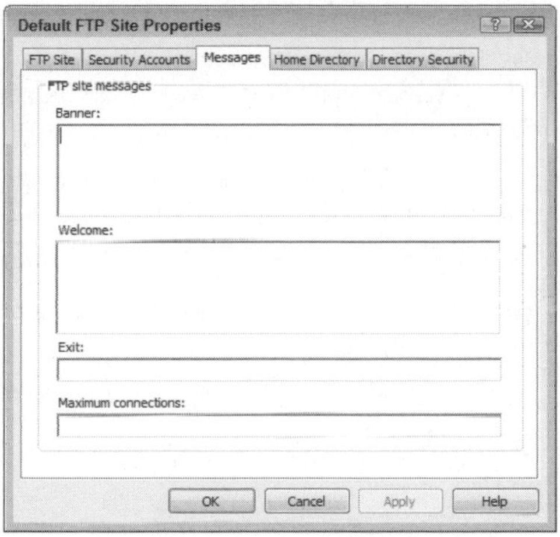

FIGURE 7.10
Provide any messages
required to identify
your Web site and
help users.

MODIFYING THE HOME DIRECTORY TAB

The Home Directory tab shown in Figure 7.11 controls the location and security settings for the home directory. Notice that you can use a local directory or a share (directory or drive) on another machine. The FTP Site Directory information includes the path to the directory and the rights the user has to the directory. Notice that you only have a choice of read, write, and log visits. The Directory Listing Style is especially important. Many FTP utilities require the UNIX style of directory listing and won't show any subdirectories until you use it. If users have problems seeing the folders or files on your FTP site, you may need to make this change.

FIGURE 7.11

The Home Directory tab controls the location and security settings of the root FTP directory.

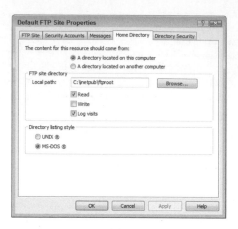

SAVING YOUR CONFIGURATION

After you create an FTP site configuration, it's time to save the configuration for later. (This technique also works for virtual directories.) You can use the configuration to create a new FTP site based on the file content or to restore a broken configuration. To save the configuration:

1. Right-click the FTP site and choose All Tasks ➤ Save Configuration to a File from the context menu. You'll see a Save Configuration to a File dialog box.

2. Type the name of the file you want to create in the File Name field.

3. Choose a location for the file in the Path field. The default setting of C:\Windows\system32\ inetsrv usually works fine.

4. Optionally, check Encrypt Configuration Using Password, type a password in the Password field, and confirm it in the Confirm Password field.

5. Click OK.

Eventually, you'll need the configuration information you stored. Follow these steps when you decide to use the configuration to create a new FTP site (or virtual directory):

1. Right-click the FTP Sites or a specific FTP site and choose New ➤ FTP Site (From File) from the context menu. When creating a virtual directory, choose New ➤ Virtual Directory (From File) instead. You'll see an Import Configuration dialog box.

2. Type the path and name of the file that contains the configuration information. This information appears in an XML file. Consequently, if you named your file Test earlier, you'd need to look for Test.XML now. The default directory for storing the configuration files is C:\Windows\ system32\inetsrv.

3. Click Read File. You see the configurations within the file appear in the Select a Configuration to Import list.

4. Click OK. IIS asks whether you want to create a new site based on the data or replacing the existing site data.

5. Choose a site creation option and click OK. IIS creates or recreates the FTP site (or virtual directory) for you.

Managing FTP Servers with the FTP Utility

At some point, you'll need to manage the content on your FTP site. You can perform this task manually using Windows Explorer or with a graphical utility, such as FTP Explorer. However, the problem with all of these utilities is that you have to be present to use them—they don't provide automation. You can automate many content management tasks using the FTP utility, which is one of the easiest ways of transferring files to literally any system. This utility uses the following syntax:

```
FTP [-v] [-n] [-i] [-d] [-g] [-s:<Filename>] [-a] [-w:<Buffer_Size>]
    [-x:sendbuffer] [-r:recvbuffer] [-b:asyncbuffers] [-A] [-?]
    [<Host>]
```

FTP uses case-sensitive switches. For example, -A isn't the same as -a. In addition, you must use the – (hyphen) sign and not the / (slash) when typing command line arguments. You need to type the command with these requirements in mind. Most of these switches also appear in the interface, so you can modify the behavior after you start the application. The following list describes each of the command line arguments.

-v   This switch disables the display of remote server responses. It comes in handy if you want the download to progress in the background without disturbing your foreground task.

-n   Use this switch to disable auto-logon on initial connection.

-i   Use this switch to remove interactive prompting during multiple file transfers. This enables you to automate the file transfer process.

-d   Use this switch to display all FTP commands passed between the client and server. This enables you to debug script files.

-g   This switch disables filename globbing (essentially, wildcard expansion), which permits the use of wildcard characters in local filenames and pathnames.

-s:*Filename*   Replace <Filename> with the name of a text file containing FTP commands. In essence, this switch enables you to create a script for your FTP download. Use this switch instead of redirection (>).

-a   This switch tells FTP to use any available interface when creating a connection to the host.

-w:*Buffer_Size*   Use this switch to change the data transfer buffer size. The default size of 4,096 bytes normally works well. However, you might want to decrease the buffer size if you experience errors on a connection or use a larger buffer size for local connections. A large buffer is more efficient, but you lose less data for each damaged packet when working with a small buffer.

-A   Use this switch to log on as an anonymous user. Note that this is the only switch typed in uppercase.

-?   Use this switch to display online help. Note that, at the time of this writing, there are typos in both the Help and Support Center document and the application-supplied help.

-x:sendbuffer   Overrides the default send buffer size of 8,192 bytes.

-r:recvbuffer   Overrides the default received buffer size of 8,192 bytes.

-b:asyncbuffers   Overrides the default number of asynchronous buffers (3 is the default).

Host   Replace this parameter with the name or address of the host you want to connect to for a file download.

The FTP utility provides a surprising array of commands you can use after you run the utility. There really are too many to list here, but you can get a list easily enough. All you need to remember is one command: the question mark (?). If you type a question mark, you see a list of all the things you can do with FTP.

TIP The FTP utility is just one of many utilities you can use to manage your server. The command line is literally brimming over with free utilities that can make management easier. You can obtain a new view of the command line through my book *Windows Administration at the Command Line for Windows Vista, Windows 2003, Windows XP, and Windows 2000* (Sybex, 2007).

Setting Security for Your FTP Site

You can control access to your FTP site using the same techniques that you use for any other part of the server. When working with an FTP site, you can set security at the following levels:

◆ FTP site

◆ Folder

◆ Virtual directory

◆ File

The FTP site, folder, and virtual directory levels all use the same technique for setting permission. Right-click the entry you want to change and choose Permissions from the context menu. You'll see the security options shown in the dialog box in Figure 7.12. Notice that this isn't the standard security dialog box. It provides additional levels of security, such as the ability to list the folder contents. Consequently, the security you set at these levels is refined without having to perform too many extra configuration steps.

FIGURE 7.12
IIS helps you set refined security for the FTP site, folder, and virtual directory.

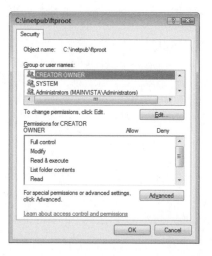

The IIS_IUSRS user doesn't have any access by default. Consequently, even if you allow anonymous access to your FTP site, you must also provide the permissions required to access it to the IIS_IUSRS user. Microsoft added this extra step as a security feature to IIS 7. Use these steps to add the IIS_IUSRS user.

1. Click Edit. You'll see the Permissions dialog box.

2. Click Add. You'll see the Select Users, Computers, or Groups dialog box shown in Figure 7.13. In many cases, you'll need to change the From this Location entry.

FIGURE 7.13
Change the From this Location field so it shows the server containing the FTP site.

3. Click Locations. No matter how you have security set on your system, you'll very likely see the Windows Security dialog box shown in Figure 7.14, even if you've provided this information in the past. This Vista security feature prevents just anyone from locating a machine on the network.

FIGURE 7.14
Provide the security information that you need to access the machine names on the network.

4. Enter your name and password. Windows displays the Locations dialog box.

5. Choose the machine that contains the FTP site and click OK. The location information changes so you can enter the IIS_IUSRS user account.

6. Type **IIS_IUSRS** in the Enter the Object Names to Select field and click OK. Windows adds the IIS_IUSRS account to the Group or User Names list in the Permissions dialog box shown in Figure 7.15.

FIGURE 7.15
Define the security settings for the IIS_IUSRS account.

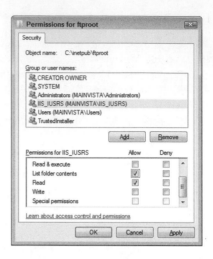

7. Check the options in the Permissions for IIS_IUSRS list.

8. Click OK twice. Windows applies the permissions you've set to the FTP site, folder, or virtual directory.

Accessing file security in an FTP site is the same as in Windows Explorer. If you can't see the files, right-click the FTP site, folder, or virtual directory and choose Explore from the context menu. Right-click the file and choose Properties from the context menu. Select the Security tab. You'll see the Properties dialog box shown in Figure 7.16. At this point, you can set security for the file just as you would for any other FTP site entity.

FIGURE 7.16
Accessing file security is slightly different from accessing other entities on an FTP site.

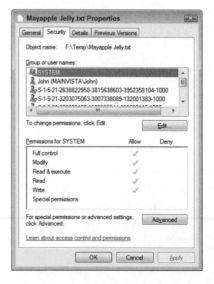

Connecting to Other Servers

Most administrators won't change the settings on their own machine—they'll want to access other machines on the network. Unfortunately, the new Internet Information Services (IIS) Manager won't let you connect to other machines and you couldn't administer older versions of IIS with it anyway. Consequently, you need to use the Internet Information Services (IIS) 6.0 Manager to create a remote connection to another machine on the network when you need to configure it. Fortunately, Microsoft makes this task easy. Simply use the following steps to create a connection to another machine.

1. Right-click the Internet Information Services entry and choose Connection from the context menu. You'll see the Connect to Computer dialog box shown in Figure 7.17.

FIGURE 7.17
Provide connection settings to another computer on your network.

2. Type the name of the server you want to access in the Connect to Computer dialog box. Click Browse, if necessary, to locate the computer using a hierarchical map of the network. During the search process, you'll very likely see the Windows Security dialog box shown in Figure 7.14, even if you've provided this information in the past. This Vista security feature prevents just anyone from locating a machine on the network.

3. Optionally, check the Connect As option and type your name and password. The connection normally relies on your Windows credentials. If the account that you're using doesn't have the required permissions on the other machine, you must supply credentials that do provide the required access.

4. Click OK. The Internet Information Services (IIS) 6.0 Manager window will change, as shown in Figure 7.18 to include the remote server. Notice that you have full access to all of the remote server features, including both Web sites and FTP sites.

FIGURE 7.18
The Internet Information Services (IIS) 6.0 Manager window displays the resources on the remote system.

Performing Common Tasks with IIS Versions 6.0 and Below

Once you establish a connection to the remote server, you'll want to begin administering it. The following sections provide an overview of the various tasks you can perform. In most cases, you'll find that the features work precisely as before with some small changes in functionality to accommodate both Vista and IIS 7. The following sections don't provide detailed configuration information, but they do provide enough to tell you about the Vista and IIS 7 changes. The sections take a hierarchical view of the Web site and start at the topmost level. These sections discuss Web site management. Managing an FTP site is the same as it is for the local connection (see the "Working with FTP Sites" section of the chapter for details).

Working with Application Pools

Applications pools are a new feature of IIS 6, and IIS 7 continues with a managed version of the same technology. An application pool is a kind of container that stores applications. Each container is separate from every other container. Consequently, applications in one application pool can't affect applications in another application pool, so a failure of an application need not affect IIS as a whole. The technical term for this technique is *worker process isolation*. Figure 7.19 shows examples of application pools.

The DefaultAppPool is the only one you'll see after setting up IIS 6. The other two application pools are for applications installed on the server. If one of these other two applications fails, they won't affect the default Web site or each other. As you can see, this technique makes your Web server considerably more reliable. The price you pay for this reliability is some increased overhead, which means a small performance hit that's very likely well worth the cost.

The applications appear below the application pool in the hierarchy. For example, the Report–Server application pool in Figure 7.19 contains two applications: Report Server Interface and Report Server. Both of these features are part of the SQL Server Report Services feature, so it makes sense to place them in the same application pool. The following sections describe how to work with application pools in IIS 6.

FIGURE 7.19
Using application pools makes your system considerably more reliable.

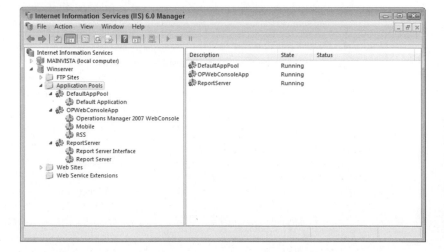

CREATING AND DELETING APPLICATION POOLS

Normally, an application will create an application pool when it installs itself on your system. However, some applications won't and you might want to separate them from other applications on the system. The following steps describe how to create a new application pool.

1. Right-click the Application Pools folder and choose New ➢ Application Pool from the context menu. You'll see the Add New Application Pool dialog box shown in Figure 7.20.

FIGURE 7.20
Define the name and basic configuration for your new application pool.

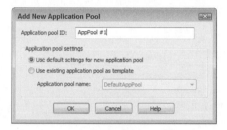

2. Type a descriptive name for the new Application Pool. In some cases, it works better to use a name without space when you must access the application pool data from within an application.

3. Choose whether you want to use the default application pool settings or use an existing application pool as a template. When you choose to use an existing application pool, you must supply the name of the application pool in the Application Pool Name field.

4. Click OK. IIS adds the new application pool.

At this point, you can configure the application pool using the information in the sections that follow. If you eventually decide to remove an application pool, right-click the entry in the list and choose Delete from the context menu. IIS 6 will ask whether you're sure that you want to remove the application pool. Click Yes to complete the process.

You can assign application pools to Web sites, folders that you convert to applications, and virtual directories that you convert to applications. The "Configuring the Home Directory Tab" section of the chapter tells how to change the application pool for a Web site. You can discover how to create an application using a folder and assigning an application pool to it in the "Creating an Application from a Folder" section of the chapter. See the "Creating an Application from a Virtual Directory" section of the chapter to learn how to assign a virtual directory application to an application pool.

CONFIGURING THE RECYCLING OPTIONS

Part of the benefit of using application pools is that they intelligently help the system heal itself when errors occur. When a worker process experiences an error, the system lets it complete the requests it has in its request queue (see the "Configuring the Performance Options" section for details) and then lets the worker process end gracefully or the system terminates the faulty worker process after the time interval you configure ends. In the meantime, the system creates a new worker process to take over from the faulty worker process. This new worker process accepts all new requests for service from clients. In short, the system recognizes a failure and fixes it for you faster than you can probably even notice that an error has occurred. Of course, you still have to step in when worker processes experience more than the normal number of failures because the system can't fix errant code. Figure 7.21 shows the recycling options that IIS provides to keep your application healthy.

FIGURE 7.21
It's important to
determine how
you want worker
processes to recycle
themselves.

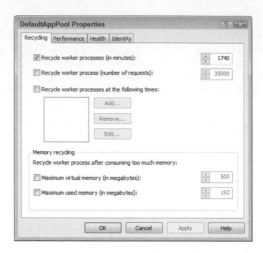

Worker processes can actually fail in subtle ways, so the system sets a recycling rate to change out old worker process code automatically. This act guarantees that the worker process continues to perform efficiently, even when the system doesn't recognize a subtle problem, such as a memory leak. You can choose to recycle worker processes after a specific time interval (in minutes), after a specific number of calls, or at certain times of the day.

The memory leak problem is so significant that IIS also provides the means to recycle worker processes after they consume too much virtual or real memory as well. If you know that your application is leaky, you can keep the system from crashing by recycling the worker processes when they use a certain amount of memory.

CONFIGURING THE PERFORMANCE OPTIONS

You don't want worker processes consuming system resources when no one is requested their services. The Performance tab contains options that help you configure worker processes so they run efficiently. These options control how the worker process performs and how much processing it can do before IIS limits it in some way. Figure 7.22 shows the performance options for worker processes.

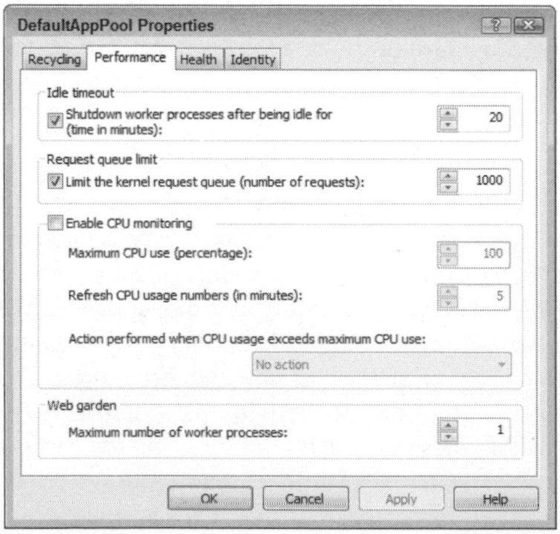

FIGURE 7.22
Tune the application
pool settings to meet
the needs of your
application.

The first setting, Shutdown Worker Processes after Being Idle for (Time in Minutes), determines how long IIS should wait before it stops a worker process that no one is using. IIS unloads the worker process from memory and frees the resources that it uses. The default setting of 20 minutes is arbitrary—you should tune it to meet the needs of your application. For example, if someone makes a request of your application every 21 minutes, waiting only 20 minutes for a request seems inefficient at best. You should decide whether to terminate the worker process immediately or wait the additional minute or two for a request.

The Request Queue Limit options let you determine how many requests a particular worker process can accumulate. When a worker request reaches its limit, then it refuses any additional requests. At this point, IIS can create another worker process to handle requests if you configure the application pool as a Web Garden (an application pool that allows more than one worker process). Setting a limit that reduces the risk of unanswered requests makes your applications more reliable, but at the cost of creating additional worker processes or refusing the request completely (the server sends a 503 error to the requestor). More worker requests can result in better performance as long as you don't overextend system resources. However, each worker process does consume system resources, so you must achieve a balance between reliability, performance, and system resource use to achieve overall application responsiveness.

The CPU Limit options monitor the application in another way. Some applications approach a certain level of CPU activity when they fail. You can monitor for this condition and cause the worker process to stop accepting requests (IIS sends a 503 error to the requestor when this situation occurs). More important, the recycle interval will recycle the worker process and create a new one that doesn't have the failure. This limit also keeps too many requests from overwhelming the server so that it can continue processing requests without crashing. Obviously, you don't want to monitor CPU performance continuously, so you also need to tell IIS how often to check the CPU statistics. The default interval of 5 minutes works well for most Web sites, but you may want to use a shorter interval on Web sites that receive a high level of activity. As an extreme measure, you can also tell the server to shut down when it receives too much activity. About the only time you want to take this approach is if you think your server's under attack (such as a DDOS attack).

The Web Garden feature is very important. Although the DefaultAppPool uses just one worker process, allowing more worker processes can have both reliability and performance benefits when you don't exceed system resources. You don't want to allow hundreds of worker processes on systems with a single CPU and limited memory because the system literally won't get anything accomplished. A better approach is to limit the worker processes to some multiple of the number of processors on your machine (with due consideration for the memory installed). For example, a four-processor system can easily run four worker processes in most cases.

CONFIGURING THE HEALTH OPTIONS

IIS needs some way to determine that the worker process is still in good health and ensure it hasn't failed in some way. The options on the Health tab shown in Figure 7.23 determine how IIS accomplishes this goal. The options also partially control what IIS does when it encounters an application pool with major problems.

The Enable Pinging options determine how often IIS checks the worker process to determine whether it's still responsive. A responsive worker process is still probably doing its job, but it may not be doing it correctly (which is why the system also requires a good recycling scheme). However, this check at least ensures that the worker process hasn't crashed and can still receive requests.

FIGURE 7.23
Use the Health tab options to check the status of the worker processes.

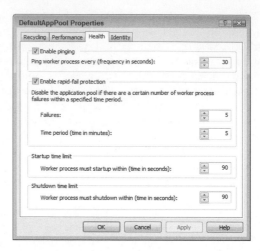

The Enable Rapid-Fail Protection options determine how IIS reacts to an application pool that has worker processes failing at an unanticipated rate. The failures need not only occur when the worker process fails to respond to a ping; they can also occur for every other reason discussed in this section so far. For example, if a worker process exceeds CPU processing limits and fails for that reason, the system still considers it a failure. The settings determine how many failures must occur within a given time frame before IIS shuts down the application pool. When the application pool shuts down, the application stops working and IIS will send a 503 error to all requestors. However, it's usually better that a single application stops working, rather than have the entire server crash.

The Startup Time Limit and Shutdown Time Limit options determine how long IIS waits for an application to perform startup and shutdown tasks. When the worker process fails to start in the time allotted, IIS considers it a failure and tries to start the worker process again. This setting is important when your worker processes must access distributed resources such as a database. Make sure you allow sufficient time for it to start under heavy load conditions or the application may fail even when there's nothing wrong with it. When the worker process fails to stop within the allotted time, IIS terminates it and considers it a failure and counts it toward the application pool total. Again, you must provide sufficient time for the worker process to stop or your application could encounter data loss and other issues related to termination, rather than a graceful shutdown.

CONFIGURING THE IDENTITY OPTIONS

The identity tab contains a simple setting for the credentials that the application pool should use when making requests on the application's behalf. The application pool can use different credentials from the application. The default setting uses the predefined Network Service account. You can use any other predefined account that you feel provides sufficient access. In many cases, you can rely on the Local Service account to improve system security without causing any problems for the application. You can also choose to use a custom account.

Modifying Web Site Settings

The Web site settings occur at two levels in IIS 6. The Web Sites folder contains the global settings for all Web sites that it contains. When you create a new Web site, it uses the settings from the Web Sites folder as a starting point. Only when you change the settings for the individual Web site do the settings vary from the global settings. Consequently, you'll want to configure the Web Sites folder settings before you begin creating Web sites and as part of your global setting configuration.

Some settings don't appear in the Web Sites folder. For example, the Web site description is always unique, so you can change this setting on a global level. Each Web site must also have a unique TCP port and so on. Consequently, when you create a new Web site, you must provide certain unique values as part of the configuration process.

The Web Sites Properties dialog box is essentially the same as the individual Web site Properties dialog boxes. IIS grays out some features because you can't set them at a global level. In addition, the Web Sites Properties dialog box contains an additional Service tab that controls how the World Wide Web Publishing Service itself performs. The following sections describe how to perform configuration changes at both levels.

CONFIGURING THE WEB SITE TAB

The Web Site tab begins by defining the Web site identification, as shown in Figure 7.24. You can't define this information globally, only at the local Web site level. The information you provide includes a Web site name, IP address, and one or two port numbers.

FIGURE 7.24

Web site configurations include a Web Site tab that determines the Web site identity.

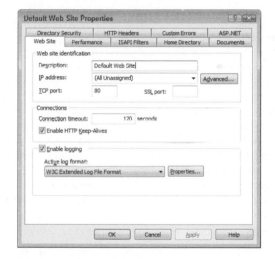

The problem is that the TCP Port field is misleading. While this number does define the default port number, it doesn't tell you about other port numbers that IIS supports natively. Click Advanced and you'll see an Advanced Multiple Web Site Configuration dialog box like the one shown in Figure 7.25. As you can see, IIS defines two ports for all Web sites: standard and secure. If you allow outside access to your Web site, you'll need to configure your firewall to accommodate both the standard port of 80 and the secure port of 443. You can create multiple standard host ports for your system. In fact, you can even remove the default setting of port 80 and use something else. However, you can only have one secure port.

The Connections section of the Web Site tab determines the connection settings. The first point of interest is the HTTP Keep-Alives Enabled option. This setting tells IIS to maintain a connection with the client during the entire client session. The advantage of this setting is that the client won't need to reestablish contact for each request. The client and server both save time, and server performance improves. The disadvantage of this setting is that IIS maintains the connection if the client inadvertently loses contact with the server. The server must wait the entire interval specified by the Connection Timeout setting before it releases the connection. The default setting of 900 seconds (15 minutes) is too long for a local connection. A setting of 400 seconds (or less) works better.

FIGURE 7.25
Web sites support both standard and secure connections, so they require multiple port numbers.

As with the FTP site settings, you can log all access to your Web site. You have the same logging choices of the W3C Extended Log File Format (default), the Microsoft IIS Log File Format, or ODBC Logging. However, in this case, you also have a choice of a National Center for Supercomputing Applications (NCSA) common log file format. This format is compatible with servers running the Apache Web server, so it's a good choice in a mixed server environment. The remaining log file choices and options are the same as they are for FTP sites.

TIP You might be tempted to think that once you select a log format you have to live with it forever. Fortunately, Microsoft provides the CONVLOG utility (located in the \WINDOWS\system32 folder) to convert IIS logs from any supported format to NCSA common log file format. The utility will convert Internet Protocol (IP) address to Domain Name Service (DNS) names. You can even convert logs from local time to Greenwich Mean Time (GMT) in order to synchronize entries from various parts of the world. Several Web sites have a description of this log file format including http://ulysses.uchicago.edu/docs/LOGS.doc2.html.

CONFIGURING THE PERFORMANCE TAB

The Performance tab helps you control the performance of the Web server as a whole and balance the resources available to individual Web sites. The Bandwidth Throttling setting controls how much data the Web server or Web site can transfer in KB/sec. The default setting doesn't place any limit on either the Web server or the Web sites it contains. You'll want to control the Web site bandwidth when a Web server hosts multiple sites to ensure that one Web site doesn't consume all of the available bandwidth. Likewise, you'll want to limit an individual Web server when you have multiple servers vying for the same bandwidth.

The Web Site Connections setting controls how many users can access the Web server or Web site at one time. Normally, IIS doesn't place any limit on the number of users. However, depending on the applications you're running, the capabilities of the server, and the number of users you anticipate accessing the server, you'll want to place limits on the number of accesses to ensure the clients receive reliable application performance.

CONFIGURING THE ISAPI FILTERS TAB

The ISAPI Filters tab contains a list of special applications for IIS (you can see a description of ISAPI filters and see how they work in IIS 7 in the "Managing ISAPI Filters" section of Chapter 6). Figure 7.26 shows the default list of filters for a simple IIS installation (Web sites don't install any ISAPI filters by default). Unless you buy a third-party package that includes ISAPI filters or you create an ISAPI filter of your own, you'll never need to look at this tab except to ensure the filters are all running. You can tell a filter is running because it has a green arrow that points up. If you see a red down arrow icon, you know the filter isn't running and you need to find out why. Filters often cause IIS to act erratically or you'll see a loss of functionality.

CONFIGURING THE HOME DIRECTORY TAB

The Home Directory tab shown in Figure 7.27 contains all of the information for the root location of the Web site. As with an FTP site, you can place the Web site on a local or remote drive. Unlike an FTP site, you can also redirect a Web site to another URL. Notice that Web sites provide a few more directory access options. Notice, also, that there's an option to protect your script source and to allow directory browsing. Directory Browsing is a nice feature to have if you want to make the Web site completely open. It helps users to search all of the available files. However, this option is harmful if you want to hide anything on your site and probably isn't a good choice for public sites.

FIGURE 7.26

The Web Sites Properties dialog box contains settings that affect all Web sites on your system.

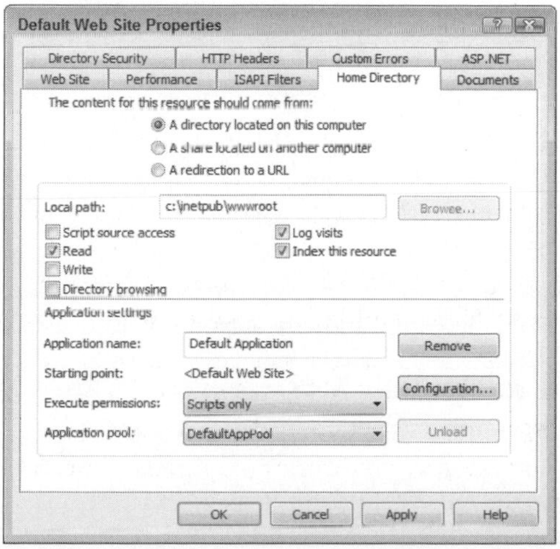

FIGURE 7.27

The Home Directory tab contains location and usage information for the Web site root.

You can tell IIS to index the Web site. The Indexing Service handles Web sites separately from local hard drives or other indexing setups you might create. This allows search pages to report only the data that appears on your site and reduces the risk of inadvertently disclosing critical information. In addition, this separation enabled you to set the indexing features separately from the rest of your system.

By default, IIS always creates a Web site as an application when you create a new one. The application name is always Default Application and it uses the DefaultAppPool. Unfortunately, if you have multiple Web sites using the same application pool, you lose some of the reliability and performance features that worker process isolation can provide. It's better to create a new application pool (see the "Creating and Deleting Application Pools" section of the chapter for details) and assign the new Web site to that pool. You can see the application pool selection in the Application Pool field. Simply choose a new application pool from the drop-down list box.

CONFIGURING THE DOCUMENTS TAB

The Documents tab contains a list of default documents. IIS chooses a default document based on the capabilities of the requesting browser and the order in which the documents appear in the list. IIS uses a default document when you check the Enable Default Document option. If you don't enable this feature, then the user will need to enter the name of a Web page precisely or they'll receive an error message. You can add and remove default documents using the Add and Remove buttons.

IIS also provides a feature for adding a default footer to every Web page. Default footers commonly contain contact information or other links on the Web site. To use this feature, check Enable Document Footer. You'll also need to supply the name of a footer file. A footer file is a standard HTML page that IIS adds to the bottom of the document.

CONFIGURING THE DIRECTORY SECURITY TAB

The Directory Security tab contains the security settings for your site. Click Edit in the Authentication and Access Control group and you'll see an Authentication Methods dialog box. IIS provides four levels of access:

Anonymous   You'll use anonymous access for a site that everyone can visit.

Basic   Basic authentication works fine for local sites, but presents a security problem for remote sites because the user passes their name and password in cleartext.

Integrated Windows   The Integrated Windows Authentication method is secure because it uses encryption for both the username and password. However, the problem with this method is that it limits access to Windows clients. This last limitation will have a greater impact on server setups than a workstation setup.

.NET Passport   The .NET Passport authentication provides considerable flexibility, but it requires that everyone get a Passport and you must trust Microsoft with the user information. You can use this approach on public Web sites where you want a verifiable method of identifying the user.

You can also set restrictions on who can access your Web server by clicking Edit in the IP Address and Domain Name Restrictions group. You'll see the IP Address and Domain Name Restrictions dialog box where you can add specific restrictions by single computer, group of computers, or by domain name. Using a domain name isn't a good choice because it incurs a performance hit—the server must perform a reverse lookup for each request.

NOTE   You won't see the Secure Communications group when accessing an IIS 6 Web server from the Internet Information Services (IIS) 6.0 Manager. If you want to add a server certificate, you must perform the task from the server, rather than from the remote location.

The Web Sites folder also contains an Enable the Windows Directory Service Mapper option. This feature lets you use Active Directory to provide a client-certificate mapping (to identify the client machine). Your server must be part of a Windows domain to use this feature.

Configuring the HTTP Headers Tab

The HTTP Headers tab shown in Figure 7.28 controls content handling for your Web site. The Enable Content Expiration is especially important if your site handles time critical information. The browser will compare the cached copy on the user's local hard drive with the expiration date to determine whether it needs to download a new copy of the page from the Web server. Using this feature effectively means reducing Web server demands, while ensuring the user always has fresh content.

FIGURE 7.28
Use the features found on the HTTP Headers tab to control content for your Web site.

The Custom HTTP Headers section contains a list of specialized headers for your Web server. An HTTP header contains information about the content that follows. For example, it could tell the client to use a particular helper application to display the content. The headers that IIS sends out are standard as of the time of release. However, as standards groups define new HTTP headers, you might want to add them to your server. This feature allows you to make the extension without much effort.

You'll use the Content Rating feature on sites that contain objectionable material that younger viewers might see. Click Edit Ratings and you'll see a Content Ratings dialog box. The Rating Service tab tells you about the ratings service. It provides a link you can visit that provides additional information and has a questionnaire you can answer about your site. The Ratings tab has settings that you can use to set the content rating for your site. There are entries for violence, sex, nudity, and language. You'll rate the level of each of the entries using a slider. The tab also contains fields for a contact address (the email address of the person who rated the site) and an expiration date for the content rating.

The final setting on the HTTP Headers tab is the MIME Map. The MIME setting determines the types of files your site supports. IIS sends this information to the client, so the client knows what to expect concerning content types. Unless you use some unusual file types, you'll never need to touch this setting. However, if you do find that you need to change something, ensure you add the standardized MIME entries for the file type available from RFC 3161 (`http://www.faqs.org/rfcs/rfc3161.html`).

CONFIGURING THE CUSTOM ERRORS TAB

The Custom Errors tab contains a list of every error that the Web server can generate, along with an associated error message. In most cases, the basic error message is pretty generic and less than helpful. However, most users find it useful enough—at least they know there's a problem. You can use the entries on this tab to define custom responses for error messages. For example, users of your Web site might run into one error more often than any other error message. Defining a custom error message could provide useful help to users who need it and reduce the number of support calls you receive.

CONFIGURING THE SERVICE TAB

The Service tab shown in Figure 7.29 only appears as part of the Web Sites Properties dialog box. You use it to configure how the World Wide Web Publishing Service works (in reality, you're tuning the interaction of the Web sites with the service).

FIGURE 7.29
Configure the interaction between the Web sites and the World Wide Web Publishing Service using these options.

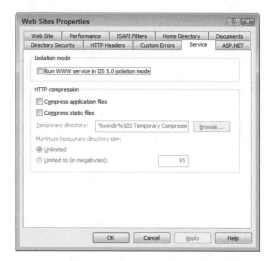

The Isolation Mode options let you control how IIS performs worker process isolation. In most cases, you'll want to perform worker process isolation as described in the "Working with Application Pools" section of the chapter to enhance system performance and reliability. However, you may have to use IIS 5 isolation mode when certain situations occur. The three most common problems appear in the following list:

Multi-instance ISAPI Extensions   Some developers wrote older ISAPI extensions so that multiple processes could load them. Each instance of the ISAPI extension runs independently and concurrently. Worker process recycling interferes with this tactic by creating a new version of the ISAPI extension that doesn't contain the state information stored by the previous instance. In addition, the process invoking the ISAPI extension isn't guaranteed to interact with that particular ISAPI extension during the entire processing cycle. The best bet, here, is to determine whether the vendor has an updated ISAPI extension you can use since these older ISAPI extensions usually had other problems too.

Out-of-Worker Process   In this case, a worker process isn't self-contained. The developer designed it to call other worker processes to perform part of its work. The concept is about the same as Word calling Excel to perform a task. Excel is an out-of-process COM object that Word uses to accomplish specific goals. Unfortunately, the only way to fix this problem is to determine whether the vendor has a newer, IIS 6 friendly, product.

Session State Persistence   As you might imagine, worker process recycling means that IIS loses the settings within the code and memory space of a particular worker process every time it recycles the worker process. The new worker process starts and has no settings to use unless it stores them in another location, such as on disk. This may or may not be a problem and you'll have to test for it. ASP.NET applications don't have this particular problem. Even if you know the application persists its session state in memory, test it with the IIS 6 setting anyway to verify that the persistence issue actually causes a problem (don't use a production server to perform this test).

The HTTP Compression feature can significantly improve application performance and make the application more responsive on the client. IIS compresses the data it sends to a compression-enabled client when you use these settings. The compressed data requires less network bandwidth, so it arrives at the client considerably faster. The client decompresses the data and displays it on screen as normal.

Of course, using HTTP compression can consume a lot of hard drive space, so you need to set limits on how much space the compression can use. The Maximum Temporary Directory Size option of unlimited probably won't work very well with a Web site that has lots of data to send. You should limit the amount of space allocated to compression to a reasonable level. Depending on other uses of the hard drive, you'll probably want to limit the cache to one or two percent of the hard drive.

CONFIGURING THE ASP.NET TAB

You can see the ASP.NET tab just fine, but you really can't do much with it. From the Web Sites folder perspective, you can identify the ASP.NET version and the virtual path information. The Internet Information Services (IIS) 6.0 Manager doesn't let you change anything from the global perspective. An individual Web site will also show you the ASP.NET version and the virtual path information. You can choose a different ASP.NET version as the default when the server has multiple versions installed, but that's it. If you want to edit the global configuration or the Web site configuration information, you must perform the task at the server.

Working with Folders

Folders are storage containers that are local to the Web site that contains them. You use folders to hold local applications, data, and other resources. The following sections describe how to work with folders.

MODIFYING FOLDER SETTINGS

When you work with folders, you have two options for modifying them. The first is to right-click the Web site or folder that holds the folder and choose Open from the context menu. When you perform this task, you'll see a new copy of Windows Explorer open and you can interact with the folder as you would any folder on your machine as long as you have the required permissions. The second is to right-click the folder in IIS and choose Properties. You'll see a dialog box like the one shown in Figure 7.30 where you can change the IIS settings for the folder.

FIGURE 7.30
Manage folder set-
tings using the same
techniques you use
with Web sites.

IIS provides the means for you to create individual settings for your Web site directories. Generally, the folder's Properties dialog box contains a subset of those found for the Default Web Site
Properties dialog box. The Documents, Directory Security, HTTP Headers, Custom Errors, and
ASP.NET tab entries work the same in both cases. The Directory tab is actually a renamed form of
the Home Directory tab. In short, working with a directory is easy once you understand how to
work with a Web site.

CREATING AN APPLICATION FROM A FOLDER

When you create a new folder, IIS treats it as a storage receptacle. You can't use it for application
storage. In fact, if you try to execute an application, such as an ASP.NET application, the application
fails. You convert a folder to an application by clicking Create in the Application Settings area
shown in Figure 7.30. At this point, you can choose the execute permission for the folder and set the
application pool it uses by changing the setting in the Application Pool field.

Working with Virtual Directories

It isn't always convenient to place data you want to see on your Web site on the local drive or even
within the \Inetpub\wwwroot folder hierarchy. A virtual directory is essentially a pointer to the
data, wherever it exists. The virtual directory makes it appear that the data is local to the Web
server, although the data might exist on a network drive. Think of a virtual directory as a sort of
shortcut for IIS. You can discover more about virtual directories by reading the IIS 7 material in the
"Adding Virtual Directories to the Web Site" section of Chapter 3.

CREATING THE VIRTUAL DIRECTORY

Creating a virtual directory is relatively easy. Right-click the location where you want to place
the virtual directory. You can place the virtual directory at any level below the Default Web Site
in the IIS hierarchy. Choose New ➢ Virtual Directory from the context menu and you'll see the
Welcome screen of the Virtual Directory Creation wizard. The following steps will show you
how to complete the virtual directory setup.

1. Click Next. You'll see a Virtual Directory Alias dialog box. The name you assign here is the
   name that IIS will use to reference the directory. It's also the name the user will need to

access the directory. Using single word directory names is usually best because using spaces causes problems for some browsers. In addition, you'll find single word directory names easier to work with when you create Web pages.

2. Type an alias for the virtual directory, and then click Next. You'll see a Web Site Content Directory dialog box. The Directory field contains the path to the physical directory location. You must type a location that appears on the server. The wizard grays out the Browse button in this case because you can't search for the physical directory location in the same context as the server will see it.

3. Provide a content directory path and name, and then click Next. You'll see an Access Permissions dialog box, as shown in Figure 7.31. Notice that the access permissions don't directly correspond with the settings from any of the tabs that we discussed earlier. The security settings are easy to understand, but you'll always want to check the settings later.

FIGURE 7.31
The security settings in the Access Permissions dialog box don't correspond to settings in the Directory Properties dialog box.

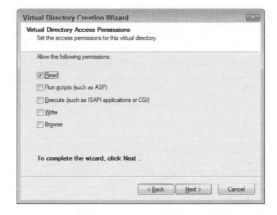

4. Choose security settings for your virtual directory, and then click Next. You'll see a completion dialog box.

5. Click Finish. IIS will create the virtual directory for you.

6. Right-click the new virtual directory, then choose Properties from the context menu. You'll see a Directory Properties dialog box that looks very much like the one shown in Figure 7.30.

7. Verify the settings for your virtual directory.

CREATING AN APPLICATION FROM A VIRTUAL DIRECTORY

Unlike a folder, you can create a virtual directory that appears as an application from the outset by choosing the Run Scripts or Execute options in the Virtual Directory Access Permissions dialog box shown in Figure 7.31 when you create the virtual directory. Even if you don't choose these options, you can always change the virtual directory to an application later. You convert a virtual directory to an application by clicking Create in the Application Settings area shown in Figure 7.30. At this point, you can choose the execute permission for the folder and set the application pool it uses by changing the setting in the Application Pool field.

Depending on how you create a virtual directory, it will very likely use the DefaultAppPool application pool at the outset. In most cases, you'll want to create a private pool for the application and assign the virtual directory to it by selecting the new application pool in the Application Pool field.

Modifying Individual File Settings

As with folders, you have two options for modifying files. You can use Windows Explorer to modify the file by right-clicking the folder that contains it and clicking Open. Alternatively, you can right-click the file and choose Properties from the context menu. This second option opens a file Properties dialog box.

The file Properties dialog box is an even smaller version of the Default Web Site Properties dialog box. It contains the same HTTP Headers, Custom Errors, and ASP.NET tabs. The File Security tab is a renamed version of the Directory Security tab with the same options. Finally, the File tab is a shortened version of the Home Directory tab. You'll see fewer options than before. For example, you can't use a share from another computer for the obvious reasons. In addition, the security options only include read and write protection. The File tab also contains options for protecting your source code and logging user visits.

Let's Start Building

Theoretically this chapter is a lot of old news for some people. You've probably performed most of the tasks in this chapter at one time or another. Vista and IIS 7 do present a few quirks in the process, but essentially everything is the same as before. In many cases, this chapter provides a short update of the skills you already possess. This chapter helps you build these skills:

◆ Configure and manage FTP sites

◆ Connect to other FTP and Web servers

◆ Use Internet Information Services (IIS) 6.0 Manager to manage older Web sites

Even if you already have a lot of experience with previous versions of IIS, you might want to spend some time working with the Internet Information Services (IIS) 6.0 Manager in IIS 7 and under Vista. Look for places where security features have changed or a management setting works a little differently than before. For anyone who is working with the Internet Information Services (IIS) 6.0 Manager for the first time, you'll want to explore all of the functionality it provides, especially when working with older servers. In addition, make sure you spend time working with the FTP utility because a command line tool can provide significant help in some situations.

Chapter 8 begins the saga of the Web page development technology that many IIS administrators will rely on to provide dynamic content to users, ASP.NET. Even though ASP.NET had a slow start, you find it used on many Web sites today. The tools that Microsoft has provided for creating and managing ASP.NET applications have improved each year. Chapter 8 begins the process that continues through Part 4 of the book. In Chapter 8, you discover the techniques you'll use to create and manage basic applications. These basic principles help you perform tasks such as installing and maintaining applications.

Part 3

Configuring Application Security

Chapter 8

Basic Application Setup

One of the bigger problems that administrators commonly face is moving an ASP.NET application from one machine to another without having to reinstall it from scratch. In some cases, just restoring the application can prove troublesome because ASP.NET requires that you do a little more than simply use XCopy to move the files into a folder. When working with an ASP.NET application, you have to consider how the application is set up, whether it appears in a folder that's set up as an application, whether the user has the proper rights, and so on.

This chapter helps you perform some basic tasks with ASP.NET applications. In it, you'll learn how to create a basic application and perform some configuration on it. You'll also discover some techniques for making applications work when you move them from one location to another. Some sections of the chapter also explore common settings you'll change when configuring an application for a particular machine. Finally, you'll discover how to use the AppCmd utility, a general-purpose IIS administration tool that can help you automate some of the tasks discussed throughout the book.

In this chapter, you will learn how to do the following:

◆ Create a new application

◆ Manage application configuration

◆ Explore and browse applications

◆ Manage the application session state

◆ Change application settings

◆ Manage the application's worker processes

◆ Use the AppCmd utility

Creating Applications

ASP.NET applications won't execute unless you turn the folder or virtual directory that holds them into an application. This requirement isn't anything new; it already existed in IIS. You can learn how to perform this task in IIS 6 by reading the "Creating an Application from a Folder" and "Creating an Application from a Virtual Directory" sections of Chapter 7. IIS 7 requires you perform the same task; it just uses a different approach to perform the task. You have some additional issues to consider in IIS 7 because it provides a higher level of security and greater flexibility than IIS 6. The concepts and the goals are the same, but some of the details are different (changed for the better).

Normally, you won't need to create an application for ASP.NET at all. The application's installation program will normally perform this task for you (along with creating required application pools, installing ISAPI filters, and other tasks). Even the Visual Studio Integrated Development Environment (IDE) creates the required application folder for you when you test an application. However, you may find that you need to create an application in certain circumstances as listed here:

◆ IIS forgets that the folder contains an application (can occur during updates).

◆ An administrator or developer configures an application incorrectly, requiring a reinstall and new configuration.

◆ You need to test a custom application on another machine.

◆ An organization sets up a server farm, requiring the same application configuration on multiple machines.

◆ Moving an application works out better than reinstalling it on the new machine.

Now that you have a better idea of what applications are about for IIS 7, it's time to see how to create them. The following sections describe how to create a new application and convert an existing folder or virtual directory to an application.

Adding a New Application

Adding a new application means creating a folder or virtual directory to hold it, as well as providing the correct configuration information for IIS. If you already have an application within a folder or virtual directory, you should follow the procedure in the "Converting a Folder or Virtual Directory to an Application" section of the chapter. You'll normally create a new application when you want to test a custom application on another server and don't already have a location for it on that server. The following steps describe how to create a new application.

1. Right-click the Web site, folder, or virtual directory that will hold the new application and choose Add Application from the context menu. You'll see the Add Application dialog box shown in Figure 8.1.

FIGURE 8.1
Define the particulars for the new application that you want to create.

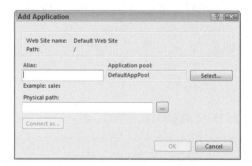

2. Type a name for the application in the Alias field. The user will use this name to access the application with a browser, so you should provide a name without spaces that the user will find easy to type.

3. Click Select to display the Select Application Pool dialog box. Choose an application pool to use for this application. If you want to create a special application pool for this application, you can create one using the techniques shown in the "Working with Application Pools" section of Chapter 13.

4. Type the physical path to the location of the data on the hard drive. You can use a UNC path, such as \\MyServer\MyDrive\Myfolder when required. When you provide a UNC path, IIS automatically enables the Connect As button. Click Connect As to set the credentials for accessing the remote location. The default setting uses pass-through authentication, which relies on the caller's credentials.

TIP One of the most common errors you'll encounter when working with a UNC path is the 500.19. This error means that the remote server didn't recognize the user's credentials. If the local user is logging onto the system as an anonymous user, the remote system may see the IIS_IUSRS account, rather than the user's true account. In this case, you can repair the problem by allowing the IIS_IUSRS account access to the remote system, setting the Web site to require security, or by setting the connection to use a specific account.

5. Click OK. IIS creates a new virtual directory with the name you provided that points to the remote location you specified.

Converting a Folder or Virtual Directory to an Application

You may have an existing folder or virtual directory that isn't an application. It may have even been an application at one time, but some type of error or failure has changed it back into a standard folder or virtual directory. You can change the folder or virtual directly back into an application using the following steps:

1. Right-click the folder or virtual directory you want to convert into an application and choose Convert to Application from the context menu. You'll see the Add Application dialog box shown in Figure 8.1. Notice that IIS fills in all of the required information automatically.

2. Change the application name found in the Alias field if necessary.

3. Click Select to display the Select Application Pool dialog box. Choose an application pool to use for this application. If you want to create a special application pool for this application, you can create one using the techniques shown in the "Working with Application Pools" section of Chapter 13.

4. Optionally, if the Physical Path field contains a UNC path, click Connect To and configure security as needed. Don't change the Physical Path field entry or you'll lose your connection to the data source.

5. Click OK. IIS converts the folder or virtual directory into an application.

Controlling Application Settings

At one time, application developers made assumptions and configured an application in a certain way without regard to the needs of the people using it. This strategy didn't work at all and developers soon found ways of exposing configuration settings to users. Unfortunately, the techniques often required the user to edit external files or fiddle with the registry. The open settings invited end users to make application tweaks that the administrator didn't want. In addition, using this approach required that the user make some kind of a decision, in some cases, so that approach didn't work very well either. COM+ started a trend where administrators use a host application to configure an underlying application. The Component Services console displays the applications that COM+ hosts and lets the administrator configure those applications from a separate location. In addition to convenience, this technique hides the configuration controls from the end user.

Today, application developers have another alternative for IIS 7 as well—they can expose settings in IIS 7 in such a way that the administrator can use the Internet Information Services (IIS) Manager to change them without doing anything extra or odd. The following sections describe how the administrator and developer can work together to provide a perfect configuration environment for ASP.NET applications.

Working with Developers to Define Application Settings

In many cases, administrators and developers turn into worst enemies because of the semantics of managing applications. They both agree that applications require settings for tuning purposes and that the administrator should have some level of control over those settings, but the means of implementing the settings isn't as clear as it could be and there are misunderstandings between the administrator and developer as well. For example, some administrators don't understand the role of session state completely (and some developers don't understand it either). In many modern applications, the session state controls what the user sees and the user often sets the session state while working with the application. For example, when you view a Web page that lets you add or remove content, the settings appear as part of the session state and the administrator won't generally need to interact with them. In fact, when the application relies on cookies, the administrator can't interact with them, which can prove frustrating when the administrator doesn't understand session state very well (see the "Managing Session State" section of the chapter for details). Consequently, part of the conversation between the developer and the administrator must focus on session state and what it means to the application.

Settings also reflect internal data that the developer should never expose. The application should appear as a black box. Sometimes a developer overcompensates for previous poor decisions and ends up overwhelming the administrator with too many choices. The settings that you choose to define with the developer should have relevance to the daily work that you perform.

It's important to remember that the settings need to be in human-readable form, even if this somehow inconveniences the developer. For example, telling the administrator to use a value of 2 when he wants a brown background isn't particularly friendly. The developer should use brown as a value instead and convert it within the application code. The code for accessing these custom variables isn't that difficult to use. For example, when working with C#, you'd use `System.Configuration.ConfigurationManager.AppSettings["MyNewSetting"];` to access a variable named MyNewSetting. Developers can read more about this feature at http://msdn2.microsoft.com/en-us/library/system.configuration.configurationmanager.appsettings.aspx.

Changing Application Behavior with Application Settings

Once you decide on which settings to create and use within an application, it's time to add them to the code and then configure them within IIS. To configure a setting for a particular application, choose the application in the Connections pane and double-click the Application Settings icon. You'll see a list of application settings, as shown in Figure 8.2.

Using the application variables is relatively easy. Any application variables that the developer has already defined appear in the list automatically. These variables have a Local entry type in most cases. Global variables that affect more than one application will have an Inherited entry type.

The task you'll perform most often is editing existing variables. To perform this task, highlight the variable you want to change and choose Edit from the Actions pane. You'll see an Edit Application Setting dialog box. Don't change the name of the variable as it appears in the Name field. However, you can change the information in the Value field to meet a particular need. Always verify that you've made the entry correctly because incorrect entries can result in a malfunctioning application.

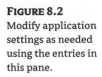

FIGURE 8.2
Modify application settings as needed using the entries in this pane.

When you do need to make an application setting, click Add in the Actions pane. You'll see an Add Application Setting dialog box. Type the name of the variable as specified by the developer (the application code must accommodate the variable or making the change won't do any good). Type an appropriate value in the Value field.

To remove a setting you no longer need, highlight the value in the Application Settings pane and then click Remove in the Actions pane. IIS will ask if you're sure you want to remove the setting. Click Yes to complete the action.

Exploring and Browsing Applications

IIS 7 provides the means to both explore and browse applications. You access these features from the Actions pane shown in Figure 8.3, just as you would when working with a folder or virtual directory.

When you click Explore in the Actions pane, IIS opens a copy of Windows Explorer with the physical location of the application as normal, and lets you make changes to the application content. Whenever you make changes to an application, the handler must determine whether the application requires compilation at the next user request. Consequently, a change in an application folder has a more significant impact than a change to a folder or virtual directory. It's normally a good idea to touch the application by opening it in a browser immediately after you make a change so any users accessing the application won't experience a delay.

Browsing an application is different from browsing a folder or virtual directory, even though they both start when you click Browse in the Actions pane. When you browse a folder or virtual directory, IIS opens the URL in a browser and attempts to show the default document or lets the user view the directory structure depending on how you've configured the settings. On the other hand, when you browse an application, IIS attempts to start the application. In many cases, this means starting an executable file, rather than simply displaying content.

FIGURE 8.3
Explore and browse your applications as needed to perform maintenance and testing.

Although exploring or browsing a folder or virtual directory is relatively innocuous, exploring or browsing an application can incur performance penalties that you might not have anticipated. An application is an executable environment where the source files provide the instructions for tasks that IIS performs through a handler to respond to a caller request. Because of the performance penalties that even small changes can incur, you'll want to make changes to an application folder only when necessary. In addition, you should follow a simple rule to ensure the caller has a good experience with your application—after you explore, make sure you browse. Browsing the application will tell IIS 7 to make any required updates, compile the application, and finally display it on screen. It's far better for you to experience a delay than to ask a caller to experience it.

Managing Session State

HTTP is a one-request protocol. The client makes a request, the server responds, and then everyone forgets that the conversation took place. Because there isn't any memory between requests, HTTP normally can't work for applications such as shopping carts or address application needs such as form-based security. However, developers have found many ways of overcoming this problem. The entire conversation between client and server becomes a *session* that can have one or more requests. Storing (remembering) the content of that conversation between requests is called the *session state* and it relies of some form of application variable storage. The following sections describe how ASP.NET manages session state and how you can configure the technique you want to use from within IIS 7.

Understanding How Session State Works

Session state is data that you store between requests. Using session state lets a client and server remember the conversation they were having between requests. In most cases, you'll find that Web applications rely on one of five methods to maintain session state:

◆ Information passed as part of the URL

◆ Information passed as part of the request headers

◆ Locally stored information in cookies

◆ Remotely stored information on a server based on user identity

◆ Dynamically configured information that appears within the body of the Web page

Most people are familiar with the first technique. In fact, some people are known to tweak the URLs provided by the server in order to derive some special benefit or to probe the server for weakness. When the caller fills out a form or makes certain requests, the URL contains the information the caller has provided (in some cases, it won't contain any information because the caller doesn't know what to request). The server sends a response that modifies the URL to show any changes due to the initial request. The next time the caller makes a request, the URL shows that the user is continuing the session. Based on the changes the caller has made to a Web page, the server can modify the URL further, perform redirections, and perform other tasks to maintain the conversation. This is the GET method of maintaining session state.

The second technique works almost the same as the first technique, except many people won't recognize it because the URL remains the same throughout the conversation, in many cases. The part of the communication that changes is the request header. A request header is a series of instructions that the server uses to know how to interact with the user. Generally, you won't see the request headers, even if you choose to view the source code for the Web page. However, the technique works the same—the caller and server make changes to the request header as needed to achieve a specific goal. If you ever decide that you'd like to see the request headers that your browser is sending, check them out at `http://web-sniffer.net/`. You can find a discussion of request headers at `http://www.faqs.org/rfcs/rfc2616.html`. The W3C site at `http://www.w3.org/Protocols/HTTP/HTRQ_Headers.html` provides a general description of the common request headers. This is the POST method of maintaining session state.

Most people also know about the third method of maintaining state information—the cookie. In fact, some people fear this form of storage so much that they'll do anything to prevent someone from storing a cookie on their system. Although cookies can't damage your system like a virus can, they can tell others a lot about the caller and some Web sites misuse them to track caller movement across the Internet. Even so, cookies are an effective way to store user data on the local system. This form of storing session state can last over multiple sessions. A user can go to your Web site and see things configured precisely the way they were in the past.

The fourth method is similar to the third method. The difference is that the server stores the information instead of the caller. Using this approach means that you must identify the user in some way. In most cases, you'll need to provide a secure logon to ensure that no one else can steal the user's settings. However, this technique does have the advantage of maintaining session state even if the caller won't accept cookies or regularly erases cookies when closing the browser.

The fifth method is unique to newer application platforms such as ASP.NET. When you view the dynamically generated source code for an ASP.NET application, you see the state information as part of the body of the Web page itself. In many cases, the state information appears as part of a hidden control, as shown in Figure 8.4. Notice the source includes two hidden controls: one at the beginning of the body and the other at the end of the body. Using this technique has the advantage of not storing information anywhere permanent and letting the client and server modify it as needed. You can easily access the information using JavaScript and other languages. In addition, using this approach means that the application can store all kinds of information, such as view state, and the data storage can change as the needs of the application change.

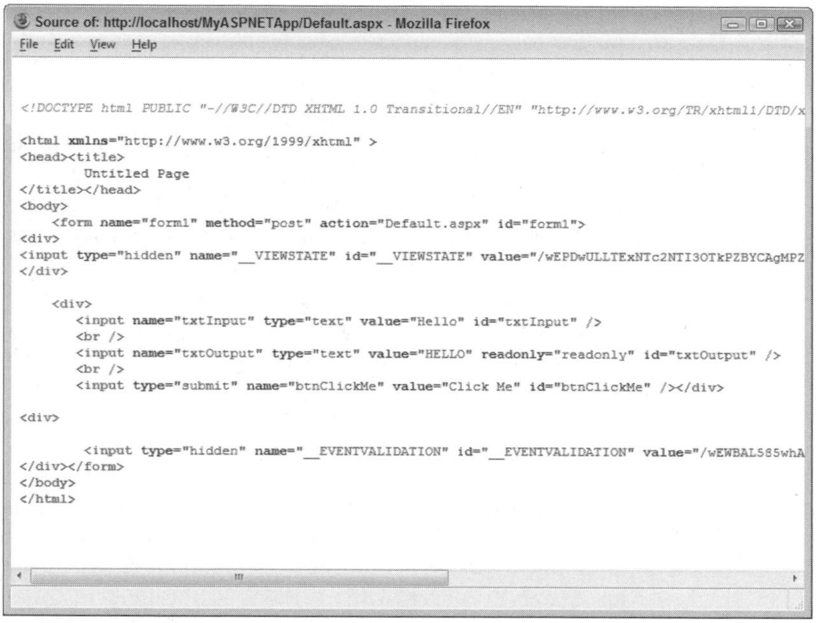

FIGURE 8.4
Dynamically generated state information has a number of advantages over the static methods of the past.

In most cases, you won't have much choice over the method an application chooses to use to store state information unless the application provides more than one method. IIS 7 focuses on state information settings for ASP.NET applications only. In all other cases, you'd need a special IIS 7 extension to provide configuration for the method an application uses to store state information— assuming that such a choice is even available.

Changing the Session State Mode

IIS 7 does provide considerable flexibility when it comes to state information for ASP.NET applications. You can view state information by choosing the ASP.NET application in the Connections pane and double-clicking the Session State icon. Figure 8.5 shows the portion of the session state information for this section, the session state mode.

The session state mode determines how IIS 7 tracks session state. The default option tracks the session state in process. In other words, the worker process actually tracks the state information as it fulfills the request of the caller. The disadvantage of this approach is that the session state information is lost when the system recycles the worker process. Of course, since the server does let the current worker process complete answering all requests in its queue, this problem may not affect your applications. However, when a user has to make many requests, such as working with a shopping cart application, it can be a problem.

FIGURE 8.5
Choosing the correct session state mode can make your applications more accessible.

You can also choose not to track session state at all. Simply select the Not Enabled option. The advantage of this option is that it actually increases application performance when an application doesn't need to maintain session state. The downside is that it prevents applications from using session state even when they do need it and a configuration error could cause your application to fail.

The Custom setting is only usable when an application developer creates a custom provider to support session state for ASP.NET applications. If your application doesn't include this feature, you don't need to worry about this setting. Normally, you'll only find this setting when working with custom applications. Commercial applications normally use a standardized method for handling session state.

A state server is a special kind of server that tracks state information. Selecting the State Server option tells IIS to rely on the `ASPNet_State.EXE` service located in the `\Windows\Microsoft.NET\Framework\v2.0.50727` folder of your hard drive. In order to use this option, you must open the Services console found in the Administrative Tools folder of the Control Panel and set the ASP.NET State Service to start automatically. After you perform the required configuration, you must decide on a timeout value for the connection. This value determines how long the server maintains the state information. If you don't set the interval long enough, you could lose state information. The Connection String field tells how to connect to the state server. In most cases, the default value works fine.

The final option is to store the state information in SQL Server. In this case, IIS stores the state information in SQL Server. This approach has the advantage of not storing state information in the worker process and making it vulnerable to worker process recycling. The technique exchanges memory as a medium of storage for hard drive space. Consequently, the storage is also more permanent. As with the State Server option, you must decide on a timeout value that reflects the needs of your application and shouldn't need to change the connection string. To enable this particular feature, you must run the `InstallSqlState.sql` script located in the `\Windows\Microsoft.NET\Framework\v2.0.50727` folder of your hard drive. If you decide that you don't want to use the standard configuration, you can check the Enable Custom Database option and create a custom setup. Generally speaking, you probably won't need this feature for anything but very large applications.

TIP   If you're creating a custom ASP.NET application and want to ensure that the state information is correct during installation, you can also configure it from the command line using the AppCmd utility described in the "Working with the AppCmd Utility" section of the chapter. Simply use the `CONFIG` object to perform the task with this command line: `AppCmd Set CONFIG /commit:WEBROOT / section:sessionState /mode:SqlServer /sqlConnectionString :string / sqlCommandTimeout: timeSpan /useHostingIdentity:True|False`. Replace the `/ sqlConnectionString` command line argument with the connection string for the database you want to use, the `/sqlCommandTimeout` command line argument with the timeout value you want to use, and the `/useHostingIdentity` argument with true or false depending on your application's needs (generally, true—see the "Considering Impersonation Requirements" section for details).

Controlling the Use of Cookies

As previously mentioned, one of the ways to store state information is cookies. Of course, you have to decide how to use cookies. For example, some Web sites insist that the caller use cookies even when the caller doesn't want to—the caller normally wins on a public Web site. You'll find the cookie settings in the Cookie Settings area shown in Figure 8.6.

FIGURE 8.6
Use the cookie settings to control how IIS works with cookies.

The first thing you have to determine is how you want your application to use cookies. The default is to use cookies even if the caller doesn't want to and, as previously mentioned, the caller usually wins that argument by leaving your Web site. You do have other options as described in the following list.

Auto Detect   You should use this setting whenever possible because it detects the caller's wishes and uses cookies only when the caller allows them.

Use Cookies   The default setting assumes that all users really do want to use cookies, whether they can support them or not. This setting irritates people who disable cookies on their browser because they'll find that they can't interact with your application unless they turn cookies on—they may choose to go somewhere else. More important, however, is that some devices can't support cookies and using this setting locks them out of your application.

Use Device Profile If you choose to use cookies even when the user doesn't want them, but you don't want to lock out devices that can't support the cookies, then you can use this setting. IIS checks the caller first to determine what kind of device is making the request. When the device doesn't support cookies, then IIS provides another means of storing the state information.

Use URI This choice avoids the whole issue of cookies. It stores the state information in the URI and then redirects the user to the original URL. The technique does require additional time and server resources to use. The caller will wait a little while longer on complex Web pages too. However, since this method doesn't require cookies, it works better when you have a public Web site.

The session identifier is a value that helps the application to detect different callers. It's a name and value pair, just like most cookies. To avoid giving the ne'er-do-wells of the world too much help, you can change the name of the session identifier from the default value of ASP.NET_SessionId. Doing so makes it harder for someone to search your Web pages for the value they need. Of course, you'll want to tell the developer about the change too since the application code may look for this value as well.

It's important to set the timeout value as well. Some individuals will attempt to obtain the session identifier and then use it to gain access to the communication between the caller and the server. In some cases, the individual will simply steal the session. Regenerating session identifiers by setting a short timeout value tends to reduce this problem. Of course, setting the timeout too short won't let you accomplish much and consumes many server resources. Microsoft recommends something shorter than the default of 20 minutes, but they don't actually tell you how much shorter to set the timeout value. A good rule of thumb is to consider the complexity of the data you're manipulating and the sensitivity of that data. A value of 5 minutes will work with some forms, but may not work very well when the user needs 10 minutes to complete a process before submitting data. Timing the interaction time with the user is probably the best way to gauge a good timeout value.

The final setting, Regenerate Expired Session ID, only applies to sessions that don't rely on cookies (the Use URI setting) unless you create specialized software to support this feature in other scenarios. Checking this option tells IIS to reject any session identifiers that don't have an active session in the database. IIS then reissues an identifier to the original caller.

Considering Impersonation Requirements

Impersonation is an important feature of Windows. If someone's logging onto the system anonymously, you don't want them to have access to everything on your network and that includes your SQL Server setup. However, when using certain kinds of session state management, the system has to access SQL Server. Since the anonymous user doesn't have access to SQL Server, gaining the required access could be a problem. That's where impersonation comes into play. The session can impersonate something that does have the required access in order to gain access to SQL Server for the session state information. Because the impersonation is under the control of the system, there isn't any security issue with this approach. The anonymous user is still locked out, the system is performing any required tasks on the user's behalf.

The Use Hosting Identity for Impersonation setting lets the system use the ASP.NET or a Windows service account to gain access to SQL Server for the purpose of maintaining session state information. If your session state strategy doesn't rely on SQL Server, you can probably clear this option. You can also clear this option when your application depends on secured sessions and you can use the user's identity to gain the required access. The time you need this option is when the user logs on anonymously or doesn't have sufficient rights to access the SQL Server setup.

Modifying Application Settings

In the "Controlling Application Settings" section of the chapter, you discover how IIS 7 lets you use application settings to control application behavior. Most applications require some form of configuration to work perfectly with your setup. The "Managing Session State" section of the chapter introduces the idea of working with settings as part of the conversation between the client and the server. This section brings those concepts together in the form of static settings required to configure the application and make the conversation between client and server flow smoothly. Applications provide both basic and advanced settings. In addition, you'll want to know how to access the settings within a virtual directory.

Changing the Basic Settings

At some point, you may need to change the location of an application (say from a beta version to the released version) or the application pool that it uses. You can perform this task by choosing the application you want to modify in the Connections pane and clicking Basic Settings in the Actions pane. You'll see a dialog box similar to the one shown in Figure 8.1. The only difference is that the Edit Application dialog box won't let you change the application name.

Changing the Advanced Settings

IIS provides access to a few more settings than the basic settings dialog box can provide. To access the additional settings, select the application you want to change in the Connections pane and click Advanced Settings in the Actions pane. You'll see the Advanced Settings dialog box shown in Figure 8.7.

FIGURE 8.7
Modify security and other advanced settings using this dialog box.

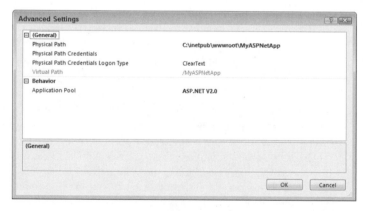

Most of these settings do appear in the Edit Application dialog box, but with different names. The Physical Path field is the same. When you click the ellipses button in the Physical Path Credentials field, you see a Connect To dialog box like the one when you click Connect To in the Edit Application dialog box. Likewise, the Application Pool fields are the same.

The one difference in this dialog box worth noting is the Physical Path Credentials Logon Type field. In this dialog box you choose the kind of logon the system performs. These selections determine how the user logs onto the system and the choices are important. The default value of ClearText isn't very secure. You can find a description of these options in the "Setting the Default Web Site Configuration" section of Chapter 2.

Managing Worker Processes

Worker processes reside within application pools. Whenever an application handles a caller request, it generates one or more worker processes to fulfill it. You access the current list of worker processes by selecting the Web server in the Connections pane and double-clicking the Worker Processes icon. Figure 8.8 shows how the Worker Processes pane appears.

FIGURE 8.8

Keep track of worker processes using the Worker Processes pane.

The essential information you receive from the Worker Processes pane includes the application pool, the PID, the state (whether or not the worker process is running), the amount of processor cycles the working process is consuming, and the amount of memory the worker process requires. By tracking these statistics, you can determine whether a worker process is running at full efficiency or has crashed. When a worker process crashes, you need to recycle it (which means that the system gets rid of the old worker process and creates a new one to replace it). The "Working with Application Pools" section of Chapter 13 describes how this process works in detail. You can see the IIS 6 version of recycling in the "Configuring the Recycling Options" section of Chapter 7.

Worker processes respond to requests. Sometimes, a worker process will have a number of requests in its queue (an empty queue is the best). To see the requests for a particular worker process, highlight the worker process you want to see and click View Current Request in the Actions pane. You'll see the Request pane shown in Figure 8.9. The longer the list of backlogged requests, the more suspicious you should be of the worker process. Of course, you have to take temporary increases in network traffic into account. The request information includes the Web site that made the request, the URL of the request, the verb used to create the request, the client IP (when known), the state of the request, and how much time has elapsed since the caller made the request.

FIGURE 8.9
Each worker process
maintains a separate
request queue.

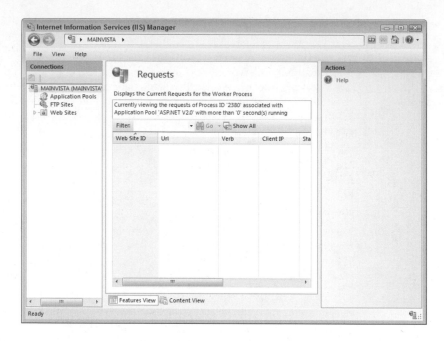

Working with the AppCmd Utility

The AppCmd utility is a general-purpose IIS administration tool that you can use to perform configuration task at the command line. In fact, this tool provides access to features you can't access from the Internet Information Services (IIS) Manager, which makes it an invaluable aid for the administrator.

Like many of the command line tools that Microsoft provides, the AppCmd utility works with objects. You can use the various objects shown in the following list to perform specific tasks.

- SITE
- APP
- VDIR
- APPPOOL
- CONFIG
- WP
- REQUEST
- MODULE
- BACKUP
- TRACE

The basic syntax for using this command is as follows:

```
AppCmd <Command> <Object> <Arguments>
```

The commands that you can use depend on the object you want to access. For example, when you use the SITE object, you have the list, set, add, delete, start, and stop commands available. The arguments also depend, in part, on the object you select. However, some arguments are usable no matter which object you select. These common arguments appear in the following list.

/? Displays a context-sensitive message. If you use this argument alone with AppCmd, you'll see a list of available objects along with some of the common arguments.

/text:value Displays the output information in text format. You can show all of the attributes for an object by using /text:*. The list you see is detailed, rather than a generic set of attributes. Display the value of a particular attribute by including its name with the command line. For example, typing **AppCmd list SITE /text:bindings** and pressing Enter at the command line displays the binding for the default Web site of http/*:80:. It's also possible, in some cases, to define a Boolean condition. For example, typing **AppCmd list SITE /serverAutoStart:True** and pressing Enter at the command line displays all Web sites where the serverAutoStart attribute is true.

/xml Displays the output information as an XML document. You can use redirection to place the output in a file for import into a database or display in a browser. It's also possible to combine this command line argument with the /in command line argument to send the output from one command to another.

/in or − Sends XML input from the standard input device to the specified command. You use this command line switch to feed information from one command to another (see the /xml command line switch for additional information).

/config:* Shows the configuration information for the specified objects. This command line argument also shows inherited configuration information. For example, a file can inherit configuration information from the file that holds it. The output from this command line argument normally appears in XML format.

/metadata Displays configuration metadata when displaying configuration information.

/commit [[site | app | url] | [apphost | webroot | machine]] Sets the configuration path where IIS saves configuration information. When working with a configuration path, you can specify the site, app, or url. When working with a configuration level, you can choose apphost, webroot, or machine.

/debug Shows debugging information for the command that you're executing. The information appears as an INFO entry. For example, if you type **AppCmd list SITE /debug** at the command prompt and press enter, you may see an INFO entry of INFO (timetaken:47, hresult:00000000, objects:2). The timetaken value tells you how long the command required to execute. The hresult value contains the numeric value of any error. The objects value tells you how many objects appear in the output.

Using the *SITE* Object

The SITE object provides access to the Web sites on your server. You use this object to perform management tasks with the Web sites, such as determining whether the Web site starts automatically when you start the system. The "Choosing the Configuration Level" section of Chapter 2 demonstrates the graphical methods for working with Web sites. The SITE object supports the following commands.

List Provides a listing of all of the virtual sites supported by a server. You can add arguments to specify a particular Web site or a property value that you want to look for. When including a property value, you must provide a value as well such as `serverAutoStart:false` to locate all Web sites that don't start automatically.

Set   Changes the configuration of the specified Web site. You must provide a Web site identifier, such as `"Default Web Site"` (the command line requires that you enclose the identifier in double quotes as shown), to use this command. In addition, you must provide the property and its associated value, such as `serverAutoStart:false` to stop the server from starting automatically.

Add   Creates a new Web site on the server. When using this command, you must provide the name of the new Web site. The command also supports optional command line arguments, as shown here.

> **/name:*WebSiteName***   Defines the name of the Web site. You must include this command line argument.

> **/id:*Number***   Specifies the numeric value of the Web site. Normally, you won't want to provide this command line argument to prevent potential conflicts with existing Web sites. IIS automatically chooses the next number in order for you.

> **/bindings:*FriendlyURL* /bindings:*RawURL***   Defines the bindings for the new Web site. The bindings determine the input requests to which the new Web site will respond. A friendly URL includes the normal protocol, domain, and port information such as `http://www.mysite.com:80`. A raw URL only includes the protocol and the port such as `http/*:80`. In this second case, the Web site listens to all incoming requests on port 80.

> **/physicalPath:*Path***   Determines the physical location of the Web site on the hard drive. For example, if you provide `C:\inetpub\mynewsite` as the path, then IIS will use the `C:\inetpub\mynewsite` directory as the root path for the server. Even though this is an optional input, you can't start a Web site without providing a physical path for it since IIS 7 won't know where to find the Web site data.

Delete   Removes the specified Web site from the server. You must provide the Web site identifier, such as `"Default Web Site"` (the command line requires that you enclose the identifier in double quotes as shown) or the Web site URL as input for this command.

WARNING   The `Delete` command is a one-way process. Once you delete a Web site, you can't undo the action. You must re-create the Web site from scratch. For this reason, you'll want to store the current Web site configuration using the CONFIG object (see the "Using the *CONFIG* Object" section of the chapter for details) before you delete it. Because the deletion affects an entire Web site, you may also want to make a backup of the entire server before you proceed. See the "Using the *BACKUP* Object" section of the chapter for instructions on creating a backup.

Start   Starts the specified Web site. You must provide an identifier or URL to start the Web site.

Stop   Stops the specified Web site. You must provide an identifier or URL to stop the Web site.

Using the *APP* Object

The APP object provides access to all of the applications on your server. You use it to access a particular application installed on a particular Web site. The "Creating Applications" section of this chapter demonstrates the graphical methods for working with applications. The APP object supports the following commands.

List   Provides, when used alone, a list of all of the applications on the server. You can list a specific application by providing its name or URL. It's also possible to filter the application list by providing a property and its associated value. For example, if you type `AppCmd List APP / apppool.name:"DefaultAppPool"` and press Enter, the AppCmd utility will list all of the applications that appear within the DefaultAppPool application pool.

Set   Changes the configuration of the specified application. You must provide an application identifier, such as `"Default Web Site/"` (the command line requires that you enclose the identifier in double quotes as shown and provide the ending slash), or an application URL to use this command. In addition, you must provide the property and its associated value, such as `/enabledProtocols:http` to set the new value.

Add   Creates a new application with the name you specify. You must provide a name as a minimum. The command also supports the optional command line arguments shown here.

> **/site.name:*SupportingSite***   Defines the Web site that hosts the application, such as `"Default Web Site"`. You must provide this argument.
>
> **/path:*Path***   Defines the virtual path to the application, such as `/app1`. You must include the beginning slash, even if the application appears at the root of the host. It's possible to bury an application as many layers deep as necessary by including more path information, such as `/MyPublicDir/app1`, which would place the application in the `MyPublicDir` folder. You must provide this argument.
>
> **/physicalPath:*Path***   Determines the physical location of the application on the hard drive. For example, if you provide `C:\MyApp` as the path, then IIS will use the `\MyApp` directory as the root path for the application. Even though this is an optional input, you can't start an application without providing a physical path for it since IIS 7 won't know where to find the application executables, data, and resources.

Delete   Removes the specified application from the Web site; however, the application's physical data remains—only the configuration information is lost. You must provide the full application identifier, such as `"Default Web Site/app1"` (the command line requires that you enclose the identifier in double quotes as shown) or the application URL as input for this command.

WARNING   The `Delete` command is a one-way process. Once you delete an application, you can't undo the action. You must re-create the application from scratch. For this reason, you'll want to store the current application configuration using the `CONFIG` object (see the "Using the *CONFIG* Object" section of the chapter for details) before you delete it. Make sure you save only the application settings and not the entire Web site settings, or you could overwrite some Web site settings when you restore the application.

Using the *VDIR* Object

The VDIR object provides access to all of the virtual directories on your server. You use it to access a virtual directory that you've attached to a particular Web site. The "Adding Virtual Directories to the Web Site" section of Chapter 3 demonstrates the graphical methods for working with virtual directories. The VDIR object supports the following commands.

List   Provides a list of all of the virtual directories on the server. You can filter the output by providing a specific virtual directory name. For example, typing `AppCmd List VDIR "Default Web Site/MyPublicArea"` at the command line and pressing Enter shows the physical location of the MyPublicArea virtual directory. You can also list virtual directory information by proving an URL to the virtual directory location.

Set Changes the configuration of the specified virtual directory. You must provide a virtual directory identifier, such as `"Default Web Site/MyPublicArea"` (the command line requires that you enclose the identifier in double quotes as shown), or an URL to use this command. In addition, you must provide the property and its associated value, such as `/logonMethod:Network` to set the new value.

Add Creates a new virtual with the name you specify. You must provide a name as a minimum. The command also supports the optional command line arguments shown here.

> **/app.name:*SupportingSite*** Defines the application that uses this virtual directory, such as `"Default Web Site/MyPublicArea"`. You must provide this argument.

> **/path:*Path*** Defines the virtual path to the virtual directory, such as /MyPublicArea. You must include the beginning slash, even if the virtual directory appears at the root of the host. It's possible to bury a virtual as many layers deep as necessary by including more path information, such as /MyPublicDir/SubDir, which would place the SubDir virtual directory in the MyPublicDir folder. You must provide this argument.

> **/physicalPath:*Path*** Determines the physical location of the virtual directory on the hard drive. For example, if you provide `C:\MyVDir` as the path, then IIS will use the `\MyVDir` directory as the root path for the virtual directory. Even though this is an optional input, you can't use a virtual directory without providing a physical path for it since IIS 7 won't know where to find the data.

Delete Removes the specified virtual directory from the Web site; however, the virtual directory's physical data remains—only the configuration information is lost. You must provide the full virtual directory identifier, such as `"Default Web Site/MyPublicArea"` (the command line requires that you enclose the identifier in double quotes as shown). You can't use an URL as input for this command.

Using the *APPPOOL* Object

The APPPOOL object provides access to the application pools on your server. It's important to remember that an application pool isn't associated with a particular Web site, but that any application, including Web sites, folders, and virtual directories, can rely on a particular application pool. Every application must have an application pool associated with it in order to execute. The "Working with Application Pools" section of Chapter 13 demonstrates the graphical methods for working with application pools. The APPPOOL object supports the following commands.

List Provides a list of all of the application pools on the server. You can filter the output by providing a specific application pool name. For example, typing **AppCmd List APPPOOL "DefaultAppPool"** at the command line and pressing Enter shows the managed pipeline mode and state of the DefaultAppPool application pool.

Set Changes the configuration of the specified application pool. You must provide an application pool identifier, such as DefaultAppPool. In addition, you must provide the property and its associated value, such as `/autoStart:false` to set the new value.

Add Creates a new application pool with the specified name. You don't have to provide anything more than a name for the new pool and then configure it using the Set command.

Delete Removes the specified application pool from the server. You must provide the application pool identifier, such as DefaultAppPool. Deleting the application pool also deletes any worker processes. The applications that rely on the application pool will stop running. Consequently, you should only use this command on application pools that aren't in use.

WARNING   The `Delete` command is a one-way process. Once you delete an application pool, you can't undo the action. You must re-create the application pool from scratch. For this reason, you'll want to store the current application configuration using the `CONFIG` object (see the "Using the *CONFIG* Object" section of the chapter for details) before you delete it. Make sure you only save the application pool information and not all of the Web site information or restoring the application pool could destroy your Web site configuration.

Start   Starts the specified application pool. You must provide an identifier to start the application pool.

Stop   Stops the specified application pool. You must provide an identifier to stop the application pool.

Recycle   Recycles the worker processes within an application pool. Recycling removes any existing worker processes after they have fulfilled all of their pending requests and creates new worker processes. You can use this command to perform tasks such as restart worker processes that have failed or to clean up memory leak problems.

Using the *CONFIG* Object

The `CONFIG` object provides access to all of the general configuration options for the server that don't fall within a particular configuration topic. You'll actually find a considerable number of options here. For example, you'll use the `CONFIG` object to change any of the server MIME settings and it provides access to the error pages for your Web site. You'll find the general configuration settings discussed throughout the book. The `CONFIG` object supports the following commands.

List   Provides a list of all of the configuration objects on the server (a very large number, so you'll normally want to filter them). You can filter the output by providing a specific site value. For example, typing **AppCmd List CONFIG "Default Web Site/MyPublicArea"** at the command line and pressing Enter shows the configuration for the MyPublicArea virtual directory. However, you'll still see a considerable amount of information, so you'll probably want to add the `/section` command line argument. Typing **AppCmd List CONFIG /section:?** and pressing Enter displays a list of available sections. If you type **AppCmd List CONFIG "Default Web Site/MyPublicArea" /section:"system.applicationHost/customMetadata"** at the command line (always include double quotes as needed to delimit the input values) and press Enter, you'll see the custom metadata for the MyPublicArea virtual directory.

Set   Changes the configuration of the specified server object (Web server, Web site, folder, virtual directory, or file). If you don't provide an identifier for a specific object, AppCmd defaults to changing the global settings. You must provide a section identifier (see the `List` command for details). The `/section` command line switch must identify the section in enough detail to set its value. The actual entry consists of a property and value pair. For example, if you want to enable the default document feature for the default Web site, you'd type **AppCmd Set CONFIG "Default Web Site" /section:defaultDocument /enabled:true** and press Enter at the command prompt. See the `Search` command for ways of obtaining precise section and property information.

Search   Displays the configuration path for a particular setting. You define the setting you want to find as a `/section` command line switch. It's also possible to filter the output by providing a specific property and value pair. For example, if you want to locate all Web sites that have the defaultDocument feature enabled, you'd type **AppCmd Search CONFIG /section:defaultDocument /enabled:true** at the command prompt and press Enter.

Lock Locks a particular configuration section so that no one can change it. This command changes a particular object and all objects that it contains including the Web server, Web site, folder, virtual directory, and file levels. For example, if you lock a section at the Web server level, then the section is locked everywhere else on the server, but if you lock it for a particular Web site, the section is only locked on the Web site. If you don't provide an identifier for a specific object, AppCmd defaults to changing the global settings. You must provide the name of a section to lock using the /section command line argument.

Unlock Unlocks a particular configuration section so that anyone with the proper credentials can make changes to it again. You must provide the same /section command line argument and level identifier you used to lock the section. See the Lock command for details.

Clear Clears the specified section of settings. The section remains in place unless you also specify the /delete command line argument, but it doesn't contain any configuration information. This command clears the configuration for a particular object and the inherited values for all objects that it contains including the Web server, Web site, folder, virtual directory, and file levels. For example, if you clear a section at the Web server level, then the section is cleared everywhere else on the server, unless you specifically set values at those other levels. If you don't provide an identifier for a specific object, AppCmd defaults to clearing the global settings. You must provide the name of a section to lock using the /section command line argument.

Reset Sets the settings in a particular section to the default values used at the time of setup. This command resets the configuration for a particular object and the inherited values for all objects that it contains including the Web server, Web site, folder, virtual directory, and file levels. For example, if you reset a section at the Web server level, then the section is reset everywhere else on the server, unless you specifically set values at those other levels. If you don't provide an identifier for a specific object, AppCmd defaults to resetting the global settings. You must provide the name of a section to lock using the /section command line argument.

Migrate Migrates the settings of an older server to a new one. You can choose to migrate all of the settings or specific settings based on the filtering criteria described in the following list.

Identifier Specifies the configuration path or URL to use to begin the migration. For example, you could choose to migrate a particular Web site or an application within that Web site. If you don't provide an identifier, AppCmd defaults to migrating all of the settings for the entire server.

/section:Path Defines the section that you want to migrate. You need to provide the specific path to the configuration setting, such as /section:defaultDocument. Unless you specify the /recurse command line argument as well, the /section command line argument only moves the settings at the current level.

/clear Clears the configuration information on the original source after migration. It's usually better to migrate the information, verify that it migrated correctly, and then manually remove the information from the original source. Using this approach reduces the potential for errors that could cripple both the originating site and the target.

/recurse Specifies that AppCmd should migrate settings at the current and all lower levels. Consequently, if you specify /section:defaultDocument with the /recurse command line argument, AppCmd won't move just the enabled property value, but all of the default documents configured for the section.

Using the *WP* Object

The WP object provides access to all of the worker processes on your server. A worker process is always associated with a particular application, but IIS 7 doesn't care where the application appears or on what Web site it executes. A worker process always appears within a particular application pool, so you'll want to spend some time reviewing the APPPOOL object as well. The number of worker processes varies over time as the applications create new worker processes to fulfill requests and the system recycles worker processes. The "Managing Worker Processes" section of this chapter demonstrates the graphical methods for working with worker processes. The WP object supports the following command.

List Provides a list of worker processes. Normally, you'll provide the PID of the process that you want to list. For example, typing **AppCmd List WP "3897"** and pressing Enter at the command prompt displays the worker process with a PID of 3897. However, most people don't know PIDs very well, so you can also use the application pool as a filter. For example, typing **AppCmd List WP /apppool.name:DefaultAppPool** and pressing Enter displays all of the worker processes in the DefaultAppPool application pool. Since this information includes the PID, you can now track a particular worker process using its PID.

NOTE The concepts behind recycling haven't changed much since IIS 6. The "Configuring the Recycling Options" section of Chapter 7 describes recycling from the IIS 6 perspective.

Using the *REQUEST* Object

The REQUEST object provides access to all of the HTTP requests on your server. The HTTP request can be of any type: static or dynamic. Any time a user requests any sort of resource on your server, the request appears within the REQUEST object. The number of requests varies over time as clients make new requests and the server fulfills them. The "Setting Failed Request Tracing Rules" section of Chapter 4 demonstrates the graphical methods for working with failed requests. The REQUEST object supports the following command.

List Provides a list of pending HTTP requests (the list is empty when the server has no pending requests, even if you have a page open in the browser). Although you can use a particular identifier to monitor a specific request, you may want to monitor the Web site as a whole or look for requests based on filters. You can use a number of filters for listing the requests so that you can find a particular request easily. The following list describes the filters you can use to locate particular HTTP requests (mixing filters is fine and you don't have to provide an identifier).

/site.name:*Name* Specifies the name of the Web site to monitor. Normally, AppCmd displays the pending requests for all Web sites. Using this filter, you can specify a particular Web site such as **/site.name:"Default Web Site"** for the default Web site.

/wp.name:*Identifier* Specifies a particular worker process to monitor. You can use this filter to monitor a Web site, application, or a single worker process of either type.

/apppool.name:*Name* Specifies a particular application pool to monitor. You can use this filter to monitor all of the worker processes within a particular application pool. When the application pool applies to a specific Web site or application, you can monitor all of the worker processes for that Web site or application without any input from other Web sites or applications.

/elapsed:*Time* Specifies a particular time interval to monitor in milliseconds. You can use this filter to locate applications that are taking too long to process requests or may have crashed. AppCmd displays all of the requests that have been executing longer than the specified time.

Using the *MODULE* Object

The MODULE object provides access to all of the modules on your server. A module provides some basic functionality for the server in handling client requests. The "Working with Response Modules" section of Chapter 4 demonstrates the graphical methods for working with modules. The MODULE object supports the following commands.

List Provides a list of all of the modules on the server. You can filter the output by providing a specific module name. For example, typing **AppCmd List MODULE UrlMappingsModule** at the command line and pressing Enter shows the module type and precondition information for the specified module. You can further filter the information by providing an /app.name command line argument. For example, typing **AppCmd List MODULE UrlMappingsModule / app.name:"Default Web Site/"** at the command line and pressing Enter would display the UrlMappingsModule information for the default Web site.

Set Changes the configuration of the module. You must provide a module identifier, such as UrlMappingsModule. In addition, you must provide the property and its associated value, such as /preCondition:integratedMode to set the new value. You can optionally include an application name so that the change only affects that application. For example, if you want to change just the Default Web Site, you might type **AppCmd Set MODULE UrlMappingsModule /preCondition:integratedMode /app.name:"Default Web Site/"** at the command line and press Enter.

Add Creates a new module entry with the specified name. This technique only lets you add modules that you've already registered with IIS 7. You don't have to provide anything more than a name for the module and then configure it using the Set command. However, you can use the /app.name command line argument to specify a particular application to receive the new module.

Delete Removes the specified module from use. You can disable any module currently installed on the server. Use the /app.name command line argument to specify a particular application from which to disable the module.

Install Installs a native module on the server. Remember that you must install managed assemblies in the Global Assembly Cache (GAC) (see the "Adding a Managed Module" section of Chapter 4 for details). You must provide the module name and path to the executable file as a minimum. Use the /app.name command line argument to specify a particular application to hold the module. The following list shows the command line arguments you can use with this command.

/name:*Name* Specifies the name of the module. You can use any name that helps you remember the module's purpose.

/image:*Path* Specifies the location and name of the executable file that IIS 7 should use for the module. IIS doesn't perform any check of this executable, so you could use any executable. The executable you choose must provide the basic functionality required to respond to HTTP requests, such as an ISAPI extension.

/add   Automatically adds the new module to the server so that IIS begins using it immediately. You should provide a specific application name when using this command line switch unless you truly want to install and use the module at the global level.

Uninstall   Removes the specified native module from the server. Remember that you can't uninstall managed assemblies directly, but must instead remove them from the GAC (see the "Adding a Managed Module" section of Chapter 4 for details). Use the `/app.name` command line argument to specify a particular application from which to remove the module. Even though the module is removed from the server, the executable file still resides on the disk and you can reinstall it later.

Using the *BACKUP* Object

The BACKUP object helps you create a backup of the server settings and then restore the backup later should you need to do so. Creating a backup of your configuration can save considerable time if your server fails for some reason (such as a hard drive crash). You can't accomplish this task using the graphical interface. The backups appear in subfolders of the `\Windows\System32\inetsrv\ backup` folder. The BACKUP object supports the following commands.

List   Provides a list of all of the backups on the server. You can filter the list by providing a specific backup name. However, if you provide a backup name, you can't use wildcards, so you must provide the precise backup name.

Add   Creates a new backup of the configuration information on the server. You can specify the name of the backup or AppCmd will generate one for you automatically. The default backup name is a series of numbers and letters like this: 20070604T123641. The name includes the year, month, day, hour, minute, and second of the backup. Consequently, the backup name is unique and relatively easy to identify once you know the secret code.

Delete   Removes a configuration backup from the list. You must specify the name of the backup you want to remove. AppCmd only lets you remove one backup at a time.

Restore   Restores the server configuration using the information found in a backup. You must provide the name of a backup to use. Make sure you actually want to restore the entire Web server. If you want to restore just part of the Web server, you could also use the other objects described in this chapter to perform a partial restore.

Using the *TRACE* Object

The TRACE object provides access to the failed request trace logs. These logs help you understand problems with your system. By automating your interactions with the logs at the command line, you can automatically place the data within a database for later analysis. The "Setting Failed Request Tracing Rules" section of Chapter 4 demonstrates the graphical methods for working with failed requests. The TRACE object supports the following commands.

List   Provides a list of all of the trace files on the server. You can filter the trace files by name. It's also possible to use the following command line arguments to filter the output.

/site.name:*Identifier*   Specifies the name of the Web site you want to search for, such as "Default Web Site".

/wp.name:*Identifier*   Specifies the PID for the worker process you want to locate.

/verb:*VerbName*   Specifies the verb that you want to search for, such as GET.

/statuscode:*Code*   Specifies the status code that you want to locate, such as 500.

Configure Enables, disables, or configures a failed request event trace. You can use any of the following command line switches to perform the configuration.

Identifier Specifies the configuration path or URL to use for tracing. If you don't provide an identifier, AppCmd defaults to working with tracing for the entire server.

/enablesite Enables failed request event buffering for the Web site that you specify with the identifier. If you don't provide an identifier, AppCmd defaults to enabling tracing for the entire server.

/disablesite Disables failed request event buffering for the Web site that you specify with the identifier. If you don't provide an identifier, AppCmd defaults to disabling tracing for the entire server.

/enable Enables a failed request event buffering rule based on the value of the /path command line argument. When you don't specify a /path command line argument, AppCmd uses * (all paths) as the basis for the new rule. You must enable tracing before you can use this command line argument using the /enablesite command line argument.

/disable Removes the specified rule based on the value of the /path command line argument. If you don't provide a /path command line argument, AppCmd disables all failed request event buffering. You must enable tracing before you can use this command line argument using the /enablesite command line argument.

/path:Rule Defines the path to use for failed request event buffering. For example, if you supply *.aspx as the path, then the server will track all incoming requests for ASPX files.

/areas:Provider Defines the provider to use to perform the trace. For example, if you use the "WWW Server" provider, the system will track static requests.

/verbosity:Level Specifies the amount of information that IIS 7 should record in the failed request event log.

/timeTaken:Time Determines whether IIS 7 tracks the events based on time. If you supply a value, then IIS will create event entries when a request requires more than the specified time to execute.

/statuscodes:Codes Determines whether IIS 7 tracks the events based on status code. If you supply a value, then IIS will create event entries when a response contains the specified status code. You can separate multiple codes with a comma.

Inspect Lets you see the content of a particular trace log. You must supply the name of the event log to inspect, such as "Default Web Site/fr000001.xml" (you must provide the double quotes when the input argument contains spaces). In addition, you can filter the output using the /name command line switch. For example, if you type **AppCmd Inspect TRACE "Default Web Site/fr000001.xml" /name:MODULE_SET_RESPONSE_ERROR_STATUS** and press Enter, you'll see all of the MODULE_SET_RESPONSE_ERROR_STATUS entries found in the fr000001.xml file for the default Web site.

Let's Start Building

This chapter has provided you with some basic information about working with ASP.NET applications. You might be surprised to discover just how many problems this information will solve. The techniques in this chapter address the most common problems that administrators must solve.

In addition, you now know about a basic administration tool that can save you many hours of work by letting you automate specific tasks. This chapter helps you build these skills:

◆ Create a new application

◆ Manage application configuration

◆ Explore and browse applications

◆ Manage the application session state

◆ Change application settings

◆ Manage the application's worker processes

◆ Use the AppCmd utility

You won't really know how to use the new techniques until you try them out. If you have a test server available, install an ASP.NET application on it. Test the application to make sure it works. Now, create a second Web site and copy the application to that second site. Use the techniques found in this chapter to configure the second application and test it to determine whether it also runs. Only by practicing these skills can you hope to become proficient in using them.

It's also important to learn how to work with the AppCmd utility—a surprisingly complex offering that provides great access to IIS 7 settings. Try some simple settings first. Make the required changes at the command line and then look for the results in the GUI. After you've worked with AppCmd for a while, try creating some batch files for automating tasks you perform all the time. You'll be surprised at just how much time a simple batch file can save in administering a server.

Chapter 9 considers ASP.NET security. Unlike other applications described so far in this book, ASP.NET provides a flexible and very detailed set of security settings that you can use to meet most threats today. Not only can you set Windows security to protect the files, but you can also configure your applications to consider particular user roles and keep less experienced users out of areas that might prove unsafe for them. In addition, you can also place security restrictions on the code itself, which means that even if the user somehow manages to gain undue access, the code can't perform tasks that you don't want it to perform. In short, this chapter demonstrates why ASP.NET security (correctly applied) might be precisely what you need to overcome threats to your Web site today.

Chapter 9

Understanding the .NET Security Model

Security is perhaps one of the most important topics on the minds of administrators today because the consequences of a break-in are so terrible. For most administrators, keeping the network secure ranks right up there (or perhaps even higher) with keeping the network running. When you work with .NET applications, you really have three layers of security to consider and each level has a specific task to perform when it comes to securing IIS.

The first level of security is Windows. You use Windows security to restrict access based on name and group affiliation, just as you would for an HTML file. In addition, you can perform auditing using Windows security. However, Windows security is a coarse tool—it doesn't let you discriminate levels of access very well. You should consider Windows security as the beginning of the setup, not the end.

The second level of security is to control code access to your system. Windows security focuses on the user, but it's easy to convince the code to perform tasks on the user's behalf. Using code-based security reduces the risk that someone will find a way around the security features you've implemented in your application.

The third level of security is role-based security. A user fulfills a specific role when performing certain tasks. Giving everyone user-level security for most tasks reduces the attack surface of your application—making it considerably harder to mount an attack on your system. You can place a user in a specific role to perform some tasks. For example, the manager role may let the user add new users to the list, but the manager role only becomes active for this one task. Likewise, a user may have a different role when accessing the application from the Internet than using the company intranet. While Windows security creates the overall level of access, role-based security further reduces access to what the user requires at given time.

This chapter also discusses a number of security utilities. The most important of these utilities is the Microsoft .NET Framework 2.0 Configuration Console. You use this console to tell the .NET Framework about the code running in IIS. This console, combined with the settings in IIS itself, determines how users interact with an application from a security perspective.

In this chapter, you will learn how to do the following:

◆ Understand and manage operating system security

◆ Understand and manage role-based security

◆ Understand and manage code-based security

◆ Use the Microsoft .NET Framework 2.0 Configuration Console to configure security

Considering Operating System Security

Windows security is vast and performs many functions within the operating system and the applications it supports. As an administrator, you have to have a good idea of how this security works (which is the purpose of this chapter), but you don't actually need to worry about the low-level details of function calls. Developers spend untold time trying to figure out the Windows 32-bit Application Programming Interface (Win32 API) with its myriad confusing calls. Even though you don't need to worry about the function calls, you at least need to know how security is organized to administer it properly, which is why this portion of the chapter delves into details at a relatively low level.

NOTE   It's important to know that developers don't rely on just one application programming interface (API) to create secure applications. You may actually have several layers of Windows-type security APIs to consider. One security API to consider relies on biometrics, the use of human body parts such as the iris and fingerprints for identification purposes. The Biometrics API (BAPI) helps programmers embed biometric technology into applications. A consortium of vendors including IBM, Compaq, IO Software, Microsoft, Sony, Toshiba, and Novell originated BAPI. Learn more about BAPI at the IO Software Web Site (http://www.iosoftware.com/pages/Products/Biometric%20API/index.asp). You can also find a biometrics standards Web site at the Biometrics Consortium Web site (http://www.biometrics.org/).

This portion of the chapter also examines two editors that Windows supplies for modifying security on your system. You already know about the Access Control Editor because you saw it discussed in the "Considering Security Issues" section of Chapter 4 (most administrators don't even know that this editor has a particular name). The Security Configuration Editor performs additional setup. It sets the policies for either a local or group setting. You can create INF files that contain the security settings you use and then import them using the Local Security Policy console found in the Administrative Tools folder of the Control Panel or using the SecEdit utility.

A Detailed View of Windows Security

The theory behind Windows security is simple. Every object has a lock and every object requestor has a key. If the requestor's key fits the lock, then the requestor gains access to the object and the resources it provides. This is token-based security. The user's token is their key to resources on the local machine, the network and intranet, and even the Internet.

It's important to understand that the user's access is limited to the combination of group and individual rights that the administrator assigns. However, most of the configuration options available to the administrator affect Windows as a whole. The "Modifying Application Settings" section of Chapter 8 describes how the administrator and developer can work together to configure the application. One of the configuration choices available to the administrator and developer is the use of Windows security to control access at a significantly improved level of detail. A developer can write code that sets Windows security for particular objects, calls, and portions of an application. When the developer couples this level of security with application settings, the administrator can achieve better security without losing any flexibility.

User-level access depends on a security ID (SID). When the user first logs into the system, Windows assigns an access token to the user and places the user's SID (stored on the domain controller or other security database) within it. The user object carries both the access token and the SID around for the duration of the session. An access token also contains both a Discretionary Access Control List (DACL) and a Security Access Control List (SACL). The combination of Access Control

Lists (ACLs) and SID within the access token is a key that allows the user access to certain system resources. Because this access lasts the entire session, the user must log out and then back into the system whenever the administrator makes a change to security; otherwise, the user won't gain additional rights that the administrator provides.

A key is no good without a lock to open. The lock placed on Windows resources is called a security descriptor. In essence, a security descriptor tells what rights the user needs to access the resource. If the rights within the ACLs meet or exceed the rights in the security descriptor, then the lock opens and the resource becomes available. Figure 9.1 shows the content of the ACL and the security descriptor used for token-based security. The following sections provide more details about how token-based security actually works, using Figure 9.1 as the point of discussion.

FIGURE 9.1
Token-based security relies on ACLs and security descriptors.

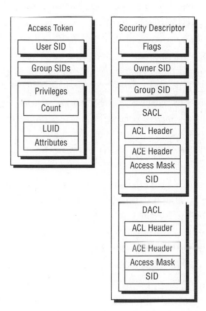

UNDERSTANDING ACCESS TOKENS

There are two ways of looking at a user's rights under Windows: individual rights and group rights. The user's SID is the account number that Windows assigns to the user during login. The access token that holds the SID also contains other structures that identify the groups the user belongs to and what privileges the user has. Each group entry also has an SID. This SID points to other structures that describe the group's rights. To understand the user's rights, you need to know both the user's individual rights and the rights of the groups that the user belongs to. You'd normally use the Local Users and Groups or the Active Directory Users and Computers Microsoft Management Console (MMC) snap-in to change the contents of this access token.

The privileges section of the access token shown in Figure 9.1 begins with a count of the number of privileges that the user has—the number of special privilege entries in the access token. This section also contains an array of privilege entries. Each privilege entry contains a locally unique identifier (LUID)—essentially a pointer to the entry object—and an attribute mask. The attribute mask tells what rights the user has to the object. Group SID entries are essentially the same. They contain a privilege count and an array of privilege entries.

One of the things that you need to know as part of working with some kinds of objects is that object rights flow down to the lowest possible node unless overridden by another SID. For example, if you give the user read and write privileges to the \Temp directory on a hard drive, those rights would also apply to the \Temp\Stuff directory unless you assigned the user specific rights to that directory. The same holds true for containers. Assigning a user rights to a container object like a Word document gives the user the right to look at everything within that container, even other files in most cases. It's important to track a user's exact rights to objects on your server using security surveys, since you could inadvertently give the user more rights than needed to perform a certain task.

UNDERSTANDING SECURITY DESCRIPTORS

At this point, you have a better idea of how the access token (the key) works. It's time to look at the security descriptor (the lock). Figure 9.1 shows that each security descriptor contains five main sections. The following list describes each section.

Header and Flags   The header consists of version information and a list of control flags. The flags tell you the descriptor status. For example, the SE_DACL_PRESENT flag indicates the presence of a DACL. If the DACL is missing, then Windows allows everyone to use the object. The basic security descriptors haven't changed since Windows 2000, so you can see a list of basic security descriptors at http://www.microsoft.com/technet/prodtechnol/windows2000serv/reskit/distrib/ dsce_ctl_qxju.mspx. The overview at http://www.microsoft.com/technet/prodtechnol/ windows2000serv/reskit/distrib/dsce_ctl_ajfg.mspx provides additional information about Windows security flags.

Owner SID   Tells who owns the object. This doesn't have to be an individual user; Windows allows use of a group SID here as well. The limiting factor is the group SID must appear in the token of the person changing the entry. In other words, you can't assign ownership to a group where you don't have membership.

Group SID   Tells which group owns the object. This entry only contains the main group responsible for the object and won't contain a list of all groups with access to the object.

SACL   Controls the Windows' auditing feature. Every time a user or group accesses an object when the auditing feature for that object is on, Windows makes an entry in the audit log. There's more than one entry in this section, in most cases, so Windows stores the information in an array.

DACL   Controls object use. Windows assigns groups and users to a specific object. There's more than one entry in this section, in most cases, so Windows stores the information in an array. A DACL can contain a custom value, a default value, a NULL (empty) value, or not appear in the security descriptor at all (this last option is rare and dangerous). You'll normally find more objects with default values than any other DACL type.

UNDERSTANDING ACLS

As previously mentioned, a security descriptor relies on a SACL and a DACL to control the security of an object. Both elements use the same basic ACL data structure, but for different purposes. An ACL consists of two entry types. The first is a header that lists the number of access control entries (ACEs) in the ACL. Windows uses this number to determine when it's reached the end of the ACE list. (There isn't any of end-of-structure record or other way to determine the size of each ACE in the structure.) The second entry is an array of ACEs.

An ACE defines the object rights for a single user or group. Every ACE has a header that defines the type, size, and flags for the ACE. It includes an access mask that defines rights a user or group has to the object. Finally, there's an entry for the user or group SID.

There are four main ACE header types (you can find the full list of ACE headers at `http://msdn2.microsoft.com/en-us/library/aa374912.aspx`). Windows currently uses three out of the four main ACE header types. The following list tells you about each of the main header types.

General Access   This header type appears in the DACL and grants object rights to a user. Use it to add to the rights a user already has for an object on an instance-by-instance basis. For example, you might want to prevent the user from changing the system time so that you can keep the machines on the network synchronized. However, there might be one situation—such as daylight savings time—when the user would need this right. You could use an access-allowed ACE to allow the user to change the time in this one instance.

Object Access   This header type helps Windows assign specific security to software objects and subobjects. A developer must provide special code to provide this access. For example, the developer could use this type of ACE to assign security to the property of a COM object. To use this type of ACE, the developer needs to obtain or create a globally unique identifier (GUID) for the object in question. Once the developer adds the required code, application settings could allow the administrator to control access to particular application features at runtime.

System Audit   This ACE header type works with the SACL. It defines which events to audit for a particular user or group. There are system audit header types for both general and object use. The .NET Framework doesn't provide a specific auditing feature, so you can use this feature when you want to know who's accessing a particular Web site feature and when they access it. This feature requires that the user log onto the system. Yes, it does work with anonymous access, but all you'll see is the anonymous user information.

System Alarm   This is the currently unused ACE type. It enables either the SACL or DACL to set an alarm when specific events happen.

THE IMPORTANCE OF ORDER FOR SECURITY

Once you know how Windows evaluates the ACEs in the DACL, you'll discover a few problem areas—problems that the Windows utilities address automatically. Order is an important consideration when working with Windows security because Windows uses a very basic method for determining how to evaluate the security elements.

Windows evaluates the ACEs in an ACL in the order in which they appear. At first, this might not seem like a very big deal. However, it could become a problem in some situations. For example, what if you want to revoke all of a user's rights in one area, but the user's list of ACEs includes membership in a group that allows access to that area? If an application places the access-allowed ACE before the access-denied ACE in the list, the user would get access to the area.

A developer who doesn't completely understand Windows security could place the ACEs in the wrong order and accidentally give the user more or less access than desired. The Windows utilities will normally point out these problems for system objects such as folders and files, but not for application objects, methods, properties, and events, so security issues can crop up. That's the reason you want to rely on code-based security whenever possible so CLR addresses these issues automatically. The SACL has the same problem, but it only affects auditing, so the effect is less severe from the system security standpoint.

The developer must also exercise care in the ordering of group SIDs. Rights that a user acquires from different groups are cumulative. This means a user who belongs to two groups, one that has access to a file and another that doesn't, will have access to the file if the group granting the right appears first on the list. In addition, if one ACE grants read rights and another write rights to a file, and the user is asking for read and write rights, Windows will grant the request.

Fortunately, developers seldom need to work with Windows at such a low level and they can rely on .NET Framework features to control many forms of access. As an administrator, you'll never have to worry about the order of the ACEs because applications decide that order at a low level. When you use the Windows utilities described in this chapter, you know that the order is correct. The only potential for problems occurs when a developer creates the ACEs in the wrong order and checking for these security issues should be part of your custom application testing.

Using the Access Control Editor

The process for using the Access Control Editor appears in the "Considering Security Issues" section of Chapter 4. The process involves locating a folder, file, or other system object you want to secure and then modifying the DACL using the Access Control Editor. The fact that this process is so common means that few administrators really know what they're doing, but now that you've read to this point in the chapter, you understand how changing the DACL for a particular object changes access to that object. You've probably used the Access Control Editor for a long time and you never even knew what to call it.

Using Windows security helps you set the baseline security for your ASP.NET application. This level of security provides control by user and group. However, this tool can also help you monitor what happens when the application makes changes to the DACL based on requirements that you set. You can use this operating system feature to verify changes made by the sample applications. Security is one of those difficult changes to verify unless the developer wants to build multiple test applications. The Access Control Editor is one of many tools that can help you check the output of any custom application. This particular tool is one of the easiest to use and the most reliable. In general, you'll want to use this tool before you use anything else.

It's also easy to use the Access Control Editor to set up test cases for custom applications when you suspect an error in the code. Developers usually need to know as much as possible about a security error to find it, so setting up test cases helps you describe the error in detail. For example, you might want to ensure that the custom application detects certain types of security changes. (This behavior often occurs when a virus is at work, so the ability of a custom application to detect odd changes is important.) The Access Control Editor enables you to make changes on a test object quickly. You can then test the custom application to see how the change affects its operation. Generally, the custom application needs to detect changes within certain ranges of approved behavior. For example, an application would want to detect files that have security turned off if the information they contain is sensitive.

Using the Security Configuration Editor

The Microsoft Security Configuration Editor is an administration tool that reduces both security management and analysis time. Initially you'll use this tool to configure the operating system security parameters. Once these parameters are in place, you can use the Security Configuration Editor to schedule periodic tests.

The overall goal of the Security Configuration Editor is to provide a single place to manage all of the security concerns for a network. However, it doesn't actually replace all the tools you used in the past—the Security Configuration Editor augments other security tools. The Security Configuration Editor also provides auditing tools that Windows has lacked in the past.

One of the unique ideas behind the Security Configuration Editor is that it's a macro-based tool. You'll create a set of instructions for the Security Configuration Editor to perform, and then allow it to perform those instructions in the background. Obviously, this saves a lot of time since you don't have to wait for one set of instructions to complete before going to the next set. You can also group tasks, which saves input time.

CONFIGURING THE SECURITY CONFIGURATION EDITOR

The Security Configuration Editor doesn't appear in the Administrative Tools folder of the Control Panel; you must configure it manually. The following steps tell you have to create the Security Configuration Editor and store it in the Administrative Tools folder. This procedure assumes that you have administrator level privileges, because the tool won't work under Vista or Windows Server 2008 unless you have the proper rights. In addition, you must open the utilities correctly or the resulting console will fail to work as anticipated.

1. Right-click the `MMC.EXE` file located in the `\Windows\System32` folder of your hard drive and choose Run As Administrator from the context menu. You'll see a blank Microsoft Management Console (MMC) window. This window acts as a host for snap-ins that you choose and is the basis for all of the consoles found in the Administrative Tools folder of the Control Panel.

2. Choose File ➤ Add/Remove Snap-in. You'll see the Add or Remove Snap-ins dialog box shown in Figure 9.2.

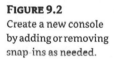

FIGURE 9.2
Create a new console by adding or removing snap-ins as needed.

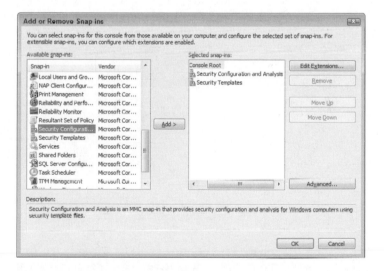

3. Highlight the Security Configuration and Analysis snap-in and click Add. Perform the same task with the Security Templates snap-in. Your display should now look like the one shown in Figure 9.2.

4. Click OK. MMC adds the snap-ins to the console. The snap-ins are ready for use, but they aren't actually configured yet. You need to perform some additional tasks to use them. These tasks appear in the sections that follow this one.

5. Choose File ➢ Save. You'll see a Save As dialog box.

6. Type **Security Configuration Editor.MSC** in the File Name field. Click Save. MMC creates a new entry for the Security Configuration Editor in the Administrative Tools folder of the Control Panel. (The actual name will appear as `Security Configuration Editor.msc` in the Administrative Tools folder—right-click the entry and choose Rename from the context menu to rename the entry to Security Configuration Editor.)

DEFINING A SECURITY SETUP

Creating a security setup begins when you choose an existing template or create a new one using the Security Templates MMC snap-in. You can find sample templates in the `\Windows\security\templates` folder of your hard drive. To add the template to the list, right-click the Security Templates entry and choose New Template Search Path from the context menu. Locate the folder that contains the templates in the Browse For Folder dialog box and click OK to add it. If you want to use an existing template as a basis for creating a new one, you can right-click on the desired template and use the Save As command found on the context menu. Microsoft supplies a variety of templates designed to get you started in creating this security database, as shown in Figure 9.3. (Vista doesn't ship with any templates, unlike Windows XP, which does provide a number of templates by default.) If you don't see a template you want to use, then you should try downloading one of the Microsoft security guides such as:

Windows 2003 Server Security Guide `http://www.microsoft.com/downloads/details.aspx?FamilyId=8A2643C1-0685-4D89-B655-521EA6C7B4DB`

Windows Vista Security Guide `http://www.microsoft.com/downloads/details.aspx?FamilyId=A3D1BBED-7F35-4E72-BFB5-B84A526C1565`

FIGURE 9.3
The Security Configuration Editor provides a number of standard templates for creating your security setup.

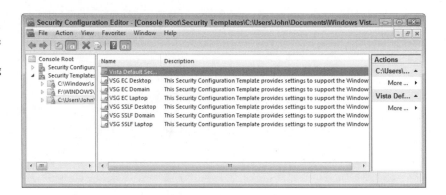

TIP You can use any existing template for Windows 2000 and above as a basis for creating your own template. In fact, many of these templates appear online. For example, the Department of Energy's (DOE) Computer Incident Advisory Capability (CIAC) Web site provides a template you can use as a starting point for checking the security of a system at `http://www.ciac.org/ciac/documents/CIACTemplates/CIACwk.inf`. Check for additional templates at `http://www.ciac.org/cgi-bin/webglimpse/www/htdocs/ciac/archive?query=Template`.

Each of the security templates serves a different purpose as indicated by the name and description. This section relies on the Vista Security Guide Enterprise Configuration for Desktops template

(VSG EC Desktop), but all of the other templates work about the same as this one. All of the templates contain the same basic elements shown in Figure 9.4. The following list describes each of these elements for you.

FIGURE 9.4
Each of the security templates contains the same security elements.

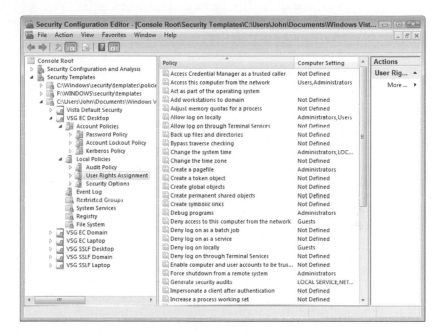

Account Policies   Defines the password, account lockout, and Kerberos policies for the machine. Password policies include items like the minimum password length and the maximum time the user can use a single password. The account lockout policy includes the number of times a user can enter the wrong password without initiating a system lockout. Kerberos policies feature elements like the maximum user ticket lifetime.

Local Policies   Defines the audit policy, user rights assignment, and security options. Audit policies determine the types of data you collect. For example, you could audit each failed user logon attempt. User rights assignments are of special interest since this policy affects the rights you can assign to a user (the access token). The security options policy contains the elements that determine how the security system will react given a set of circumstances. For example, one policy will log off a user when their usage hours expire.

Event Log   Defines how the event log stores data and for how long. These policies also determine maximum event log size and event log viewing rights.

Restricted Groups   Defines groups that can't access the workstation or server at all, or restricts the amount of access they can obtain.

System Services   Displays a list of the system services on the target machine. Double-clicking a service displays a dialog that allows you to set the policy for that service and allows you to adjust the startup mode for the service. Normally, you'll leave the icons in this policy alone. However, you can safely change any system service DLLs you create.

Registry   Contains all of the major registry hives. Double-clicking a branch displays a dialog you use to set the security for that branch. In addition, you can choose the method of security inheritance by children of this branch.

File System   Contains protected file system entries. You can add new files to the list or modify existing entries. Double-clicking a file system entry displays a dialog you use to set the security level for that file system member. In addition, you can choose the method of security inheritance by children of this file system entity (applies only to folders).

Active Directory Objects   This entry is only available if you have Active Directory enabled (which means you must have a domain controller set up). It allows you to edit the security settings for any Active Directory objects, including users and groups.

CREATING A SECURITY DATABASE AND USING IT

The templates that Microsoft provides are a good starting point, but you'll want to customize them for your particular needs. Simply go through the list of objects and define policies as you would using the Local Security Policy or Group Policy Object Editor (GPEdit.MSC) consoles. After you perform this task, save the template to disk by right-clicking it and choosing Save As from the context menu.

The templates don't do much good until you implement them. To create a new implementation, you must create a new database. The following steps tell how to perform this process.

1. Right-click the Security Configuration and Analysis snap-in entry and choose Open Database from the context menu. You'll see an Open Database dialog box. It's impossible to open a database that's currently in use, such as the SecEdit.SDB file located in the \Windows\security\database folder, but you can create a new database.

2. Locate the folder you want to use to store the database. Type the name of a database you want to create in the File Name field and click Open. You'll see an Import Template dialog box.

3. Locate the folder that contains the template you created. Highlight the template you want to use and click Open. The Security Configuration Editor will create the new database for you.

At this point, you can perform a number of tasks using the new security database. One of those tasks is to check the server for potential security problems as defined by the template you loaded. To perform this task, right-click the Security Configuration and Analysis entry and choose Analyze Computer Now from the context menu. You'll see a Perform Analysis dialog box. Type the name and location of a log file in the Error Log File Path field and click OK. You'll see an Analyzing System Security dialog box. When the dialog box closes, you can compare the template settings to the computer settings, as shown in Figure 9.5.

You can also use the database to configure the computer. This feature makes it possible to fix major security issues very quickly. Consequently, even if IIS or the server as a whole fails to meet security requirements, you can quickly reconfigure the computer so it does pass. The other options let you import and export templates, and view the error log when necessary. Overall, this tool provides a very fast method of checking IIS for security issues without a lot of work on your part once you set the required security policies. The odd thing is that Microsoft hides the tool from view.

FIGURE 9.5

Analysis helps you understand where the security of a particular system is weak.

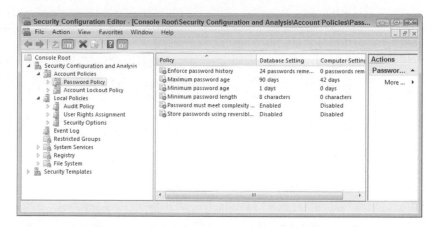

Configuring Local Security Policies with the SecEdit Utility

The Security Configuration Editor is a great tool to use when you need to create a security database or set up a new template. It's not a bad tool to use when you need to check system security. However, most administrators are going to need to automate the security analysis process, which means working at the command line. The Security Edit (SecEdit) utility helps you analyze and manage security policies on your system using the same techniques as the Security Configuration Editor. This utility uses the following syntax:

```
secedit /analyze /db FileName [/cfg FileName] [/overwrite]
[/log FileName] [/quiet]
secedit /configure /db FileName [/cfg FileName ] [/overwrite]
[/areas Area1 Area2 ...] [/log FileName] [/quiet]
secedit /export [/db FileName] [/cfg FileName]
[/mergedpolicy] [/areasArea1 Area2 ...] [/log FileName] [/quiet]
secedit /import /db FileName.sdb /cfg FileName [/overwrite]
[/areas Area1 Area2 ...] [/log FileName] [/quiet]
secedit /validate FileName
secedit /GenerateRollback /CFG FileName /RBK SecurityTemplatefilename
  [/log FileName] [/quiet]
```

The following list describes each of the command line arguments.

/analyze   Performs an analysis of the security policy on a system by comparing it to the settings in a database.

/db FileName   Specifies the database used to perform the analysis, configuration, or other tasks.

/cfg FileName   Specifies a security template to import into the database before the utility performs a task. You can create a security template using the Security Template Microsoft Management Console (MMC) snap-in.

/overwrite   Overwrites any existing database entries before the utility imports the security template. Otherwise, the utility adds the settings in the security template to the existing database.

/log *FileName*   Specifies the file to use for logging purposes. The log receives the status of the configuration process. If you don't specify this command line switch, the utility uses the SCESrv.LOG file located in the \WINDOWS\security\logs folder.

/quiet   Performs the analysis without displaying any comments.

/configure   Performs a security configuration based on the content of the specified security database.

/areas *Area1 Area2 ...*   Specifies the security areas to manage. If you don't include this command line switch, the utility manages all security areas. You can specify multiple areas by separating each area with a space. The following list contains the valid security areas.

> **SECURITYPOLICY**   Defines the user security policy, which includes account policies, audit policies, event log settings, and security options.
>
> **GROUP_MGMT**   Defines the restricted group settings.
>
> **USER_RIGHTS**   Defines the user rights assignments to system objects.
>
> **REGKEYS**   Defines the registry permissions.
>
> **FILESTORE**   Defines the file system permissions.
>
> **SERVICES**   Defines the system service settings.

/export   Exports the security settings to a database file.

/mergedpolicy   Creates a merged database file that includes both local and domain security settings.

/import   Imports the security settings from a database file. You can use a template file to provide overrides for settings in the database.

/validate *FileName*   Validates the contents of a security template. Use this option to reduce syntax-induced errors.

/GenerateRollback   Generates a security rollback based on the content of a security rollback template. The system offers you the opportunity to create a rollback template when you apply a security update to the system. This rollback template will return the system to the state it was in before the security update.

/RBK *SecurityTemplatefilename*   Specifies the name of the file that contains the security rollback template.

Understanding Role-Based Security

When Microsoft started designing .NET, the world of computing was moving from the local area network (LAN) and wide area network (WAN) to the Internet. The individual user and group approach used by Windows didn't necessary reflect the best way to pursue security in a distributed environment. In addition, the current environment was too open to potential attacks from outside.

Microsoft had actually begun working on the whole issue of one-size-fits-all security sometime earlier with COM+. In COM+, an administrator could configure applications to provide specific levels of access based on a user's role. You created roles, assigned users to those roles, and defined the applications and methods that the role could access. Consequently, a manager could have access to methods that a general user didn't. However, the COM+ version of role-based security didn't always work very well with the Internet and it wasn't as flexible as administrators would like. In addition, developers had to use convoluted tactics to make COM+ security work properly.

The following sections describe how .NET role-based security reflects its COM+ heritage and where it differs. More important, the following sections describe how you can work with role-based security to improve the overall security of your system. You'll also learn about some of the tools that Microsoft provides for working with role-based security.

An Overview of .NET Framework Security Features

To overcome the security problems inherent in Windows, Microsoft enhanced the role-based security approach originally found in COM+ to work as a general programming methodology. The managed environment also maintains better control over resources that tend to create problems in the unmanaged Windows environment. These two security changes, along with the object-oriented programming strategy of the .NET Framework, summarize what you'll find as security enhancements in the .NET Framework. Here's a list of the critical security enhancements for the .NET Framework.

Evidence-Based Security   This feature determines what rights to grant to code based on information gathered about it. CLR examines the information it knows about an assembly (.NET executable file) and determines what rights to grant that code based on the evidence. Using the information it has obtained, CLR matches the evidence against a security policy, which is a series of settings that define how the administrator wants to secure a system.

Code Access Security   CLR uses this feature to determine whether all of the assemblies in a calling chain (stack) have rights to use a particular resource or perform a particular task. All of the code in the calling chain must have the required rights. Otherwise, CLR generates a security error that you can use to detect security breaches. The purpose of this check is to ensure that someone can't intercept rights that they don't deserve.

Defined Verification Process   Before the just-in-time (JIT) compiler accepts the Microsoft Intermediate Language (MSIL) assembly, it checks the code the assembly contains for type safety and other errors. This verification process ensures that the code doesn't include any fatal flaws that would keep it from running. The checks also determine whether an external force has modified strongly named code. After JIT performs these checks, it compiles the MSIL into native code. CLR can run a verified assembly in isolation so that it doesn't affect any other assembly (and, more important, other assemblies can't affect it).

Role-Based Security   If you know how role-based security works in COM+, you have a good idea of how it works in .NET. Instead of assigning security to individuals or groups, you assign it based on the role that an individual or group will perform. The Windows SID security is limited in that you can control entire files, but not parts of those files. Role-based security still relies on identifying the user through a logon or other means. The main advantage is that you can ask the security system about the user's role and allow access to program features based on that role. An administrator will likely have access to all of the features of a program, but individual users may only have access to a subset of the features.

Cryptography   The advantages of cryptography are many. The concept is simple—you make data unreadable by using an algorithm, coupled with a key, to mix up the information. When the originator supplies the correct key to another algorithm, the original data is returned. Over the years, the power of computers has increased, making old cryptology techniques suspect. The .NET Framework supports the latest cryptographic techniques, which ensures your data remains safe.

Separate Application Domains   You can write .NET code in such a way that some of the pieces run in a separate domain. It's a COM-type concept where the code is isolated from the other code in your program. Many developers use this feature to load special code, run it, and then unload that code without stopping the program. For example, a browser could use this technique to load and unload plug-ins. This feature also works well for security. It helps you run code at different security levels in separate domains to ensure true isolation.

Defining Membership and Evidence

For many people, the word *evidence* brings up the vision of a court with judge and jury. The term is quite appropriate for the .NET Framework because any code that wants to execute must present its case before CLR and deliver evidence to validate any requests. CLR makes a decision about the code based on the evidence and decides how the evidence fits within the current policies (laws) of the runtime as set by the network administrator. Theoretically, controlling security with evidence as CLR allows applications built on the .NET Framework to transcend limitations of the underlying operating system. Largely, this view is true. However, remember that CLR is running on top of the underlying operating system and is therefore subject to its limitations. Here's the typical evidence-based sequence of events.

1. The assembly demands access to data, resources, or other protected elements.

2. CLR requests evidence of the assembly's origins and security documents (such as a digital signature).

3. After receiving the evidence from the assembly, CLR runs the evidence through a security policy.

4. The security policy outputs a permission based on the evidence and the network administrator settings.

5. The code gains some level of access to the protected element if the evidence supports such access; otherwise, CLR denies the request.

Note that the assembly must demand access before any part of the security process occurs. The Win32 API normally verifies and assigns security at the front end of the process—when the program first runs. (A program can request additional rights later or perform other security tasks.) CLR performs verifications as needed to enhance system performance.

CLR defines two kinds of evidence: assembly and host. Any custom evidence resides within the assembly as assembly evidence. CLR also ships with seven common evidence classes that cover most needs. These seven classes provide host evidence because Microsoft implemented them as part of the host (CLR).

◆ `ApplicationDirectory`

◆ `Hash`

◆ `Publisher`

◆ `Site`

◆ `StrongName`

◆ `URL`

◆ `Zone`

The `ApplicationDirectory`, `Site`, `URL`, and `Zone` classes show where the code came from. The `Publisher` and `StrongName` classes tell who wrote the code. Finally, the `Hash` class defines a special number that identifies the assembly as a unique entity—it shows whether someone has tampered with the content of the assembly.

Understanding Permissions

So far, you've learned about the kinds of security you can use, how the system uses evidence, and how to determine membership in a particular code group. All of these facts help you understand how security works, but your application still doesn't have permission to perform any tasks. When CLR loads an assembly, the assembly lacks any rights—it can't even execute code. Consequently, the first task CLR must perform with the assembly is to use the evidence and the code group memberships to determine what permissions the assembly has. To perform this task, CLR must run the evidence through the policies set up by the network administrator.

The developer and the administrator must work together to assign permissions to an application. The developer begins by declaring security requirements for the application within the code. These declarations tell the administrator what the application must have in order to run. For example, the application may require access to a particular folder on the hard drive to use for data storage. In addition, the application user must also have access to this directory so the application and the user can perform required tasks. Declarations in the application code make this requirement known to the administrator.

Meanwhile, the administrator must also configure the application to respect certain policies. For example, the administrator may give permission to use a particular subdirectory, but not the parent directory that contains it in order to promote separation of applications running on the server. The network administrator sets these policies using the Microsoft .NET Framework 2.0 Configuration console described in the "Using the Microsoft .NET Framework 2.0 Configuration Console" section of the chapter. It's possible to view the existing set of permissions using the Permissions Calculator utility (`PermCalc.EXE`) described in the "Using the Permissions Calculator Utility" section of the chapter. Earlier versions of the .NET Framework relied on the Permissions View utility (`PermView.EXE`), which works almost exactly the same as the Permissions Calculator utility, except that it has fewer command line options. If you'd like to get the developer eye view of permissions, the excellent short article at `http://www.codeproject.com/useritems/Permviewexe.asp` provides a good start.

Using the Permissions Calculator Utility

Configuring the environment to support an assembly properly is just fine if you know what the assembly needs. However, you may never meet the developer who created your application. This lack of communication can cause problems because the network administrator might not have any clue as to what the program needs. (This is another good reason to declare security requirements in your code.) Fortunately, the Permissions Calculator utility can help.

Unlike many of the .NET utilities described in this book, the Permissions Calculator utility doesn't come with the .NET Framework itself. Instead, this tool comes with the .NET Framework 2.0 Software Development Kit that you download from `http://www.microsoft.com/downloads/details.aspx?FamilyID=fe6f2099-b7b4-4f47-a244-c96d69c35dec`. After you download and install the SDK, you'll find this tool in the `\Program Files\Microsoft Visual Studio 8\SDK\v2.0\Bin` folder of your hard drive.

The Permissions Calculator looks inside the assembly for special entries the developer has made. Depending on the command line switches you choose, it displays output information about the assemblies that the assembly requires to execute, writes the security information to an XML file, and displays that XML file on screen. You can also choose how the Permissions Calculator interprets entries within the assembly. This utility uses the following syntax:

```
PermCalc [Options] <assembly> [<assembly> ...]
```

The following list describes each of the command line arguments.

-CleanCache   Forces the utility to reconstruct all of the cache files from scratch. It's important to clean out the cache to ensure that you get a correct reading of the security requirements for an assembly. In addition, you always want to clear the cache after the developer has made changes to the assembly. Otherwise, the output could reflect the prior version's requirements, rather than the current requirements.

-HostProtection   Displays information about the Host Protection Attributes (HPA)–protected categories within the assembly. When the assembly doesn't contain any HPA-protected categories, the command line displays an error message, "An error has occurred: Object reference not set to an instance of an object." The HPA-protected categories include a number of special programming constructs such as shared state information (where the assembly uses static variables that don't change state between calls), synchronization (where two or more threads within the assembly must run in a synchronized state), and external process management (where the assembly provides a means to control the host process externally). The HPA-protected categories have a definite impact on other Microsoft products such as SQL Server, so you need to know whether an assembly supports them. You can discover more about this feature by reading about the `System`
`.Security.Permissions.HostProtectionAttribute` class at `http://msdn2.microsoft.com/`
`en-us/library/system.security.permissions.hostprotectionattribute.aspx`.

-Internet   Sometimes the developer won't provide precise permission values. This command line switch attempts to make up for the lack of security information by interpreting assembly requirements using the Internet zone as an estimate. The default overestimates assembly requirements by using an unrestricted permission state (which could give an IIS application too many rights).

-Out *Filename*   Specifies the name of the file to use for output purposes. The default filename combines the assembly name, PermCalc, and the XML file extension such as `Declarative.exe`
`.PermCalc.xml`.

-Sandbox   Reports the minimum set of permission that will allow the application to run, rather than the permissions specified by the assembly itself. The result of this report is a listing of minimum requirements that provide maximum security, but could result in an assembly that won't work due to lack of resources. Generating this report is helpful when you want to understand the difference between what the assembly requests and what CLR thinks the assembly needs.

-Show   Displays the PermCalc XML file output in a browser when the utility completes the analysis.

-Stacks   Displays the call stack for the assembly and shows the permissions for each level of the call stack. A call stack is a listing of the series of calls that an assembly makes. For example, when an assembly needs code in another assembly, it calls a method within that assembly, which creates two levels in the call stack—the original assembly and the method it calls. Call stacks can become quite complex, but displaying the call stack information can tell you precisely where a particular security requirement occurs and allows you to precisely tune the security requirements for an application.

-Under   Sometimes the developer won't provide precise permission values. This command line switch attempts to make up for the lack of security information by underestimating requirement permissions (using a very restricted review of required rights). The default overestimates assembly requirements by using an unrestricted permission state (which could give an IIS application too many rights). The assembly may not run when you configure security based on the output of this command line switch. When working with IIS, it's far better to use the `-Internet` command line switch to estimate required rights when the developer doesn't provide enough information within the assembly.

-Assembly Displays the assembly-level permission requests using a number of permission sets including minimum, optional, and refused. As an administrator, you'll always include this command line switch because you can't truly discover the IIS security requirements for an assembly without it.

You can use the Permissions Calculator utility in several ways. Always include the -Assembly command line switch to obtain a complete view of the assembly requirements. It's important to include the -Show command line switch when you want to view the results of an analysis immediately (the utility always outputs the results to a file). Make sure you also clean the cache whenever there's a concern about contamination from a previous version of the same assembly. Given these minimum requirements, type **PermCalc -Show -CleanCache -Assembly -Internet** *Filename* at the command prompt to detect the assembly level security information. Figure 9.6 shows the assembly level output for the example in this section.

FIGURE 9.6

Add assembly level information to your application for general security needs.

The command contains a plain-text header, followed by XML entries for each security requirement. Notice that the Permission View Tool outputs three sections of information.

Minimum Permission Set Contains the minimum rights the program can accept for normal execution. The program must have these to do anything at all, even if it's at a reduced operating level.

Optional Permission Set Defines the rights the program would like to have, but doesn't necessarily need. Your program may need these rights to perform ancillary or enhanced functionality tasks.

Refused Permission Set Includes all of the permissions that the operating system could bestow on the program, but you don't want the program to have. For example, you might not want the program to have the right to skip verification or allow the user to access the program from the Internet.

NOTE Working with IIS 7 means that you must know a little about XML. This chapter assumes that you already know about XML. However, you can find an excellent XML tutorial on the W3Schools Web site at `http://www.w3schools.com/xml/default.asp`. Another tutorial appears on the ZVON Web site at `http://www.zvon.org/xxl/XMLTutorial/General/book_en.html`.

As you can see, the output can be a little difficult to read. In this case, the minimal permission set contains a `<PermissionSet>` element. Within that `<PermissionSet>` entry is a single permission (`<IPermission>`) element. This permission is based on the `System.Security.Permissions.SecurityPermission` class and it requests that the assembly be granted permission to execute (as specified by the `Flags` element). So, in order for this assembly to do anything, you must grant it permission to execute, which seems pretty minimal. The optional permission set doesn't contain any entries, but the refused permission set does. In this case, the assembly has refused to allow CLR to skip the verification process. You don't have to do anything about a refused right, CLR takes care of it automatically for you. However, because CLR must verify the assembly every time it runs, the assembly will require more time to load and execute. The benefit of verification is that CLR instantly notices any tampering and you receive an alert the second it happens.

Because the command line contains the `-Show` command line switch, you'll also see a browser display like the one shown in Figure 9.7 that describes the assembly in detail. Again, this is an XML file that's hard to read in some cases, but not if you know what to look for. The XML file contains two sections. The `<Demand>` section tells you about specifics that the developer has identified within the file. You always accommodate these requirements to make the application run. The `<Sandbox>` section tells you about the CLR mandated requirements for the assembly. The developer didn't specify these requirements, but CLR has determined that you should meet them anyway to ensure the assembly can run.

FIGURE 9.7

Make sure you understand all the assembly requirements as specified by the developer.

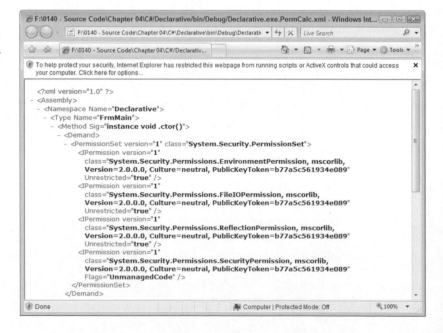

As with the command line output, you'll see a `<PermissionSet>` element that contains one or more `<IPermission>` elements. The `<IPermission>` element class tells you about the request. For example, the `System.Security.Permissions.EnvironmentPermission` class tells you that the assembly requires access to environmental variables, while the `System.Security.Permissions` `.FileIOPermission` class tells you that the assembly will work with files. This second class can prove problematic when you don't specify the `-Stacks` command line switch. When you use the `-Stacks` command line switch, you can determine that the assembly actually requires access to the `C:\` folder as shown here:

```
<IPermission version="1" Append="C:\" Read="C:\"
  class="System.Security.Permissions.FileIOPermission, mscorlib,
  Version=2.0.0.0, Culture=neutral, PublicKeyToken=b77a5c561934e089"
  Write="C:\" PathDiscovery="C:\" />
```

The details provided by the `-Stacks` command line switch tell you that the assembly requires `Append`, `Read`, `Write`, and `PathDiscovery` rights to the `C:\` folder. You may choose to grant or deny access to precisely that folder and no other folder given the information in the output. If you deny access, the assembly won't work as expected and could fail completely. When you grant access to just the location that the assembly requires, you reduce potential security problems because the assembly has such strict restrictions placed on it.

Understanding Principal and Identity Objects

Much of the conversation in this chapter has dealt with the code calling a method. Code access security is the main component you'll use to ensure the safety of the applications in a distributed environment. In addition, you'll use role-based security to ensure the caller has the proper credentials. Principal and identity objects generally relate to users or at least a caller of some type. You'll find the essentials for these two categories of objects in the `System.Security.Principal` namespace.

An *identity* object represents the user. It includes the user's name, credentials, and other personal information that belongs to the user. On the other hand, a *principal* object is the security context in which the user is operating. The security context varies by location, application, and other criteria. The combination of identity and principal objects determines the user's rights to use resources and request services.

Fortunately, you can use the principal and identity objects for more than checking the user's identity and verifying they're in a specific role. For example, using a simple login mechanism is great when a system setup confines the user to their local machine. It begins to break down a little as the user moves on to the LAN. When you get to a fully distributed environment where the user could be anyone with the right password, the whole idea of validating a user with a password alone seems absurd.

Principal and identity objects help you maintain a secure environment in a distributed application. The developer can add code to an application that demands certain credentials for an application to accept a request. For example, the developer can add code for a link demand that has a strong name identity permission requirement. This requirement is a special kind of security key that someone would have a very hard time guessing. It's a numeric password of a sort, but a numeric password that the user doesn't supply—instead, the code making the call supplies the password. Consequently, the link secures itself by supplying a special password that only the link knows. The developer can include other kinds of security checks within the code to make it very hard for anyone to do anything even if they gain access to the application.

The permissions can have other ramifications too. For example, your Web site downloads a component to the user machine and the machine executes that component to perform certain tasks. In times past, someone could attempt a remote execution scheme of virus-laden code to circumvent any protections that the component might contain. Working with principal and identity objects, the developer can create the component in a way that it only executes locally or only executes remotely. This kind of protection is called a zone identity permission.

UNDERSTANDING ZONES

The zone from which code loads determines a basic level of security. For example, code contained on your local machine is generally safer than code downloaded from the Internet. Knowing the original location of code can help you determine its trustworthiness. By default, CLR defines five different zones (most of which look familiar to anyone who uses Internet Explorer).

◆ MyComputer

◆ Intranet

◆ Trusted

◆ Internet

◆ Untrusted

◆ NoZone

Anything that resides on the local machine is in the MyComputer zone. The Intranet zone includes any code downloaded using a UNC location such as \\ServerName\Drive\Folder\Filename.TXT. CLR also uses the Intranet zone for code downloaded from a Windows Internet Name Service (WINS) site, rather than a standard IP site, such as a local Web server. Anything outside of these two zones is in the Internet zone. Initially, the Trusted and Untrusted zones are empty. However, the network administrator can place sites that are normally in the Internet zone into either the Trusted zone (to raise its confidence level) or the Untrusted zone (to lower its confidence level). The NoZone zone is a temporary indicator for items that CLR has yet to test. You should never see this zone in use.

Understanding Code-Based Security

As previously mentioned, code-based security works with the code, rather than the user. You use code-based security to ensure that the code can't perform any tasks that you wouldn't normally allow the user to perform and that the code shouldn't perform on the user's behalf. For example, you probably won't want anonymous users to access the company database to obtain a list of products. However, you can allow the code to perform that task on the user's behalf. Reading the database shouldn't pose a problem. Writing to the database could present a problem, however, so you'd use code-based security to ensure that the code can read the database on the user's behalf, but not write to it. The use of code-based security is important because it restricts applications from performing tasks incorrectly, even when someone tries to use an application flaw to force the code to perform the task.

Why Use Code-Based Security?

Before you proceed any further, it's important to realize that the .NET programs you use always include both code access and role-based security. Even if the developer doesn't include a single line of security code in the program, .NET provides default levels of security for the application. Therefore, the advantage in asking the developer to add security code to the application isn't one of adding security—it's already there. The real advantage is controlling security, which is what everyone should be worrying about now.

You probably have a good understanding of user issues, but code access security can present a problem because no one has had to work with it in the past. At one time, every piece of code you ran on a computer came from one source. There was no need to worry about online connections, email, and nefarious individuals knocking on your firewall door. Today, users face a deluge of code from myriad sources. Sometimes the code enters a system without anyone knowing. Code can also enter from a welcomed source such as a Web service, and cause considerable damage to your system because someone has compromised the third-party source. In short, code could be trusted at one point, but you don't have that luxury anymore.

Systems are also more complex today. The advances in computer speed and resources have fueled unheard levels of development. This places a burden on you, as an administrator, to protect users of your code. The second reason you want to use code access security is to ensure that no one uses the code incorrectly in the applications you support. Code access security defines how someone can use the code and, more important, what types of tasks they can't use the code to perform. For example, if you decide that your code should never access the hard drive, you can tell .NET that you don't want it to perform that task.

One of the special features that you probably won't see mentioned a lot is that your code can insist that a user have a digital signature. In addition, a vendor can provide a digital signature as evidence for gaining access to specific resources. The application code can actually check for a particular strong name. Although digital signature technology has flaws, it's considered very reliable. Using a digital signature is only an option when the developer adds the correct code to the application, which means the developer has to become proactive.

Another good reason to declare security requirements is error handling. When the developer doesn't define the security requirements for the code, CLR assumes the current environment meets all the code requirements when it runs the application. Unfortunately, the environment varies by user, mode of access, and a number of other characteristics that the developer can't determine when writing the application.

When to Use Code- or Role-Based Security

It's important to consider when you should use a particular mode of security. One of the tendencies that developers have today is to create a secure user environment by restricting user activities to the point where the user can't do much at all. However, by restricting both the user and the code, an application can provide flexibility and secure access. Look at the issue from this perspective. If you know that the developer has signed all of the code on your system, then any unsigned code probably came from a nonsecure source and you shouldn't execute it. This is an oversimplification of the problem, but it often helps to look at issues from this perspective. Because any code you execute can check the security of other .NET code, it becomes possible to maintain good security even when the user downloads a virus from the Internet.

Using the Code Access Security Policy Tool

The Code Access Security Policy (CASPol) tool is a command line utility you can use to add and remove policies from a system, as well as make other adjustments. Normally, you want to use the .NET Framework Configuration tool demonstrated in the "Using the Microsoft .NET Framework 2.0 Configuration Console" section of this chapter to make changes, but this tool can come in quite handy for a number of tasks. Generally, you won't use it directly at the command prompt, but will call on the CASPol tool from a batch file or a program to perform specific types of tasks automatically. The following sections describe CASPol and provide a few basic usage techniques.

USING CASPOL

The Code Access Security Policy (CASPol) utility helps you set the code access security for an application. You can perform all of the same tasks at the machine, user, and enterprise levels. This utility uses the following syntax:

```
caspol -en[terprise] <args> ...
caspol -m[achine] <args> ...
caspol -u[ser] <args> ...
caspol -cu[stomuser] <path> <args> ...
caspol -a[ll] <args> ...
caspol -ca <path> <args> ... or caspol -customall <path> <args> ...
```

The following list describes each of the request levels for a command.

-en[terprise]   Performs a task that affects the system at the enterprise level.

-m[achine]   Performs a task that affects the system at the machine level.

-u[ser]   Performs a task that affects the system at the user level.

-cu[stomuser] *path*   Performs a task that affects a user other than the one currently executing CASPol. You must specify a path to the user's settings file to perform this task.

-a[ll]   Performs a task that affects the enterprise, machine, and user levels. The user level change affects the current user. If you want to change another user, you must use the -customuser or -customall command line switch.

-ca *path* or **-customall** *path*   Performs a task that affects the enterprise, machine, and user levels of a custom security configuration file. You must specify a path to the custom security configuration file to perform this task.

Once you define the level you want to work with, you can specify a particular action that you want to perform. The default level is machine for most commands. To obtain information at a different level, precede the action with a level command line switch. For example, typing **CASPol -enterprise -list** at the command line displays all of the security settings for the current user at the enterprise level. The following list describes each of these actions.

-l[ist]   Lists all of the security settings.

-lg or **-listgroups**   Lists the code groups.

-lp or **-listpset**   Lists the permission sets.

-lf or **-listfulltrust**   Lists the full trust assemblies.

-ld or **-listdescription**   Lists the code group names and descriptions.

-cft or **-checkfulltrust**   Checks the full trust list. The utility displays a list of any discrepancies it finds in the full trust list.

-ap { *named_xml_file* | *xml_file name* } or **-addpset** { *named_xml_file* | *xml_file name* } Adds a named permission set to the policy file. The permission set must appear as an XML file. When the permission set is a named permission set, all you need to provide is the name of the file. Otherwise, you must provide both the name of the file and a name for the permission set. You can find the XML file specification at http://msdn2.microsoft.com/en-us/library/thd4h5h0(vs.71) .aspx. Another good place to look for examples is the Security.CONFIG file in the \Documents and Settings*User Name*\Application Data\Microsoft\CLR Security Config*.NET Framework Version*\ folder on your hard drive.

-cp *xml_file pset_name* or **-chgpset** *xml_file pset_name*   Modifies the named permission set. The permission set must appear as an XML file. You must specify the name of the permission set you want to change. See the **-addpset** command line switch discussion for details on creating a permission set.

-rp *pset_name* or **-rempset** *pset_name*   Removes the specified permission set.

-af *assembly_name* or **-addfulltrust** *assembly_name*   Adds the specified full trust assembly. The assembly must have a strong name (the vendor must sign the assembly). Generally, you'll use this command line switch with assemblies that implement a custom security feature. You must add any referenced assemblies to the full trust list before you add the specified assembly.

-rf *assembly_name* or **-remfulltrust** *assembly_name*   Removes the specified full trust assembly.

-rg {*label* | *name*} or **-remgroup** {*label* | *name*}   Removes the code group with the specified label or name. The CASPol utility automatically removes any child groups.

-cg {*label* | *name*}{*mship* | *pset_name* | *flag*}+ or **-chggroup** {*label* | *name*}{*mship* | *pset_name* | *flag*}+   Changes the code group with the specified label or name. You may modify the membership, permission set, or flags. See the discussion of the membership and flag values later in this section. The permission set is a string indicating an existing permission set.

-ag {*parent_label* | *parent_name*}*mship pset_name* [*flag*] or **-addgroup** {*parent_label* | *parent_name*}*mship pset_name* [*flag*]   Adds a new code group to the specified parent. You may specify the parent name or label. You must specify the membership and permission set. Setting the flags argument is optional. See the discussion of the membership and flag values later in this section. The permission set is a string indicating an existing permission set.

-rsg *assembly_name* or **-resolvegroup** *assembly_name*   Lists the code group associated with the specified assembly.

-rsp *assembly_name* or **-resolveperm** *assembly_name*   Lists the permissions associated with the specified assembly.

-s[ecurity] { **on** | **off** }   Enables or disables .NET Framework security. The default setting is enabled.

-e[xecution] { **on** | **off** }   Enables or disables the right to run checking that CLR performs when starting an application. The default setting is enabled.

-pp { **on** | **off** } or **-polchgprompt** { **on** | **off** }   Enables or disables the policy change prompt that appears every time you change a policy. The default setting is enabled.

-q[uiet]   Disables the policy change prompt for the current command.

-r[ecover]   Recovers the most recently saved version of the enterprise, machine, or user level. This feature is a type of undo.

-rs or **-reset**   Resets the enterprise, machine, or user level to its default state. This feature removes any changes you've made since installing the .NET Framework.

-rsld or **-resetlockdown**   Resets a level to its default lockdown state.

-f[orce]   Forces CASPol to perform a save without performing a self-destruct check. The utility normally verifies that a policy change won't prevent it from running. Using this feature could disable CASPol functionality.

-b[uildcache]   Builds the security policy cache file.

Some of the command line switches that you use with the CASPol utility require that you specify a membership. The membership command line switches appear in the following list.

-allcode Specifies the All Code membership.

-appdir Specifies the Application Directory membership.

-custom *xml_file* Specifies a custom membership. You must define the details within an XML file. See the discussion on the MSDN Web site at `http://msdn2.microsoft.com/en-us/library/hh1y1b72(vs.71).aspx` for details on this technique.

-hash *hashAlg {-hex hashValue | -file assembly_name}* Specifies a Hash membership. You must provide the name of the algorithm used to create the hash. In addition, this membership requires the actual hash value as a hexadecimal number or the name of the assembly file that contains the hash.

-pub *{-cert cert_file_name | -file signed_file_name | -hex hex_string}* Specifies a Software Publisher membership. You must provide a certificate filename, a signed filename, or a hexadecimal string to identify the publisher identity. In all cases, the input is based on a digital signature.

-gac Specifies a GAC membership.

-site *website* Specifies a Site membership. Normally, you must provide the site domain such as www.mysite.com.

-strong *{-file assemblyfile_name | -hex public_key}{name | -noname}{version | -noversion}* Specifies a Strong Name membership. You must specify three pieces of information. First, you must identify the assembly using an assembly name or a public key token. Second, you must specify the assembly name or tell the utility that you don't want to provide a name using the -noname command line switch. Third, you must provide a version number or indicate that you don't want to provide a version number using the -noversion command line switch.

-url *url* Specifies a URL membership. When specifying a URL on the Internet, you must provide the protocol as part of the URL. For example, you could use `http://www.mysite.com/`. When specifying a UNC URI, you must include the information using the standard UNC format such as \\myserver\myshare.

-zone *zone_name* Specifies a Zone membership. The zone values can include any member of the following list.

- MyComputer
- Intranet
- Trusted
- Internet
- Untrusted

Some of the command line switches that you use with the CASPol utility require that you specify a flag value. The flag value command line switches appear in the following list.

-exclusive {on|off} Sets the policy statement Exclusive flag.

-levelfinal {on|off} Sets the policy statement LevelFinal flag.

-n[ame] *name* Sets the code group name to the specified value.

-d[escription] *desc* Sets the code group description to the specified value.

LISTING THE PERMISSIONS AND CODE GROUPS

Even a default .NET Framework setup includes a number of policies and code groups, so listing them at the command prompt is often useful. For that reason, it's usually better to list them to a file using the **CASPol -list >>** *Filename* command, where Filename is the name of the file you want to use. The default setup includes all policies and code groups for all levels. CASPol formats the file so that you can potentially parse it using an external program.

You can reduce the amount of information by specifying a particular level. For example, typing **CASPol -user -list** displays just the policies and code groups at the user level. Of course, now you can't compare differences between levels, but you do gain access to all of the information at one level.

Another way to list policies and code groups is by type. For example, you can type **CASPol -enterprise -listgroups** to list just the enterprise groups. Typing **CASPol -machine -listdescription** displays a description of the various groups, as shown in Figure 9.8. You also have options for listing all of the permissions (the -listpset switch) and all of the assemblies that have full trust (the -listfulltrust switch). The combination of all these switches provides relatively full access to all of the security information for the .NET Framework. Unfortunately, you have to issue the commands one at a time—you can't combine them to create custom listings in a single pass.

FIGURE 9.8
Employ various lists as needed to see a snapshot of the information on your system.

NOTE Many of these switches also come in a shortened version that you can use to reduce your typing. For example, you could type the command in this example as **CASPol -m -ld**. The chapter uses the longer form to make the meaning of the command line entries clearer.

This command is particularly handy when you want to see the hierarchical structure of the zones. Notice that there are actually subzones in some cases. For example, the My_Computer_Zone entry includes Microsoft_Strong_Name and ECMA_Strong_Name entries.

Of course, the question remains as to why you'd want to use this approach to list the various security elements when you can use the .NET Framework Configuration Tool. As you work with the various outputs, you'll notice that they're structured, which means you can process the output information in a variety of ways. The simple text makes it easy to manipulate the entries for storage in a permanent form in either a database or a written report.

Using this utility is also the only way to obtain information when you use a remote connection that doesn't have the bandwidth required to use the .NET Framework Configuration Tool. A text interface is faster and uses fewer resources. These reasons keep many developers using text-based utilities, even when GUI alternatives exist.

MAKING GROUP MODIFICATIONS

The .NET Framework security features work like a hierarchical database in some respects. Consequently, you can add and delete entries as needed to create new policies and setups. You can also modify existing policies. For example, you can add a new permission set to an existing group. This is one area where CASPol really shines. Imagine having to set up a new server using the .NET Framework Configuration Tool. Yes, you can eventually do it, but it's going to take considerable time (assuming you can keep the network administrator awake). A simple batch file lets CASPol perform the required configuration for you using a single command.

The reason that I mentioned the hierarchical database approach is that you can visualize how a change will affect the system better when you use this perspective. Look again at the hierarchy in Figure 9.8. You can add a new code group at any point along that hierarchy. For example, if you wanted to add a super secret strong naming convention to the `Microsoft_Strong_Name` entry, you could type the following command: `CASPol -addgroup 1.1.1. -zone MyComputer FullTrust -name MyStrongGroup -description "This is a special group."`, CASPol will display the security policy message. Type **yes** (lowercase and the full word) and CASPol will display the success message shown in Figure 9.9.

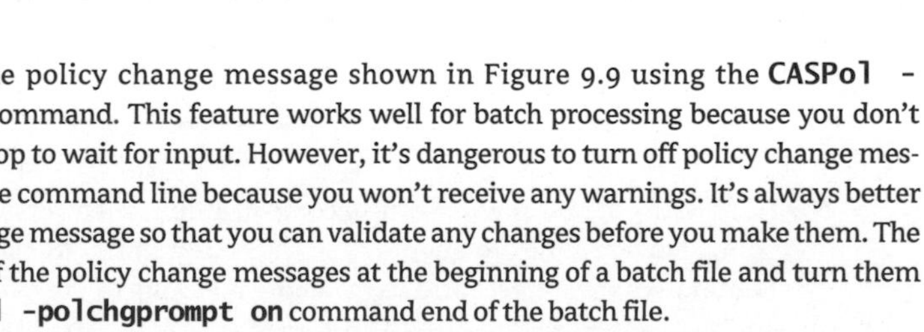

FIGURE 9.9

When adding a new group, CASPol asks whether you want to change the security policy.

TIP   You can turn off the policy change message shown in Figure 9.9 using the `CASPol -polchgprompt off` command. This feature works well for batch processing because you don't want the processing to stop to wait for input. However, it's dangerous to turn off policy change messages when working at the command line because you won't receive any warnings. It's always better to receive the policy change message so that you can validate any changes before you make them. The best method is to turn off the policy change messages at the beginning of a batch file and turn them back on using the `CASPol -polchgprompt on` command end of the batch file.

Removing a group is actually easier than adding one. All you need is either the hierarchical level or the code group name. Type `CASPol -remgroup MyStrongGroup` to remove the MyStrongGroup added earlier. CASPol will ask you whether you're sure about making the change as it did before. After you type **yes**, CASPol will remove the group and display a success message.

WARNING   The -remgroup command is a one-way process. Removing a group is permanent and there's no undo command. Make sure you actually want to remove a group before you execute this command.

Using the Microsoft .NET Framework 2.0 Configuration Console

The .NET Framework Configuration Tool has a lot to offer the administrator. It's a tool that you should spend time learning, even if you aren't using it for security needs. For example, this tool lets you view registered assemblies and add new ones using a graphical interface, as shown in Figure 9.10.

FIGURE 9.10

Add the .NET Framework Configuration Tool to your list of security aids.

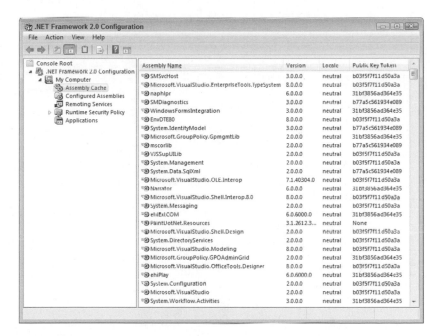

Using this tool is easier than using utilities such as GACUtil (Global Assembly Cache Utility), which you use to register assemblies with strong names for global use. The following sections describe the security uses of the .NET Framework Configuration Tool.

Working with Code Groups

The "Defining Membership and Evidence" section discusses the idea of code groups. The .NET Framework only comes with one code group by default, the All_Code group. The Enterprise, Machine, and User policies all support this code group and you'll generally use it for all local programs. However, you can modify how the code groups work and even add new code groups as the need arises. Any new code group you add will appear below the All_Code group in the hierarchy.

When you first select the Runtime Security Policy\<Level>\Code Groups\All_Code entry in the left pane of the .NET Framework Configuration Tool, you'll see a help screen. This screen contains options for adding new code groups or configuring the existing code group, as shown in Figure 9.11. (This figure also shows the location of the All_Code entry in the hierarchy.)

FIGURE 9.11
Add or Edit code
groups using this
help screen.

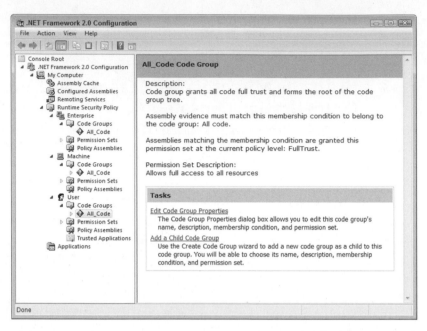

You can use one of three ways to create a new code group. Click the Add a Child Code Group link and you'll see a Create Code Group dialog box. This dialog box contains an option to create the code group manually, or you can import an XML file that contains the code you want to use. The third method is to right-click an existing code group and choose the Duplicate entry from the context menu. This technique creates a code group with the same characteristics as the parent.

When you choose to create a code group manually, you pass through several dialog boxes. Each dialog box asks a question about the new code group including the condition type (such as Application Directory, Zone, or Hash) and the permission set (such as Full Trust, Execution, or Internet).

Editing a code group means changing features such as the condition type and the permission set. When you click Edit Code Group Properties on the help screen, you see a Properties dialog box similar to the one shown in Figure 9.12.

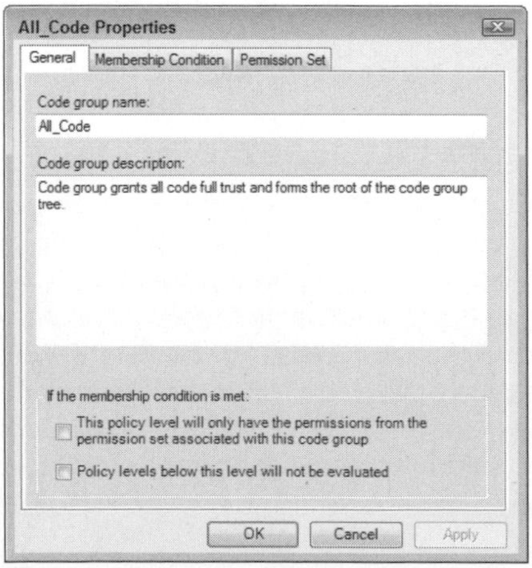

FIGURE 9.12
Use this dialog box to
change the character-
istics of a code group.

Notice that you can use this dialog box to determine how the code group will work with the policy levels. The first check box lets you set the code group to use permissions associated with the permission set for the code group exclusively. The second tells CLR not to evaluate policy levels below the existing policy level. In other words, this check box creates an exclusive code group.

Creating and Defining Permission Sets

The .NET Framework comes with a standard set of permissions. You can create additional permission sets as required to meet specific programming needs. In addition, you can modify the definitions for existing permissions. However, modifying a current permission isn't a good idea because that action will change the default meaning of the permission and could cause applications written by other developers to fail. (CLR prevents you from changing .NET Framework specific permission sets.)

You have the same options for creating a new permission set as described in the "Working with Code Groups" section. When you create a new permission manually, you'll see the Create Permission Set dialog box. The first screen asks for a name and description for the permission set. The second screen asks you to define the permission for the permission set, as shown in Figure 9.13.

NOTE   The top of the screenshot shown in Figure 9.13 contains a black area. This black area only appears in Vista and in Windows Server 2008. When you open the same screen in Windows XP or Windows 2003 Server, the black area contains explanatory text. Hopefully, Microsoft will eventually fix this problem.

FIGURE 9.13
Define the permissions for your new permission set carefully to avoid security breaches.

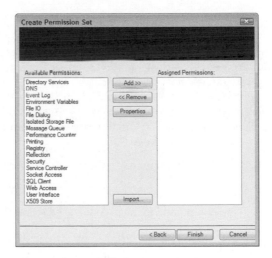

Whenever you add a new permission, the .NET Framework Configuration Tool displays a Permission Settings dialog box that helps you configure that particular permission. The dialog boxes vary by permission. For example, the File IO permission includes a setting that lets you define individual permissions for each drive you want the permission set to access, or you can grant unlimited drive access. You can click Import to import an XML file containing the permissions you want to use. Custom permission sets include a help screen that lets you view, change, and rename the permission set.

Defining Policy Assemblies

Policy assemblies contain the code used by CLR to evaluate the evidence presented by an object to obtain a permission. The default .NET Framework configuration is all you need unless the developer who creates a custom application for you designs a special policy that requires additional code. If you need to create a unique policy, then you must add the assembly to the appropriate list or the evaluation will always fail. Unfortunately, you may find that .NET is less than helpful in telling you about the problem. It always appears as a security error.

Adding Configured Applications

The Applications folder isn't strictly a security setting, but entries in this folder can affect individual applications. When you look at the help screen for the Applications folder, you see two entries. The first helps you add a new configured application to the list. The second helps you fix the configuration of an application. For example, the developer of an application may design it to use an assembly that isn't available or is outdated.

You need to consider two configured application features. First, this utility lets you change the code bases for the application. Several of the applications in this chapter rely on the code base provided by the application, so it's easy to see how changing the code base could affect the security of the application as well.

The second feature appears on the Properties dialog box for the application. To display this dialog box, right-click the application entry and select Properties from the context menu. The .NET Framework Configuration Tool normally checks the Enable Publisher Policy check box by default. However, it's possible that someone could clear this check box, which will affect the security of the application. You could find that the application fails because someone has turned off the publisher policies.

Let's Start Building

This chapter has demonstrated three levels of security you can use to protect ASP.NET applications in IIS. You won't use just one level to create a complete security solution—you need all three. The methods you use depend on the requirements of the application, the needs of the user, your corporate culture, the skills of the developers, and the threats your organization faces. As noted many times in this chapter, Windows security, role-based security, and code-based security have many overlaps that provide you with the flexibility you need to implement a security plan. This chapter helps you build these skills:

◆ Understand and manage operating system security

◆ Understand and manage role-based security

◆ Understand and manage code-based security

◆ Use the Microsoft .NET Framework 2.0 Configuration Console to configure security

Now that you have a better idea of just how much flexibility you have in configuring ASP.NET applications, it's time to begin exploring that security. The best way to begin is by exploring the tools that Microsoft provides. You won't gain a full appreciation for the security features of Windows and the .NET Framework until you understand the tools at your disposal. Make sure you actually try using the tools on a test machine. Try various security settings and then test them using applications you install. Otherwise, it's very hard to begin seeing how a security change you make affects an application you install.

Although this chapter provides a lot of good practical advice on security, it doesn't provide the IIS security story. Chapter 10 uses the information you learned in this chapter to show you how to perform security setups within IIS itself. Configuring Windows and the applications you use is a first step, but you must also configure IIS to obtain complete protection.

Chapter 10

Configuring Application Security

Chapter 9 told you all about .NET security—how it works, how to monitor it, when to use it in place of Windows security, and so on. Of course, knowing about the security and setting it are two different things. This chapter shows how to set various kinds of security for ASP.NET applications. You'll begin by working with authentication settings that can affect any application and then move on to defining authorization rules. Authentication, the act of verifying a caller, is probably the most important security act because it can stop someone at the door—before they've accessed your server. Authorization is the next step in the process—it defines what the user can do now that you know who they are. The combination of authentication and authorization provides the user with access to your server.

The next two sections of the chapter discuss Secure Sockets Layer (SSL)—the kind of security that most users already know about when they access a Web site using HyperText Transfer Protocol Secure (HTTPS). The first step in implementing SSL is to obtain and install a server certificate. If you're working with a public Web site, you'll obtain the certificate from a third party such as VeriSign, but you can use a self-signed certificate for intranet purposes. After you install the certificate, you can use it to secure an application with SSL. Of course, that means setting up a secure site to use the SSL.

At this point, you've stopped intruders at the door and you've secured the connection between the caller and the server. The next three sections discuss securing the application. As described in Chapter 9, you use three levels of security for ASP.NET applications. Chapter 4 already discusses the first level, which is Windows security. This chapter discusses rule- and code-based security. As part of configuring rule- and code-based security, you must also configure users.

The final section of the chapter describes the last part of the application equation, saving user settings with a profile. It's important to store user settings so the user doesn't have to configure everything from scratch during every visit. However, you must perform this task in a secure manner. This chapter explores only one of many alternatives that you have—the user profile. User settings occur at two levels: global and group. Using the right setting in the right place is an essential part of maintaining a secure environment.

In this chapter, you'll learn how to do the following:

- ◆ Manage authorization settings
- ◆ Define authorization rules
- ◆ Manage server certificates
- ◆ Use SSL to secure an application
- ◆ Configure .NET users

◆ Configure role-based security settings

◆ Configure code-based security settings

◆ Save user settings

Setting Authentication Requirements

Authenticating users is an important task in letting them gain access to server resources—at least, when those resources require some kind of security. You need to know that the caller requesting access has a legitimate reason to do so and is on the list of those who should have access. Even though most of your callers will be humans, today there isn't any reason to expect that the caller is human. Your Web service may receive a request from another computer or even another kind of device. The access could occur without any human intervention at all. The following sections describe the various types of authentication IIS supports, tells you how to configure each type, shows how to enable and disable authentication, and considers the response types.

Considering the Authentication Types

Not all forms of authentication are secure. For example, anonymous authentication doesn't perform any validation of the user at all. Basic authentication is only slightly more secure and it's full of so many security holes that most experts consider it useless for all but the least secure tasks. Set up correctly, Windows authentication can be quite secure, but then you need to know precisely who will log into the system at all times—it's not very flexible. All of these authentication types have purposes and you may require more than one type on your server, depending on your application needs.

In all cases, you configure an authentication type by choosing the connection level in the Connections pane and the authentication type in the Authentication pane. When you see Edit as one of the options in the Actions pane, you can click the entry and see the configuration information. Some authentication types, such as Windows authentication, require no configuration because they rely on the user's personal credentials. The following sections describe the particulars of each authentication type.

ANONYMOUS AUTHENTICATION

Everyone must log into the server, which seems like a contradiction when you don't know who the user is. Anonymous authentication lets the caller log in using a default account. You don't know who the caller is, so you let them use a known account on the server—hopefully one that has very limited rights. Anonymous authentication is the only authentication option enabled by default and it's the type used on just about every public Web site except those that require you to log in. Figure 10.1 shows the Edit Anonymous Authentication Credentials dialog box where you configure the anonymous authentication.

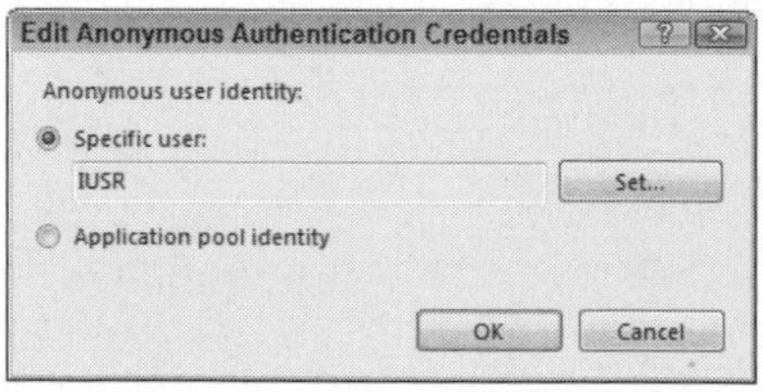

FIGURE 10.1
Configure the credentials used for anonymous authentication.

When you want to change the Specific User setting, click Set. You'll see a Set Credentials dialog box where you type the username, password, and then confirm the password. Click OK to complete the action. Every user who accesses the connection uses the same authentication. The default setting is to use the IUSR account, which has minimal rights and works fine for public Web sites.

As an alternative to a specific user, you can choose the Application Pool Identity option. This option depends on the application pool that the connection uses for authentication purposes. The anonymous user has the same rights as the application pool, which means that the user will have more rights than normal or the application pool will have fewer rights than normal. You can learn more about application pools in the "Working with Application Pools" section of Chapter 13. However, it's important now to know how to set the authentication for an application pool as described in the following steps.

1. Select Application Pools in the Connections pane.

2. Highlight the application pool you want to modify and click Advanced Settings in the Actions pane. You'll see the Advanced Settings dialog box shown in Figure 10.2.

FIGURE 10.2
Select an identity for the application pool.

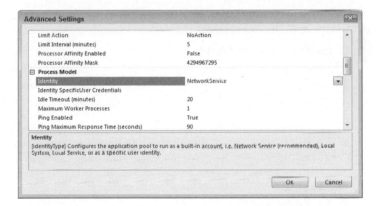

3. Locate the Identity field of the Process Model group, as shown in Figure 10.2.

4. Set the identity you want to use for the login—don't select one of the system accounts unless you're working with an intranet. Remember that this identity affects the application pool as well as the user logging into the server. In this case, the user would have the same privileges as the NetworkService account, which is too high for any anonymous user.

5. Choose SpecificUser in the Identity field when you know the standard accounts provide too many rights.

6. Highlight the Identity SpecificUser Credentials field and click the ellipsis on the right side of the display. IIS displays a Set Credentials dialog box where you type the username and password and then confirm the password. Click OK to complete the action.

ASP.NET IMPERSONATION

ASP.NET impersonation relies on credentials other than those offered by the authentication built into the .NET Framework. When working with the default setting, IIS authenticates the user through a secure connection and relies on the user's credentials for authentication purposes. The user's credentials also provide the means for running an application, so the application doesn't run under the standard ASP.NET account and the capabilities of the application reflect the user's rights to perform tasks.

You can use this feature to enable or disable features based on the user's name or group affiliation. Figure 10.3 shows the configuration options for ASP.NET impersonation.

FIGURE 10.3
Use ASP.NET impersonation to run applications using something other than the default account.

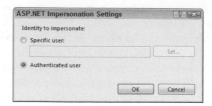

You also have the option of running the application using a specific set of credentials, other than the default credentials. This option comes in handy when the application requires more rights than the user has when logging into the system and the default credentials won't provide the required access either. When you want to change the Specific User setting, click Set. You'll see a Set Credentials dialog box where you type the username, password, and then confirm the password. Click OK to complete the action.

BASIC AUTHENTICATION

Basic authentication has a host of security problems associated with it and you shouldn't rely on it for authentication purposes in most cases. The default basic authentication setup passes the username and password in cleartext using Base 64 encoding, which is easily decoded. In addition, this form of authentication can expose the name of your domain to outsiders, making it easier for them to gain unauthorized access to your server. You can make this form of authentication a little safer by using an SSL connection between the client and the server. Figure 10.4 shows the Edit Basic Authentication Settings dialog box used to configure basic authentication.

FIGURE 10.4
Basic authentication isn't a particularly safe authentication option.

You should provide the Default Domain field entry. This field provides a domain that IIS can use for authentication purposes when the user doesn't provide a domain name as part of the login information. If you don't provide this entry and the user also doesn't provide a valid domain, IIS will reject the user's credentials even when the username and password are correct.

The Realm field is an optional entry that contains the DNS domain name or Web address that will use the credentials. When you configure this option, the DNS domain name or Web address appears on the user's login dialog box for informational purposes. IIS doesn't use this information to authenticate the user. If you provide the default domain name in the Realm field, the user will see the domain name when logging into the system and you'll potentially expose this important information to the outside world. In most cases, you don't want to include anything in the Realm field since it doesn't help authenticate the user.

DIGEST AUTHENTICATION

Digest authentication is slightly more secure than basic authentication. It uses the same techniques as basic authentication, except, instead of sending the user credentials in plain text, the digest authentication sends an MD5 hash value. MD5 is a standardized method of turning login information into a 128-bit numeric value. You can see the standard at `http://www.ietf.org/rfc/rfc1321.txt` and a human-readable version at `http://en.wikipedia.org/wiki/MD5`. When you open the Edit Digest Authentication Settings dialog box, you see a single field for the authentication realm.

Unlike basic authentication, the Realm field is a required entry for digest authentication that contains the DNS domain name or Web address that will use the credentials. When you configure this option, the DNS domain name or Web address appears on the user's login dialog box for informational purposes. IIS also uses this information to authenticate the user. If you provide the default domain name in the Realm field, the user will see the domain name when logging into the system and you'll potentially expose this important information to the outside world.

FORMS AUTHENTICATION

Forms authentication is one of the more secure authentication mechanisms available to the administrator, especially when coupled with SSL. Instead of relying on a standard operating system authentication technique, forms authentication relies on the application to perform the authentication instead. This authentication type can maximize use of the features in the .NET Framework to ensure the identity of a caller using secure methods. The application can use any level of encryption deemed necessary to protect user information. In addition, the credentials can contain more information than IIS normally requests for authentication purposes, which means the application can interrogate the caller in depth before allowing access to the server. The Edit Forms Authentication Settings dialog box appears in Figure 10.5. Notice that this form of authentication requires substantially more configuration than other types.

FIGURE 10.5
Use forms authentication to let the application perform the authentication.

Unlike most of the authentication types discussed so far, forms authentication relies on redirection as part of the authentication process. When the caller can't provide an authentication token, the system redirects the caller to the Web page defined by the Login URL field. The default setting for this field is `Login.ASPX`. When the user sees the login Web page and provides the correct credentials, the application performs any required checks and then passes back an authentication token that allows access to the requested resources. The access expires the moment the cookie expires or the user deletes it. Any request to the application that doesn't include the authentication token automatically displays the login page. The Authentication Cookie Time-Out (In Minutes) field determines how long the authentication token is valid.

Fortunately, you don't have to rely on the cookies to store the authentication token. The Mode drop-down list defines the method used to store the authentication token. Choose the Don't Use Cookies to avoid all of the problems that cookies can present in storing information. (Remember that using cookies can provide a performance and resource usage benefit, however, so not using cookies also presents a trade-off.) The Name field defines the name of the cookie when stored on the user's machine. There isn't a good reason to change the default name except to keep the information a little more private.

The Protection Mode field defines how IIS protects the authentication token. It's usually a good idea to maintain the default setting of Encryption and Validation because it's more secure. Again, there's the performance penalty to consider and you can possibly gain a little performance benefit for less secure applications by using one of the other settings. You can further protect the authentication token by checking the Requires SSL option. In addition to encrypting the authentication token using Triple-DES encryption and relying on a validation screen to ensure no one has tampered with the cookie, SSL encrypts the entire communication stream, making it quite unlikely that someone will tamper with the authentication process.

The Extend Cookie Expiration On Every Request option provides a means of creating a continuous session. The caller maintains a logged in status as long as it makes requests before the authentication token expires. You'll normally keep this option checked unless you want to ensure that the sessions always expire after a certain time.

WINDOWS AUTHENTICATION

Windows authentication doesn't require any special configuration. When you enable this form of authentication, IIS relies on the user's Windows identity for authentication purposes. In addition, any application that the user starts will run using the Windows identification, which means the application features will reflect the user's rights.

Enabling and Disabling an Authentication Type

Before you can use a method of authentication, you must enable it at the level where you need it. Some administrators enable all of the authentication methods they require at the server level, which often leaves the server vulnerable to a host of attacks from outside sources. When you disable an authentication method, you close an opportunity for someone even to open the door to the server. Consequently, the lower the level at which you enable a particular authentication type, the less likely it is that someone will gain entry to a major portion of your Web server.

The enable and disable feature is a toggle. When you enable an authentication type, the Disable option appears in the Actions pane. Likewise, disabling an authentication type displays the Enable option in the Actions pane. To enable or disable an authentication type, highlight its entry in the Authentication Type field and click Enable or Disable in the Actions pane as required.

Understanding the Response Types

The Authentication pane in Figure 10.6 shows the various authentication types, whether they're enabled or disabled, and a response type column. You can't change the response type field and for good reason—it determines how the authentication takes place. When a browser sees a particular response type, it performs an action, such as displaying a login dialog box. The response type is actually a kind of instruction and sometimes an error. It signals the need for additional information, which is the reason you can't change it.

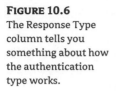

FIGURE 10.6
The Response Type column tells you something about how the authentication type works.

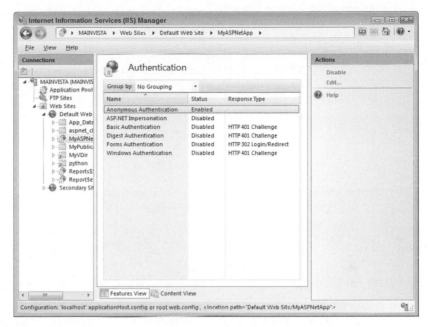

Anonymous authentication doesn't require a response type because IIS doesn't ask the user for any additional information. The ASP.NET impersonation option doesn't require any additional information either since the system provides the information it needs. The most common response type, HTTP 401 Challenge, is actually an error designation that tells the browser to display a login dialog box. The only other default response type, HTTP 302 Login/Redirect, is for forms authentication. By observing the response types that IIS uses, you can learn a little about how an authentication works, which can come in quite handy when you install a custom authentication.

Modifying the Authorization Rules

While authentication determines who has access to IIS, authorization tells what a user can do once they gain access. To access the authorization rule, select the connection level you want to change in the Connections pane. Double-click the Authorization Rules icon and you'll see the Authorization Rules pane shown in Figure 10.7. The sections that follow describe how to work with the rules used to control what callers can do with resources on your Web site.

Understanding the Difference between Authorization and Security

It's important not to confuse authorization and security. Authorization may stipulate that a user can use the GET verb to obtain a Web page from a particular Web site. Security may determine that the user only has rights to see summary data and not all of the available information. Authorization always involves some kind of action—it uses verbs to define particular actions. Security always involves objects and restrictions—it uses locks and keys to restrict access to particular objects based on the caller's rights. Consequently, authorization gives a caller access, while security removes unneeded access.

FIGURE 10.7
Use the Authorization Rules pane to control what callers can do with the Web server, Web site, and applications.

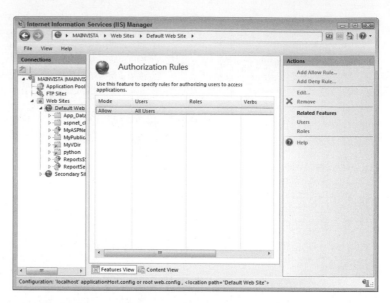

Authorization is also different from security in context. The authorization rules you set only affect Web site users, while security affects everyone who accesses the server. For example, when you set an authorization rule denying access to a folder, only callers who access the folder through a browser or other Web application see the effect of the access rule. Users who access the server directly through a network connection still have access to the folder.

The biggest hint that security and access are different is the way in which IIS handles them. (You can test this out by setting a test Web site to disallow anonymous users and then by trying to log on as an anonymous user.) When a user tries to access a Web page that you haven't authorized them to see, IIS displays the 401.2 error message shown in Figure 10.8.

FIGURE 10.8
When IIS encounters an authorization issue, it displays a 401.2 error message.

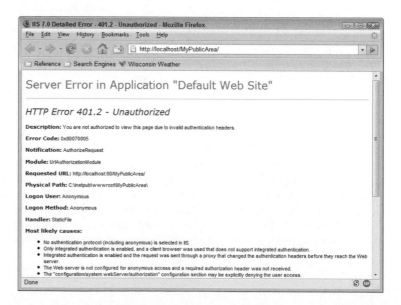

When you log on locally, you can see all of the details for this error, including the fact that the system is using the StaticFile handler. IIS provides the username and method. In this case, both are set for Anonymous. The Notification field shows that this is an AuthorizeRequest. The result is that the user hasn't gained access, but the message clearly shows an authorization problem.

If you reset the authorization to allow anonymous users, but set security so that neither the Users nor the IIS_IUSR account can access the folder, you'll see the 500.19 error message shown in Figure 10.9. In this case, the Notification field shows that the error occurs at BeginRequest. IIS can't even provide access to the `Web.CONFIG` file, so IIS can't tell you anything about the request—it hasn't occurred yet. This is an example of a security problem instead of an authorization problem.

FIGURE 10.9

When IIS encounters an authentication issue, it displays a 500.19 error message.

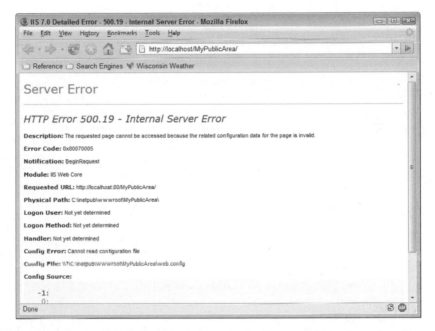

Whether you use authorization or security to block access to the directory depends on the effect you're trying to achieve. Authorization lets the Web site continue working and, because you're dealing with a 401 error, could allow authentication to occur (see the "Understanding the Response Types" section of the chapter for details). When a 500.19 error occurs, IIS completely blocks access because it never gets the chance to authenticate the user. Consequently, you could use security to provide a block for a particular folder unless the user is already logged onto the system, but you could use authorization to force the user to log onto the system for authentication purposes.

At this point, try giving yourself access to the folder, but block access to a single file within that folder. When you are authorized to see the folder (and its contents), authenticated to do so, and the administrator hasn't set any security roadblocks in the way, access occurs as normal. However, IIS blocks access to the one file due to the security setup as shown in Figure 10.10. Notice that the Notification field tells you that this is an AuthenticateRequest, not an AuthorizeRequest. Consequently, the error number is 401.3, not 401.2. As you can see, authorization and security may seem to achieve the same objectives, but they're quite different in effect.

FIGURE 10.10

Authorizing someone access to a folder, but denying access to a resource, produces a 401.3 error.

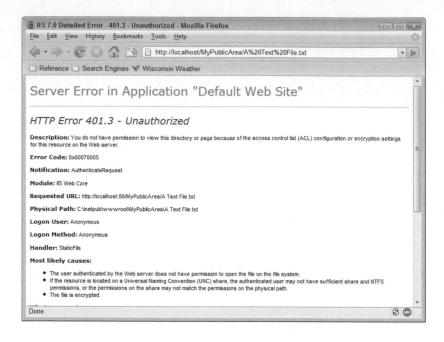

Understanding Allow and Deny Rules

Allow and deny rules tell IIS what the caller is authorized to work with based on the caller's identity. For example, when you log onto the system as an anonymous user, you have different authorization than when you log on as the administrator. The authorization affects the Web server, Web site, folder, or application. You can't set authorization for a single file. To remove access to a particular file, you must set security on it (see the "Understanding the Difference between Authorization and Security" section of the chapter for details on getting authorization and security to work together properly).

You use an allow rule to authorize a caller to use the resources within a particular connection. Likewise, you use a deny rule to prevent a caller from using resources within a particular connection. IIS doesn't make the allow or deny rule an all-or-nothing decision—you allow or deny access based on the verbs the caller provides. For example, you can allow a caller to GET a particular resource, but not to POST it. The standard verbs (as defined by the HTTP 1.1 specification at `http://www.w3.org/Protocols/rfc2616/rfc2616-sec9.html`) include:

- GET
- HEAD
- POST
- PUT
- DELETE
- TRACE
- CONNECT

When you choose not to include one or more specific verbs, the allow or deny rule affects all of the verbs. Since there are many nonstandard verbs, creating a rule that affects all verbs can have unexpected effects. Some of the nonstandard verbs include OPTIONS, PATCH, PROPFIND, PROPPATCH, MKCOL, COPY, MOVE, LOCK, and UNLOCK.

Rules need not affect individuals; you can also specify groups and roles. The use of roles to create authorization scenarios is important because a role doesn't reflect the rights of a particular user or the rights of the user's group connections, but it depends on what the user is doing at a particular time. By setting authorization according to a role, you can give the user authorization to use only what's needed to accomplish a given task.

Adding Allow or Deny Rules

At some point, you'll very likely need to add new allow or deny rules. To perform this task, you open the Authorization Rules pane and click Add Allow Rule or Add Deny Rule in the Actions pane. You'll see an Add Allow Authorization Rule dialog box when you click Add Allow Rule as shown in Figure 10.11. The corresponding Add Deny Authorization Rule dialog box looks the same except for the title bar.

FIGURE 10.11
Add allow or deny rules to control authorization on your server.

The first task is to apply the rule to a specific group. You can choose any of the following groups:

All Users Creating an all users rule affects all of the users for the system. It doesn't matter whether the IIS has authenticated the user as an anonymous user, a specific account, as part of a group, or in a particular role. The rule you create affects everyone, so you need to use this group carefully, especially when you define a deny rule.

All Anonymous Users This group affects only anonymous users. Anyone who's logged in using an individual account, as part of a group, or in a specific role is unaffected. You can use this kind of rule to deny access to the public to a particular Web site feature, while granting access to callers who have logged in.

Specified Roles or User Groups This group affects a particular role or a group of users. You must define the role using the role-based security features provided with IIS (see the "Setting Role-based Security Using .NET Roles" section of the chapter for details). Define any user groups using standard Windows security features. When working in a domain, you should define the groups using Active Directory. When supplying more than one role or user group (you can mix them within a single rule), you must separate each role or user group with a comma or IIS tends to get confused and treat the entire list as a single entry.

Specified Users This group only affects a particular user. You define the user as part of the Windows security or as part of the .NET Users pane. (See the "Managing .NET Users" section of the chapter for details on working with .NET users.)

The second task is to determine whether the rule applies to all verbs or specific verbs. To apply the rule to a specific verb, check the Apply this Rule to Specific Verbs option. Type the verbs you want to use in the edit box. Make sure you separate each verb with a comma or IIS has a tendency to treat all of the verbs as a single massive verb (even though you place spaces between the verbs).

It's important to realize that deny rules always take precedence over allow rules. The order of the rules in the list doesn't make any difference. Consequently, when you add a deny rule that affects all verbs for someone at a specific level, you can't use an allow rule to give them authorization for specific verbs.

The entries at a higher level don't affect the entries at a lower level. Consequently, you can give only GET access at a higher level and then authorize additional verbs at a lower level. This approach lets you provide maximum protection for the server and the individual sites, while giving access to all of the required verbs to use an application.

Editing Existing Allow or Deny Rules

By default, IIS provides the Allow All Users rule shown in Figure 10.7. This rule lets any user do anything once IIS authenticates them. Obviously, if you're running a public Web site and allow anonymous users, you really don't need anything else. However, when you're running a secure Web site, you need something better than authorizing every user to perform any task. At the very least, you need to add rules that only allow access to the verbs that your application supports.

Depending on how you want to set up your server, you may actually want to remove this rule, but you can also edit it. To edit a rule, highlight its entry in the Authorization Rules pane. Click Edit in the Actions pane. You'll see a dialog box that looks like the one shown in Figure 10.11. The only difference is that the title bar will say Edit Allow Authorization Rule or Edit Deny Authorization Rule. You have the same options when editing a rule as you do when adding one. See the "Adding Allow or Deny Rules" section of the chapter for details.

NOTE When you look at the Authorization Rules pane, you'll notice that the Entry Type field tells you whether a rule is inherited or local. You can't edit or delete inherited rules. However, you can override inherited rules by defining a rule of your own. Whenever you work with an inherited rule, make sure you test the application thoroughly to ensure you receive the results you expect from overriding it.

Removing an Allow or Deny Rule

Eventually, you'll need to remove rules you no longer need from the list, rather than edit them to meet specific requirements. To remove a rule from the list, highlight its entry in the Authorization Rules pane and click Remove in the Actions pane. IIS will display a Confirm Remove dialog box. Click Yes to complete the action. You can't remove inherited rules—you can only remove local rules.

Working with Server Certificates

The term *certificate* is appropriate. A server certificate is a kind of document that identifies the server. Normally, this certificate comes from a third party that performs a verification process to determine that you are who you say you are. When someone makes a sensitive request for information from your Web site, you present the certificate to them so that they know you're actually the one receiving the information, rather than someone else posing as you. A third party that the caller trusts signs the certificate, so the caller trusts you, as well, because the trusted third party has vouched for you. Because the Internet is so impersonal, it's important to know whom you are working with at any time, making certificates an essential tool.

Sometimes you don't need a trusted third party to vouch for you—all you really need is a certificate that identifies your organization in some way. For example, a partner company already knows and trusts your organization, but you want to be sure that they know they're working with you and not someone else. Using a self-signed certificate can work, in this case, because the certificate is still unique and it specifically identifies your organization. It's possible for someone to impersonate someone else using a self-signed certificate, which is why you always want the third party verification included for public uses such as Web sites.

No matter how you create certificates, you need them to perform some tasks in IIS. For example, if you want to set up an SSL connection, you need a certificate of some type to do it. The SSL protocol is based on the concept of creating a secure connection between parties based on a certificate that positively identifies at least one of those parties—normally the server. To access the server certificates, select the server entry in the Connections pane and double-click the Server Certificates icon. You'll see the Server Certificates pane shown in Figure 10.12. The following sections describe working with certificates.

FIGURE 10.12

Server certificates provide identification between two parties on the Internet.

Importing an Existing Certificate

Whenever you receive a certificate from a third party, you must import it into your server in order to use it. In addition, you'll export and then import a certificate when you want to move a certificate from an existing server to a new one. The following steps show how to import a certificate.

1. Click Import in the Actions pane. You'll see the Import Certificate dialog box shown in Figure 10.13.

FIGURE 10.13
Import existing certif-
icate files into your
server to use them.

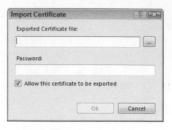

2. Type the path for the certificate you want to import. You can also click the ellipsis to display an Open dialog box you can use to locate the Personal Information Exchange (PFX) file containing the certificate.

NOTE The PFX file format is the only one that IIS accepts. You can't use an alternative format such as PKCS #12 (P12), ARM, Privacy Enhanced Mail (PEM), or Distinguished Encoding Rules (DER). There's some confusion as to whether PFX and P12 are two different versions of the same Public Key Cryptographic System (PKCS #12) standard, but the two file formats aren't the same. Consequently, IIS won't accept a P12 file in place of a PFX file even if both truly are following the same standard. You can see a list of all of the PKCS standards at `http://en.wikipedia.org/wiki/PKCS`. There's a PKCS FAQ at `http://www.drh-consultancy.demon.co.uk/pkcs12faq.html` that attempts to make some sense out of the whole mess.

3. Type the password for the certificate in the Password field. The password must match exactly (even with capitalization).

4. Check the Allow this Certificate to be Exported option if you want to allow someone to export the certificate. This option is beneficial when working with a locally generated certificate. However, it's a good idea to secure your third-party certificate by clearing this check box and locking away the original file where no one but authorized personnel can get to it.

5. Click OK. IIS imports the certificate and it appears in the Server Certificates pane.

Creating a Certificate Request

Before you can obtain a certificate from a third party, you must create a request for it. The certificate creation process generates a file that you send along with other information to the third party. The amount of information you must supply depends on the third party's requirements and the kind of certificate you request. The following steps describe how to create a certificate request.

1. Click Create Certificate Request in the Actions pane. You'll see the Request Certificate dialog box shown in Figure 10.14.

2. Type a name for the certificate in the Common Name field. Make sure this name reflects the name that your organization wants to use for the certificate since anyone who works with it will need to know the name.

3. Provide your organizational information. You must use full names, no abbreviations. The certificate must contain full information in every one of the fields, including the Organizational Unit field. If you have a small company, you'll need to provide either your company name or something like main office.

FIGURE 10.14
Define a name for the certificate and the identifying information for your organization.

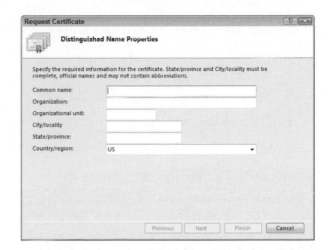

4. Click Next. You'll see the Cryptographic Service Provider Properties dialog box shown in Figure 10.15.

FIGURE 10.15
Define the characteristics of the certificate.

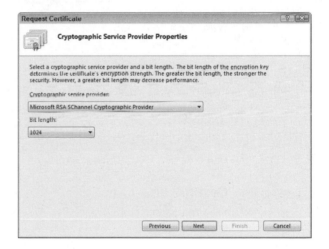

5. Choose a cryptographic service provider. The Microsoft Rivest-Shamir-Adleman (RSA) SChannel Cryptographic Provider works well in most cases. It provides support for hashing, data signing, and signature verification. You can read a complete description of this cryptographic service provider at http://msdn2.microsoft.com/en-us/library/aa386988 .aspx. The Microsoft Diffie-Hellman (DH) SChannel Cryptographic Provider provides support for a number of additional needs. The most important reason to use this cryptographic service provider is when you need to exchange private keys on a nonsecure network. However, you'll also find that this cryptographic service provider suffers from a number of flaws, one of which is speed. The other problem is that this cryptographic service provider only supports 512- and 1,024-bit keys. You can read more about this cryptographic service provider at http://msdn2.microsoft.com/En-US/library/aa386984.aspx. In most cases, you'll want to use the default setting of Microsoft RSA SChannel Cryptographic Provider.

6. Choose a key length in the Bit Length field. The rule of thumb here is that a longer key provides better security and a shorter key provides better performance. You need to choose a key length that reflects the security requirements for your organization. In most cases, the 1,024-bit key length for a Microsoft RSA SChannel Cryptographic Provider and the 512-bit key length for Microsoft DH SChannel Cryptographic Provider works well.

7. Click Next. You'll see a File Name dialog box.

8. Type the name of the file you want to use to save the request.

9. Click Finish. IIS generates a text file you can use to request a certificate.

Completing a Certificate Request

After you supply all of the information that a third party requires to generate a certificate, you'll receive a Certificate (CER) file. You use this file to install the certificate on your server. The following steps help you perform this process.

1. Click Complete Certificate Request in the Actions pane. You'll see the Complete Certificate Request dialog box shown in Figure 10.16.

FIGURE 10.16

Tell IIS where to locate the CER file containing the third-party certificate authority response.

2. Type the location of the CER file. You can also click the ellipsis button to display an Open dialog box you can use to locate the file.

3. Type a friendly name for the certificate in the Friendly Name field. Make sure the friendly name reflects the actual certificate use.

4. Click OK. IIS imports the certificate and it appears in the Server Certificates pane.

Creating a Domain Certificate

A domain certificate is very much like a third-party certificate, except that you use the domain certificate server to sign the certificate, rather than rely on a third party. Consequently, you can use this certificate with partners who already trust you, but it isn't a good choice for a Web site where you must provide a certificate that callers who don't know you will trust. The following steps tell how to create a domain certificate.

1. Create Domain Certificate in the Actions pane. You'll see a Create Certificate dialog box that looks like the one shown in Figure 10.14 (except for the title bar).

2. Type a name for the certificate in the Common Name field. Make sure this name reflects the name that your organization wants to use for the certificate since anyone who works with it will need to know the name.

TIP   Developers who use localhost for testing and want to see the Web site precisely the way the user will see it should create a certificate with the name of localhost. Provide localhost as the entry for both the Common Name field (step 2) and also as the certificate's friendly name (step 6). This process creates a certificate with the correct values for the browser to acknowledge the certificate as coming from the correct Web site.

3. Provide your organizational information. You must use full names, no abbreviations. The certificate must contain full information in every one of the fields, including the Organizational Unit field. If you have a small company, you'll need to provide either your company name or something like main office.

4. Click Next. You'll see the Online Certificate Authority dialog box shown in Figure 10.17. This dialog box identifies the certificate authority used to sign the certificate. When creating a certificate using a certificate server on your network, provide the location of the certificate server.

FIGURE 10.17
Provide the name and location of the certificate server used to sign the certificate.

5. Type the name of the certificate authority on the server, followed by a backslash, followed by the server name. For example, if the certificate authority name (as you provided it during installation) is MyCA and the name of the server is MyServer, you would type **MyCA\MyServer**. If you've forgotten the certificate authority name, open the Certificate Authority console found in the Administrative Tools folder of the Control Panel on the server. The certificate authority name appears directly after the Certification Authority entry in the Certification Authority console (see Figure 10.18).

USING DOMAIN CERTIFICATION AUTHORITY CERTIFICATES

You must install the certificate authority certificate in the Trusted Root Certification Authorities store on the IIS server system before the system will trust the domain certification authority. To perform this task, you must export the certificate authority server certificate and then import the certificate into the IIS server. Use the following steps to export the certificate authority server certificate.

1. Right-click the certificate authority name shown in Figure 10.18 and choose Properties from the context menu. You'll see a certificate authority Properties dialog box.

2. Choose the General tab. You'll see one or more CA certificates (normally just one).

3. Highlight the certificate you want to use and click View Certificate. You'll see a Certificate dialog box.

4. Choose the Details tab and click Copy to File. You'll see the Certificate Export Wizard.

5. Follow the steps to create a domain certificate (CER) file. Any of the output formats should work fine for this task.

Now that you have a CER file to use, you need to install it on the IIS server. The following steps accomplish this task.

1. Double-click the certificate entry in Windows Explorer from the IIS server. Windows will ask whether you're sure that you want to open the file.

2. Click Open to see the certificate.

3. Verify the information is correct and then click Install Certificate. You'll see the Certificate Import Wizard.

4. Click Next. You'll see the Certificate Store dialog box.

5. Choose the Place All Certificates in the Following Store option.

6. Click Browse and choose the Trusted Root Certificate Authorities option.

7. Click OK. You'll see the store added to the Certificate Stores dialog box.

8. Click Next. You'll see a summary dialog box.

9. Click Finish. You'll see a Security Warning dialog box telling you that you're about to install a certificate from a certificate authority.

10. Verify the information and click Yes. The domain controller will now appear within the trusted list for the IIS server.

6. Type the friendly name for the certificate. The friendly name is the name you'll use to reference the certificate on your machine. Use a name that reflects that this certificate is a domain certificate, rather than one issued by a third party such as VeriSign.

7. Click Finish. Even on a lightly loaded system, the certificate signing process can require several minutes. Be patient because interrupting the process simply means that you have to start it over again. When the certificate is signed, it appears in the Server Certificates pane. In addition, you'll see the certificate information in the Issued Certificates folder of the Certification Authority console as a Web Server certificate as shown in Figure 10.18. The certificate type appears in the Certificate Template column of the entry. The remainder of the entry tells about the certificate—who requested it, how long the certificate will last, and all of the identifying information found in the original certificate request.

FIGURE 10.18

The Certificate Authority console will show the certificate you created using IIS.

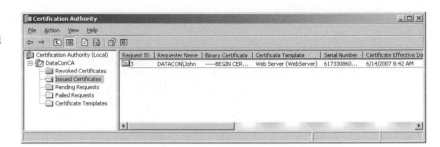

RENEWING CERTIFICATES

Unlike most of the certificates you see in the Server Certificates pane, a domain certificate includes an additional entry in the Actions pane. The Renew action lets you renew a certificate when it becomes outdated. The following steps describe how to review your domain certificate.

1. Highlight the outdated certificate and click Renew in the Actions pane (if this action doesn't appear, then the certificate you have highlighted isn't renewable using this technique). You'll see the Renew an Existing Certificate wizard.

2. Choose the Renew an Existing Certificate option and click Next. You'll see a Specify Online Certificate Server Authority dialog box.

3. Type the name of the certificate authority on the server, followed by a backslash, followed by the server name. This field contains the same information as when you originally requested the certificate.

4. Click Finish. After a long wait, IIS will update the certificate information in the Server Certificates pane.

On rare occasions, renewing a certificate directly will fail. In this case, you can try creating a certificate request, handling it on the certificate authority server, and then installing it on the IIS server using the other options in the first page of the Renew an Existing Certificate wizard. Use the Create a Renewal Certificate Request option to create the request and the Complete a Certificate Renewal Request option to install the certificate. If you still can't obtain satisfactory results, delete the old certificate and create a new one using the procedure in this section of the chapter.

Renewing certificates normally won't work for third-party certificates because you have no direct connection to the certification authority server. Follow the third-party recommendations for renewing a third-party certificate.

Creating a Self-Signed Certificate

A self-signed certificate is good for a number of tasks. If someone already knows you and simply needs to know that they're talking with you, a self-signed certificate can do the job. You'll also find self-signed certificates used for testing purposes. There isn't a good reason to purchase a certificate from VeriSign for your test server. In most cases, all you really need is something to let you test your applications. After all, you already test yourself. The following steps tell you how to create a self-signed certificate.

1. Click Create Self-Signed Certificate in the Actions pane. You'll see the Create Self-Signed Certificate wizard shown in Figure 10.19.

FIGURE 10.19
Use self-signed certifi-
cates for partner,
local, or testing needs.

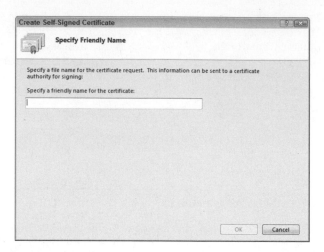

2. Type a friendly name for the certificate. The name should be something that positively identifies the certificate as self-signed so you don't confuse it with another certificate.

3. Click OK. IIS generates the certificate for you and automatically installs it in the Server Certificates pane.

NOTE Developers who use a self-signed certificate for testing purposes will see an error when viewing the Web site in a browser. Most modern browsers will complain that the name on the certificate doesn't match the name of the Web site when working with localhost. This error won't affect your testing results in most cases, but the browser displays may not precisely reflect what the user sees. See the procedure found in the "Creating a Domain Certificate" section of the chapter to overcome this problem.

Configuring an Application to Use SSL

One of the main reasons to obtain a server certificate is to create an SSL setup. In some cases, you'll secure the whole server, but in other cases you'll secure only specific applications or even specific Web pages. What you secure depends on the situation. For example, a public Web site may only secure the Web pages used to log in for premium information, while a shopping cart application may use SSL for the entire shopping experience. A private Web site may secure the entire Web site to ensure no one can intercept messages between the client and the server. No matter what reason you have for securing a Web site or its elements, the following sections will get you started.

Creating an HTTPS Binding

Before you can use SSL at all, the Web site must support an HTTPS binding. The HTTPS protocol relies on SSL to secure the communication between the client and the server. It's important to remember that only the communication is secure—you still need to include appropriate security to secure the Web site or application as needed. For example, when working with a shopping cart application on a public Web site, all you need to secure is the communication using HTTPS, but when working with a private Web site where access is limited, you also need to provide security.

When you create a Web site, you normally assign it an HTTP binding (see the "Adding a Web Site" section of Chapter 2 for details). The default port for this binding is port 80, but you can use any port desired. HTTPS binding works the same way, except it has a default port of port 443. You can use another port number if desired for additional security. In this case, you're adding a second binding to an existing Web site. The following steps show how to add an HTTPS binding after you install a server certificate on the server.

1. Select the Web site you want to modify in the Connections pane.

2. Click Bindings in the Actions pane. You'll see the Web Site Bindings dialog box shown in Figure 10.20.

FIGURE 10.20
View the existing bindings for a Web site using this dialog box.

3. Click Add. You'll see an Add Web Site Binding dialog box similar to the one shown in Figure 10.21.

FIGURE 10.21
Add the HTTPS binding to the Web site for secure communications.

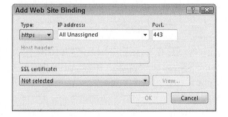

4. Choose the HTTPS entry in the Type field. The dialog box changes so it looks like the one shown in Figure 10.21.

5. Provide an IP address in the IP Address field or use the All Unassigned setting as shown. Choose a port for the secure communication. The default setting is port 443.

6. Choose an SSL certificate in the SSL Certificate field.

7. Click View to see the certificate so you can ensure that this is the correct certificate for the Web site in question. You'll see a Certificate dialog box that contains all of the certificate details. Click OK to close the Certificate dialog box.

8. Click OK. IIS creates the new binding. You can see it in the Web Site Bindings dialog box.

9. Click Close to close the Web Site Bindings dialog box.

Defining the Server Settings

After you install a certificate and configure the appropriate bindings, you can begin using SSL. Even though all of the infrastructure is in place, you still have to configure the Web site, folder, or application to use SSL. To perform this task, select the Web site, folder, or application you want to configure in the Connections pane and double-click the SSL Settings icon. You'll see the SSL Settings pane shown in Figure 10.22.

FIGURE 10.22
Configure a Web site, folder, or application to rely on SSL for communication security.

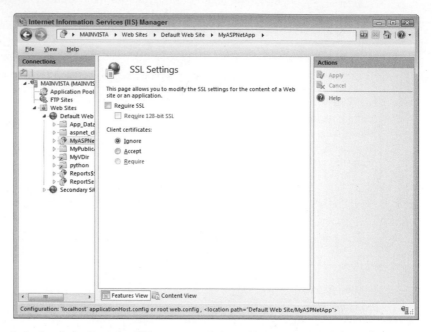

All you need to do is check the Require SSL option and then click Apply in the Actions pane to implement SSL. The default SSL provides 40-bit encryption, which works fine for most applications. It's important to remember that even 40-bit encryption will slow the connection dramatically and use more server resources as well. Theoretically, it's possible for someone to break 40-bit encryption, however, so you might need additional encryption.

When the situation requires tougher security, you can click the Require 128-bit SSL option. This option makes it incredibly unlikely that someone will intercept and decrypt your communication. However, it also presents problems for browsers that don't support 128-bit encryption and slows your server down even more.

You can also require that the client provide a certificate to prove their identity. A client certificate provides an additional level of security because now both ends of the conversation have proof of the other's identity. You can either accept the client certificate when available or require the certificate as part of the SSL setup using the options shown in Figure 10.22. Using the client certificate does provide a significant boost in security, but using the client certificate also impacts system performance even more than using 128-bit SSL encryption. You should only require a client certificate in the most secure communications.

Defining the Client Settings

The client will also need to make some changes to use SSL. If a client attempts to access an SSL page using the HTTP protocol, they receive error message 403.4, which signifies that IIS has forbidden access. Under the most likely causes for this issue, you'll find that enabling SSL ranks at the top. The client must access the Web page by directly typing HTTPS as the protocol since most browsers assume the client will use HTTP.

Most browsers also display a message box when the user attempts to access the Web site for the first time, like the one shown in Figure 10.23. Unfortunately, no matter how the browser developer words the message, most users just don't understand what is happening and refuse to accept the certificate. You can overcome this problem by pre-installing the certificate on the user's machine whenever possible.

FIGURE 10.23
Browsers display a message box telling the user about the SSL certificate.

When you require a client certificate, you'll need to ensure that the client knows about the client and that the client has the certificate installed using the procedures for their particular browser. Because only private Web sites are likely to require client certificates, you can make this procedure part of any Web site documentation for your organization. The important issue is that the client must have a certificate installed in the browser and not just on the machine. Browsers that support certificates provide the means for viewing existing certificates and installing new ones. If the user encounters problems accessing your application, ask them to view the certificate they have installed on their machine and ensure it meets any access requirements for your server.

Managing .NET Users

The list of .NET users you create for a Web site or application helps determine who can log onto the Web site or application. However, before you can add .NET users to your setup, you need to enable forms-based authentication (see the "Setting Authentication Requirements" section of the chapter for details). You should also disable any other form of authentication for an application or the application may not work as anticipated.

TIP The techniques for working with forms-based applications aren't very hard and they're considerably more reliable than other techniques you've used in the past. My books *Mastering Web Development with Microsoft Visual Studio 2005* (medium- to large-sized enterprise development) and *Mastering Microsoft Visual Web Developer 2005 Express Edition* (personal and small business development) both show how to create forms-based applications.

A developer must also create an application in such a way as it supports forms-based authentication. The process isn't hard, but the application will end up with a Login.ASPX file and some database entries that control user access. Once you enable forms-based authentication and have a suitable application, you can begin adding users to the list. Choose the application you want to configure in the Connections pane and then double-click the .NET Users icon to display the .NET Users pane shown in Figure 10.24. The following sections describe how to manage .NET users.

FIGURE 10.24
Use the .NET Users
pane to manage
users for an ASP.NET
application.

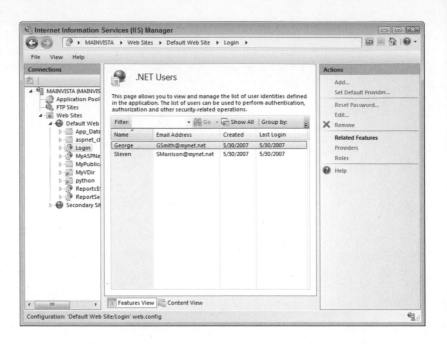

NOTE   You may have noticed the Reset Password action in the Actions pane. Clicking this action
displays a dialog box that tells you the user's question and answer are required to reset the password. As an administrator, you can't do anything with the password; the application that the
developer creates must include the functionality required for the user to make this change. In
fact, if you look at the user entries in the SQL Server database, you'll find that the .NET Framework encrypts much of the information, making it impossible for the administrator to peek at the
information. The .NET Framework also supports functionality that lets a user recover a password. The user provides the answer to a question and the application automatically sends the
password to the user's email account.

Adding Users

One of the first tasks you'll perform with the new application is add a list of users that can access
it. Some applications will include functionality for you to add new users using the application itself.
In fact, some applications may ask the user to provide their own information and gain acceptance
through administrator approval. Theoretically, you may never see any of the user's information
except for a name and other nonsensitive data. Follow these steps when you want to add the users
directly from IIS.

1. Click Add in the Actions pane. You'll see the Add .NET User dialog box shown in Figure 10.25.

2. Type the user's information in the various fields. You must provide input for every blank.
   Make sure that the blanks contain valid information because you can't edit the information
   later. In fact, you can't see any of the information later, not even for verification purposes, so
   getting it right the first time is essential.

FIGURE 10.25
Provide the username
and other essential
input information—
all blanks must have
an entry.

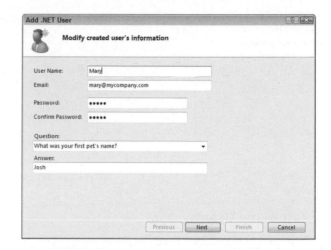

3. Click Next. You'll see the .NET User Roles dialog box shown in Figure 10.26.

FIGURE 10.26
Configure the
user's access to an
application based on
their role.

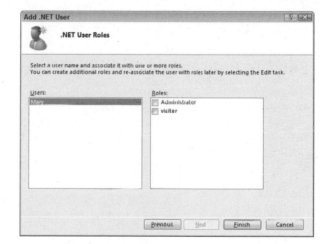

4. Check each of the roles that the user will fulfill in the organization.

5. Click Finish. IIS will add the new user to the list.

Editing Users

You can edit users for a particular ASP.NET application—you simply can't change very much
information about them. When you click Edit in the Actions pane, you'll see an Edit .NET User dialog box like the one shown in Figure 10.27. This dialog box lets you change the user's email address
and set new roles for the user. Otherwise, you can't make any changes to the user's settings.

FIGURE 10.27
IIS won't let you
change very many
.NET user settings.

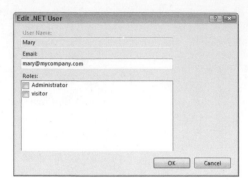

Removing Users

Because of the restrictions placed on administrators, it's very likely that you'll need to remove a user at some point. Although the security restrictions that IIS places on administrators are warranted (and even good), user idiosyncrasies will make it necessary to remove an account and then re-create it from time to time. To remove a .NET user entry, highlight the entry you want to remove and click Remove in the Actions pane. You'll see a dialog box asking whether you're sure you want to remove the user. Click Yes to complete the action.

Setting Role-Based Security Using .NET Roles

The roles you create for an application depend on the application itself since the developer must add code to the application to act on the roles. Consequently, you'll probably see the roles already configured when you install a new application and you'll have to work with the developer before you can change any of them. To see the roles associated with an application, choose the application in the Connections pane and then double-click the .NET Roles icon to display the .NET Roles pane shown in Figure 10.28.

FIGURE 10.28
Use the .NET Roles
pane to view the roles
associated with a particular application.

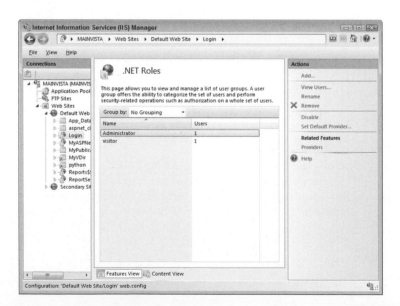

It's important not to change any of the settings in the .NET Roles pane without understanding the consequences of doing so. For example, when you click Rename, IIS turns the Name field of the selected entry into an edit box and you can change the role name. Unfortunately, if the application doesn't have a similar change, it won't recognize the user's role and won't work as expected. Removing roles can have a similar effect and adding roles is useless when the application doesn't support the role.

This pane does have one particular feature that will appeal to administrators. You can highlight a role and click View Users in the Actions pane. IIS will display a .NET Users pane that's filtered to show just the users that fulfill the specified role. This view can prove useful when you need to make changes to every one of the users in a particular role or simply need to perform an inventory of them.

Setting Code-Based Security Using .NET Trust Levels

The .NET trust level determines how much trust you can place in the code for a particular application. This setting complements the code-based security settings defined by the developer (see the "Understanding Code-Based Security" section of Chapter 9 for details on code-based security). In some cases, the setting will override the developer setting by placing greater restrictions on the code. The purpose of this setting is to restrict the code so that an outsider can't fool the code (by using an exploit or other trick) into performing a task that the original developer never intended. To access the .NET trust level, select the application you want to configure in the Connections pane, and then double-click the .NET Trust Levels icon to display the .NET Trust Levels pane shown in Figure 10.29.

FIGURE 10.29
Choose the level of trust required to run an application, but not let it perform unexpected actions.

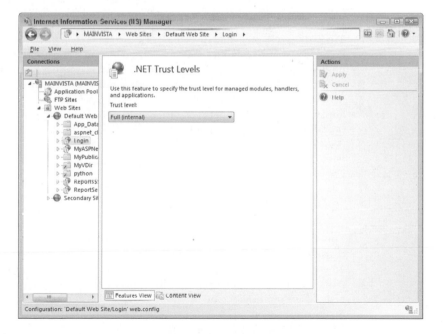

The setting is a single drop-down list box that defines how much trust you can place in the code in a given circumstance. The following list describes each of the settings.

Full (internal)   Gives the code unrestricted permissions, which means that it can do anything on the server. The application can perform any task and access any resource on the server unless the developer has included restrictions that reduce application trust or you configure the application using other means, such as the Microsoft .NET Framework 2.0 Configuration console described in the "Using the Microsoft .NET Framework 2.0 Configuration Console" section of Chapter 9. You should never use this setting for an application that has outside access, and you may not want to use it on internal applications unless required.

High (web_hightrust_config)   Provides the application with maximum access to system resources and allows it to perform most common tasks. This level of security normally works fine for internal networks and some applications on private network. You don't want to use this setting with a public connection unless absolutely required because it still provides the application code with considerable access to the server. An application with this setting cannot perform the following tasks directly (however, it can request that another application perform the task indirectly, which gives you an added layer of control).

- Call unmanaged code using the Platform Invoke (P/Invoke) functionality

- Call serviced components

- Write to the event log

- Access Microsoft Message Queuing (MSMQ) service queues

- Access Open Database Connectivity (ODBC), Object Linking and Embedding – Database (OLE-DB), or Oracle data sources

Medium (web_mediumtrust_config)   Provides the application with a moderate level of access to system resources, but restricts actions that the application can perform to a greater degree. This level of security normally works well on private networks where outside access is questionable and can work on some public networks. However, when working with a public network, you must also work with the developer to ensure all inputs are checked and that the application provides internal restrictions as needed to prevent unauthorized actions. In addition to the restrictions of the High access level, the Medium access level provides these restrictions (it's usually not possible to perform these tasks indirectly either).

- Access files outside the application directory

- Access the registry

- Make network or Web service calls (even internal Web services)

Low (web_lowtrust_config)   Provides the application with restricted access to resources and considerable restraints on actions that it can perform. Use this level of security for public networks where you have no reason to believe there's any chance of securing the application otherwise. About the only task this application can perform is serving data to the user. In addition to the restrictions of the High and Medium access levels, the Low access level places these restrictions on the application.

- Write to the file system

- Call the Assert method (the Assert method is used by developers for debugging purposes)

Minimal (web_minimaltrust_config)   At this level, the application can only execute. You can't use it to serve data or perform other tasks. However, this level is useful for situations where you really do need the application to execute and rely on its internal data. For example, you could create an online game using this approach. The application can also store information on the user's machine using cookies, so it can still function and maintain state.

Storing User Settings with the .NET Profile

The .NET profile works like a setting, except that it's on a per-user or per-role basis in many cases. The profile helps you configure an application to meet the needs of a particular group and it helps you perform on-the-fly configuration of specific application features. For example, administrators may need to see specific information that the average user may not need to see. However, when you're performing system maintenance, you may not want anyone to see the settings, so you can temporarily disable administrator access as well. The entries can affect a particular user and you can also create global settings that affect everyone. The basic difference between a profile and an application setting is that a profile configures user access while an application setting configures application functionality.

Normally, an application will come configured with all of the required profile settings. However, you'll want to view and become familiar with these settings so you can modify them as needed later. To view the profile settings for an application, choose the application in the Connections pane and double-click the .NET Profile icon. You'll see the .NET Profile pane as shown in Figure 10.30.

FIGURE 10.30
Use profiles to modify user access to application functionality.

Adding a Global Property

Global properties affect everyone who uses the application. For example, you might use this feature to change the message that the application displays to greet the user. To add a global property, click Add Property in the Actions pane. You'll see the Add .NET Profile Property dialog box shown in Figure 10.31.

FIGURE 10.31
Define property values that reflect activities that application can perform.

Because the application needs to interact with the property, you can't simply define a property without working with the developer. Once the application has the property in place, you can provide a property name, data type, and serialization (how the data is stored) option based on the developer's input. (Developers will usually choose String serialization because it's convenient, but may choose XML for complex data or binary for sensitive data.) You should also provide a value based on the range of values that the developer tells you the property can accept.

The Read Only option lets you make the property unchangeable by the user. When the user tries to make a change, IIS retains the old value. Of course, setting the property to read only can also hinder the application from working, so you need to check with the developer about when this option is appropriate.

The Available for Anonymous Users option is a security feature. Normally, IIS keeps this option cleared. If your application services anonymous users, however, you can check it to be sure they see the effects of the property as well.

Adding a Group

Groups are any entity that the application is designed to recognize. A group could be a Windows user group, an individual user, a .NET role, or any other designation that somehow separates one group of users from another. The properties you set for one group won't affect any other group. To create a new group, click Add Group in the Actions pane. You'll see an Add Group dialog box where you can type the group name. Click OK to complete the action.

Adding a Group Property

Properties can appear globally or as part of a group. When they appear as part of a group, they only affect that group. To add a new property to a group, click Add Property to Group in the Actions pane. You'll see a dialog box like the one shown in Figure 10.31. Use the same technique as you would for adding a global property (see the "Adding a Global Property" section of the chapter for details).

Removing Groups or Properties

It's important to exercise care in removing groups or properties because an absent group or property can cause the application to work incorrectly. To remove a group or property, highlight the group or property you want to remove and click Remove in the Actions pane. You'll see a warning message asking whether you're sure you want to remove the group or property. Click Yes to complete the process. Deleting a group removes any properties contained within the group as well.

Editing Properties

You can edit any part of a property except the property name. To edit a property, highlight the property you want to change and click Edit in the Actions pane. You'll see a dialog box like the one shown in Figure 10.31. Use the same technique to edit the property as you would for adding a global property (see the "Adding a Global Property" section of the chapter for details).

Generally speaking, the only safe edit is one where you change a property value within the limits set by the developer. For example, a `System.Boolean` property can have a value of `True` or `False`. A `System.String` property may have a specific set of values (as in a configuration option) or may allow any value you want to provide (such as a string that defines an application greeting). Numeric properties will always require a number as a value, but you need to know the valid range before you make a change to it.

Serialization, the method of storing the value on disk, can change because some types of serialization are more efficient than others in certain circumstances. A serialization change does require changes in the application code, so you can't make them unless the developer also changes the application. The method of serialization doesn't change the value or data type of the property, so a developer may very well ask you to change this setting. As always, exercise care in making changes because even serialization can cause application problems.

Developers rarely change the data type of a variable. When they do make a data type change, they also change the name of the variable to show the change in type. If someone tells you to change a data type, you'll want to verify the action before you make the change.

Renaming Properties

Renaming a property can have the same devastating effects as removing one. The application may not be able to find the data it needs to complete a task. Consequently, you should only rename properties when required by application changes. To rename a property, highlight the property you want to change and then click Rename in the Actions pane. The Name field entry will turn into an edit box. Type the new property name and press Enter.

Let's Start Building

The chapter has focused on implementing security. While Chapter 9 helped you understand how security works and how to monitor it, this chapter has helped you gain the knowledge required to secure your ASP.NET applications. Good security is an essential part of any application strategy today because the penalties for lax implementation are so incredibly high. It's important to remember to secure the door, secure the communications channel, secure the user, secure the code, and secure the application settings so that few opportunities exist for someone with ill intent. This chapter helps you build these skills:

◆ Manage authorization settings

◆ Define authorization rules

◆ Manage server certificates

◆ Use SSL to secure an application

◆ Configure .NET users

◆ Configure role-based security settings

◆ Configure code-based security settings

◆ Save user settings

Now that's you've seen how security works, take time to plan a secure setup for your application, implement the security settings, and test them. Of course, the result is going to appear perfect to you because you planned it and used every resource at your disposal to make sure it works. Now it's time to ask a third party to poke holes in your security scheme. When there are no more holes to poke, consider asking a security professional to examine your setup as well. Even after you have gone to these extremes, remember one last important piece of advice—every security scheme has holes. No matter how well you plan and implement your security scheme, someone else will find a way to poke holes in it. The goal is to create the best security scheme you can and then monitor it. When someone does poke a hole in your security scheme, take time to find out how they did it. Patch the new hole, but always assume that someone else will find a new way to get in.

Chapter 11 discusses database connectivity. IIS 7 uses databases for a considerable number of tasks, so you already have some level of database connectivity. However, applications require their own connections to the database and that's the focus of Chapter 11. You'll use the information you learn in Chapter 11 to create connections that will work well for your applications.

Chapter 11

Defining Database Connectivity

Very few computers lack a database. Even home users have databases, often several of them, installed on their computers. Of course, a database offers little when you can't connect to it. Consequently, it's hardly surprising that database connectivity would be one of the issues that face someone using IIS. Not only does IIS 7 use SQL Server to handle its own storage needs, but you'll also find databases of all kinds used with the applications that run on IIS. It's important to realize that the world doesn't rely on just one database, so the IIS administrator will commonly find a need to connect to databases other than Access or SQL Server, despite Microsoft's desire that everyone use its products exclusively.

Administrators need to consider multiple levels of connectivity for the Web server, Web sites, and applications. The level at which a connection appears determines its visibility, accessibility, security exposure, and other factors. IIS is also set up to work exclusively with SQL Server. If you want to use another database, you have to learn the arcane art of the connection string. The access isn't impossible; Microsoft simply wants to remind you that SQL Server is their product. This chapter helps you discover the art of creating a custom connection string that should let you access any common database. Of course, once you create a connection string, you'll want to add it to IIS and manage it in some way.

A database is an essential part of almost any Web site. It is also the most valuable part of any Web site and you're exposing that value to potential loss. It's very hard not to read about database losses in the trade press papers anymore. Few weeks go by without some mention of someone losing thousands of records containing essential data such as social security numbers. Even if you don't store such sensitive information in your database, your data has value and you must do everything you can to protect it. Although a section of a chapter can hardly do justice to the entire topic of database security, this chapter does provide some essentials you need to know when working with IIS 7.

In this chapter, you will learn how to do the following:

- ◆ Define the requirements for making a database connection

- ◆ Manage the providers required for IIS

- ◆ Define and use the elements of a connection string

- ◆ Create a list of connection strings

- ◆ Develop security requirements for database connections

NOTE A few definitions are in order before you begin this chapter. A *database* is a storage container for data—it includes tables, indexes, views, scripts, and other database elements. A *database manager* is a special piece of software that organizes and manages the content of the database on behalf of the organization. A *database management system (DBMS)* is a vendor-produced product that includes the database manager and any required support databases. It's easy to confuse these terms because they sound so much alike and some people use the terms in more than one way.

Understanding Database Connectivity Requirements

Applications can create connections to databases in many ways. The most efficient approach is to use a direct connection. That's the kind of connectivity described in this chapter. You create a connection to the database using the IIS application. When the caller makes a request, the Web application responds by querying the database, retrieving the required data, and formulating a response. Usually, this approach is the most efficient way to work and many Web applications use it without any problem at all.

ASP.NET provides special resources for working with a direct connection. When the developer creates the application, the Web.CONFIG file for it contains a new connection string. The connection string is a combination of XML and data required to make a connection to the database that looks like this (the connection string appears on one line in the file, even though it appears on multiple lines in the book).

```
<add connectionString="Server=MAINVISTA\SQLEXPRESS;
    Database=ReportServer$SQLExpress;Integrated Security=true"
    name="MySQLConnection" />
```

This is a SQL Server Express connection, but other databases use a similar approach (the "Considering the Elements of a Connection String" section of the chapter describes how to create connection strings for almost any database). Even though the developer created this string, you can modify the string using the Internet Information Services (IIS) Manager (see the "Managing Connection Strings" section of the chapter for details). You can also modify the strings directly using a standard text editor. The point is that the connection information is a string that you can modify as needed. To read the string, the developer uses the following call:

```
System.Configuration.ConfigurationManager.
    ConnectionStrings["MySQLConnection"].ConnectionString
```

TIP Developers can discover more about connection string management basics at http://msdn2.microsoft.com/en-us/library/ds20z471.aspx. You can also find an interesting article about using connection strings for Web farms at http://www.codeproject.com/aspnet/WebFarmConnStringsNet20.asp.

The example shown is for the SQL connection described earlier. The point is that developers can implement the connection string in such a way that the application doesn't care where the database appears—the only consideration is finding it. Consequently, when working with direct connections, the administrator has considerable control over the location of the database and the developer doesn't have to do anything special when that location changes. The code handles any changes automatically.

Direct connections are nice when you're working with ASP.NET and they're even usable when working with other language products. Because the data appears in a standard XML file, you can use the connection in any language product that supports XML. Even scripting languages, such as VBScript and JavaScript, provide support for XML, so the connection string is usable for any direct connection in any modern language.

However, the flexibility that direct connections can provide also causes security problems. The Web.CONFIG file is text. Anyone who gains access to the Web server will know where you store the data. They don't even have to jump through the firewall to gain this information. Although this chapter doesn't discuss indirect access techniques, you should consider using them for sensitive data such as social security numbers. Using indirect access techniques, you can hide everything about the database access behind a firewall—making it considerably more difficult for someone to compromise your data.

Indirect techniques rely on a middle-level business component. For example, you could implement all of the required business logic as part of a COM+ application. The COM+ application can appear behind the firewall. Your Web application simply calls the COM+ application and asks it to perform the required access. The Web application receives the data as normal and forms it into a Web response. Now all the outsider knows is that you can make a series of calls to get data, but that's it.

By adding logic to the middle-level component that checks requests for irregularities, you can further restrain outside access to just the expected data. In other words, anything unexpected sets off alarms and rejects the request for data, so you have considerably better control over how outsiders access the data. Through good input-checking techniques, you can restrict the kinds of requests that callers make and thwart efforts such as script injection attacks.

It's important to remember that there isn't a free ride of any sort in Web site management. Every level of indirection causes performance hits, so your Web server needs more power to work with these indirect requests. Using indirect requests also reduces the reliability of your Web site because the Web site now has more software that can break and the software exists on multiple machines, which also adds a hardware reliability hit. The indirection can also have unintended effects. For example, it makes good sense to use at least one level of indirection for a shopping cart application because the data exchange includes sensitive information such as credit card numbers. However, the indirection increases the shopper wait time, so you'll also lose sales when shoppers quit before making their purchase due to delays in Web site response.

Managing Providers

At one time, you had to create a connection string to perform just about any task using ASP.NET. Someone at Microsoft finally figured out that developers were spending a great deal of time re-creating the same connections repeatedly. A *provider* is a special kind of service that manages certain kinds of data storage. For example, IIS relies on a provider to store role information for a user. Don't confuse an IIS provider with a database provider, which is a special kind of software that creates a connection between the application and the database manager.

Using providers can save developers a great deal of time. For example, when a developer adds login controls to a Web page to implement forms-based security, the login controls actually rely on the System.Web.Security.SqlMembershipProvider class as a provider in most cases. This class provides membership information using a SQL Server database. As an alternative, the developer can use the System.Web.Security.ActiveDirectoryMembershipProvider, which provides membership information from Active Directory. The point is that the developer simply uses the services of the provider, rather than having to code the database connectivity by hand.

IIS includes some default providers. You can also add providers through applications. The providers that you'll consider in this chapter fulfill three needs: .NET Roles, .NET Users, and .NET Profile. ASP.NET does support other providers (see the "Adding New Providers" section of the chapter for details). You can add providers as needed to the Web server, Web site, or application. It's important to remember that the .NET focus on providers doesn't prevent you from using them for other programming languages when the programming language provides the correct linkage.

To access the providers, select the level you want to work within the Connections pane and double-click the Providers icon. You'll see the Providers pane shown in Figure 11.1. The figure is showing the .NET Roles feature, but you can also choose to view the .NET Users or .NET Profile features. Each feature provides access to a particular IIS element. The following sections describe providers in detail and help you understand how they help you create a connection to your database.

FIGURE 11.1
Use the Providers pane to manage the providers on your Web site.

Understanding the Purpose of a Provider

Applications use connection strings that you create separately from a provider. The connection string tells the application where to locate the data the application requires. Likewise, a provider requires a connection string as input to describe the connection to the database manager. All providers in IIS 7 are .NET classes. Providers provide three features (or you could say they fall into three groups):

.NET Roles   This feature implements any role-based need. You'll find everything from the provider for the .NET Roles feature to providers used for role-based security. The default provider is the `System.Web.Security.SqlRoleProvider` class.

.NET Users   This feature implements any user or membership need. If you were to create your own user database, such as for a forms-based application, the resulting provider would appear as part of this feature. The default provider is the `System.Web.Security.SqlMembershipProvider` class.

.NET Profile   This feature implements any profile storage. You can use to it to store any global or group profile information. The default provider is the `System.Web.Profile` `.SqlProfileProvider` class.

TIP   Developers can find a good two-part article that describes providers at `http://odetocode` `.com/Articles/427.aspx` and `http://www.odetocode.com/Articles/428.aspx`. The Microsoft documentation for Web security classes appears at `http://msdn2.microsoft` `.com/en-us/library/system.web.security.aspx` and you'll find the profile classes at `http://msdn2.microsoft.com/en-us/library/system.web.profile.aspx`.

Every feature has a default provider. When you select the default provider, IIS 7 tells you that it's the default provider, as shown in Figure 11.1. You can't edit, rename, or remove the default provider because IIS 7 requires it to perform tasks. The default provider is also the one that applications are most likely to use for specific purposes, such as managing user accounts or working with roles.

Whenever a developer creates a .NET application with database requirements, Visual Studio provides the means to include the correct connection string within the `Web.CONFIG` file. However, you may find that the default providers don't appear as part of your IIS 7 installation or they become corrupted. You can recreate the database and its required tables using the ASPNet_Reg-SQL utility with the –A command line option. For example, if you want to re-create the database required for the `System.Web.Security.SqlRoleProvider` class, you would type **ASPNet_ RegSQL -Ar** at the command line and press Enter. The ASPNet_RegSQL utility appears in the `\Windows\Microsoft.NET\Framework\v2.0.50727` folder of your hard drive. Here are the most common command line options for recreating the provider information.

-Aall   Re-creates all of the application services options.

-Am   Re-creates the membership (.NET Users) options.

-Ar   Re-creates the role manager (.NET Roles) options.

-Ap   Re-creates the profiles (.NET Profile) options.

-Ac   Re-creates the application personalization options.

-Aw   Re-creates the SQL Web event provider.

Viewing Connections Associated with a Provider

A provider isn't very helpful without connections. It's important to remember that the provider only includes software, not the actual connection. The connection string you create provides the information required to create the connection using the provider software. To see the connections associated with a particular provider, highlight the provider in the Providers pane and click Connection Strings in the Actions pane. You'll see a list of connections like the one shown in Figure 11.2. You can use the techniques described in the "Managing Connection Strings" section of the chapter to change the connection information when necessary.

Adding New Providers

In some cases, you may need to add a new provider to IIS. For example, an application you want to install may use Active Directory, rather than SQL Server, to store .NET User information. Table 11.1 shows the standard providers used by ASP.NET and IIS. Third parties can create custom providers as well, so you may see other options in your IIS installation.

FIGURE 11.2
Providers rely on con-
nections to perform
any useful work.

TABLE 11.1: ASP.NET 2.0 Provider Types and Associated Classes

PROVIDER TYPE	ASSOCIATED CLASSES
Role Management (.NET Roles)	`System.Web.Security.AuthorizationStoreRoleProvider`
	`System.Web.Security.SqlRoleProvider`
	`System.Web.Security.WindowsTokenRoleProvider`
Membership (.NET Users)	`System.Web.Security.ActiveDirectoryMembershipProvider`
	`System.Web.Security.SqlMembershipProvider`
Profile (.NET Profile)	`System.Web.Profile.SqlProfileProvider`
Site Map	`System.Web.XmlSiteMapProvider`
Session State	`System.Web.SessionState.InProcSessionStateStore`
	`System.Web.SessionState.OutOfProcSessionStateStore`
	`System.Web.SessionState.SqlSessionStateStore`
Web Events	`System.Web.Management.EventLogWebEventProvider`
	`System.Web.Management.SimpleMailWebEventProvider`
	`System.Web.Management.TemplatedMailWebEventProvider`
	`System.Web.Management.SqlWebEventProvider`
	`System.Web.Management.TraceWebEventProvider`
	`System.Web.Management.WmiWebEventProvider`

TABLE 11.1: ASP.NET 2.0 Provider Types and Associated Classes *(CONTINUED)*

PROVIDER TYPE	ASSOCIATED CLASSES
Web Parts Personalization	`System.Web.UI.WebControls.WebParts.SqlPersonalizationProvider`
Protected Configuration	`System.Configuration.DPAPIProtectedConfigurationProvider`
	`System.Configuration.RSAProtectedConfigurationProvider`

Make sure you choose the correct provider type for any applications you install. The following steps tell how to add a new provider to the list shown in the Providers pane.

1. Choose the provider type in the Feature field and click Add in the Actions pane. When working with .NET Roles or .NET Profile, you'll see the Add Provider dialog box shown in Figure 11.3. (You'll learn about .NET Users differences at the end of this procedure—the actual installation process is the same.)

FIGURE 11.3
Provide the required information for either a .NET Roles or .NET Profile provider.

2. Choose a provider class from the Type field. The Type field contents changes according to the kind of provider you want to install. If you don't see the provider class you need, it means that you're installing the wrong provider type or that you haven't registered the provider on the current system. The provider must appear in the GAC to appear in the list.

3. Type a name for the provider. The provider name is important because the developer may use it to reference the provider.

4. Type the name of the connection string in the ConnectionStringName field. Don't type the connection string here, just the name of the connection string. You must configure the connection string separately (see the "Managing Connection Strings" section of the chapter for details).

5. Type the name of the application (if any) that will use the provider in the ApplicationName field. When working with a provider in an application, you type that application's name. Don't include an application name when multiple applications will use the same provider. Make sure you check with the developer when creating this entry to ensure you include the name of an application when one is required and you're not creating the provider entry in

an application folder. If you don't provide an application name, then the provider defaults to using the value in the `HttpContext.Current.Request.ApplicationPath` property supplied as part of the caller request (making it possible to determine the application name when the application runs).

6. Type a description for the provider in the Description field. A description may not seem very exciting or useful, but you really need to include one unless you expect other administrators to delete the provider accidentally. Only a properly documented provider has any chance of survival.

The .NET Users version of the Add Provider dialog box contains some additional entries, as shown in Figure 11.4. The entries from Figure 11.3 are also present, so you supply them as you normally would. The Behavior section entries in Figure 11.4 control how the provider performs certain tasks. The following list describes each of these options.

FIGURE 11.4
The .NET Users provider requires additional settings to work properly.

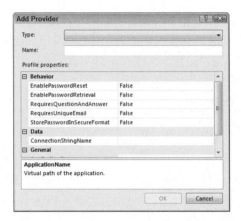

EnablePasswordReset This setting determines whether the application can reset a password using the provider's `ResetPassword()` method. In general, you want the user to change the password or tell the application to provide the password through email, rather than allowing the application to reset the password (a potential security hole). The default setting is `False`. You should set this value to True when the application includes an administrator or user feature to reset the password.

EnablePasswordRetrieval This setting determines whether the user can ask the application to retrieve a password using the `GetPassword()` method. This feature appears on many Web sites where the user can click a link that sends a forgotten password to their email account. Given that users are likely to forget their password at some point, this feature can reduce support calls. However, someone could theoretically use this feature to bypass security (it would be very hard because they'd have to know the user's question and answer, along with having access to their email account). The default setting is `False`.

RequiresQuestionAndAnswer Normally, when a user wants to reset or retrieve their password, they must supply an answer to a question. In fact, that's the default behavior for a forms-based application. This setting determines whether the user must actually supply an answer to a question. In all cases, you should change this setting to `True` for any user activity. The default setting is `False`.

RequiresUniqueEmail Generally, forms-based security requires a unique email because otherwise multiple users could send their password information to a single email address when retrieving it. In all cases, you should change this setting to True for any user activity. The default setting is False.

StorePasswordInSecureFormat The SQL Server database used to store the password information normally stores it as a hash, which means that no one can read it. The hash works by creating an encrypted form of the user's information. When the user enters the same information, the hash routine creates precisely the same hash. This technique ensures that the application can store the user's password without actually storing the human-readable form. Always change this setting to True to maintain good Web server security. The default setting is False.

Editing Existing Providers

You may make a mistake when creating a new provider or find that you need to modify a setting to reflect changing environmental needs. IIS lets you edit any provider except the default provider, which you can never change. To edit a provider, highlight the provider's entry in the Providers pane and click Edit in the Actions pane. You'll see a dialog box similar to the one shown in Figure 11.3 (.NET Roles and .NET Profile) or 11.4 (.NET Users). IIS lets you modify all of the settings except the Type and Name fields.

Removing Unneeded Providers

At some point, you may need to remove a provider you no longer need. You can remove any provider except the default provider. To remove a provider, highlight the provider entry in the Providers pane and click Remove in the Actions pane. IIS will display a dialog box asking you to confirm that you want to remove the provider entry. Click Yes to complete the process.

Considering the Elements of a Connection String

Connection strings cause a lot of woe for administrators and developers alike because they're not well documented and Microsoft's manner of handling them makes things worse. Fortunately, the connection string itself is easy to figure out once you know a few tricks and have a little more information than Microsoft commonly provides. The following sections describe connection strings from a number of perspectives.

Understanding the *Web.CONFIG* Entries

A connection string defines the data source used by the application. Depending on what data source you want to use, the connection string can contain a significant number of elements. For example, you may need to tell IIS which provider to use when working with the connection. However, a minimal connection requires at least the name and connectionString attributes.

The connection string appears in a special section of the Web.CONFIG file. You'll find it nestled within the <configuration> element, as shown here (the connection string appears on one line in the file, even though it appears on multiple lines in the book).

```
<configuration>
    <connectionStrings>
        <add connectionString="Server=MAINVISTA\SQLEXPRESS;
            Database=ReportServer$SQLExpress;Integrated Security=true"
            name="MySQLConnection" />
    </connectionStrings>
</configuration>
```

A `<connectionStrings>` element can contain any number of entries. In addition, you can use special elements to modify the entries. For example, when an application inherits a connection it doesn't need, the developer can remove it. The valid elements include:

add   Adds the connection string to the collection of connection strings. You perform this task with the graphical interface by adding a new local connection. The connection string must include the `name` and `connectionString` attributes as a minimum.

clear   Clears all of the connection strings inherited from a previous level. For example, when this entry appears in an application, the application won't include any references from the Web server or Web site levels. In addition, it removes references from any application folders that are higher in the hierarchy. You can't perform this task using the graphical interface. This element doesn't include any attributes.

remove   Removes an existing inherited connection string from the connection string collection. You perform this task with the graphical interface by removing an inherited connection. This element only requires the `name` attribute to identify the connection you want to remove.

Understanding the Attributes

The connection string includes a number of attributes that define its behavior. As previously mentioned, the shortest connection string you can create includes the `name` and `connectionString` attributes. However, you can include any number of attributes needed to define the connection fully. Here's a list of the connection string attributes.

connectionString   This attribute defines the connection. It includes information such as the name of the database and the security used to access it. The connection string provides input for the database manager—it helps the database manager decide whether to provide access to the requested information. When the database manager does decide to provide the information, the connection string also provides information on the method for providing the information. For example, many modern databases can provide output in XML format. The precise connection string contents depend on the DBMS you use—every vendor provides different name/value pairs to define the connection. However, this section does describe a few of the more common setups that you'll encounter. You must provide the `connectionString` attribute as part of the `<add>` element. The default value is an empty string.

name   Provides the name of the connection. Developers use the connection name to access the `connectionString` and other attributes. You must use a unique name for each connection. You must provide the `name` attribute as part of the `<add>` and `<remove>` elements. The default value is an empty string. When you create a local connection with the same name as an inherited connection, the local connection overrides the inherited connection.

providerName   Defines the database provider to use to create the connection. Don't confuse this setting with the provider described in the "Managing Providers" section of the chapter. A database provider is the software that creates a connection between the application and the database manager. It's not an IIS service. The default database provider is `System.Data.SqlClient`. The following list describes the common database providers for ASP.NET.

System.Xml   Provides support for XML databases, which includes the output of most Web services.

System.Data.OleDb   Provides support for Object Linking and Embedding – Database (OLE-DB) data sources. For the most part, you'll find that OLE-DB includes support for SQL Server, Access, and Oracle.

System.Data.SqlClient   This is the default database provider. It provides support for most versions of SQL Server. Microsoft has optimized this database provider for use with SQL Server 7.0 and later.

System.Data.Odbc   Provides support for any ODBC database. The ODBC database provider is the most flexible of them all. You can provide drivers for just about every database made. Although the connection is a little slow (most drivers aren't optimized), the connections are reliable. If you can't find a database provider for your database, try locating an ODBC driver for it and use the System.Data.Odbc database provider. You don't need to define a data source for ODBC using the Data Sources (ODBC) console located in the Administrative Tools folder of the Control Panel as you did in the past.

System.Data.OracleClient   Provides support for Oracle databases.

lockAllAttributesExcept   Locks all the attributes of the parent element, except those provided in the list. This attribute appears as part of the parent attribute—you can't lock parent attributes at the child level. You can include multiple attributes in a comma-delimited list.

LOCATING OTHER DATABASE PROVIDERS

You aren't stuck using the database providers that Microsoft supports. In fact, you may be surprised at the number of database providers available for the .NET Framework. The following list provides just a few of the database providers you can add to your ASP.NET setup to access alternative databases.

DB2 Provider IBM DB2 iSeries   http://www.ibm.com/developerworks/db2/2

Firebird SQL .NET Provider   http://firebirdsql.org/dotnetfirebird/

MySQLDirect .NET Data Provider (CoreLab.MySql)   http://www.crlab.com/mysqlnet/

Oracle .NET Data Provider (Oracle.DataAccess.Client)   http://www.oracle.com/technology/pub/articles/cook_dotnet.html

OraDirect .NET Data Provider (CoreLab.Oracle)   http://www.crlab.com/oranet/

PostgreSQLDirect .NET Data Provider (CoreLab.PostgreSql)   http://www.crlab.com/pgsqlnet/

Sybase Adaptive Server (ASE) Enterprise .NET Data Provider (Sybase.Data.AseClient)   http://www.sybase.com/detail?id=1028614

System.Data.SQLite   http://sqlite.phxsoftware.com/

VistaDB (VistaDB.Provider)   http://www.vistadb.net/

Make sure you also visit alternative ways of implementing the entire ADO.NET solution. For example, you can find an open source solution at http://www.mono-project.com/ADO.NET. The bottom line is that you should be able to find a database provider for almost any modern database and more than a few ancient databases as well.

---

lockAllElementsExcept   Locks all the child elements of the parent element, except those provided in the list. This attribute appears as part of the parent attribute—you can't lock child elements at the child level. You can include multiple attributes in a comma-delimited list.

lockAttributes Locks the specified attributes of the parent element. This attribute appears as part of the parent element—you can't lock parent attributes at the child level. You can include multiple attributes in a comma-delimited list.

lockElements Locks the specified child elements of the parent element. This attribute appears as part of the parent element—you can't lock child elements at the child level. You can include multiple attributes in a comma-delimited list.

lockItem Locks the entire element when set to `True`. The default setting is `False`.

Working with the Connection String

The `connectionString` attribute requires additional explanation because it contains a host of entries. Each of these entries is separated by a semicolon and defines a different element of the connection. The connection string elements contain name/value pairs. You set a property name equal to a particular value. For example, in this SQL Server connection string:

```
Server=(local);Database=MyDatabase;Integrated Security=true
```

contains three name/value pairs. The Server property tells the DBMS to choose the (local) instance of SQL Server. The Database property tells the database manager to provide access to the MyDatabase database. Finally, the Integrated Security tells the database manager to rely on Windows security to provide the credentials for the connection.

Most connection strings are more complicated than the one for a SQL Server connection. For example, when you want to create an ODBC connection, you must supply the name of the driver, as well as other configuration information, as shown here (the connection string appears on one line in the file, even though it appears on multiple lines in the book).

```
Driver={SQL Server};Server=MyServer/SQLInstance;Database=MyDatabase;
Uid=MyUsername;Pwd=MyPassword
```

In this case, the ODBC connection relies on the SQL Server driver. The server is on MyServer and the connection relies on the SQLInstance of SQL Server. The connection relies on MyDatabase. In this case, the connection string includes the username (Uid) and password (Pwd), rather than rely on integrated Windows security.

You'll find some variances between connections, even when you use the same connection type. For example, here's an ODBC connection string for Sybase System 11.

```
Driver={Sybase System 11};SRVR=mySybaseServerName;DB=myDatabaseName;
UID=myUsername;PWD=myPassword
```

The differences are subtle, but you must pay attention to them or the connection won't work. Some ODBC drivers require specific capitalization—UID isn't the same as Uid. Every ODBC connection string includes the Driver property and this one points to the Sybase System 11 driver. This driver relies on SRVR to provide the server name and DB to provide the database name. The UID and PWD properties perform the same tasks as before, but because the driver capitalizes the strings, you should also capitalize them in your connection string.

Connection strings vary even when working with newer technologies such as OLE-DB. For example, here's a connection string for an Access database.

```
Provider=Microsoft.Jet.OLEDB.4.0;Data Source=C:\myPath\myJet.mdb;
User ID=Admin;Password=MyPwd
```

When working with OLE-DB, every connection string sports a Provider property that tells which provider to use. In this case, the provider is for Microsoft Access. The Data Source property defines where to locate the MDB file containing the data. This connection string also provides a User ID and Password property for credentials. However, you don't have to provide these properties when the database lacks security settings (the default). Contrast the Access OLE-DB connection string with this connection string for Sybase.

```
Provider=Sybase ASE OLE DB Provider;Data Source=MyDataSourceName;
Server Name=MyServerName;Database=MyDatabaseName;
User ID=myUsername;Password=myPassword
```

Unlike ODBC, there are more similarities than differences, but there are still differences. In this case, the Provider, Data Source, User ID, and Password entries work as before. Of course, you have to provide entries that make sense for the particular DBMS. This connection string also includes a Server Name property that identifies the server and a Database property that identifies a particular database.

The problem with connection strings is that they aren't standardized, so there isn't a precise formula you can follow to create them. However, most vendors make the connection string requirements clear and you'll find that creating a connection string is a variant of the examples described in this section of the chapter.

Managing Connection Strings

Before you can make a connection to a database, you need a connection string. While it's possible to define the connection string within the application, it's a lot more flexible to define it within the Web.CONFIG file. By placing the connection string within the Web.CONFIG file, you can ensure that both developers and administrators have equal access to the connection string, making it far more likely that database changes will flow down to the application where the user needs them.

To access the connection strings, select the level you want to work within the Connections pane and double-click the Connection Strings icon. You'll see the Connection Strings pane shown in Figure 11.5. IIS 7 includes a default connection named LocalSqlServer that it uses to store IIS configuration information. The following sections describe how to add, edit, rename, and remove connection strings.

Adding a New Connection String

You can define a connection string using a number of different techniques. The easiest method is to define a connection to SQL Server because you can do it with a few simple entries. The harder method applies to everyone else because you have to create the connection string by hand. The "Working with the Connection String" section of the chapter describes some of the issues to consider when creating a connection string by hand. Once you become familiar with the methods your DBMS uses, creating a connection string by hand isn't hard, but the first few can prove troublesome.

FIGURE 11.5
Use connection strings to create connections between applications and databases.

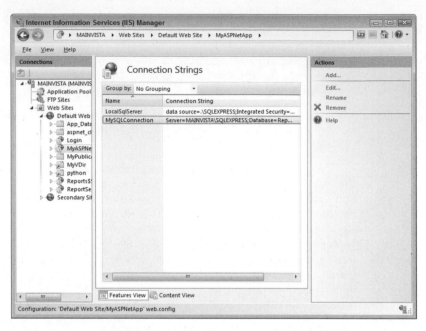

Fortunately, the developer will normally create and test the connection string as part of creating the application. Consequently, you won't normally need to create a new connection string, but may have to edit a connection string to match a new database location or other requirements (such as password, timeout, or other requirements to gain access to the data). The following steps tell you how to create a basic connection string in IIS.

1. Click Add in the Actions pane to create a new connection string. You'll see the Add Connection String dialog box shown in Figure 11.6.

FIGURE 11.6
Define the connection string using the SQL Server defaults or a custom connection string.

2. Type a name for the connection in the Name field. The name has to match the connection that the application expects to use. If you don't provide the correct name, the application won't find the data it requires to perform tasks.

3. Select the SQL Server or Custom option. The SQL Server option only works for SQL Server databases. You must use the Custom option when working with every other kind of database. When you choose the Custom option, type the connection string for the database and click OK to create the connection. Otherwise, continue to the next step of this procedure.

4. Type the name of the server that has the data you want to use in the Server field. Notice that IIS automatically adds the Server property to the edit box in the Custom area for you.

5. Type the name of the database you want to use in the Database field. Notice that IIS automatically adds the Database property to the edit box in the Custom area.

6. Choose Use Windows Integrated Security to pass the caller's credentials to SQL Server or Specify Credentials to provide specific credentials to SQL Server. You must always specify the credentials when working with anonymous connections. Follow these additional steps when you choose the Specify Credentials option

   A. Click Set. You'll see the Set Credentials dialog box shown in Figure 11.7.

FIGURE 11.7
Provide the credentials that SQL Server requires to access the database.

B. Type the username. Type the password twice. Click OK. IIS adds the credentials to the Specify Credentials field. Notice that IIS automatically adds the User ID and Password properties to the edit box in the Custom area and removes the Integrated Security=True entry.

7. Click OK to add the new connection.

Editing Existing Connection Strings

Editing a connection string is very much like adding a connection string. You still see the dialog box shown in Figure 11.6 when you edit a connection string and have all of the same options to change except for the connection name. IIS won't let you change the connection name—see the "Renaming Connection Strings" section for details about renaming a connection string.

To edit the connection string, highlight the entry you want to modify in the Connection Strings pane. Click Edit in the Actions pane. Use the procedure found in the "Adding a New Connection String" section of the chapter to modify the entry.

Renaming Connection Strings

IIS lets you modify the name of any connection string except the default connection string, LocalSqlServer. To rename a connection string, highlight the connection string you want to modify in the Connection Strings pane. Click Rename (if you don't see the Rename action, you can't rename the connection string). IIS turns the Name field into an edit box. Type the new name and press Enter to complete the process.

Removing Connection Strings

Generally speaking, it's far easier to edit a connection string than to remove it and create a new one simply because the connection strings can prove troublesome to create. Whenever possible, try to edit the connection string before you delete it when you plan to replace one connection string with another.

You can remove any connection string including the default connection string (something you should never do). To remove a connection string, highlight the connection string entry in the Connection Strings pane and click Remove in the Actions pane. IIS will display a dialog box asking you to confirm that you want to remove the connection string. Click Yes to complete the process.

Considering Security Issues for Database Connections

As mentioned several times in the chapter, databases are the lifeline of most companies today. The information contained in a database is of more value than any other aspect of an application setup. A company could lose hardware or personnel, or even the software, before they can afford the loss of data. The database has importance not only to the company but to the people who visit the company's Web site as well. If someone loses your social security number or credit card information, then there are potential losses to your financial welfare, required credit monitoring, potential identity theft, and all kinds of other ramifications too ghastly to think about (but as an IT professional, you must think about them).

The trade press magazines do a good job of telling everyone about everyone else's security mistakes, so it's best to leave the scare tactics to them. The question is how to prevent security breaches or at least keep them from wrecking everyone's reputation. The biggest thing you must remember is that someone who's determined to break in will do so. Consequently, you have to make life as difficult as you can for the person breaking in and then deny them the data any way you can once they achieve their goal. The following sections include some ideas for securing your data.

Encrypt the Data

The best way to deny someone access to the data is to encrypt it. Microsoft sets IIS to encrypt much of the data it uses by default. You actually have to go out of your way to create a setup that doesn't include the required encryption. When you open the ASPNETDB.MDB file for an application, what you see are hashes for a number of the personal questions, as shown in Figure 11.8 for the aspnet_Membership table. A hash provides a 128-bit equivalent for essential data—you can't even decrypt it. To use a hash, the application asks the user for input, creates a hash from it, and compares the resulting hash to the hash in the database—simple and effective. Hashes work best for situations where the user must provide identifying information such as a password or the answer to a question.

You can also rely on standard encryption techniques for the database. Both the .NET Framework and SQL Server support a number of encryption techniques. Always use the Advanced Encryption Standard (AES) when you can because there are ways to break the Data Encryption Standard (DES). You can learn more about AES at `http://csrc.nist.gov/CryptoToolkit/aes/ rijndael/`. The point is to expect someone to break into your system and even overcome all of your other carefully defined roadblocks. Properly defined encryption denies the person access to the data without going through the software you support, which should include features that deny unauthorized access.

FIGURE 11.8
Encrypt the data so that even if someone does steal it, the data is useless.

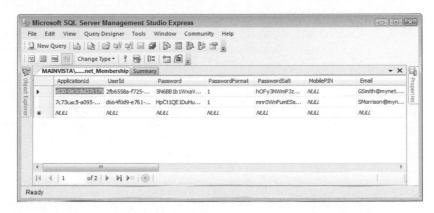

The downside to encryption is that it slows your application. Consequently, along with the encryption you must provide enough server capacity to ensure the application works as anticipated. Yes, some companies are struggling right now to provide enough capacity to support the application without added encryption, but you can't afford not to support encryption given the cost of letting data out. In fact, encryption will likely become mandatory, at some point, so it's better to get started now.

Install All Required Patches and Updates

Many security breaches occur because the company didn't install a required patch or update. Because databases rely on several layers of software, it's especially easy to find a security hole when the company doesn't patch the application at every level:

- Operating System
- IIS
- Application
- Middleware
- Database Manager
- Client Operating System
- Client Application
- Network

Yes, that's a lot of patching and updating, but you can't avoid it if you want to maintain a secure setup. Your application should check the client for required patches because the client is potentially the largest security hole. Deny access when you find that the client is accessing your system with an outdated and potentially dangerous browser. It's your data; you should maintain control over it because if you don't, you may very well appear as the highlight of one of those trade press articles.

Use Middleware When Possible

Direct database access is nice because it makes your application perform well, but it's also dangerous. Hide your database on the other side of the firewall whenever possible. Place the database on another server whenever you can. Make the person breaking into your system work to locate the database. Use middleware to provide the required access to your application and then make sure the middleware is robust enough to detect unauthorized access. The harder you make it for anyone trying to access the system the better because making things hard buys you time. However, time alone isn't enough—make sure you monitor absolutely everything when it comes to your database. Look for people sneaking around in places they shouldn't be. Active security is the only way to prevent accidental data spillage because someone with the proper motivation will find a way inside your server.

Rely on Proper Security

Chapters 9 and 10 tell you all about ASP.NET security. The "Considering Security Issues" section of Chapter 4 provides additional information about Windows security. Make sure you use this information to define proper security for the database. Don't allow just anyone to access that database and certainly don't provide more than read access whenever possible. If you don't secure your database properly, then you have no one else to blame when someone comes in and simply copies the database from your server (yes, it has actually happened to some people).

Part of proper security is to rely on impersonation whenever necessary to provide database services. Don't give the user logging into the application from the Internet the rights to work with the data directly. Give this right to the application instead so that you can place roadblocks to access and monitor the access when it does occur. If the application alone has the right to access the database, then users who somehow gain access to your server's hard drive won't gain much.

Don't stop with impersonation, however. Make sure the application only has the access rights it actually requires to get the job done. If your application can get by with just read rights, that's great. Use another application, one that's installed on your private network behind the firewall, to make changes to the database whenever possible. Lock down the system as much as possible to ensure that no one can gain unauthorized access.

TIP You'll find many helpful security articles for IIS on the Internet. For example, the article on the Information Security Web site at `http://infosecuritymag.techtarget.com/articles/september01/features_IIS_security.shtml` provides a number of very helpful tips that can make your IIS setup considerably more secure. Another good article appears on the GovernmentSecurity.org site at `http://www.governmentsecurity.org/articles/DatabaseSecurityPart1.php`. You can find additional GovernmentSecurity.org articles at `http://www.governmentsecurity.org/MSIISInformation.php`.

Test Your System

Testing is probably the least performed yet most helpful part of securing the databases on your system. Don't assume that someone can't access your data—test the system. Better yet, hire one of the many Internet security companies to test your system. These companies hire security specialists that can help you detect and fix many common security problems. These problems can prove extremely hard for someone who works with the system every day to find, yet prove extremely easy for outsiders to find. Take every precaution to ensure that if someone breaks in, they have to work hard to do it.

Don't trust just anyone to test your system. Make sure you use a reputable security company—one that has insurance to protect you should one of their employees decide to take a joy ride on your server. Look for other people who have used the service and get their feedback on the services that the company has provided. It's important to know that you can trust the company testing your system because some nefarious individuals pose as legitimate companies and then suddenly disappear after they've gotten all of your data.

Keep the Databases Small

Some developers want everything in the universe to appear in a single database, which obviously makes the database quite large. It's better to use multiple small databases than to use a single large database. Using small databases reduces the attack surface of your application. If the attacker can only obtain a subset of the application data, the information might not even make sense because the attacker will see it out of context. When possible, store the data in multiple, physically separate locations and use middleware code to combine the data into a cohesive entity.

Interrogate the User

One of the more successful techniques for overcoming security problems is to interrogate the user randomly. Sometimes the application can do it at the beginning, sometimes in the middle. Ask a question that only the user, not someone outside the company, will know. Better yet, ask the user a personal question that someone inside the company is unlikely to know. Make sure you have several of these questions (ten or more is a good idea)—things that the user is unlikely to forget, but someone else is unlikely to know, so the user has no reason to write the material down. Use the questions randomly, so that it becomes harder for someone to look over someone else's shoulder to guess the next question.

Don't Break Integrity

One of the most essential database security rules is not to break the integrity of the system by doing foolish things. For example, there isn't any reason to store a copy of the database on someone's laptop. Doing so exposes the database to instant compromise by anyone who steals the laptop. Companies come up with a lot of reasons why the database has to appear on the user's machine, but most of them aren't worth it when the data is compromised. If a sale requires a few extra seconds to complete, the cost is worth it when compared to the cost of providing free credit services to customers who probably won't want to deal with your company again.

If you absolutely must place part of the database on a user's laptop to ensure that the user can access data as needed, don't include the whole database. Only include the part of the database that the user actually requires. Any unusual or nonstandard request should go through your company anyway for verification purposes. Control the amount of data that you let off the server because control is the best way to avoid compromise in the first place.

Make sure you secure the database on the user's machine. If possible, use new Microsoft technologies such as BitLocker to encrypt the entire hard drive, making the hard drive useless to someone who steals it. Encrypt the database to ensure that even if someone does gain access to the hard drive, they have to deal with the encrypted database as well. Always make life difficult for the person who wants to steal your data.

Let's Start Building

This chapter has demonstrated techniques for creating database connections, safeguarding the database once you connect to it, and managing the connection over the life of the application. You've also discovered how to create connections to all kinds of databases, not just SQL Server. This chapter helps you build these skills:

♦ Define the requirements for making a database connection

♦ Manage the providers required for IIS and applications

♦ Define and use the elements of a connection string

♦ Create a list of connection strings

♦ Develop security requirements for database connections

Obviously, this chapter can't tell you about the specific database for your application. To obtain all of the information you need, it's important to work with the developer. In many cases, you'll find that at least a preliminary connection comes with the application that you can modify to meet your needs. This chapter also doesn't provide a full discussion of database security. Since your data is so important, it's essential that you create a complete plan for protecting it. Creating the right connection and protecting the data after you connect to it should be two essentials on your list whenever you install a new application. Don't forget to review the setup as often as needed to ensure the data remains safe because new security leaks appear often.

Up to this point, the book has described a number of ways to configure IIS 7 using the graphical utilities. Although it's possible to perform most tasks using this approach, you must perform some tasks at the command line. In addition, sometimes it's simply more convenient to use the command line to make a change using batch files. Chapter 12 introduces you to IIS at the command line and shows how you can use the command line to perform a number of tasks. Of course, part of the command line is the files you've been changing using the graphical utilities. Chapter 12 explains these files in detail and tells how you can make similar changes simply by editing the text in the files.

Chapter 12

Modifying the Application Configuration Files

Most of this book has concentrated on the graphical tools that Microsoft provides. For the most part, the graphical tools do work well and you shouldn't need to use anything else. However, sometimes you'll run into a situation where you'll want to work with the configuration files directly. For example, some settings aren't easily accessible from the graphical interface, so you need to change those settings by modifying the configuration file directly. One such change is configuring the Web server or individual Web sites to use a different logging methodology.

Not all of the configuration files appear in the \inetpub\AdminScripts folder; several of them appear in the \Windows\System32\inetsrv folder. This chapter introduces you to a number of configuration files that you might not even know about. You should use the graphical utilities whenever possible to edit these files; however, this chapter points out instances where using the graphical utilities simply won't accomplish the task.

Previous chapters of the book have introduced you to some command line utilities you need to know about. For example, you'll find the XCopy utility in Chapter 4, the FTP utility in Chapter 7, and the AppCmd utility in Chapter 8. This chapter introduces you to a number of additional utilities and scripts. One such script, ADSUtil.VBS, provides you with significant flexibility and you can use it within batch files or other scripts to perform extensive configuration. You'll also discover specialty scripts, such as ClusFTP.VBS, which help you configure FTP servers for cluster scenarios.

In this chapter, you will learn how to do the following:

◆ Modify the Web.CONFIG file using a text editor

◆ Modify security settings using a text editor

◆ Modify application settings using a text editor

◆ Perform tasks at the command line

Understanding the *Web.CONFIG* File

The Web.CONFIG file appears more than once on your server. In fact, you'll see one Web.CONFIG file for each Web site and application. Every virtual directory includes a Web.CONFIG file as well. In fact, you'll run into the Web.CONFIG file so often, it's easy to become confused. The sections that follow describe some of the issues you need to consider when working with Web.CONFIG, tell you the easiest way to make the changes, and describe some of the most common elements that you'll modify.

NOTE IIS 7 doesn't use the metabase and it has a considerable number of other changes too. You may find that old tools and utilities don't work as they once did. Make sure you check out the list of breaking changes in IIS 7 at `http://www.iis.net/default.aspx?tabid=2&subtabid=25&i=1236&p=2`. If your application requires FrontPage extensions, make sure you check out the fix for this issue at `http://www.iis.net/articles/view.aspx/IIS7/Deploy-an-IIS7-Server/Installing-IIS7/Install-FrontPage-Server-Extensions`.

Understanding Hierarchy

IIS starts out with basic settings. These settings don't appear in any of the standard folders for the Web site. You'll find them in the `\Windows\Microsoft.NET\Framework\v2.0.50727\CONFIG\` folder on your system, which is the starting point for all of the `Web.CONFIG` settings. When you need to make a server-level setting change, you must open the server-level `Web.CONFIG` file to do it. Any settings you make in this `Web.CONFIG` file affect every other level unless you provide a specific override at that level.

TIP If you ever make a mistake in the `Web.CONFIG` file for the Web server that completely disables the Web server (or, at least, damages it in such a way that fixes are difficult), you'll find a `Web.CONFIG.Default` file in the `\Windows\Microsoft.NET\Framework\v2.0.50727\CONFIG\` folder on your system. Copy this file to the `Web.CONFIG` file. Don't simply rename the `Web.CONFIG.Default` file because you won't have a backup for later. Using this approach resets the server to defaults—you'll lose all of your settings, but you'll regain access to the server and be able to restart it. Use this technique as a last ditch fix for severe configuration problems.

The next level is the Web site. The root folder for the Web site contains the Web site settings. The default Web site settings appear in the `\inetpub\wwwroot` folder. Any other Web site you create has a `Web.CONFIG` file in its root folder. Any changes you make to these files affect the entire Web site, including all applications, unless you specifically override them at the folder or application level. These changes also override any settings you define at the Web server level. The important point is that these files affect the next level in the Web server hierarchy, even though they don't appear at the next level in the Windows folder hierarchy. The two hierarchies are different and it's important not to confuse them.

Folders and applications come next. When a folder or application appears within the Windows folder hierarchy, it's easy to determine that folder's or application's position in the Web server hierarchy as well. However, folders and applications can rely on virtual directories. When you use a virtual directory for the folder or application, the `Web.CONFIG` file appears in the root folder of that virtual directory. Again, even though the Windows hierarchy differs from the Web server hierarchy, the Web server hierarchy is the one that matters. Folder and application `Web.CONFIG` file settings always override those of the Web site and the Web server.

Using XML Notepad to Modify *Web.CONFIG*

You can edit the `Web.CONFIG` file using Notepad or any other editor that produces pure text. Of course, applications such as WordPad don't produce pure text—they product formatted text and the formatting codes will interfere with the `Web.CONFIG` file. Unfortunately, using Notepad isn't a very easy way of modifying the file. The text is very hard to make sense of and you can't see the `Web.CONFIG` hierarchy at all, as shown in Figure 12.1.

A better way to edit the Web.CONFIG file is to use an XML file editor. You can find a number of paid products on the market. One of the best options for the devoted XML file user is XML Spy (http://www.altova.com/products/xmlspy/xml_editor.html). In most cases, you won't need the full capabilities of such an editor. Microsoft produces XML Notepad, which works fine in most cases, and you can download it free from http://www.microsoft.com/downloads/details .aspx?familyid=72d6aa49-787d-4118-ba5f-4f30fe913628. Figure 12.2 shows how the same Web.CONFIG file appears in XML Notepad.

FIGURE 12.1

You can use Notepad to edit the Web.CONFIG file, but you won't enjoy it.

FIGURE 12.2

XML Notepad makes it considerably easier to view, edit, and manage the Web.CONFIG file.

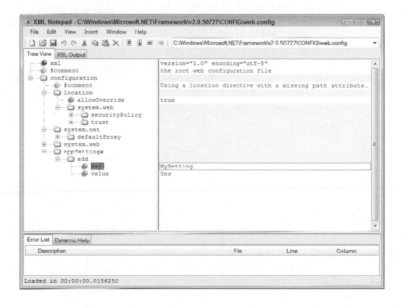

Figure 12.2 shows the main reason to use an XML editor such as XML Notepad. You can easily see the hierarchy of the various elements, making it considerably harder to introduce errant text into the file. However, you can still introduce errors, which brings up the second reason to use an XML editor. An XML editor can employ an Extensible Stylesheet Definition (XSD) file to ensure the accuracy of the information you place in the file. This technique isn't failsafe, but it does reduce the risk of introducing errors considerably. The XML editor compares special information in the XSD file with the contents of your `Web.CONFIG` file to search for errors. You can learn more about XSD at `http://www.w3schools.com/schema/default.asp`.

To work with XSD, you must have an XSD file. The best file is the one supplied with Visual Studio. If you know of someone who has Visual Studio, you'll find the required `DotNetConfig.XSD` file in the `\Program Files\Microsoft Visual Studio 8\xml\Schemas` folder of the hard drive. Of course, you might not have access to Visual Studio, so you need an alternative source for the XSD file. Microsoft doesn't publish the file anywhere. The best place to obtain a third-party file is at `http://www.radsoftware.com.au/articles/intellisensewebconfig.aspx`. Unfortunately, the author hasn't completely updated this file for ASP.NET 2.0, but it does provide enough functionality for most purposes.

Add the XSD file to XML Notepad by choosing View ➢ Schemas. You'll see the XML Schemas dialog box shown in Figure 12.3. Type the location for the XSD file in the Filename field or click the ellipsis button to display an Open dialog box you can use to search for the file. Click OK. Remove any XSD entries you don't need by highlighting them and pressing Delete or disable the XSD entries by checking the entry in the Disabled column. Click OK and you'll have the required XSD support for the `Web.CONFIG` file.

The XSD support immediately changes the way XML Notepad works. For example, when you add a new element, XML Notepad now tells you which options you have, as shown in Figure 12.4. In this case, XML Notepad tells you that when working with the `appSettings` element, you can provide `add`, `clear`, and `remove` child elements.

The XML Notepad editor can also help you locate errors and tell you how to fix them, as shown in Figure 12.5. In this case, the `Web.CONFIG` file contains an errant entry. Instead of adding an `add`, `clear`, or `remove` child, the `Web.CONFIG` file now contains an `Error` child. The error appears in the Error List tab. Double-click the error and XML Notepad takes you directly to the error entry. You can then double-click the errant entry to see the list of possible options for it.

FIGURE 12.3

Add XSD support for the Web.CONFIG file to reduce the potential for errors.

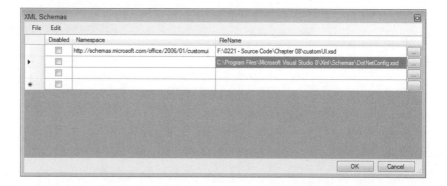

FIGURE 12.4
XML Notepad tells you which elements and attributes you can add to avoid errors.

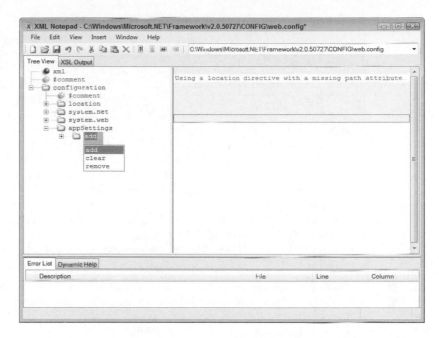

FIGURE 12.5
Use the XML Notepad features to locate errors and fix them.

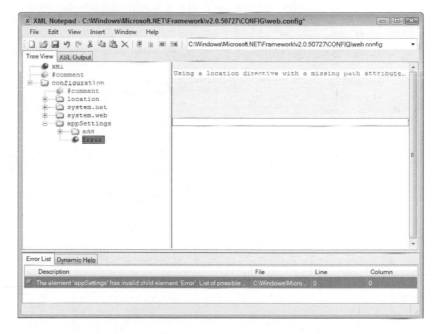

An Overview of the *Web.CONFIG* Elements

It's time to put a number of puzzle pieces together to obtain a better understanding of how things work with the `Web.CONFIG` file. The "Understanding Friendly Names and Configuration Names" section of Chapter 1 describes how you can view configuration names whenever necessary using the Internet Information Services (IIS) Manager. These configuration names actually have counterparts in the `Web.CONFIG` file and you can use the XML Notepad to search for them.

The important issue to remember is that only changed items appear in the `Web.CONFIG` file. For example, if you choose to open the .NET Compilation pane shown in Figure 12.6 and change the Maximum Size of Batch entry to something like 2,000, then you'll see the change in the `maxBatchSize` element of the `Web.CONFIG`, as shown in Figure 12.7. The `\Windows\Microsoft.NET\Framework\v2.0.50727\System.Web.DLL` file contains the default values that the system uses. You can also find a complete listing of all of the default values in the `\Windows\Microsoft.NET\Framework\v2.0.50727\CONFIG\Web.CONFIG.Comments` file.

Microsoft provides a complete listing of the various `Web.CONFIG` elements at `http://msdn2.microsoft.com/en-us/library/ms228147(VS.80).aspx`. You'll also want to view the entries at `http://msdn2.microsoft.com/en-us/library/1fk1t1t0(VS.80).aspx`. The default settings for the Web server include these elements:

location Determines whether the administrator can override the settings provided as child elements. The default value is True. Any elements contained within this element are subject to the override setting. You can learn more about this element at `http://msdn2.microsoft.com/en-us/library/b6x6shw7(VS.80).aspx`.

system.net Determines the basic settings for Internet applications. The most common child element is `defaultProxy`, which determines the proxy used to handle HTTP requests. You can learn more about this element at `http://msdn2.microsoft.com/en-us/library/6484zdc1.aspx` or `http://msdn2.microsoft.com/en-US/library/aa309410(VS.71).aspx`.

FIGURE 12.6
Only modified entries appear in the `Web.CONFIG` file.

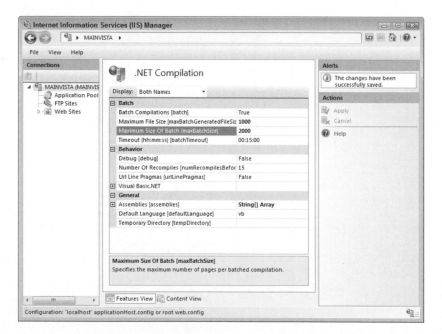

FIGURE 12.7
The changes appear in
the Web.CONFIG file
using the configura-
tion name.

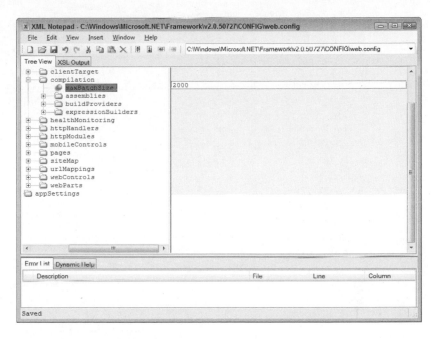

system.web Defines the settings for the ASP.NET application environment. For example, this
element contains child elements that control both authorization and compilation of ASP.NET
applications. You can learn more about this element at http://msdn2.microsoft.com/en-us/
library/dayb112d.aspx or http://msdn2.microsoft.com/en-us/library/
dayb112d(VS.71).aspx.

The Web server settings tend to define the big picture—how the Web server will react with all of the
Web sites and the applications they contain by default. Once you move past the Web server, to the Web
site, you'll see other elements. The two default elements are system.web and system.webServer. The
system.web entries tend to define the ASP.NET application environment in more detail.

The system.webServer settings are the root entries for the IIS 7 configuration. These settings control the Web server engine and modules. In some cases, these settings used to appear in the binary
database that IIS used to hold metadata, but these settings all appear in XML form now. For example,
this is where you'll find the default document, directory browsing, failed request tracing, and the
handler mappings. You can learn more about this element at http://msdn2.microsoft.com/
en-us/library/ms689429.aspx.

There aren't any default elements for folders and applications. The elements you see depend on
the configuration requirements of the folder or application. In many cases, folders won't require
any settings at all. Applications generally require settings to perform tasks. The system.webServer
element will contain a defaultDocument child element that contains the default document for the
application, as shown in Figure 12.8. Because this is an ASP.NET application, the default document
is default.aspx, as shown in the figure. The Visual Studio environment automatically changes
this entry as needed to match the default document set by the developer.

FIGURE 12.8
Applications normally contain some default elements designed to make them work.

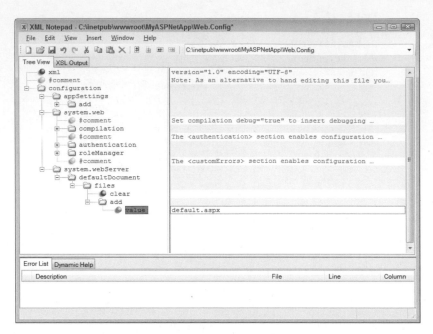

The configuration element normally contains a system.web element as a minimum. Notice the comments shown in Figure 12.8. These comments provide instructions that help you modify the entries correctly. For example, the compilation element normally contains a debug attribute that determines whether the application is using a debug or release compilation. This same setting appears in the graphical interface as part of the .NET Compilation pane. You change it using the Debug property.

In many instances, applications also contain an authentication element. Most ASP.NET applications rely on forms authentication, so you'll see the mode attribute set to Forms. The other valid options include None, Windows, and Passport. The interesting part about this setting is that it includes the Passport option, which doesn't appear in the Authentication pane. However, it doesn't include the basic or digest authentication options, which do appear in the Authentication pane of the graphical tool, so there isn't a one-to-one correlation between the graphical tool and the Web.CONFIG file.

When you choose the basic or digest options, the mode attribute contains the Windows option. Of course, this makes it impossible to know where the basic and digest settings actually appear since IIS 7 does rely on XML for all settings. It turns out that implementing basic or digest security requires additional entries that you'll find in the \Windows\System32\inetsrv\config\ApplicationHost.CONFIG file (see the "Working with the *ApplicationHost.CONFIG* File" section of the chapter for details on working with this file).

Changing Security Settings

ASP.NET and IIS 7 offer a number of security configuration options. You have already seen many of the common techniques in play in other chapters of the book (most notably Chapters 8 and 9). However, the graphical interface doesn't quite provide complete access to all of the security settings. In some cases, you must change the security for an application using the Web.CONFIG file. The following sections describe some of the configuration tasks you can perform using files instead of the graphical interface.

Denying Access to a Particular File

One of the most common restrictions is to keep certain groups from viewing a particular file. The most common way to perform this task is to use the techniques found in the "Considering Security Issues" section of Chapter 4. However, ASP.NET provides another way to perform the task. You can open the Web.CONFIG file and add a file entry to deny access to it. To perform this task, you need to add some elements to the Web.CONFIG file, as shown in Figure 12.9.

FIGURE 12.9
Reduce access to a file based on specific criteria.

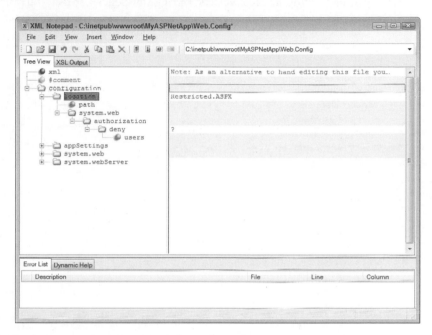

In this case, you begin by creating a location element and then adding the other elements shown in the figure. The location element also has an attribute named path. You set the value of path to the name of the file you want to protect—Restricted.ASPX in this case. The deny element also has an attribute named users. The value of ? addresses anyone who isn't logged into the system. The XML version of this technique looks like this:

```
<location path="Restricted.ASPX">
  <system.web>
    <authorization>
      <deny users="?"></deny>
    </authorization>
  </system.web>
</location>
```

You can add as many location elements as needed to protect individual files within a Web application. The authorization element can contain as many deny or allow elements as needed to protect the file fully.

Changing the Security Policies

In many cases, you can obtain information from the `Web.CONFIG` file and use it to locate other files you need. The `\Windows\Microsoft.NET\Framework\v2.0.50727\CONFIG\Web.CONFIG` file contains the listing of security policy files, as shown in Figure 12.10. These policies appear in the .NET Trust Levels pane as a drop-down list of security policies you can use. The "Setting Code-Based Security Using .NET Trust Levels" section of Chapter 10 describes this particular feature in detail. However, using the graphical tool, you can't change the policies. In fact, you really don't know what the polices are because Microsoft doesn't describe them in any detail and you can't see the content of the policy files using the graphical utility. In short, you must accept the Microsoft view of what security policies are good for your server, which may not be the best idea for a private Web site.

FIGURE 12.10
Find the locations of the security policy files and use them to modify the security policy for your server.

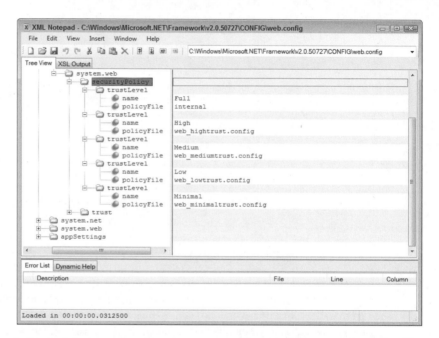

You can approach this task in two ways. First, you can modify an existing security policy file. This option has the advantage of giving other people a familiar set of policies to use. However, it also means that you won't have the default settings available should you need them for any of a number of purposes, including troubleshooting security on your Web site. Second, you can create a custom security policy file based on an existing file and require administrators to use it. This option has the advantage of letting you experiment with settings, diagnose any problem areas, and then implement the security policy as needed. The second approach is probably better because it provides you with the greatest flexibility. The following sections discuss this second approach.

UNDERSTANDING THE SECURITY POLICY FILE FORMAT

The security policy files have a specific format, as shown in Figure 12.11. In this case, you're looking at the `MySecurityPolicy.CONFIG` file that I created as an example for this chapter. By using an existing security policy file as a template, you can avoid having to create everything from scratch.

FIGURE 12.11

Use an existing security policy file such as web_ hightrust.config as a template and modify it as needed.

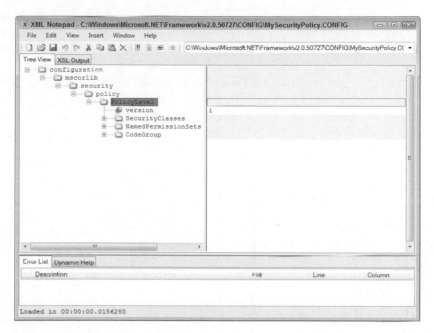

The actual configuration begins at the PolicyLevel element. You must include a version attribute that includes the version number of the policy. Make sure you keep the policy version number updated to reduce the chance that someone will use an outdated policy. The child elements describe different aspects of a security policy as described in the following list.

SecurityClasses   Each SecurityClass element contained in the SecurityClasses element describes a different .NET assembly used for security purposes. You probably won't need to add an entry to this list unless your company creates a special security assembly. The assembly must appear in the GAC. The Description attribute of the SecurityClass element provides the namespace, full assembly name, version number, culture information, and the public key token (used for the assembly's strong name).

NamedPermissionSets   The named permission sets work very much the same as permission sets you create using the Microsoft .NET Framework 2.0 Configuration Console (see the "Using the Microsoft .NET Framework 2.0 Configuration Console" section of Chapter 9 for details). The only difference is that you define each PermissionSet element using attributes, as shown in Figure 12.12. You must include the information shown in the figure for each custom permission set you want to create. The article at http://msdn2.microsoft.com/en-us/library/aa302425.aspx provides details on PermissionSet element basics. Some PermissionSet elements include IPermission children that describe permissions for individual assemblies. You can see a discussion of this form of PermissionSet element at http://msdn2.microsoft.com/en-us/library/ms916848.aspx. Microsoft doesn't provide an actual documentation page, so these two articles are the best information on the topic of defining a PermissionSet element as of this writing.

CodeGroup   The CodeGroup element also contains features based on the entries you create using the Microsoft .NET Framework 2.0 Configuration Console. Besides the references for permission sets, the best reference for the CodeGroup element is at http://msdn2.microsoft.com/en-us/library/ms154466(SQL.90).aspx. The CodeGroup element includes class, version, and PermissionSetName attributes, as shown in Figure 12.13. The class attribute defines an assembly name you provided in the `SecurityClasses` element. The version attribute is a simple number defining the version number of the code group. The `PermissonSetName` attribute must contain the name of a permission set found in the `PermissionSets` element.

FIGURE 12.12
Use permission sets to control the code access security on your server.

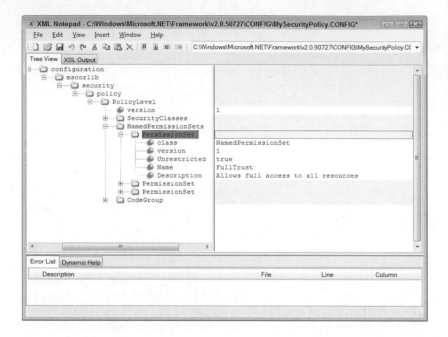

FIGURE 12.13
Define code groups based on the assemblies and permission sets you've defined.

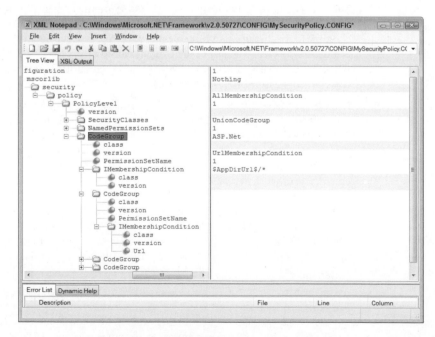

DEFINING A NEW *SECURITYCLASS* ELEMENT

When you need to define a new `SecurityClass` element, you must obtain the namespace from the developer. However, you can obtain all of the other information you need from the `\Windows\ assembly` folder on your hard drive, as shown in Figure 12.14. The assembly name, version, and public key token information appear as shown. Use a value of `neutral` for the culture when you don't see an entry in the Culture column. A complete `Description` attribute entry includes the following information (all entered on one line).

```
System.Web.AspNetHostingPermission, System, Version=2.0.0.0,
Culture=neutral, PublicKeyToken=b77a5c561934e089
```

MAKING A SECURITY PROFILE AVAILABLE FOR USE

After you create your new security policy, you need to provide a method for accessing it. To perform this task, you add a new `trustLevel` element to the `Web.CONFIG` file, as shown in Figure 12.15. Notice that the `trustLevel` element includes both `name` and `policyFile` attributes to define the new trust level. You can see the new security policy in the .NET Trust Level pane of the Internet Information Services (IIS) Manager (see the "Setting Code-Based Security Using .NET Trust Levels" section of Chapter 10 for details).

FIGURE 12.14
The `\Windows\ assembly` folder tells you all about the assemblies in the GAC.

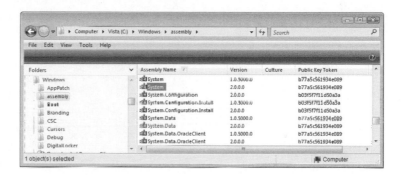

FIGURE 12.15
Make the new security policy accessible by adding it to the `Web.CONFIG` file.

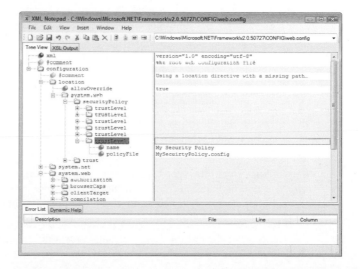

Changing Application Settings

You'll make most application settings changes found in the following sections using the Internet Information Services (IIS) Manager. That's because these files replace binary files used to store information in the past. However, because the files are in XML format and not a binary database, knowing about these files can be useful. A developer can create custom management applications for you based on their content and you can locate errant settings with greater ease when using an editor. For example, you may have defined an incorrect URL in multiple locations—using the Internet Information Services (IIS) Manager to change these settings is time consuming, but using an editor can be quite fast.

Working with the *ApplicationHost.CONFIG* File

The \Windows\System32\inetsrv\config\ApplicationHost.CONFIG file contains a number of settings that don't appear in the individual Web.CONFIG files. The Web.CONFIG files normally contain managed settings, while the ApplicationHost.CONFIG file contains native code settings of various sorts. For example, when you use basic or digest authentication, the settings appear in the ApplicationHost.CONFIG file, rather than the Web.CONFIG file, as shown in Figure 12.16.

FIGURE 12.16
The ApplicationHost.CONFIG file normally contains native code settings.

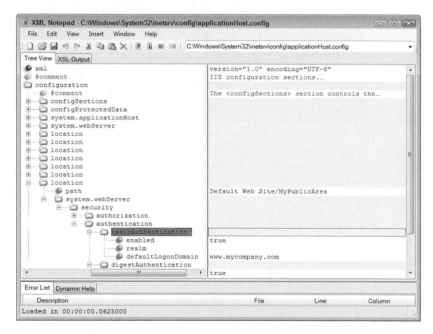

Even though the file appears quite complex, you can break the ApplicationHost.CONFIG file into five major areas. Once you know which area to view for a particular kind of data, working with the file becomes considerably easier. The following list describes each of the major areas.

configSections The configSections element defines the sections within the configuration file. You'll never need to change anything in this element because IIS depends on a specific configuration to accomplish tasks and you'll use other means to configure custom applications.

configProtectedData The configProtectedData element contains the security provider information for the system. You normally won't need to change this information unless you obtain a third-party provider (there aren't any available for IIS 7 at the time of this writing). If you do obtain a third-party provider, it's likely that the provider's installation program will make all of the appropriate entries for you. In sum, you probably won't need to change the settings in this element.

system.applicationHost The system.applicationHost element is a configured section—one that doesn't necessarily have to appear by default, but you'll normally see it. This element contains a number of interesting configuration options that include the application pools, custom metadata, listener adapters, log file settings, and some Web site settings. A number of these settings are impossible to set using the graphical utilities. For example, you can't set the log file settings using the graphical interface, but you can set them quite easily using the settings in this file. The Web site settings include the Web site bindings, failed request logging, and application location information.

system.webServer The system.webServer element is a configured section—one that doesn't necessarily have to appear by default, but you'll normally see it. Many of these entries look like they came directly from the graphical interface. For example, you'll find the CGI settings here, as well as the default Web page and directory browsing settings for the Web server as a whole. Some settings aren't available from the graphical interface. For example, you can set up ODBC logging using elements contained within this element. One of the performance options you'll want to check is caching. You can enable or disable caching for the Web server as a whole or for the kernel.

location Every time you create a new location in IIS, IIS creates a new location element to hold it. The location element contains a path attribute as a minimum that describes the location. For example, you'll find an entry for the Default Web Site in the list. Every application, virtual directory, or folder with special settings appears in the list. A common child element is system.webServer. This element may contain any number of child elements or no child elements at all. The elements you see depend on the special settings for the location. When working with an application, it's common to see elements for setting the security, default directory, and handlers.

Working with the *Administration.CONFIG* File

The \Windows\System32\inetsrv\config\Administration.CONFIG file contains administrative settings for the server. For example, you'll configure the actual list of administrators here and define the list of administrator providers you want to use, as shown in Figure 12.17. As with the ApplicationHost.CONFIG file, the Administration.CONFIG file contains a number of required entries that you probably won't change, including the configSections element.

The main item of interest is the moduleProviders element. It contains a list of modules that IIS uses to perform useful work. You can't access these providers from the graphical interface—they affect IIS at a relatively low level. IIS sorts them by server and ASP.NET modules. As with the security profiles, the modules you use must appear in the GAC. You can add new modules by registering the module in the GAC using the GACUtil utility and then adding the appropriate entry to the moduleProviders element (see the "Defining a New *SecurityClass* Element" section of the chapter for details on the information you must provide).

Simply adding an add element to the moduleProviders element won't make the provider accessible to the server. You must link the provider to a particular location, which is where the location element comes into play in this file. When you open the location element, you'll find that it contains a modules element that has a list of modules for that location. You simply refer to the name of the element you created in the moduleProviders element. When you remove an element from this list, the server no longer uses the module provider for that particular location, but it remains configured for use later. The default IIS setup only includes one location, the Web server itself.

FIGURE 12.17
The Administration
.CONFIG file contains
administrative
settings.

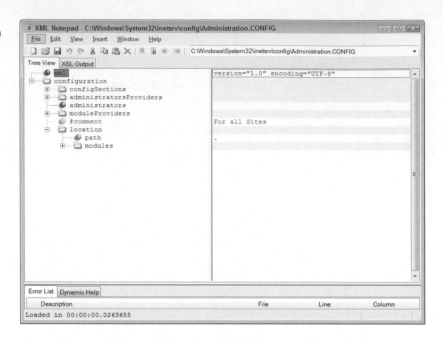

Performing Configuration Tasks without the GUI

Most organizations shovel their Web server into a closet somewhere or put it in a special computer center. No matter where you hide your server, you don't have direct access to it normally. When an error occurs, you might not have access to it using the graphical utilities either. That's when you need to log in using the command prompt and rely on command line utilities to get the job done. Command line utilities also make it considerably easier to automate tasks using scripts or batch files. In short, even though command line utilities might seem unimportant, you really need to know how to use them in order to work with IIS in some cases. The following sections provide tips and techniques for working with IIS at the command line.

NOTE　You'll find a few executables in the \Windows\System32\inetsrv folder that aren't explained in this book. Don't ever use the ASPNetCA.EXE, IISRSTAS.EXE, IISSetup.EXE, INetInfo.EXE, or WMSvc.EXE programs because Microsoft hasn't designed them for stand-alone use. Make sure you know precisely how the utility works before you use it.

USING WINDOWS POWERSHELL TO CONFIGURE IIS

Vista doesn't currently include Windows PowerShell as a default feature and it's uncertain whether Windows 2008 Server will include this feature. Instead, you have to download Windows PowerShell and install it as a separate feature. You can obtain Windows PowerShell from http://www.microsoft .com/technet/scriptcenter/topics/msh/download.mspx.

Using Windows PowerShell has some similarities to the command line, but there are also significant differences—too many differences to describe in a section of a chapter. My book, *Windows Administration at the Command Line* (Sybex, 2007) provides two chapters on Windows PowerShell that will make working with it significantly easier.

Windows also doesn't come with the cmdlets required to administer IIS 7. You can learn how to write these cmdlets at http://www.iis.net//articles/view.aspx/IIS7/Use-IIS7-Administration-Tools/Scripting-IIS7/Writing-PowerShell-Command-lets-for-IIS7. If you'd like to see a short tutorial on using Windows PowerShell to manage IIS, check out the Channel 9 presentation at http://channel9.msdn.com/Showpost.aspx?postid=256994.

In general, overcoming the obstacles to using Windows PowerShell to manage IIS is probably worth the effort if you plan to use the command line almost exclusively. However, there's a lot to learn if you only plan to use the command line occasionally and the standard command line that comes with Windows will prove far easier to use.

Using the W3WP Utility

Normally, you won't worry about launching a worker process at all—you'll let IIS do it. However, the World Wide Web Worker Process (W3WP) utility can help you launch a worker process manually. The only times you'd need this utility are to determine why a worker process isn't working properly or to perform a remote execution from the command line (rare). This utility uses the following syntax:

```
W3WP -debug [-s <site id>]
W3WP -h [Application Host File] [-w <Root Web.CONFIG File>]
     [-in <Instance Name>]
```

The following list describes each of the command line arguments.

-debug   Use this argument to launch a worker process using the default application host configuration file. The default settings use the default Web site (*site ID 1*). You can modify this behavior using the -s argument.

-s *SiteID*   Defines the site identifier to use for launching the worker process. Getting the right site identifier is important. The easiest way to find this number is to choose the Web site in the Connections pane of the Internet Information Services (IIS) Manager. Click Advanced Settings in the Actions pane and you'll see the Advanced Settings dialog box. The site identifier appears in the ID field. You can also locate this information in the \Windows\System32\inetsrv\config\ApplicationHost.CONFIG file. The information appears in the configuration\system .applicationHost\sites element as one of the site element entries.

-h [*ApplicationHostConfigurationFilename*]   Launches a worker process using the specified application host configuration filename. If you don't specify a filename, then the utility uses the default Web site (*site ID 1*).

-in *InstanceName*   Defines the instance name to use. The default setting uses HWC- followed by the process identifier (PID) for the worker process. Consequently, when the instance has a PID of 1001, you'll see a name of HWC-1001 for it.

-w *RootWebConfigurationFilename*   Defines the root Web configuration file to use when launching the worker process.

Command Line Switches for the Graphical Utility

Normally, you'll run the Internet Information Services (IIS) Manager as a .NET-managed executable. That's the default setup when you start it using the Internet Information Services (IIS) Manager applet found in the Administrative Tools folder of the Control Panel. You can also run the Internet Information Services (IIS) Manager directly from the \Windows\System32\inetsrv folder by typing **InetMgr** and pressing Enter. It turns out that the utility sports two command line switches that can make a difference in how you use them, as shown here.

/MMC   Runs the Internet Information Services (IIS) Manager as an MMC snap-in, instead of as a regular application. This approach has advantages and disadvantages. When working with Internet Information Services (IIS) Manager as a snap-in, you can combine it with other utilities for a combined approach to working with various IIS elements. The downside is that the MMC version lacks a few of the amenities of the application version. You'll find out more about these issues later in this section.

/Reset   Resets the MMC interface to a known good state. You can use this command line switch with the /MMC command line switch to repair any errors in creating an MMC version of the display.

The MMC version of Internet Information Services (IIS) Manager does lack a few features of the application form. For example, when you select the Help menu, you won't see the IIS help you're used to seeing. What you'll see instead is a list of MMC help. The File menu doesn't include the option to save connections. In addition, the View menu is missing completely. Even so, you can right-click on every object in both versions of the applications and perform all of the tasks that you expect, so the MMC deficiencies shouldn't prove troublesome for most people.

The fact that the Internet Information Services (IIS) Manager works just fine as a MMC snap-in makes it possible for you to create your own utility for managing IIS. The trick is to create your own console and not rely on the one that Microsoft creates for you. A console you create on your own provides author mode access, which makes it possible to author a particular view or add other snap-ins as needed. The following procedure tells you how to create a combined Internet Information Services (IIS) Manager and Internet Information Services (IIS) 6.0 Manager console.

1. Choose Start ➤ Run. You'll see the Run dialog box.

2. Type **MMC** in the Open field and click OK. You'll see a blank copy of MMC open.

3. Choose File ➤ Add/Remove Snap-in. MMC presents the Add or Remove Snap-ins dialog box shown in Figure 12.18.

FIGURE 12.18
Add the snap-ins you want to use for management purposes to the console.

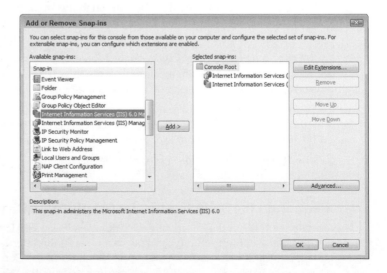

4. Double-click the Internet Information Services (IIS) 6.0 Manager and Internet Information Services (IIS) Manager snap-ins (along with any other snap-ins you want to add). MMC adds these snap-ins to the Selected Snap-ins list shown in Figure 12.18.

5. Click OK. MMC will display the two snap-ins in the new console, as shown in Figure 12.19.

FIGURE 12.19

The new console contains both managers.

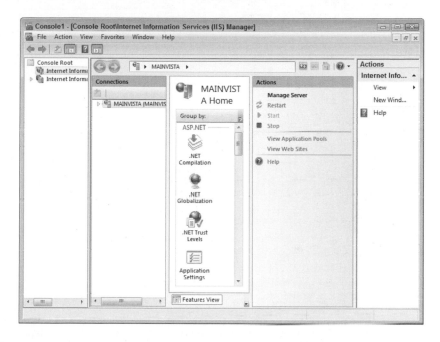

6. Choose File ➤ Save. MMC displays a Save As dialog box.

7. Type a name for the new console and click Save. The new console appears in the Administrative Tools folder of the Control Panel.

The Internet Information Services (IIS) 6.0 Manager appears normally, but the Internet Information Services (IIS) Manager appears squashed. You can easily overcome this problem by choosing View ➤ Customize in the Actions pane. MMC presents the Customize View dialog box shown in Figure 12.20. Clear the checks next to features you don't need in order to give the Internet Information Services (IIS) Manager more desktop space and click OK. Clearing the Console Tree and Action Pane options presents precisely the same view that you've always seen. If you need some of the features back later, simply reopen the Customize View dialog box and place checks next to the options you need. You can also open the Customize View dialog box by choosing the View ➤ Customize menu option. It's also possible to display the Customize View dialog box by clicking the button in the upper left corner of the console and choosing Customize View from it.

FIGURE 12.20
Modify the view so it appears the same as the original console if desired.

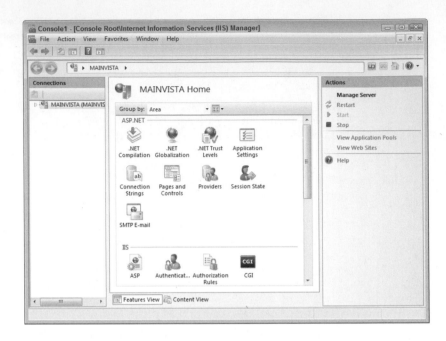

EXTENDING IIS

Unlike previous versions of IIS, the use of XML and managed code in IIS 7 makes it a lot easier to extend. The features you've seen throughout the book are the defaults. However, you can change those defaults to meet any need your organization has. This book can't provide complete details on writing IIS 7 extensions because that topic requires an entire book by itself, but it's important to know the capabilities exist.

You may decide at some point that you want to at least see what's available. You can find good presentations on IIS extensions at `http://www.iis.net/default.aspx?tabid=2&subtabid=26&i=1177` and `http://channel9.msdn.com/ShowPost.aspx?PostID=215282`. There's also an interesting blog entry detailing some of the issues behind IIS extensions at `http://mvolo.com/blogs/serverside/archive/2006/10/22/Extending-your-IIS-7-server-with-.NET.aspx`.

Performing Configuration with the *ADSUtil.VBS* Script

The `ADSUtil.VBS` file contains a script that you can use to modify the contents of the `\Windows\System32\inetsrv\config\ApplicationHost.CONFIG` file without using an XML editor. This utility originally worked with the binary metabase used by IIS, but now it works with the XML files supplied with IIS 7. In some cases, the utility changes settings in other files as well, but all of the common settings appear in the `ApplicationHost.CONFIG` file.

You won't find a one-to-one correlation between the settings either. For example, the `W3SVC/1/ServerBindings` path used by the ADSUtil utility actually appears in the `configuration\system.applicationHost\sites\site\bindings` element in the `ApplicationHost.CONFIG` file for the host site with an `id` attribute value of 1. Even so, if you're used to the old binary metabase, this utility can save you significant time. This utility uses the following syntax:

```
CScript ADSUTIL.VBS <cmd> [<path> [<value>]]
```

The path argument tells the ADSUtil utility where to look for information. The value argument tells the ADSUtil what setting to use when changing a particular path value. The following list describes each of the commands.

HELP   Provides extended help information. You don't need to provide a path or value for this command. The extended help information will tell you about any new features that Microsoft adds to the ADSUtil utility.

APPCREATEINPROC, APPCREATEOUTPROC, and APPCREATEPOOLPROC   Creates a new application based on the virtual directory. At one time, IIS supported the COM concept of in-process and out-of-process applications, so you needed separate commands for creating in-process and out-of-process COM applications. Then, Microsoft introduced the pooled application. IIS 7 doesn't support the COM in-process or out-of-process applications any longer, but ADSUtil continues to support the commands for backward compatibility reasons. Consequently, whether you type `CScript ADSUtil.vbs APPCREATEINPROC W3SVC/1/Root/MyVDir`, `CScript ADSUtil.vbs APPCREATEOUTPROC W3SVC/1/Root/MyVDir`, or `CScript ADSUtil.vbs APPCREATEPOOLPROC W3SVC/1/Root/MyVDir`, you still end up with a pooled application named MyVDir. The resulting application relies on the DefaultAppPool. If you want to change the application pool, use the SET command to define the name of the application pool for the AppPoolId property for the application. For example, to change the MyVDir application to use the Classic .NET AppPool, you'd type `CScript ADSUtil.VBS SET /W3SVC/1/root/MyVDir/AppPoolId "Classic .NET AppPool"` and press Enter.

TIP   If you have a hard time figuring out the paths for applications, you can obtain help from the \Windows\System32\inetsrv\config\ApplicationHost.CONFIG file. Look in the configuration\system.applicationHost\customMetadata element for a key element with a path attribute that matches your application.

APPDELETE   Removes an application but not the associated virtual directory. For example, if you type `CScript ADSUtil.vbs APPDELETE W3SVC/1/Root/MyVDir` and press Enter, you'd remove the MyVDir application. However, the MyVDir virtual directory would still appear on the server. To remove the associated virtual directory, use the DELETE command.

APPDISABLE, APPENABLE, and APPGETSTATUS   Disables an application, enables an application, and reports an application's status. Unfortunately, none of these three commands appear to work with IIS 7, but they do continue to provide output. Type `CScript ADSUtil.VBS APPDISABLE /w3svc/1/root/MyASPNetApp` and you'll see an application disabled message. The ADSUtil utility even changes the required entries in the C:\Windows\System32\inetsrv\config\ApplicationHost.CONFIG file, but IIS 7 appears to ignore them. Type `CScript ADSUtil.VBS APPENABLE /w3svc/1/root/MyASPNetApp` and you'll see an application enabled message. In addition, the utility removes the property that disables the application. Type `CScript ADSUtil.VBS APPGETSTATUS /w3svc/1/root/MyASPNetApp` and you'll see application status information, which is always a 0 under IIS 7.

APPUNLOAD   Unloads an application from memory. You can use this to force a reload of the application when memory corruption or another fault occurs. Normally, you won't need to use this command because the server performs the task for you automatically. In fact, it's probably better not to use this command on a production server at all because you could end up with data damage and other nasty surprises.

CONTINUE_SERVER   Continues server operation after a pause. IIS 7 doesn't support pausing or continuing—you must start or stop the server instead. Using this command will start the server after a stop, but then the ADSUtil utility freezes and you must press Ctrl+C to continue.

COPY/MOVE   Even though these commands appear on the list of tasks you can perform, the current implementation of the ADSUtil utility doesn't actually provide support for them.

CREATE   Creates a new property value, property, or schema element. For example, if you type **CScript ADSUtil.VBS CREATE W3SVC/1/DefaultDoc/** and press Enter, you'll add a path named W3SVC/1/DefaultDoc/ to the Web server. The Web server has to support a particular path to use it. Consequently, adding new paths at random won't accomplish much.

CREATE_VDIR   Creates a new virtual directory. You can use the resulting virtual directory as a data source or as an application. To use it as an application, you must create an application using the APPCREATEPOOLPROC command. Defining a virtual directory is actually a two-step process using the ADSUtil utility. First, you must create the virtual directory entry using a command such as **CScript ADSUtil.vbs CREATE_VDIR W3SVC/1/Root/MyVDir**. You won't be able to see the virtual directory in the graphical utilities at this point, but you can enumerate it using the ENUM command. After you create the virtual directory, you must assign a path to it using a command such as **CScript ADSUtil.VBS SET /W3SVC/1/root/MyVDir/Path F: \Temp**. At this point, you can see the virtual directory in Internet Information Services (IIS) Manager.

CREATE_VSERV   Creates a new Web site. However, this isn't a single-step process. In order to create a new Web site, you must perform a number of additional configuration tasks. For example, to create a new Web site named MyServer that's the third Web site on a server and has a binding with port 82, you'd use the following command sequence.

1. Type **CScript ADSUtil.VBS CREATE_VSERV W3SVC/3** and press Enter. ADSUtil creates the new Web site.

2. Type **CScript ADSUtil.VBS SET W3SVC/3/ServerComment "MyServer"** and press Enter. ADSUtil assigns the Web site a name.

3. Type **CScript ADSUtil.VBS SET W3SVC/3/ServerBindings "*:82:"** and press Enter. ADSUtil creates a binding for the Web site.

4. Type **CScript ADSUtil.VBS CREATE_VDIR W3SVC/3/ROOT/** and press Enter. ADSUtil creates the root directory object for the Web site.

5. Type **CScript ADSUtil.VBS SET W3SVC/3/ROOT/Path "C:\ThirdSite"** and press Enter. ADSUtil defines the root directory path for the new Web site. At this point, you can view the new Web site in Internet Information Services (IIS) Manager.

6. Define the remaining server features. You'll need to use various SET and CREATE commands to configure the server as required.

DELETE   Removes a property value, property, or schema element. This particular command is very powerful, so you need to use it with care. In most cases, you only want to use this command to modify a property value. For example, if you type **CScript ADSUtil.VBS DELETE W3SVC/1/DefaultDoc** and press Enter, you'll remove all of the default documents for the default Web site. On the other hand, if you type **CScript ADSUtil.VBS DELETE W3SVC/1/DefaultDoc/** and press Enter, you'll remove a path named W3SVC/1/DefaultDoc/ from the Web server. You'd then need to use the SET command to add the default documents that you wanted to use back into the metabase. In some cases, the ADSUtil utility reports that it completed an action, but IIS automatically reverses that action, which means it didn't actually occur. Verify changes using the GET command.

ENUM Obtains a list of schema elements, their associated properties, and values. For example, if you type **CScript ADSUtil.VBS ENUM W3SVC/1** and press Enter, the ADSUtil utility displays the schema for the entire default Web site. Use redirection to place this information in a file if desired. You can't use the ENUM command to display property values—use the GET command instead. If you want to see only the path information for a particular Web site, use the /P command line switch.

TIP If you want to get a fuller view of the schema for your Web server, try typing **CScript ADSUtil.VBS ENUM** and pressing Enter. You'll see the top-level information for the Web server including a number of interesting paths. For example, if you want to control logging, try the logging path. The FTP server appears as part of the MSFTPSVC path.

FIND Determines whether a particular property exists. The FIND command can potentially do more, but the additionally functionality appears broken in IIS 7. Even so, you can type **CScript ADSUtil.VBS FIND W3SVC/3/ROOT/Path** and press Enter to determine whether the Path property exists. When this property exists, you'll see a message such as "Property Path found at: W3SVC/3/ROOT." You can also simply type **CScript ADSUtil.VBS FIND Path** and press Enter to locate all of the Path properties, as shown in Figure 12.21.

FIGURE 12.21
The FIND command is exceptionally useful in helping you navigate the complex paths.

GET Obtains the value of a particular path and displays it on screen. You use this command only with properties, not with the schema itself. For example, when you type **CScript ADSUtil.VBS GET W3SVC/1/ServerBindings** and press Enter, you'll see an output value of 80 for the default Web site. The ServerBindings portion of the path is a property. However, if you want to obtain part of the schema, you must use the ENUM command instead.

PAUSE_SERVER Pauses server operation. IIS 7 doesn't support pausing or continuing—you must start or stop the server instead. Using this command will stop the server, but then the ADSUtil utility freezes and you must press Ctrl+C to continue.

SET Defines the value of a property. You must supply a valid path that points to a property value, rather than part of the schema. For example, when you type **CScript ADSUtil.VBS SET W3SVC/1/ServerBindings "*:82:"** and press Enter, the ADSUtil utility sets the HTTP protocol for the default Web site to use a port of 82, instead of the normal port 80. In addition, the asterisk

(*) indicates that the setting is for all IP addresses. If you want to use a specific IP address, you use it in place of the asterisk like this: `"127.0.0.1:82:"`. It's important to remember that the binary metabase has unique names for the HTTP and HTTPS protocols. When you want to change the HTTPS protocol binding instead, you specify the SecureBindings property instead.

START_SERVER   Starts the server. For example, if you type `CScript ADSUtil.VBS START_SERVER W3SVC/1` and press Enter, the ADSUtil utility will start the default Web server. You'll see a successful start message when the action is finished.

STOP_SERVER   Stops the server. For example, if you type `CScript ADSUtil.VBS STOP_SERVER W3SVC/1` and press Enter, the ADSUtil utility will stop the default Web server. You'll see a successful stop message when the action is finished.

Let's Start Building

This chapter has helped you understand the role that the command line plays in working with IIS. If nothing else, you now know how to use all of those scripts and executable files in the `\Windows\System32\inetsrv` folder. You've also discovered some interesting new ways to work with the graphical utility. Using the MMC version of the Internet Information Services (IIS) Manager does provide some flexibility that you don't get with the application version. This chapter helps you build these skills:

- Modify the `Web.CONFIG` file using a text editor
- Modify security settings using a text editor
- Modify application settings using a text editor
- Perform tasks at the command line

You can have quite a bit of fun discovering new IIS features using the information found in this chapter. Of course, you never want to experiment on your production server—always use a test server to work with new utilities and to try new settings. After you confirm (after thorough testing) that a new setting does help performance, improve reliability, or make your server more secure, test it on your production server as well. This chapter has also shown you a new view of the Internet Information Services (IIS) Manager that you should try out. You may discover that you really like the MMC version of the utility.

Chapter 13 introduces a topic that all administrators have to deal with at some point, performance. Application performance is a complex topic because performance means so many different things to different people. For the most part, you can view performance as a balanced approach to managing application speed, reliability, and security. You've already discovered just how secure you can make IIS in Chapters 8 and 9, so Chapter 13 concentrates on the speed and reliability legs of the performance triangle.

Chapter 13

Improving Application Performance

Administrators use the term *performance* to mean different things. To some, the term simply means accomplishing the task in any way possible. Completing the task is obviously a requirement, but it's not the only requirement. Most administrators equate speed and performance, but that's not accurate either. Doing something fast doesn't mean doing it well. This chapter helps you define performance in a more scientific manner. Yes, the application needs to complete the task and complete it as quickly as possible, but it must also complete the task well in order to produce worthwhile results.

Part of the performance picture in IIS is the use of application pools, performance monitoring, and application behavior modification to achieve specific results. This chapter explores all three issues and helps you come up with a plan for your organization. It would be nice if there were a canned plan that worked for everyone, but every organization has different goals and needs, so it's important to consider performance from your organization's perspective.

Finally, IIS 7 supports feature delegation. Sometimes, feature delegation is a necessary requirement unless you want to micromanage every Web site and application on a server. However, sometimes feature delegation can turn into a huge performance hit. This final section of the chapter delves into how feature delegation can be a friend or foe.

In this chapter, you will learn how to do the following:

◆ Define a performance plan based on the performance triangle

◆ Manage application pools

◆ Define and manage performance monitoring

◆ Modify application behavior

◆ Define the performance implications of feature delegation

Understanding the Performance Triangle

Performance is a measure of how well your computer accomplishes a given task, not how fast it accomplishes the task. Sure, it's always nice to get the job done quickly, but quickly doing it wrong doesn't accomplish much. An IIS configuration that performs well provides these elements:

◆ Security that makes sense given the tasks you're trying to accomplish

◆ Reliable operation and data handling

◆ Efficient resource usage, resulting in better speed

Any performance plan must consider performance as a triangle of security, reliability, and speed. A change in one leg of the triangle affects the other two legs in some way. When you make your server too secure, speed drops to zero because no one can accomplish any work. Because no one can accomplish any work, reliability becomes a nonissue. Likewise, if your entire focus is on reliability, you'll sacrifice some speed and security to obtain it. A balanced view is best, but what *balanced* means depends on the needs of your organization. A banking Web site will almost certainly consider security as the high priority while a gaming Web site will deem speed as most important.

A Web site can become too finely tuned as well. It may not seem possible, but tuning requires time and patience. You focus your attention on performance needs, rather than other requirements, making your Web site brittle. The finely honed performance edge offsets other needs that you haven't addressed. The following sections discuss both performance and the need to maintain perspective when considering performance.

Balancing Security, Reliability, and Speed

As previously mentioned, performance is a triangle consisting of security, reliability, and speed. You must balance all three to achieve a system that performs well. The following sections describe these three topics in the order that you should consider them when creating a performance plan for your system.

FOCUSING ON SECURITY

Security is a critical part of any system that performs well. After all, a system that lacks security invites intruders who will be happy to damage any work the system accomplishes. Most of the chapters in this book provide some advice on security for your system. Of course, the two security chapters (Chapters 8 and 9) provide the most discussion of the topic, but because security is such an important issue, you'll find it discussed just about everywhere in the book.

The goal of security for the purposes of performance is to keep the work that applications accomplish safe. The work appears as

- Data stored on the system
- Access the system provides to the data
- The integrity of the environment in which users interact with the applications and the data they support

Consequently, security isn't simply a matter of protecting the data to the point that no one can do anything with it. Security from a performance perspective involves measured risk—it requires that you determine how much risk the system can accommodate before it fails to provide the security leg of the performance triangle. The amount of risk your application can sustain depends on the kind of application—the sensitivity of the environment and the needs of the user. Obviously, whenever you make the data more secure, the user is less able to work with it.

Access to the data is the critical part of the performance picture for security. It's important that the user receive proper access or authorization to work with the data or the application is useless. Authenticating the user and securing the network connection are the pathways to authorizing the user with lower risk. Most users will accept an up-front security check and it actually makes some users feel more secure. Using biometrics probably isn't an answer, in most cases, but you can also do better than a simple name and password.

Users often give away the most secure passwords, but they don't tend to give away the answers to questions you might ask, especially when they don't know the questions in advance. During a job interview, it's possible to note many things about the user—things the user will always remember, but that other people won't know. For example, you could ask the user about their first job out of high school. Yes, it's common knowledge, but hardly something that another individual will memorize and you can place a time limit on answering. A bank of 10 random questions and their encrypted related answers can provide an amazing amount of security when done correctly.

Once you authenticate a user and know that it is, indeed, the person you think it is, you can rely on SSL, encrypted tokens, and other standard methods for securing the conversation. Again, the means you use to secure the connection depend on the sensitivity of the data. SSL places a significant burden on the server and client alike, but it provides nearly flawless security. Encrypted tokens work very well too and place a smaller load on the server and client. At some point, you have to make a determination of how much speed and reliability the user is willing to give up in the name of security.

ADDING RELIABILITY

Reliability is a measure of access. You use it to determine how well users can access the system. A hardware failure will certainly cause access problems, so a server that has a hardware failure will also have a reliability problem. A software failure can also cause access problems. When an application freezes, the user can no longer access the system. Security can also cause access problems. When a user enters a name and password, but the server doesn't provide access, the user tends to see the Web site as unreliable. Many administrators are used to viewing reliability as uptime, but a server that's up and doesn't provide access is no more useful than one that's failed completely. Consequently, equating reliability with access provides another way to view the whole issue and makes it apparent that good hardware isn't sufficient.

It might not seem obvious, but whenever a server is stressed—lacking resources to accomplish a given task—it also becomes less reliable. The user still has access, but the access is slower and therefore less reliable. Reliability measurements have degrees, just as many other server criteria do. Just how unreliable your server becomes depends on the kind, duration, and intensity of the stress. For example, your system will freeze completely when you run out of memory and there's no recovery for the problem. Windows will usually try to warn the administrator about the problem, but administrators seldom monitor the server so closely that they even see such messages until it's too late.

Stress need not be as severe as complete loss of memory to cause problems, however. For example, try defragmenting your hard drive when the free hard drive space is less than 10 percent and you'll find it takes a long time to complete (if it ever does complete). The problem is a lack of hard disk resources. Even though your hard drive has 10 percent free space, the disk defragmenter might not have enough space to move large data segments around and will spend its time thrashing (a condition where an application tries to find enough hard drive space to perform a task to no avail).

Sometimes reliability problems occur even when the system seems to have enough resources, but you haven't optimized it. For example, some applications begin to act oddly when they can't request large enough pieces of memory, even though enough memory is available to answer the request. Windows memory can fragment over time and running the many applications that servers do at once only makes the problem worse. The long uptimes of servers exacerbates the problem, making it nearly impossible to avoid.

In a world where 24/7 Internet connectivity is considered essential, administrators often keep their servers running all of the time and never perform any maintenance on them—at least not until they fail completely. Fortunately, vendors have made hardware a little easier to maintain over the years and administrators have more software tools as well. Maintenance need not mean downtime and it's always possible to take one server offline at a time when working with a server farm. Optimizing your server can make applications more reliable. Of course, there are various kinds of reliability, and you'll want to ensure your optimized system provides them all:

◆ The application starts without displaying weird resource messages.

◆ The application runs without crashing (even gracefully).

◆ The server tracks user settings properly and the application accepts changes as anticipated.

◆ All data remains accessible and intact.

◆ Data updates always occur as anticipated.

◆ None of the other running applications experience problems after starting a new application.

MAKING THE SERVER FAST

Only after you make your server secure and reliable should you consider making it fast. In fact, when you make your server secure and reliable, it's going to be faster by default, but not due to any actual increase in system speed. The increase in speed will come because you spend less time trying to accomplish a task and fixing system errors. You might be surprised if you monitor the time lost due to various inefficiencies today. However, the fact remains that you can usually speed up your server once you have all of the other problems under control.

Server performance increases usually begin with good maintenance. Make sure you install all required patches and updates for all of the software on your system. Of course, you'll want to test the patches and updates first on a test system that has the same configuration as your production server. Otherwise, you might encounter nasty surprises when an update or patch conflicts with other software on the system. Even so, some exploits now appear on the same day that a vendor releases a patch or update, so you can't take a lot of time testing them either. If the problem is severe enough and the vendor releasing the patch or update notes that you can remove it if necessary, you might want to risk installing the patch or update immediately.

Use application pools to your benefit. One of the new performance enhancers for IIS 7 is the considerable amount of control you have over the application pools, which means that you can easily control memory. The most critical resource on any server is memory—controlling it effectively makes a big difference in the performance of your applications. The "Working with Application Pools" section of the chapter provides details on controlling application pools. Along with application pools, the application settings make a considerable difference in performance. Make sure you combine the application pool information with the compilation settings found in the "Compiling the Application" section of Chapter 5.

Monitoring is the next step in making your application run faster. You can't optimize the applications on your server until you know which ones are running slowly and how they're running slowly. The tool might seem old, but the Reliability and Performance Monitor console provides the best means of checking for optimization issues. "Implementing Performance Monitoring" provides details on the IIS 7 counters you can use to measure performance more accurately. After you accumulate enough information about application performance problems, you can work with the developers to overcome the issues. Developers can also add performance counters to applications, so it's important that you also discuss adding such counters when the performance data you collect doesn't point to a specific source of potential problems.

Collecting all of this information and making all of these preliminary changes to the system might seem like a lot of effort to gain a little extra performance out of your server. It's also important that any conclusions are preliminary—the developer still needs to make changes to any custom application to test theories of why a particular application runs slowly. Considering the amount of time and effort spent, you have to consider whether the performance problem is enough of an issue to pursue. It's not always a good idea to throw additional hardware at a software problem, but sometimes it's the most efficient course of action.

Considering the Effects of Too Much Speed

The answer to the question of whether an application can run too quickly might seem obvious. For most administrators, more is better. The "Balancing Security, Reliability, and Speed" section of the chapter already considers two of the problems with emphasizing speed over any other consideration. A server that emphasizes speed will almost certainly have both security and reliability problems. Most companies today can't allow either problem to exist, so too much speed can be a problem before you even consider focusing on it.

Too much speed can also cause a number of other problems. For example, an application tuned to the very edge of performance can use processing cycles, memory, and hard drive resources wastefully. The cost in terms of resources for the additional speed is very high when compared to the additional throughput the application provides. At some point, the cost/performance curve becomes too high to support any additional application speed. Fortunately, the cost of any speed gain is decreasing as hardware becomes increasingly less costly, but you still need to consider the cost of the speed gain.

Speed increases for one application normally spell a proportionate decrease in speed for all other applications on the server, unless you can pay for the speed gain by using resources more efficiently. Consequently, any speed increase you obtain will very likely make users of that application happy and all other users less happy because they'll spend more time waiting for the application to perform a task. Of course, you have to weigh the needs of users against each other. An emergency room doctor's need for a speedy application is probably higher than that of the maintenance person. On the one hand, you're looking at a life and death situation and in the other, you're looking at a clean floor.

A potential reliability problem when tuning for speed is that you end up taxing the server's capacity for work. When the server experiences an overload, such as from an external attack or a demand for additional content from the Web site, it lacks the resources to perform efficiently (if at all). In some case, the server will actually freeze from the stress and become unavailable to perform any tasks at all. Consequently, you need to include an engineer's skeptical view of resource usage. Monitoring can help you determine the maximum server load in any area. Naturally, your normal load should be half of this amount. In addition, you should consider at least a 20 percent surplus over the maximum load to handle surprises. Depending on your situation, you may want to include an even larger surplus to ensure that any overload scenarios don't turn into server crashes and other problems.

Interestingly enough, some effects of too much speed are hard to measure, but they do exist. For example, causing the server hardware to work extra hard generates more heat. The added heat requires more air conditioning for cooling and, given the ever-increasing price of electricity, translates into increased costs, even though these costs are partially hidden. Of course, you may have anticipated the extra electrical costs, but the extra heat also degrades components faster and you may end up with more server downtime. Obviously, you have to consider the costs, both visible and hidden, of tuning exclusively for speed.

Working with Application Pools

The idea behind application pools is a good one. The applications on your server execute within a particular area of memory defined by an application pool. Applications from different application pools don't interact and, consequently, can't cause damage to each other. In addition, because each application can have its own application pool, you can control the memory used by that application, among other things. In short, application pools provide an environment in which applications can execute safely, reliably, and efficiently. The following sections describe in detail how to work with application pools.

Understanding the Purpose of Application Pools

At one time, applications ran in a single large memory space. An application with memory problems could easily overwrite the memory used by another application, causing it to crash. The problem could continue, causing a cascade reaction until the server simply gave up and froze. Immediately after the reboot, the whole process could begin anew. You'd think that Microsoft would come up with a foolproof way of fixing the problem, but they really haven't. Memory errors still occur. However, the combination of the managed environment and application pools do make memory corruption unlikely— someone would have to make an effort to make it occur. The immediate benefit of using a combination of managed applications and application pools, then, is to ensure that one application can't cause another application to crash, at least through memory corruption. Separating one application from another is a very good idea.

IIS 7 wasn't the first version of IIS to use application pools. They first appeared in IIS 6. In fact, you can read about the IIS 6 version of application pools at `http://www.microsoft.com/technet/prodtechnol/WindowsServer2003/Library/IIS/93ddbb51-5826-4ebd-a434-24c5fd103d3a.mspx`. The problem with IIS 6 was that it still relied on the native code model, so memory corruption was still possible despite Microsoft's best efforts. In addition, the use of application pools wasn't mandatory. Consequently, you still had a bunch of code on the server that didn't follow the application pool pattern. In fact, administrators could place their server in IIS 5 isolation mode and prevent anyone from using the beneficial features of application pools at all (see the "Configuring the Service Tab" section of Chapter 7 for details).

An Overview of the Default Application Pools

The application pools appear in their own area of the Internet Information Services (IIS) Manager. To see the application pools, select the Application Pools entry in the Connections pane. Figure 13.1 shows that you'll see a list of default application pools, along with any application pools you create. The basic listing tells you the application pool name, status (started or stopped), .NET Framework version number, management pipeline mode (integrated or classic), the application pool credentials (normally Network), and the number of applications associated with the application pool.

Unlike IIS 6, IIS 7 can't function without application pools. Consequently, you'll always see some application pools in the list. The application pools normally run in integrated mode, which means that all of the underlying code is managed, making your system considerably more stable and secure. You can also choose to run the application pool in classic mode. In this case, the IIS and ASP.NET code run in separate pipelines. The ASP.NET code runs through a separate `ASPNET_ISAPI.DLL`, which is the same technique used in IIS 6. Microsoft provides classic mode for compatibility purposes and you should use integrated mode whenever possible. The following list provides an overview of the default application pools.

FIGURE 13.1
IIS provides a number of default application pools for use in IIS and applications you install.

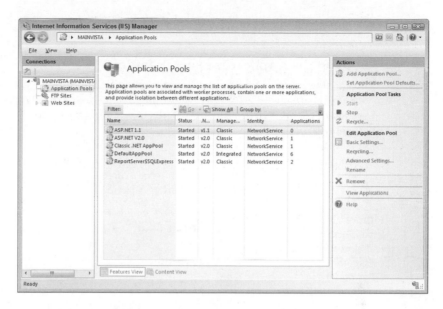

ASP.NET 1.1   The default pool for all ASP.NET 1.1 applications. It provides support for .NET Framework 1.1 in classic mode, which ensures maximum compatibility. In most cases, you won't have a choice about running a .NET Framework application in classic mode, but you should create a new application pool for each application on your server to provide maximum protection. This application pool has no default applications associated with it.

ASP.NET V2.0   The default pool for all ASP.NET 2.0 applications. It provides support for the .NET Framework 2.0 in classic mode. Because most ASP.NET 2.0 applications can run in integrated mode, you should try creating a new application pool for each ASP.NET 2.0 application that uses the integrated mode. This application pool has no default applications associated with it, but Visual Studio .NET automatically selects this application pool when it deploys the application to the server.

Classic .NET AppPool   This is the default pool for all virtual directories that you convert into applications. It provides support for the .NET Framework 2.0 in classic mode. This application pool may not provide any of the right settings for your virtual directory and you should create an appropriate application pool for it. This application pool has no default applications associated with it, but IIS automatically selects this application pool when you convert a virtual directory into an application.

DefaultAppPool   This is the default pool for all Web sites and applications that you install on IIS 7 outside of the Visual Studio deployment. It provides support for the .NET Framework 2.0 in integrated mode. Normally, you can maintain the default Web site in this application pool without any problem, but you may want to give each of the other Web sites their own application pool. This application pool contains the default Web site when you install IIS and IIS always adds other Web sites to it.

You may see a number of additional application pools that could almost fall into the default category. For example, since you must install SQL Server to perform many tasks, you may see one or more SQL Server related application pools such as the ReportServer$SQLExpress application pool shown in Figure 13.1. The appearance of these other application pools depends on the applications and application features you install. Normally, you won't use them for your own applications and should let the application manage them.

Setting the Application Pool Defaults

IIS 7 makes working with application pools significantly easier than working with them in IIS 6. To see a comparison of the two environments, you can review the "Working with Application Pools" section of Chapter 7. You can set defaults that automatically configure new applications that you create with basic settings. Of course, you can change any of the settings in the application pool that you create—these defaults simply give you a starting point so that you don't have to spend as much time in the configuration process. To display the application pool defaults, click Set Application Pool Defaults in the Actions pane. You'll see a dialog box like the one shown in Figure 13.2. The sections that follow describe each of the major sections shown in Figure 13.2.

FIGURE 13.2
Set application defaults to reflect your most common installation options to save time.

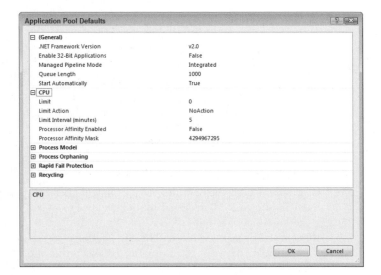

CONFIGURING THE GENERAL OPTIONS

This section contains settings that control the general functionality of the application pool. The following list describes each of the options.

.NET Framework Version   Defines the version of the .NET Framework to use for application pools. Most application pools in IIS 7 rely on the .NET Framework 2.0 by default. You should change this value when you use a different version of the .NET Framework. It's also possible to choose No Managed Code when the application pool supports applications written in other languages.

Enable 32-bit Applications   Used only with 64-bit operating systems. This property determines whether the application pool runs under Windows on Windows 64 (WOW64) mode. The resulting application pool supports only 32-bit applications.

Managed Pipeline Mode   Determines whether the application runs in integrated or classic mode. Application pools configured for classic mode rely on a separate pipeline that uses ASPNET_ISAPI.DLL, which is the same technique used in IIS 6. Microsoft provides classic mode for compatibility purposes and you should use integrated mode whenever possible.

Queue Length   Defines the number of requests that HTTP.SYS will accept for the application pool. When the number of requests exceeds the queue length, the caller will receive a 503 error message that states the service is unavailable.

Start Automatically   Determines whether the application pool starts automatically when the server starts. Normally, you'll set the application pool to start automatically for any application you want to make available to anyone calling the server. Special applications may require a separate start in response to a special event, so you won't start them automatically.

CONFIGURING THE CPU OPTIONS

The settings in this section control how the application pool interacts with the CPU. For example, you may not want an application pool to use all of the CPUs on a system. Most systems today include multiple CPUs, so controlling this feature can significantly affect application performance. The following list describes each of the options.

Limit   Determines the amount of CPU processing time that the application pool can use in 1/1,000ths of a percent. Consequently, a value of 1,000 would equal 1 percent. IIS monitors the percentage of usage over the interval defined by the Limit Interval property. When an application exceeds the percentage of CPU processing time allowed over the specified interval, IIS writes an event to the event log. In addition, it performs the task specified by the Limit Action property. Setting this property to 0 means that the application pool can use all of the CPU processing time over any interval. You'd use this setting to ensure that a single application can't monopolize the server and bring all of the other applications to a halt. The effect is similar to bandwidth throttling on a network and can improve overall server performance, but can diminish the ability of a single application to respond quickly.

Limit Action   Determines the action that IIS will take when an application pool exceeds the limits you place on it. The default action is to perform no action at all. You can also choose the KillW3WP (Kill World Wide Web Worker Process) option, which prevents the application pool from executing for the duration of the time set by the Limit Interval property. Using the KillW3WP option generates an event log entry.

Limit Interval (Minutes)   Defines the monitoring period for CPU throttling. Each time the interval expires, IIS sets the processing time monitor for the application pool back to zero and the application again has its full share of CPU processing time. Setting this property to 0 disables CPU throttling. The default value is 5 minutes.

Processor Affinity Enabled   Determines whether IIS assigns the application pool to use certain processors on a multiprocessor machine. Using this approach prevents an application from monopolizing the server. Careful CPU assignment can make it possible to even out application execution on multiprocessor systems and improve overall system performance. In some cases, using a single processor can also fix errors in applications that don't respond well to a multiprocessor environment. Select one or more processors using the Processor Affinity Mast property.

Processor Affinity Mask   Defines the processors used to service a particular application pool when you enable processor affinity. The default value of 4294967295 means that the application pool can use any of the CPUs on the server. The mask is a bitmap, so you have to use binary to define the mask. You can define a maximum of 32 processors using a 32-bit number. The first processor is CPU 0, while the last processor is CPU 31. Consequently, if you want the application pool to use CPUs 1, 2, and 4, you'd define a bitmap like this:

```
0b 0000 0000 0000 0000 0000 0000 0001 0110
```

that has a hexadecimal value of 16h or a decimal value of 22. You'd type 22 in the Processor Affinity Mask field to use CPUs 1, 2, and 4 for your application pool. When you set the Processor Affinity Enabled property to True, a value of 0 in this property will generate an error.

CONFIGURING THE PROCESS MODEL OPTIONS

The settings in this section control the process model for the application pool as shown in Figure 13.3. The upper half of the dialog box contains the same options that appear on the Identity tab of the application pool Properties dialog box for IIS 6 (see the "Configuring the Identity Options" section of Chapter 7 for details). The lower half contains worker process health options. For example, you can use it to control the number of worker processes that the process model supports and how much idle time must pass before the worker process shuts down. These options work very much like those found on the Health tab of the application pool Properties dialog box in IIS 6 (see the "Configuring the Health Options" section of Chapter 7 for details).

Some of the settings are precisely the same as before. For example, you can still control the startup and shutdown times. In a few cases, Microsoft has added more settings for better control. For example, you can now control the maximum response time for a ping, which means that the system will wait a specific time for a worker process to respond to a ping before it recycles the worker process.

FIGURE 13.3
Set the process model options to control recycling based on worker process health.

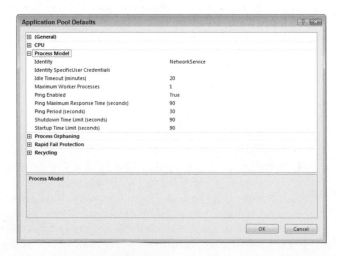

The Web garden feature, originally located on the Performance tab (see the "Configuring the Performance Options" section of Chapter 7 for details) now appears on this tab as well. As with IIS 6, IIS 7 defaults to one worker process per application pool, but you can set the number higher when necessary.

CONFIGURING THE PROCESS ORPHANING OPTIONS

It's possible for an application to abandon a worker process when certain types of errors occur. In this case, you may want the system to run an application to diagnose the problem. For example, you might want to run the Windows Symbolic Debugger (NTSD.EXE) to diagnose the error. The following list describes each of the options.

NOTE Windows doesn't have NTSD.EXE installed by default. You must download one of the debugger patches found at http://www.microsoft.com/whdc/devtools/debugging/default.mspx to obtain it. The Network World article at http://www.networkworld.com/news/2005/041105-windows-crash.html provides some useful tips for using the symbolic debugger.

Enabled Determines whether IIS uses this feature. The default setting is False, which means that nothing happens when an application orphans a worker process. You only need to enable this feature when you want to perform debugging when an application orphans a worker process.

Executable Defines the path of the executable file to load to debug or otherwise manage an orphaned worker process. The most common choice is to call NTSD.EXE, but you can use any executable designed to work with the worker process. For example, you may simply want to log the occurrence in the event log.

Executable Parameters Defines the arguments used with the executable program. The arguments you use depend on the executable program. The article at http://msdn2.microsoft.com/En-US/library/ms951776.aspx describes how to use common Windows NT Symbolic Debugger (NTSD) command line arguments (Microsoft has actually dropped the abbreviation, but it helps to know when it was in the past).

CONFIGURING THE RAPID FAIL PROTECTION OPTIONS

As with IIS 6, IIS 7 provides rapid failure protection. However, the level of protection has improved as shown in Figure 13.4. These options work very much like those found on the Health tab of the application pool Properties dialog box in IIS 6 (see the "Configuring the Health Options" section of Chapter 7 for details).

The IIS 7 extras include the ability to run a program when a failure occurs. You can define any kind of executable along with the parameters required to execute it. In addition, the settings now include the ability to define the response type for the service unavailable message. You have a choice between an HTTP or TCP message.

CONFIGURING THE RECYCLING OPTIONS

As with IIS 6, you can set recycling options for the application pools in IIS 7. In fact, many of the settings are the same they just have different names. For example, the Recycle Worker Processes (in Minutes) setting is now the Regular Time Interval (minutes) setting as shown in Figure 13.5. The theory behind recycling is precisely the same as well (see the "Configuring the Recycling Options" section of Chapter 7 for details). You can also choose to recycle application pools based on memory use. For example, the Maximum Virtual Memory (in megabytes) setting in IIS 6 is now the Virtual Memory Limit (KB) setting in IIS 7.

FIGURE 13.4
Define the parameters the tell IIS how to protect against rapid or cascade failures.

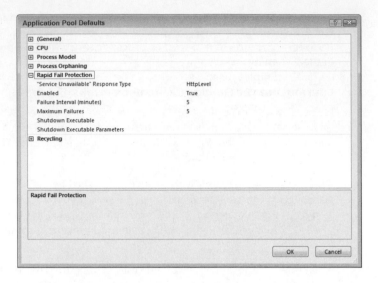

FIGURE 13.5
Recycling works about the same in IIS 7 as it does in IIS 6, but there are a few more options.

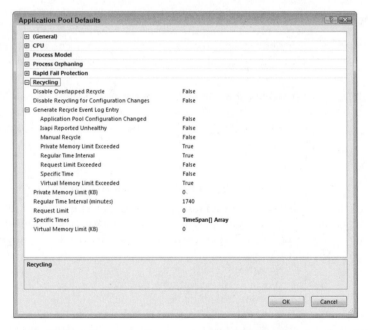

IIS 7 does fix a few issues from IIS 6. For example, some applications don't support multiple instances. In IIS 6, this limitation can cause problems when IIS creates a new application pool before it deletes the old application pool. By setting the Disable Overlapped Recycle property to True, you prevent IIS from creating a new application pool before it deletes the old one.

Some administrators also complained that a configuration change automatically generated an application pool recycle. The applications running at the time could lose data or even freeze in some cases. Setting Disable Recycling for Configuration Changes to True tells IIS to wait until the application pool has completed its pending requests before it recycles the application pool to incorporate the configuration changes.

Perhaps the most important change, and the one that's most helpful from a performance perspective, is that you can now ask IIS to create event log entries for the events shown in Figure 13.5. You have complete control over how IIS tracks application pool activity and can use the event log entries to tune your configuration. For example, if you notice that an application consistently exceeds its virtual memory limit (causing a recycle), you can work with developers to track down the problem and fix it. Fixing the memory error will almost certainly improve performance, if for no other reason than the changes you make will reduce the number of application pool recycles and the application will use memory more efficiently.

Creating New Application Pools

You'll eventually need to create new application pools on your server. For maximum efficiency, you'll probably want to create a new application pool for every major application your server supports. In addition, you'll want to create new application pools for each language type in most cases. Separate application pools can also assist in keeping Web sites separate and helping provide a specific level of service to each of the Web sites. The following steps help you create a new application pool.

1. Click Add Application Pool in the actions pane. You'll see the Add Application Pool dialog box shown in Figure 13.6.

FIGURE 13.6
Create new application pools on your server as needed to support applications and Web sites.

2. Type a name for the application pool in the Name field. Make sure the application pool name matches its purpose. For example, if you create an application pool for the MyApp application, you might want to call it MyApp Application Pool.

3. Choose one of the versions of the .NET Framework installed on the system in the .NET Framework Version field. When the application pool supports a non-.NET application, make sure you choose the No Managed Code option. Choosing this option helps your application perform better.

4. Choose either Classic or Integrated in the Managed Pipeline Mode.

5. Check the Start Application Pool Immediately option when you're creating a common application pool for a Web site or application that normally runs when you start the server. Clear this option for special purpose applications and Web sites that you want to start manually.

6. Click OK. IIS creates the new application pool for you using the default settings for the Web server. You can control these settings using the procedures found in the "Setting the Application Pool Defaults" section of the chapter.

Setting the Basic Application Pool Configuration

You may eventually decide that the standard settings for the application pool aren't working. To change the basic application pool settings, highlight the application pool you want to change and click Basic Settings in the Actions pane. Use the procedure found in the "Creating New Application Pools" section of the chapter to change the settings.

Setting the Advanced Application Pool Configuration

The default settings you configure for the server will work for most application pools, but not for all of them. In this case, you need to edit the application pool settings after you create the application pool using the procedure found in the "Creating New Application Pools" section of the chapter. To change the application pool advanced settings, highlight the application pool you want to change and click Advanced Settings in the Actions pane. Use the procedures found in the "Setting the Application Pool Defaults" section of the chapter to change the advanced settings.

Changing the Application Pool Recycling Interval

You may not like the new method of setting the recycling options for an application pool described in the "Configuring the Recycling Options" section of the chapter. In this case, IIS 7 provides a method for setting the recycling options using a dialog box that almost precisely matches the one found in IIS 6. To use this feature, highlight the application pool you want to change and click Recycling in the Actions pane. You'll see the Edit Application Pool Recycling Settings dialog box shown in Figure 13.7. Use the methods found in the "Configuring the Recycling Options" section of Chapter 7 to perform the required configuration changes.

FIGURE 13.7
Use the IIS 6 method to modify the application pool recycling options.

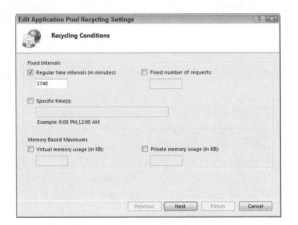

Viewing the Applications Associated with an Application Pool

Application pools support one or more applications. Sometimes, it's helpful to view the applications associated with a particular application pool when making configuration decisions. To perform this task, highlight the application pool in the Application Pools pane and click View Applications in the Actions pane. You'll see the Web Application pane shown in Figure 13.8. Notice that the resulting Actions pane only contains an option for changing the application pool of the selected application. When you finish viewing the applications and possibly changing their application pool, click Back (the left-pointing arrow) to return to the Application Pools pane.

FIGURE 13.8
View the applications associated with a particular application pool.

Removing an Application Pool

At some point, you'll want to remove application pools that you no longer need. Perhaps you removed the application that the application pool supported from the system. To remove an application pool, highlight the application pool entry in the Application Pools pane and click Remove in the Actions pane. IIS 7 will ask whether you're sure that you want to remove the application pool. Click Yes to complete the action.

Implementing Performance Monitoring

Good performance management begins with performance monitoring. You can't know what to change on a server if you don't know which application or service has problems. This chapter doesn't provide a complete tutorial on using the Reliability and Performance Monitor found in the Administrative Tools folder of the Control Panel, but it does discuss some of the objects and counters that you should know about.

NOTE It's impossible to provide full coverage on performance monitoring in a single section of a chapter. A book I wrote with Mark Minasi, *Mastering Windows Vista Business: Ultimate, Business, and Enterprise,* provides considerable information about the Reliability and Performance Monitor in Chapter 25.

The Reliability and Performance Monitor provides access to a considerable number of performance monitoring objects. Each object provides information about a certain aspect of the system. Some of these objects, such as Processor, are generic in nature and you'll rely on them to perform a number of performance monitoring tasks. However, some performance monitoring objects work well for checking IIS 7 performance as described in the following list (the descriptions also provide information on helpful counters).

Active Server Pages   Provides counters for ASP applications on a system. This object includes a number of error counters that can prove helpful in locating error conditions before they begin crashing the server. The Request Wait Time counter is quite revealing because it can help you understand server load. In fact, you'll find a number of request-related counters that can make performance optimization tasks significantly easier. When working with database applications, make sure you track the transaction counters as well.

ASP.NET   Provides counters that monitor global ASP.NET application performance. You can check overall application performance and potential error indicators such as the Request Wait Time counter. However, because this object works at the global level, you can only use it to monitor system performance and not to pinpoint precise application problems. Use the ASP.NET Applications object to pinpoint problems instead.

ASP.NET Applications   Provides counters that monitor individual application performance. As with the ASP object, you can monitor specifics about each application such as the amount of time each application waits. This object also provides useful counters for checking security problems. For example, the Forms Authentication Failure counter can tell you the number of times someone requests access and fails to obtain it. A high number with this counter could indicate undesirable external activity and definitely indicates a potential performance problem. For example, users might find that it takes several tries to gain access, which means you need to provide application changes that make login easier.

ASP.NET State Service   Outputs simple information about ASP.NET application state. This object provides an overview of ASP.NET state and provides counters that tell you the number of abandoned, timed out, active, and total sessions.

FTP Service   Indicates the health of the network when used for FTP communications. You can obtain statistics about FTP communications such as the number of anonymous and nonanonymous users. This object helps you determine whether a potential performance problem is network or application based.

HTTP Service   Indicates the health of the network when used for HTTP communications. The majority of the counters help you determine the number of cache hits and misses, which not only tells you about the network connection but the state of server memory as well. A high hit rate means that the server is accessing the disk relatively often and isn't performing efficiently. This object helps you determine whether a potential performance problem is network or application based.

HTTP Service Request Queues   Outputs simple information about the HTTP requests that the server receives. This is an overview of how well the server is handling requests no matter what those requests might be. A high rate of rejected requests (RejectionRate counter) may indicate error problems, failed logins, crashed applications, or other problems on your server. Consequently, this object is very good for a quick check of server health.

Internet Information Services Global   Provides an overview of both the FTP and HTTP services on the server. The most useful counters show cache statistics, network bandwidth information, and URI statistics. Monitor this object to obtain an overview of server health as a whole. You can't use these counters to perform any level of troubleshooting—they merely indicate potential server health problems.

Web Service   Provides detailed information about how the Web service is working with users and applications. For example, you can use the counters to determine the number of CGI requests and how many users are authenticated. You can use these counters to tell you about the current number of connections, determine how many people are attempting to make a connection, and detect whether the connection attempts are successful. Overall, this object helps you understand how outsiders are using your server, which can help you identify potential external threats, such as a DDOS attack.

Web Service Cache   Outputs simple information about how the Web service is reacting to a specific load. For example, you can detect how often the Web service is able to respond to a particular request using the cache. However, the counters don't just look at the cache as a whole, you can determine some specifics such as metadata cache hits. This object tends to focus on the Web service from an operating system perspective.

In addition to these objects, make sure you check out any objects associated with applications you use. For example, if you have SQL Server installed, you'll find that it provides a considerable number of objects you can use to monitor SQL Server performance. Even though SQL Server isn't part of IIS, it can affect the performance of any application that relies on it—even through intermediate resources. You may also find objects associated with other application languages or even other components installed as part of IIS, so it pays to look through the Reliability and Performance Monitor object list.

Defining Application Behavior Using Pages and Controls

The Pages and Controls pane provides settings that control ASP.NET applications. If you don't use ASP.NET applications, you can skip this section. To view the Pages and Controls pane, choose the Web server, Web site, or application level you want to change in the Connections pane. Double-click the Pages and Controls icon to display the Pages and Controls pane shown in Figure 13.9. The following sections describe the Pages and Controls pane configuration options in detail.

FIGURE 13.9
Configure the use of page and control features in ASP.NET to support users efficiently.

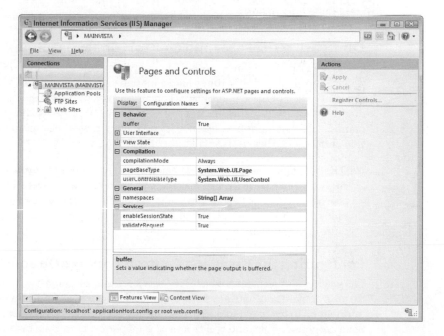

Configuring the Pages and Controls Behavior Options

The behavior options define how ASP.NET applications work and therefore have the biggest effect on application performance. For example, if you want your application to perform well, you should set the buffer property to True because this setting maintains a copy of the page in memory. However, if the application provides a unique page to everyone who requests information, then buffering the page may not be a good idea—in fact, it may cause the application to use memory inefficiently. Don't confuse unique pages with dynamic content. When a page is likely to provide the same content to callers over time but changes as needed to reflect new conditions, it's merely dynamic and buffering does work well.

The user interface settings control the master page and stylesheet used for Web page presentation. These settings don't affect performance, but they do affect the appearance of the Web page that the user sees. A developer must configure the application to use these settings, but it's always a good idea to make them accessible. A simple change here can redefine the entire appearance of a Web site without making any changes to the application code, which means Web site designers can improve Web site appearance without developer help.

Normally, allowing view state is a good idea because it maintains the content of controls so that the server doesn't have to keep uploading the entire Web page. However, when the view state includes a lot of information that changes frequently, it actually increases the network traffic required to update the Web page and creates a significant performance hit. Work with the developer to determine whether enabling view state makes sense for your application.

Configuring the Pages and Controls Compilation Options

The compilation section determines how CLR compiles the Web page code. In most cases, you'll want to use the developer recommendations for this setting. Generally speaking, you should always compile the Web page code to improve application performance.

Configuring the Pages and Controls General Options

The general section defines the .NET Framework namespaces that IIS loads to support a particular application. The default settings load a lot of namespaces, most of which your application won't use. Since each of these namespaces consumes system resources, they can create a small performance hit and reduce the efficiency of your server. Work with the developer to create a list of namespaces that the application needs and then remove the namespaces that it doesn't need to run. The performance benefit is small but noticeable.

NOTE Changing the list of loaded namespaces can improve performance, but it can also backfire on you. If you change the list, make sure you also keep in contact with the developer about any new namespaces that an application might require after coding changes. When an application suddenly stops working after a code change, look into a lack of namespace support as a potential cause of the problem.

Configuring the Pages and Controls Services Options

The services section defines which .NET services the application uses. Microsoft sets all of these services to true by default, but you may not actually need them. For example, if your application simply presents information to the user and doesn't require any user feedback in return, you can set the enableSessionState property to False and realize a significant performance gain because the server will use network and memory resources more efficiently.

Always set the validateRequest option to true. This feature helps reduce the potential for invalid user input. Sometimes the input is accidental and other times it's on purpose. In either case, you want the server to recognize this input to keep the application from crashing and prevent damage to the server. Even though setting this property to False can help you realize a performance gain, the gain leaves a security hole in your application and isn't a good value.

Considering Feature Delegation

Feature delegation is a touchy subject in IIS 7. On the one hand, you control the overall flexibility of the server with this feature. Web site administrators must have a feature delegated to them before they can use it. On the other hand, every feature you delegate to Web site administrators increases the risk of security, reliability, and even speed problems. You must delegate some features and the default IIS setup provides these features to Web site administrators by default. Some features you don't want to delegate for any reason because they could cause significant problems. To access the Feature Delegation pane shown in Figure 13.10, choose the Web server entry in the Connections pane and double-click the Feature Delegation icon.

FIGURE 13.10
Delegating features wisely can provide flexibility while preserving performance.

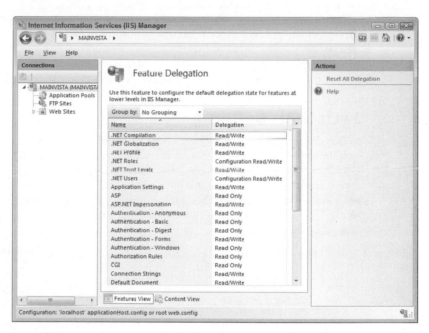

The settings that you delegate depend on the kind of applications you plan to run on the server. For example, if you don't plan to run CGI applications, then you should remove the delegation from that feature because setting up CGI incorrectly can cause all kinds of security and reliability problems. In addition, CGI applications tend to use resources inefficiently. A Web site administrator could decide to install and use a CGI application without permission when you provide the required delegation.

Delegating the SSL features might seem like a good idea. However, SSL can chew up a considerable number of resources on a server. If your server only supports informational public Web sites, there's little reason to delegate authority to use this feature to Web site administrators. In general, provide Web site administrators with the security features they need to provide a robust environment for users, but don't give them rights to do too much with the server that could result in a speed drop for everyone.

It's not always necessary to remove delegation of a feature. When you want Web site administrators to use a feature, but don't want them to change the feature settings, you can set the feature to provide read-only delegation. Using this approach lets Web site administrators know what they can do, without exposing your server to potential security, reliability, or speed-crushing settings changes. Of course, if you use the read-only approach, you also need to provide administrators with a means of requesting changes because changes do happen.

One of the default settings that could kill server performance is Failed Request Tracing Rules. This particular feature is only used for diagnosing errors. When you provide hosting space for several Web sites, you really don't want the administrators to turn on debugging because failed request tracing can kill server performance. Not only does it consume many resources, but also the Web site might not even be able to use the information they obtain.

Public Web sites may also wish to limit the use of Session State settings. Relying on cookies does make your server more efficient, but can kill user participation. It's important to define a policy that makes sense for everyone and then enforce that policy by setting this particular feature to read-only (or not delegating it at all).

You can't apply a specific set of rules to feature delegation. In most cases, you'll need to set up the server using a restrictive set of delegation rules, and then relax those rules as needed to meet specific needs. The important point to remember is that it's easier to give a Web site administrator more flexibility in managing a Web site than it is to remove some of that flexibility. Erring on the side of conservative management lets you add flexibility as needed and keep everyone happy.

Let's Start Building

In this chapter, you've discovered a new meaning for performance that will make it easier for you to define specifically what the term means for your organization. Using a common definition for performance is essential if you want to achieve the highest system efficiency possible. You've also discovered some tools to monitor the performance of your system and some techniques for making your system perform better. Most important, you've discovered that feature delegation can be a two-edged sword and that you need to manage this part of your server carefully. This chapter helps you build these skills:

◆ Define a performance plan based on the performance triangle

◆ Manage application pools

◆ Define and manage performance monitoring

◆ Modify application behavior

◆ Define the performance implications of feature delegation

Some administrators take a shotgun approach to performance and security alike. Every article they read that contains some interesting new tip or setting ends up appearing on their server. The result is a mess. Before you go any further, you need to create a performance plan for your system, just as you have created other plans for it. An unmanaged performance change is worse than not checking performance at all. Make sure you spend some time planning the performance changes, verifying that you can modify the system in an acceptable way, and considering both security and reliability concerns in addition to raw speed before you make any physical changes. Once you do have a security plan, make sure you implement it a step at a time and verify the effects of each change.

Chapter 14 considers the issue of globalization. If you have a public Web site, you must assume that anyone can access it, no matter what language they speak. Most Web sites today provide a single language version of their content, and that might work fine for you. However, if you really do need to address the needs of people who speak languages other than your own, globalization is one of the issues you must address and Chapter 14 provides some basic guidelines for you.

Chapter 14

Considering Globalization

Globalization brings up pictures of foreign locations, exotic ports of calls, and nations halfway around the world. However, globalization of a Web site is far more than simply addressing the needs of another country. Even for Web sites used exclusively in the United States, there's a need to support globalization, in some cases, because you can't always be certain that the person viewing the Web site speaks English. In fact, you have to assume that a public Web site is going to attract attention from people in other countries.

IIS provides limited support for globalization—of the three globalization components, internationalization, localization, and translation, IIS only provides limited support for localization. In short, you can't simply adjust a few settings in IIS and hope to have a complete solution. Obviously, the Web site content must reflect the language that the viewer uses. In addition, you have to consider a wealth of other requirements—everything from addressing local units of measure to supporting the viewer's customs and biases. A truly effective globalization makes the viewer comfortable, which is often hard to achieve when you don't know the country (speaking the language is usually not enough).

All of the standard .NET Framework DLLs come in a language-invariant version, which means that they don't cater to a particular language. However, in many cases, DLLs do support a specific language and you need to choose the right one. The selection of a language for a DLL or any other part of an application is part of the culture selection for the DLL or application. In addition, you must encode documents correctly so that the recipient can decode them. These and many other mechanical aspects to globalization can cause companies considerable trouble—you must test and tweak your applications to meet specific application requirements.

The final section of the chapter describes how you can modify the IIS settings to meet globalization requirements. As previously mentioned, these settings aren't enough to provide a full solution, but they are part of the solution.

In this chapter, you will learn how to do the following:

◆ Choose a globalization strategy for your organization

◆ Define the limits of globalization in IIS

◆ Choose appropriate culture settings

◆ Use document encoding properly

◆ Manage .NET application globalization settings

Considering Globalization Requirements for Your Organization

You've probably heard the term *global economy*, at some point, and may assume that everyone speaks English (at least as a second language). The global economy is more like a global shark fest with various countries contending for the prize. Unfortunately, your company is one of the sharks and your Web site is part of the bait. If you want to get your piece of the prize, you must attract enough fish to your Web site and you need the right kind of bait to attract the right kind of fish to your Web site. Once you've attracted some attention to your Web site, you'll discover that when it comes to globalization, your company has to consider a number of issues including:

- Your visitor may speak another language.

- Your visitor's country may use a different measurement system.

- Your visitor's country probably works with a different currency.

- Your visitor may wish to see dates and numbers in a different format.

- The visitor's language may use a different character set.

- Cultural references that work in your country may not work in another country.

- Colors may have different symbolism in the visitor's culture.

The fact of the matter is that few companies provide a comfortable place for people outside their country to obtain content, which may mean lost sales and missed opportunities. Depending on your product, service, or market, you may not be able to make use of the opportunity anyway, so it may not be a big deal. For example, if you make widgets, but can't ship them to Country A, then there's no point in attracting potential customers from Country A. The crux of the matter then is what kind of fish are you hoping to attract? The bait you use in the form of globalization will determine which fish you attract.

Many Web sites now have a handle on the language issue, even if the translations border on terrible. All you need to do is detect the user's language using the various clues provided in the request header and then substitute the appropriate language strings in your response. The technique is relatively simple. Unfortunately, that's where most Web sites stop, which means that the designers haven't gone far enough.

Web site visitors move on to the next Web site with just a click or two. Encountering metric measurements that need to be converted to U.S measurements before placing an order for anything or seeing that the Web site uses a poor translation means losing visitors. No one's going to take time to convert your country's units of measure into something they understand. You have to perform the required work. The same conversions apply to numbers and dates. It's important to pay close attention to formats for dates, numbers, units of measure, and so forth to ensure there's no room for misunderstanding on your Web site.

Likewise, someone in Asia looking for a product might be attracted to a Web site in France. Unfortunately, all of the prices appear in Euros, which might work fine in Europe, but have no meaning in Asia. The interesting problem for Web sites that do provide price conversion is that they require the user to perform extra work to get the information. When you read the caller's request header, you can normally obtain enough information for a conversion and should perform the task automatically. If the caller wants to use another currency, you can certainly provide that feature, but making the user perform extra work to get a price shouldn't happen. Always remember that the Web site with the correct pricing information is one click away.

Very few Web sites get encoding—the use of the proper characters—correct. In some cases, the problem is minor because people are used to reading between the lines to obtain the correct meaning. However, in many languages, the use of the correct diacritical marks is essential to providing the accurate information to the viewer. The topic of encoding is important enough that it appears in a separate section of this chapter, "Understanding the Use of Encoding."

One of the most explosive problems with Web sites that attempt to serve people in multiple countries is that of understanding the cultural differences. Humor is an exceptionally problematic issue because humor varies from place to place, even within the same country. Just what someone will find funny depends on their personal biases and there isn't any way you can know what those biases are going to be when the caller makes a request. However, cultural references are difficult even when they aren't an attempt at humor. When you hear the word *football*, do you think of soccer or the American version of the game? Sometimes pictures can overcome the difficulties people have understanding cultural references, and you should use graphics whenever possible to help overcome potential confusion.

Of course, all this brings back the original message of this section. The globalization you implement depends entirely on the kind of fish you're trying to attract. The bait you use has to make the fish feel comfortable and it has to be something the fish wants. If you use the wrong bait or present it in the wrong way, the fish will almost certainly go for someone else's hook.

CONSIDERING APPLICATION ACCESSIBILITY

Many administrators and developers don't consider those with special needs. For example, it doesn't take much to support someone who is blind, but the increase in traffic on your Web site is measurable when you choose to support this group as part of your globalization effort. By adding special attributes to HTML tags, a person using a screen reader can visualize the page content and interact with it.

Of course, you can always do more than simply adding special attributes and HTML tags. While this is certainly one definition of accessibility, it's also the least productive and most narrow-minded interpretation. Unfortunately, it's the most prevalent view of accessibility used by government and industry today because it's the viewpoint that enjoys legal status. A broader definition helps everyone because most people have some type of special need—it might simply be the need to enlarge text when their eyes are tired, but the need is still real and Web sites that cater to this need have a distinct advantage.

The best way to view accessibility is as a means of making people comfortable, not as an extra expense that the business or individual must bear. A business that pursues accessibility as a means for attracting and keeping new clients is certainly going to see a profit from their efforts. In addition, studies have shown that when a company pays attention to accessibility issues, the company's employees benefit from better health, which in turn pays dividends in reduced sick time for the company. An application, whether desktop or Web based, that's accessible is easier to use than one that lacks accessibility features. You might even find that adding accessibility features pays for itself by reducing application support costs.

Including the Alt attribute and bubble help (tooltips) in an application may seem like something that no one would use—especially with graphics—because the administrator or developer assumes that the user can see the image on screen. The fact is that some applications and Web sites alike present many images in such a way that deciphering them is difficult. The Alt attribute and bubble help provide clues for those with good vision, as well as those who might require a little additional help. The pop-up explanation becomes a source of additional information that everyone can use. In addition, it's quite possible that the browser won't download the image due to security concerns—the description acts as a replacement in this environment.

Wrist problems are one of the scourges of our society. For office workers who are prone to these problems, heavy use of the keyboard and mouse can cause a flare-up of their wrist condition. The accessibility requirements designed to ease access for those who lack good coordination also help those who have normal use of their arms by reducing the effort required to input information. A business could easily write off the cost of improving the accessibility of their software by reducing the work time lost to wrist problems, not to mention the cost of medical care. In fact, because of the high cost of medical assistance, preventing even one case of wrist problems could pay for the required upgrades and anything after that would be money saved.

Even the colors used to present information on screen can affect the productivity of those who use the application. For example, many of the same color combinations that cause problems for those with color blindness also cause eyestrain for those with normal vision. Meeting accessibility requirements for color composition can also net surprising results in reduced headaches and time off spent recovering from symptoms such as dry eyes.

Accessibility is a special kind of globalization. It's a globalization for those with special needs in your community. No, you don't have to provide a language translation or convert numbers into another form, but the idea is the same. You're providing a comfortable environment for someone with a different perspective from your own. It's the same goal as globalization in many respects—simply a different audience.

Understanding the Limitations of Globalization in IIS

Any thought that IIS provides a complete globalization solution is simply wrong. In fact, IIS brings very little to the table when it comes to globalization. If you're working with a non-ASP.NET application, IIS presents a nearly invisible level of support. The only globalization you're going to see is when the user requests something that IIS or a supporting managed component provides directly. Otherwise, any globalization must occur with the application you create. A minimal application configuration will include:

- Understanding the appropriate request encoding
- Providing the appropriate response encoding
- Using the appropriate encoding for data files on the server's hard drive
- Incorporating the correct content strings for the requested language
- Considering the cultural elements for the requestor as part of the response

ASP.NET applications fare considerably better when it comes to IIS globalization. You can configure the ASP.NET application settings using the .NET Globalization pane (see the "Changing the .NET Globalization Settings" section of the chapter for details). Because you can define the application globalization requirements, the developer can intercept the information and provide the appropriate code within the application to handle globalization. The settings also let you change the encoding directly, so the developer doesn't need to worry about this particular requirement in the code.

Many of the output methods for the .NET Framework provide an `IFormatProvider` interface entry (see the Microsoft Developer Network, MSDN, site at `http://msdn2.microsoft.com/en-us/library/system.iformatprovider(VS.80).aspx` for details on this interface). The `IFormatProvider` entry is important because it lets the developer write code that automatically changes the output of some items such as numeric and date information. The application can also choose language strings and other output features based exclusively on the information it receives from the HttpRequest object provided as input to the application (see http:// msdn2.microsoft.com/en-us/library/system.web.httprequest(VS.80).aspx for details). Most important of all, the developer can read the settings you provide within the Web.CONFIG file using the same techniques described throughout the book. In short, ASP.NET developers have access to a considerable amount of information about the caller through IIS. However, that's where the IIS support ends.

When working with an ASP.NET application, the developer still requires assistance from a number of experts to create a complete solution. Sure, the .NET Framework will provide all of the required caller information and can even provide format conversions for numeric and date information, but the developer still needs to include those language strings with the application and provide other resources as well.

One of the big issues for many Web sites is currency conversion. Fortunately, ASP.NET applications can handle Web services with aplomb and there are a number of currency converters on the Internet. One of the easier-to-use free currency converters appears on the WebserviceX.NET Web site at http://www.webservicex.net/WS/WSDetails.aspx?CATID=2&WSID=10. This Web service even uses Web Services Description Language (WSDL) and Simple Object Access Protocol (SOAP), the favorite technologies for ASP.NET. Any developer should be able to connect to the Web service with relative ease to perform currency conversions.

Choosing Appropriate Culture Settings

You must consider several forms of culture as part of Web applications. The chapter has already discussed one form, the use of words and phrases to express ideas that another culture can understand. Talking about football without providing context can have several meanings depending on which country the caller calls home. The second form of culture is the means of identifying a particular group of people. People have defined all kinds of systems to perform this task, but the one used for Web pages is quite simple. The combination of country and language defines the person's culture when it comes to a Web page.

It may almost seem as if the country and the culture would end up being the same given the criterion for determining it. However, many countries speak English, so using English alone is not enough to identify the culture. Likewise, people in India speak many languages, so India alone isn't enough to identify the culture. Saying that the culture represents an English speaker in India, however, conveys considerably more information, so you must consider both issues when creating an application for IIS.

Most programming languages equate a culture setting to a locale and assign it a standardized Locale Identifier (LCID). You can find these standardized numbers in many locations on the Internet. For example, the International LCID site at http://krafft.com/scripts/deluxe-calendar/ lcid_chart.htm provides most of the standard LCIDs in use today. Setting your application to use the appropriate LCID is part of the globalization for that application.

ASP.NET application developers have more choices than those offered by LCID at their disposal. The .NET Framework also provides a number of resources for working with locale as part of method calls. You can see how to set the culture for an ASP.NET application in the "Changing the .NET Globalization Settings" section of the chapter. In fact, you can even create custom cultures to meet special needs. The article at http://msdn.microsoft.com/msdnmag/issues/05/10/ Globalization/default.aspx provides a developer's eye view of the locale support features of the .NET Framework.

Understanding the Use of Encoding

Encoding differs from the culture settings in that encoding defines text from the computer's perspective. From the computer's perspective, characters are actually numbers. Encoding assigns letters to specific numbers so that the output from an application displays the correct letter. The decoding process converts numbers into letters so that you can read the associated content. Some people have a hard time understanding that, at the basic level, computers only understand 0 and 1. Computers can manipulate huge groups of 0's and 1's quite quickly, but they have no concept of letters and don't need to understand letters. A computer can compare, modify, delete, add, and otherwise work with letters without ever seeing them as anything more than numbers.

The most common form of encoding today is Unicode Transformation Format 8-bit (UTF-8). You'll also find that IIS 7 supports UTF-7, UTF-16, UTF-32, and UTF-32BE in the Unicode formats. You can read about these formats at `http://unicode.org/faq/utf_bom.html`. IIS 7 supports the UTF-8 format by default, but the UTF-8 format doesn't work for double-byte character set (DBCS) languages such as Japanese and Chinese. In this case, you'll want to change the setup to use UTF-16 or UTF-32.

It would be nice if there was only one standardized encoding technique, but there isn't. The UTF specification is commonly used for Web pages, but not for your hard drive and the hard drive must also encode information. In this case, the most common format is a Windows specification such as the Windows 1252 format shown at `http://www.microsoft.com/globaldev/reference/sbcs/ 1252.mspx`. In fact, you can drive yourself crazy trying to keep track of all of the encoding techniques in use today. You can see a wealth of them at `http://www.i18nguy.com/unicode/codepages.html`.

In theory, encoding should be a very simple act. You assign a number to a letter and then use software to create a visualization of that letter on screen. The only problem is that many countries don't use the same letters and many rely on diacritical marks to provide emphasis. For example, the German language uses the umlaut (see `http://dictionary.reference.com/search?q=umlaut` for an example of an umlaut and its use) and the English language doesn't. Consequently, the encoding for German is different from English. The Windows format even sports specific encodings for languages such as Greek, Arabic, and Hebrew.

Of course, if you speak Chinese or Japanese, your language doesn't even use letters—it relies on characters that represent entire words or syllables instead (see `http://www.wsu.edu/~dee/ANCJAPAN/ WRITING.HTM` for a discussion of how Japanese writing evolved). Obviously, an encoding system based on letters won't work for a language that uses characters. A lettered system can usually achieve its ends with 256 numeric combinations (8 bits). The character system requires far more, which is why Chinese and Japanese require DBCS, which allocates 16 bits (65,536 combinations) for each character. The encoding is also very different from what an English speaker might use.

When working in other languages, there's still a need to symbolize some concepts in English because the other languages may not include a word that corresponds to the computer jargon term, for example. Consequently, most of the encoding techniques for other languages include some means of working with English words as needed. For example, the CP-950 encoding technique (`http://www.microsoft.com/globaldev/reference/dbcs/950.mspx`) includes alphanumeric characters in the usual positions. However, the upper characters are for Chinese characters. For example, click on the B0 link (`http://www.microsoft.com/globaldev/reference/dbcs/950/ 950_B0.mspx`) and you'll see a number of Chinese characters, as shown in Figure 14.1. The point is that even if someone had wanted to create a single encoding system, it wouldn't have worked out because human language contains too many variances.

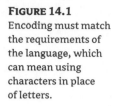

FIGURE 14.1
Encoding must match
the requirements of
the language, which
can mean using
characters in place
of letters.

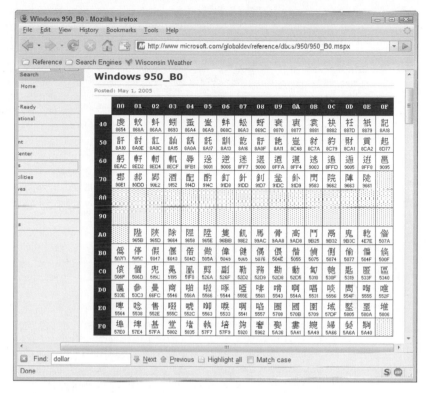

Changing the .NET Globalization Settings

As with many IIS settings, you can configure the globalization settings at the Web server, Web site, folder, or application levels. An important thing to remember with IIS 7 is that the globalization settings tend to affect .NET applications. When you want to create settings for other application types, you'll normally need to rely on the globalization features of that application to do it. The exception is the support IIS provides to the application. Because the IIS modules rely on the .NET Framework, any changes you make the .NET Globalization settings affect the IIS modules. Consequently, when a feature relies on IIS modules, rather than the application, you'll see the effects of globalization settings you provide.

These settings do affect any ASP.NET applications you install on IIS and you'll probably want to make changes at the application level, in many cases, for that reason. The Web server settings should be general enough to support any application and you should refine the settings as you move down each level. The application developer can use the globalization settings to:

- Provide locale-specific functionality through method calls (many of the .NET Framework calls support globalization directly)

- Load custom DLLs for that language

- Load and use custom strings for a particular language (allows customized prompts and explanatory text)

- Redirect the user to language- or culture-specific locations on the Web site

To access the .NET Globalization settings, choose the level you want in the Connections pane and double-click the .NET Globalization pane. You'll see a .NET Globalization pane, as shown in Figure 14.2. The following sections describe these settings in detail.

FIGURE 14.2
Use the .NET Globalization settings to help the application provide language- or culture-specific output.

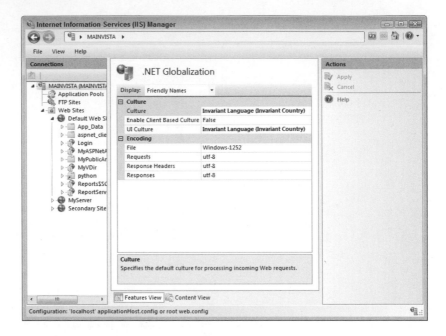

Changing the Culture Settings

As described in the "Choosing Appropriate Culture Settings" section of the chapter, cultural settings define elements of a Web page other than language that affect the viewer's perception of content. For example, someone in Germany will use a different notation for formatting numbers than someone in the United States. Normally, .NET applications don't rely on cultural information, making them culturally neutral. To enable the cultural settings for .NET applications, you must set the Enable Culture Based Client property to True.

TIP You may find that you still need additional tutorials and help with IIS 7 due to all of the changes it provides, especially when it comes to globalization. DABCC is one of the few companies as of this writing to provide a full list of IIS 7–specific tutorials and classes. You can learn more about this company at http://www.dabcc.com/channel.aspx?id=189.

Once you've enabled the culture settings, you can choose a culture for the application to use. It's important to remember that some application features will work without much in the way of developer assistance. The developer can pass any culture setting to any .NET Framework method that supports it without knowing which culture you'll select in advance. However, other features require more developer support. For example, you can choose Hindi all you want, but the application prompts won't appear in that language unless the developer provides support for the proper application prompts in that language. The same holds true for custom DLLs—you must have a DLL for the required language before you can provide cultural support for it.

To change the cultural setting for an application, click the drop-down list in the UI Culture field. You'll see a list of what appear to be language settings, as shown in Figure 14.3. However, once you start looking through the list, you'll notice that these are actually culture settings. For example, you'll find more than one English entry because many countries speak English. The culture settings for English in India vary from those for English in Jamaica, and India speaks more than one language, so it has more than one language setting. The combination of language and country often form the basis for the culture setting.

FIGURE 14.3
Choose the appropriate culture setting for your application.

Changing the Encoding Settings

As described in the "Understanding the Use of Encoding" section of the chapter, encoding defines how characters appear within a file. As shown in Figure 14.1, the default encoding for IIS 7 relies on a standard Windows encoding for files and the UTF-8 encoding for both requests and responses. The reason for using Windows encoding for files is that they appear on the local drive. In most cases, you won't need to change this setting unless your system uses a different encoding. You can see the Windows-1252 encoding at `http://www.microsoft.com/globaldev/reference/sbcs/1252.mspx`.

The Web server receives requests using the encoding shown in the Requests field. This field only defines the default encoding. A request normally includes an encoding value as part of its header, which means the request header normally defines the encoding that the caller uses, rather than the value in the Requests field. The only time IIS relies on the value in the Requests field is when the caller doesn't provide a preference. You can learn more about the content of the request header on the W3C site at `http://www.w3.org/Protocols/HTTP/HTRQ_Headers.html` and `http://www.w3.org/Protocols/rfc2616/rfc2616-sec14.html`.

A response requires two entries. The first, found in the Response Headers field, defines the response header encoding. The second, found in the Responses field, defines the response body encoding. IIS always uses these two fields to define the output of the response unless the developer overrides the default in the application. Normally, you'll set the response header and response body to use the same encoding. In fact, it doesn't really make sense to do otherwise in most cases.

Sometimes administrators really do have a hard time figuring out what their server is sending and receiving. You can see the request and response headers for a particular Web site by using an external product such as Web sniffer (`http://web-sniffer.net/`). This particular tool is exceptionally easy to use. Simply type the URL you want to see and click Submit. Figure 14.4 shows the request header from a Firefox browser contacting my personal Web site at `http://www.mwt.net/~jmueller`. Notice the `Accept-Charset` entry, which defines the encoding the caller can accept.

The response header shows the information about the server, as shown in Figure 14.5. In this case, my personal Web site is hosted on an Apache server, but the same technique and information applies to IIS servers as well. In fact, that's one of the benefits of using this particular product—it works fine with any platform, not just IIS. Some of the information will differ between platforms, but using this tool lets you verify that the settings you think you're using are the ones that the user is actually seeing.

FIGURE 14.4
The request header information tells you what the caller is sending.

FIGURE 14.5
The response header information tells you how the server responds to the caller request.

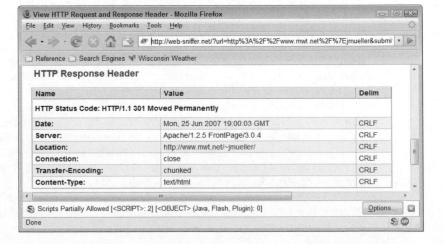

IIS 7 supports a huge list of encoding methods. It's important to note that IIS 7 overrides the value found in the `Accept-Charset` entry of the request. This means that some callers could experience problems accessing your Web site when you use the wrong encoding because the ASP.NET application never sees the value of the `Accept-Charset` entry. Unfortunately, users who contact you about contact problems won't have any idea of what you're talking about when you ask them what encoding they're using. Sending them to the Web sniffer site will help you get valid request information immediately so that you can repair any potential problems.

Response headers can actually contain a lot of information, so it pays to know how to read them. You can learn about the valid response header information for IIS at `http://msdn2.microsoft.com/en-us/library/ms537417.aspx`. Normally, a combination of the developer, .NET Framework, and IIS will create the response header information. Errors in the response header or settings that the user can't accept can cause an otherwise functional application to fail. When an error occurs, you need to locate the actual error information and then the source of that error. Fortunately, because everything is pretty much standardized, you'll seldom run into problems with either request or response headers.

Let's Start Building

This chapter has explored the rather complex topic of globalization. You've discovered where IIS can help and where it falls short. The discussion is an overview and you're definitely going to require other skills to create a complete solution. This chapter helps you build these skills:

- Choose a globalization strategy for your organization

- Define the limits of globalization in IIS

- Choose appropriate culture settings

- Use document encoding properly

- Manage .NET application globalization settings

Now that you have an idea of what IIS can do for you, it's time to define the solution for your company. You need to consider what IIS can and can't do to help you create a globalization solution. It's also important to define the language and culture skills your company requires to create a complete solution. Remember, the idea isn't simply to convey information, but to make the user comfortable with that information.

Congratulations! You've come to the last chapter of the book. What you see in this book is my experiences with IIS 7, those of the various editors, and those of the beta readers. Obviously, IIS 7 is a complex product and your experiences may differ from ours—we all learn from experience. If you want to share your experiences with me, please contact me at `JMueller@mwt.net`. I always want to hear about your experiences, good, bad, or indifferent. Let me know what you think of the book as well. I always incorporate reader comments into the next edition of the book, so your input will help me create a better book.

Glossary

This book includes a glossary so that you can find terms and acronyms easily. It has several important features you need to know about. First, every nonstandard acronym in the entire book appears here. I've left common acronyms out of the glossary. (The glossary excludes common acronyms such as units of measure and most file extensions because these terms are easy to find in other sources and most people know what they mean.) This way, there isn't any doubt that you'll always find everything you need to use the book properly.

Second, these definitions are specific to the book. In other words, when you look through this glossary, you're seeing the words defined in the context in which they're used in this the book. This might or might not always coincide with current industry usage since the computer industry changes the meaning of words so often.

Finally, I've used a conversational tone for the definitions in most cases. This means that the definitions might sacrifice a bit of puritanical accuracy for the sake of better understanding. The purpose of this glossary is to define the terms in such a way that there's less room for misunderstanding the intent of the book as a whole.

WHAT TO DO IF YOU DON'T FIND IT HERE

While this glossary is a relatively complete view of the words and acronyms in the book, you'll run into situations when you need to know more. No matter how closely I look at terms throughout the book, there's always a chance I'll miss the one acronym or term that you really need to know. In addition to the technical information found in the book, I've directed your attention to numerous online sources of information throughout the book, and few of the terms the Web site owners use will appear here unless I also chose to use them in the book. Fortunately, many sites on the Internet provide partial or complete glossaries to fill in the gaps:

Acronym Finder `http://www.acronymfinder.com/`

Free Online Dictionary Of Computing (FOLDOC) `http://nightflight.com/foldoc/`

Microsoft Business Users Glossary `http://www.microsoft.com/atwork/glossary.mspx`

Microsoft Encarta `http://encarta.msn.com/`

Microsoft .NET Glossary `http://www.microsoft.com/NET/basics_glossary.aspx`

Microsoft Security Glossary `http://msdn.microsoft.com/library/en-us/dnanchor/html/securityanchor.asp`

TechEncyclopedia `http://www.techweb.com/encyclopedia/defineterm.jhtml?term=COM`

Webopedia `http://webopedia.internet.com/`

yourDictionary.com `http://www.yourdictionary.com/`

Some entries in this list are quite specialized. For example, the Microsoft Security Glossary discusses the Microsoft view of security terms. You can find other Microsoft glossaries listed at `http://www.microsoft.com/resources/glossary/default.mspx`. If you still don't find what you need, try the Microsoft Search page at `http://search.microsoft.com/`, type the word glossary, add a specific area such as network, and click Go.

A

Access Control Entry (ACE)

Defines the object rights for a single user or group. Every ACE has a header that defines the type, size and flags for the ACE. Next comes an access mask that defines the rights a user or group has to the object. Finally, there's an entry for the user's or group's Security IDentifier (SID).

Access Control List (ACL)

Part of the Windows-based operating system security application programming interface (API) used to determine both access and monitoring properties for an object. The ACL originally appeared in Windows NT. Each ACL contains one or more access control entries (ACEs) that define the security properties for an individual or group. There are two major ACL groups: Security Access Control List (SACL) and Discretionary Access Control List (DACL). The SACL controls Windows auditing feature. The DACL controls access to the object.

Access Token

A definition of the rights that a service or resource requestor has to the operating system. This is the data structure that tells the security system what rights a requestor, such as a user, has to access a particular object. The object's access requirements are contained in a security descriptor. In short, the security descriptor is the lock and the access token is the key.

ACE

See Access Control Entry

ACL

See Access Control List

Active Server Pages (ASP)

A special type of scripting language environment used by Windows servers equipped with Internet Information Server (IIS). This specialized scripting language environment helps the developer create flexible Web applications that include server scripts written in a number of languages such as VBScript, JavaScript, JScript, and PerlScript. The use of variables and other features, such as access to server variables, helps the developer create scripts that can compensate for user and environmental needs as well as security concerns. ASP uses HTML to display content to the user. The newer ASP.NET technology is slowly replacing ASP and acts as the basis for IIS 7. Despite the similarities in names, ASP.NET is a new managed code technology that works with the .NET Framework.

Advanced Encryption Standard (AES)

The mathematical basis for performing symmetric encryption and decryption of data. The algorithm originally appeared as the Rijndael algorithm, after it's inventors (Joan Daemen and Vincent Rijmen). This is a block cipher that can accept a number of data block sizes and key lengths. Many companies now use this algorithm as a replacement for the DES and Triple DES algorithms.

AES

See Advanced Encryption Standard

AJAX

See Asynchronous JavaScript and XML

API

See Application Programming Interface

Application Programming Interface (API)

A method of defining a standard set of function or method calls and other interface elements. It usually defines the interface between a high-level language and the lower level elements used by a device driver or operating system. The ultimate goal is to provide some type of service to an application that requires access to the operating system or device feature set.

ASP

See Active Server Pages

Asynchronous JavaScript and XML (AJAX)

A technology that combines the JavaScript language and XML data storage to create a desktop application feel for Web applications. The technology works with most browsers, but the client must install a special AJAX engine to make the technology work. Besides the look-and-feel issues, the major feature of this technology is that it reduces network traffic by making requests only as needed. An application can replace part of a page, rather than request the entire page from the server. In addition, requests occur asynchronously, which means both client and server can handle information as time permits, rather than immediately.

Auditing (Security)

A technique for monitoring the security of a system, rather than controlling accessing to system resources. An audit can show whether the requestor access succeeds or fails and it's often possible to define monitoring on objects at several levels. Auditing can affect any system object, including logging into the system, using files, and executing applications. Any activity that generates an event provides a basis for auditing. However, not every object provides complete auditing, normally because the object doesn't require such detailed scrutiny.

Authentication

The act of validating the identity of a caller. This task can include any of a number of validation techniques, such as the use of passwords or biometric techniques. Most forms of authentication return a token that provides unique caller identification and lasts for a specific interval before becoming invalid.

Authentication Scheme

The methodology used to perform verification of a caller's identity. The methodology includes the input requirements from the caller, the method used to perform the verification, and the response the server provides to the caller. Many authentication schemes require a username and password, but other techniques are becoming available. Some servers provide multiple authentication schemes, each of which has particular requirements and represents trade-offs between security and ease of use.

Authorization

The act of providing access to specific services or resources based on the authenticated identity of a caller or other entity. Authorization gives the requesting party permission to use the specific service or resource.

B

Bandwidth Throttling

A method of reducing the amount of bandwidth used by a device or application during transmission. Bandwidth throttling places a limit on the amount of bandwidth any particular device or application can use. Even if the network has additional bandwidth, the device or application can't use it to perform tasks. The purpose behind bandwidth throttling is to reduce the risk that one device or application will use all of the available bandwidth and starve other devices and applications for communication needs.

BAPI

See Biometrics Application Programming Interface

Biometrics

A statistical method of scanning an individual's unique characteristics, normally body parts, to ensure that they are who they say they are. Some of the scanned elements include voiceprints, irises, fingerprints, hands, and facial features. The two most popular elements are irises and fingerprints because they're the two that most people are familiar with. The advantages of using biometrics are obvious. Not only can't the user lose their identifying information (at least not very easily), but with proper scanning techniques the identifying information can't be compromised either.

Biometrics Application Programming Interface (BAPI)

A special set of programming constructs that help developers embed biometric technology into applications. A consortium of vendors including IBM, Compaq, IO Software, Microsoft, Sony, Toshiba, and Novell originated BAPI.

Buffer

The area in memory where program variables, data, or executable code is stored. Buffers often act as a means of caching data or code. For example, word processing applications will normally read more than one page from a document to improve performance. The applications stores pages in addition to the one currently viewed by the user in the buffer until needed. Buffering is also used in applications where long request delays are anticipated, such as applications based on Web services.

C

Cache

A storage area for data, code, or other resources normally associated with memory or a special file on a hard drive. Both hardware and applications rely on the cache to improve performance. Unlike a buffer, which can store settings or even bits of information, a cache is normally associated with an entire object. However, some people use the terms interchangeably.

Cascading Style Sheets (CSS)

A method for defining a standard Web page appearance using formatting information. The formatting may include headings, standard icons, backgrounds, and other features that would tend to give each page at a particular Web site the same appearance. The reasons for using CSS include speed of creating a Web site (it takes less time if the developer doesn't have to create an overall design for each page) and consistency. Changing the overall appearance of a Web site also becomes as easy as changing the style sheet instead of each page alone. CSS is also a standards-supported technology, so it represents an easy method for developers to create Web pages that will work in standards-compliant browsers.

CGI

See Common Gateway Interface

Chunked Encoding

A method used to convert the body of a Web page into small pieces that the server can send to the caller more efficiently than sending the entire Web page. In addition, the caller receives a little of the Web page at a time so it's easier to see progress as the Web page loads. This technique relies on the RFC 2616 standard.

CIAC

See Computer Incident Advisory Capability

CLR

See Common Language Runtime

Code-Based Security

A method of restricting access to resources through the application's code, rather than the requestor, such as a user. By placing restrictions on the code, in addition to the user, the system becomes more secure because the code can no longer request access to resources it doesn't need to perform tasks. For example, if a piece of code doesn't need to write to the hard drive, then it shouldn't have access to the hard drive. Using this approach defeats many schemes for gaining access to the operation system through flaws in the code.

Code Page (CP)

A standardized method of representing characters both printed and abstract using codes. Another term applied to this form of communication is encoding—assigning a numeric value to letters, characters, and symbols to define human-readable data in a form the computer can manipulate. Other forms of character representation include American Standard Code for Information Interchange (ASCII). IBM originated the CP format and named it for the tabular form in which the encoding information appears when printed.

COM

See Component Object Model

Command Line Switch

An element provided to an application in a non-graphical interface to modify its behavior or fulfill required data needs. The command line switch normally appears with a dash (-) or slash (/), followed by a keyword or symbol, and a data value in some cases. For example, the common /? command line switch forces an application to display help information, rather than perform its normal task.

Common Gateway Interface (CGI)

One of the oldest common methods of transferring data from a client machine to a Web server on the Internet. CGI is a specification that defines how a Web server can launch EXEs and communicate with them. A CGI application is normally written with a low-level language such as C/C++ or Practical Extraction and Reporting Language (PERL). However, it's possible to use nearly any executable file with CGI. CGI receives input through the standard input device and output data through the standard output device. There are two basic data transfer types. The user can send new information to the server or can query data already existing on the server. A data entry form asking for the user's name and address is an example of the first type of transaction. A search engine page on the Internet (a page that helps the user find information on other sites) is an example of the second type of transaction. The Web server normally provides some type of feedback for the user by transmitting a new page of information once the CGI application is complete. This could be as simple as an acknowledgment for data entry or a list of Internet sites for a data query.

Common Language Runtime (CLR)

The engine (pronounced clear) used to interpret managed application tokens within the .NET Framework. All Visual Studio .NET languages that produce managed applications can use the same runtime engine. Visual Studio .NET calls on the just-in-time (JIT) compiler to compile the source code into a special tokenized form called Intermediate Language (IL) and CLR interprets the IL. (It's also possible to access the JIT compiler outside of Visual Studio .NET at the command line.) The major advantages of this approach include extensibility (you can add other languages) and reduced code size (you don't need a separate runtime for each language).

Component Object Model (COM)

A Microsoft specification for a binary-based, object-oriented code and data encapsulation method and transference technique. It's the basis for technologies such as OLE (Object Linking and Embedding) and ActiveX (components and controls). COM is limited to local connections.

Computer Incident Advisory Capability (CIAC)

An office of the United States Department of Energy (DOE) tasked with tracking viruses, Trojan horses, worms, system vulnerabilities, common patches, and other security-related information.

CP

See Code Page

CSS

See Cascading Style Sheets

D

DACL

See Discretionary Access Control List

Data Encryption Standard (DES)

An unsafe method of data encryption that relies on symmetric key encryption. This methodology was oringially introduced in 1975 and standardized by ANSI in 1981. As computer technology has improved, the encryption technique has become easier to crack, making it an unreliable means of protecting data.

Database Management System (DBMS)

A method for storing and retrieving data based on tables, forms, queries, reports, fields, and other data elements. Each field represents a specific piece of data, such as an employee's last name. Records are made up of one or more fields. Each record is one complete entry in a table. A table contains one type of data, such as the names and addresses of all the employees in a company. It's composed of records (rows) and fields (columns), just like the tables you see in books. A database may contain one or more related tables. It may include a list of employees in one table, for example, and the pay records for each of those employees in a second table. Sometimes also referred to as a Relational Database Management System (RDBMS) that includes products such as SQL Server and Oracle.

DBCS

See Double-Byte Character Set

DBMS

See Database Management System

DCOM

See Distributed Component Object Model

DDoS

See Distributed Denial of Service

Denial of Service (DoS)

A type of Web-based attack intruders perpetrate against larger organizations such as companies and standards groups. The intruder attempts to flood organization routers with useless requests in order to cause the router to crash or make it unavailable for legitimate requests. The attack often depends on servers from other organizations and individuals (known as zombies) that the intruder has infected and taken over. These other servers all generate random messages with improper content in an attempt to overload the target systems. DoS attacks also rely on viruses created by the intruder that install the zombie program on the host computer.

DES

See Data Encryption Standard

DER

See Distinguished Encoding Rules

Digital Certificate

A specially encoded key pair used for identification. A certificate authority (CA) issues the digital certificate on behalf of the requestor after verifying the requestor's identity. The recipient of the digital certificate must trust both the requestor and the CA before digital certificate can lend credence to the source of the transmitted data. For this reason, self-signed certificates don't work for public purposes because they don't require any verification from a trusted third party. Digital certificates appear in many applications, everything from email applications to SSL.

Discretionary Access Control List (DACL)

A Windows security component. The DACL controls access to an object. You can assign both groups and individual users to a specific object.

Distinguished Encoding Rules (DER)

A technique for exporting a digital certificate from a memory or other data store to disk. The most common way to use this technique is to encode ASN.1 objects into a sequence of octets. DER provides unique encoding for all ASN.1 values. This is one of several forms of X.509 certificate.

Distributed Component Object Model (DCOM)

A binary data transport protocol that interacts with the Component Object Model (COM), and is used for distributed application development. This protocol enables data transfers across the Internet or other non-local sources, but is usually limited to a local area network (LAN) or wide area network (WAN) environment. DCOM adds the capability to perform asynchronous, as well as synchronous, data transfers between machines. The use of asynchronous transfers prevents the client application from becoming blocked as it waits for the server to respond.

Distributed Denial of Service (DDoS)

A specialized form of denial of service attack where the intruder relies on a multitude of zombie (remotely controlled) machines to perform a denial of service attack on a target network. The intruder may not even know how many machines are involved in the attack since this technique often relies on virus programs to install the required software on an unsuspecting host.

DLL

See Dynamic Link Library

DNS

See Domain Name System

DOE

Department of Energy

Domain Name System (DNS)

An Internet technology that allows a user to refer to a host computer by name rather than using its unique IP address. The DNS server translates the human-readable Web site name into an IP address.

DoS

See Denial of Service

Double-Byte Character Set (DBCS)

A character encoding technique that requires two bytes for each character instead of the one character used for the American Standard Code for Information Interchange (ASCII) and other character sets. The DBCS allows an application to display words using character sets from non–English speaking countries.

Drill-Down Approach

A technique for interacting with data where the viewer begins at an overview level and progressively selects more detail. At each level of detail, the viewer determines whether the display contains the required amount of information. When the viewer requires additional information, selecting a component of the current information set presents more information about that component. Consequently, the activity presents a visual metaphor of someone drilling through the information to locate a specific detail.

Dynamic Link Library (DLL)

A specific form of application code loaded into memory by request. It's not a stand-alone executable like an executable (EXE) file. A DLL does contain one or more discrete routines that an application may use to provide specific features. For example, a DLL could provide a common set of file dialogs used to access information on the hard drive. More than one application can use the functions provided by a DLL, reducing overall memory requirements when more than one application is running. DLLs have a number of purposes. For example, they can contain device specific code in the form of a device driver. Some types of COM objects also rely on DLLs.

E

Encode

The process of transforming a printable or abstract character into a coded format.

Extensible Markup Language (XML)

1. A method used to store information in an organized manner. The storage technique relies on hierarchical organization and uses special statements called tags to separate each storage element. Each tag defines a data attribute and can contain properties that further define each data element 2. A standardized Web page design language used to incorporate data structuring within standard HTML documents. For example, you could use XML to display database information using something other than forms or tables. It's actually a lightweight version of Standard Generalized Markup language (SGML) and is supported by the SGML community. XML also supports tag extensions that allow various parts of a Web-based application to exchange information. For example, once a user makes a choice within a catalog,

that information could be added to an order entry form with a minimum of effort on the part of the developer. Since XML is easy to extend, some developers look at it as more of a base specification for other languages, rather than a complete language.

F

File Extension

The characters used to define the kind of data the file contains. For example, the TXT extension identifies files with text (string) data in them, usually in human-readable form. The file extension appears after a final period in the filename such as MyFile.TXT. Windows relies mainly on three letter file extensions, but file extensions with four or more letters are becoming more common. For example, you'll find four-letter file extensions in common use with Office 2007 and Visual Studio .NET applications use some five-letter extensions.

File Transfer Protocol (FTP)

One of several common data transfer protocols for the Internet. This particular protocol specializes in data transfer in the form of a file download or upload. The site presents the user with a list of available files in a directory list format. An FTP site may choose DOS or UNIX formatting for the file listing, although the DOS format is extremely rare. Unlike HTTP sites, an FTP site provides a definite information hierarchy using directories and subdirectories, much like the file directory structure used on most workstation hard drives. In times past, FTP transfers required a special application, but many browsers now include this capability. FTP transfers occur without encryption, so security is an issue unless the owner of the FTP site encrypts the individual files.

Filtering (Data)

A technique for reviewing raw data and creating a data view that only includes records that meet specific criteria. For example, filtering a database would display only the records within the database that met the query requirements. Filtering a user interface displays only the user interface elements that meet the specified criteria. Filtering works with lists or any other organized form of data display.

Firewall

Hardware or software (or a combination of both) used to prevent unauthorized access to a private network. The firewall can use any of a number of techniques to detect unauthorized packets and deny access to them. Most firewalls not only check incoming packets but outgoing packets as well. There are many types of firewalls including packet filter, application gateway, proxy server, and circuit-level gateway. For maximum protection, the proxy server normally works best in a hardware configuration.

Folder

A specialized area (container) for storing files on the hard drive. Folders help you manage both data and applications by breaking them up into smaller and easier to recognize groups. The folder acts as a storage receptacle. The DOS and command prompt equivalent term for folders is directories; the same term used by many other operating systems.

FTP

See File Transfer Protocol

G

GAC

See Global Assembly Cache

Global Assembly Cache (GAC)

A central repository used by the .NET Framework for storing public managed components. The GAC contains only components with strong names, ensuring the integrity of the cache. In addition, the GAC can hold multiple versions of the same component, which ensures that applications can access the version of a component that they need, rather than the single version accessible to all applications. The GAC normally appears within the \WINDOWS\assembly folder of the hard drive.

Globalization

The act of converting an application of any type to support multiple languages and cultures. Simply providing multiple languages isn't enough in many cases, the application must provide any support that the user would normally expect of an application originally created for the user. For example, the application must provide properly formatted numbers and dates, present financial data in the proper way, and consider the social taboos of the viewer. A globalized application will make users in a number of countries feel comfortable using the application in their own language.

Globally Unique Identifier (GUID)

A 128-bit number originally used to identify a Component Object Model (COM) object within the Windows registry. Microsoft now uses the GUID wherever a system requires a unique identifier. When working in COM, the system uses the GUID to find the object definition and allow applications to create instances of that object. However, the system can use the GUID for other purposes as well. GUIDs can include any kind of object, even nonvisual elements. In addition, some types of complex objects are actually aggregates of simple objects. For example, an object that implements a property page will normally have a minimum of two GUIDs: one for the property page and another for the object itself.

Graphical User Interface (GUI)

1. A method of displaying information that depends on both hardware capabilities and software instructions. A GUI uses the graphics capability of a display adapter to improve communication between the device and its user. Using a GUI involves a large investment in both programming and hardware resources, but reduces overall system complexity for the user. 2. A system of icons and graphic images that replace the character-mode menu system used by many older devices. The GUI can ride on top of another operating system (such as DOS, Linux, and UNIX) or reside as part of the operating system itself (such as the Macintosh and Windows). Advantages of a GUI are ease of use and high-resolution graphics. Disadvantages include cost, higher workstation hardware requirements, and lower performance over a similar system using a character mode interface.

GUI

See Graphical User Interface

GUID

See Globally Unique Identifier

H

Hash

A technique for generating a number based on the content of string. The hash is significantly smaller than the string and of a consistent size making it useful for indexing tasks. Larger hashes tend to provide unique values for strings and are used for security purposes. A special application takes the string as input and outputs a numeric value for it. Using the hash value for comparison with a known good value (such as a password) doesn't compromise original value. The hash value is called a message digest and the hashing algorithm determines value of this digest.

Hierarchical

1. A method of arranging data within a database that relies on a tree-like node structure, rather than a relational structure. 2. A method of displaying information on screen that relies on an indeterminate number of nodes connected to a root node. 3. A chart or graph in which the elements are arranged in ranks. The ranks usually follow an order of simple to complex or higher to lower.

Host Protection Attribute (HPA)

Special instructions provided with a .NET API for the application that hosts the CLR environment. These attributes help the host application manage the API in various ways. For example, the SharedState HPA indicates whether the API provides the means to create or manage shared state information using features such as static fields. As another example, the Synchronization HPA indicates whether the API allows the host to perform synchronization between threads.

HPA

See Host Protection Attribute

HTML

See Hypertext Markup Language

HTTP

See Hypertext Transfer Protocol

HTTPS

See Hypertext Transfer Protocol Secure Sockets

Hypertext Markup Language (HTML)

1. A data presentation and description (markup) language for the Internet that depends on the use of tags (keywords within angle brackets <>) to display formatted information onscreen in a non-platform-specific manner. The non-platform-specific nature of this markup language makes it difficult to perform some basic tasks such as placement of a screen element at a specific location. However, the language does provide for the use of fonts, color, and various other enhancements on screen. There are also tags for displaying graphic images. Scripting tags for using scripting languages such as VBScript and JavaScript are available, although not all browsers support this addition. The <OBJECT> tag addition allows the use of ActiveX controls. 2. One method of displaying text, graphics, and sound on the Internet. HTML provides an ASCII-formatted page of information read by a special application called a browser. Depending on the browser's capabilities, some key words are translated into graphics elements, sounds, or text with special characteristics, such as color, font, or other attributes. Most browsers discard any keywords they don't understand, allowing browsers of various capabilities to explore the same page without problem. Obviously, there's a loss of capability if a browser doesn't support a specific keyword.

HyperText Transfer Protocol (HTTP)

One of several common data transfer protocols for the Internet. HTTP normally transfers textual data of some type. For example, the HyperText Markup Language (HTML) relies on HTTP to transfer the Web pages it defines from the server to the client. The XML and Simple Object Access Protocol (SOAP) also commonly rely on HTTP to transfer data between client and server. It's important to note that HTTP is separate from the data it transfers. For example, it's possible for SOAP to use the Simple Mail Transfer Protocol (SMTP) to perform data transfers between client and server.

Hypertext Transfer Protocol Secure Sockets (HTTPS)

A secure form of HyperText Transport Protocol (HTTP) that relies on the Secure Sockets Layer (SSL) encryption technology to transfer data.

I

IANA

Internet Assigned Numbers Authority

IBM

International Business Machines Corporation

IIS

See Internet Information Server

Interface

The connection between two programs, two program elements (such as classes), a person and the machine, or any other place where two entities touch. An interface defines the rules for contact between the two entities. For example, a software interface normally defines the properties and methods used to initiate contact between two software elements.

Internet Information Server (IIS)

Microsoft's Web server that runs under the Windows operating system. IIS includes all of the standard Web server features including File Transfer Protocol (FTP) and HyperText Transfer Protocol (HTTP), along with both mail and news services in older versions of the product. The latest version of IIS concentrates on developer requirements and doesn't provide mail and news services. This newer version of IIS relies on a modular approach that depends on the .NET Framework, rather than the monolithic architecture used in older versions of IIS.

Internet Server Application Programming Interface (ISAPI)

A set of function calls and interface elements designed to help developers create applications for Microsoft's Internet Information Server (IIS). Essentially, this set of API calls provides the programmer with access to the server itself. This technology makes it easier to provide full application access to the Internet server so the developer can perform tasks such as Web page redirection, security checks, and incoming data parsing. There are two forms of ISAPI: filters and extensions. An ISAPI extension replaces script-based technologies such CGI. Its main purpose is to provide dynamic content to the

user. An ISAPI filter can extend the server itself by monitoring various events like user requests for access in the background. You can use a filter to create various types of new services like extended logging or specialized security schemes. Most developers use technologies such as Active Server Pages (ASP) or the newer ASP.NET in place of ISAPI because these technologies are easier to use. However, ISAPI is still used for a few speed critical applications such as the Simple Object Access Protocol (SOAP) listener used by some SOAP implementations. Expect to see ASP.NET replace ISAPI at some point because ASP.NET is based on a newer managed code technology.

ISAPI

See Internet Server Application Programming Interface

ISO

International Standards Organization

J

Java Runtime Environment (JRE)

Another name for the Java Virtual Machine (JVM). This set of files provides Java support on the host machine allowing it to run Java applications.

Java Server Pages (JSP)

A technology developed by Sun for combining HTML tags with script to produce dynamic Web content. The technology isn't that much different from ASP in concept. (In fact, Sun developed JSP as an alternative to ASP.) In theory, the Web server translates the JSP into a Java servlet before it runs the resulting application. The main reason to use JSP is the simplicity it offers over creating a Java servlet.

JIT Compiler

See Just-in-Time Compiler

JRE

See Java Runtime Environment

JSP

See Java Server Pages

Just-in-Time Compiler (JIT Compiler)

The component of the .NET Framework that transforms the .NET application tokenized executable files into native executables.

L

LAN

See Local Area Network

LCID

See Locale Identifier

Local Area Network (LAN)

Two or more devices located in a relatively small physical area connected together using a combination of hardware and software. The devices, normally computers and peripheral equipment such as printers, are called nodes. A Network Interface Card (NIC) provides the hardware communication between nodes through an appropriate medium (cable, wireless, infrared, microwave transmission, or other means). There are two common types of LANs (also called networks). Peer-to-peer networks allow each node to connect to any other node on the network with shareable resources. This is a distributed method of files and peripheral devices. A client-server network uses one or more servers to share resources. This is a centralized method of sharing files and peripheral devices. A server provides resources to clients (usually workstations).

Local Security Authority (LSA)

The portion of Windows that monitors local security activities.

Locale Identifier (LCID)

A number that uniquely identifies a country, language, or other nationalistic information. An application, online resource, or data manager uses the LCID to provide specific information, services, or resources in a form that the user can understand. For example, many applications support more than one language and the application would use the LCID to change the prompts to match the user's language.

Locally Unique Identifier (LUID)

Essentially a pointer to an object, the LUID identifies each process and its associated resources for security purposes. In other words, even if a user opens two copies of precisely the same resource (such as a document), both copies would have a unique LUID. This method of identification prevents some types of security access violation under Windows.

LSA

See Local Security Authority

LUID

See Locally Unique Identifier

M

Managed Module

A DLL or other application element that relies on the Microsoft .NET Framework for resources, the garbage collector associated with the .NET Framework for memory management, and other elements that reflect the .NET manner of performing tasks. Using managed modules relieves the developer from performing most memory management tasks, simplifies the development environment, and hides some development details. A developer compiles managed module code into tokenized Intermediate Language (IL) form, which is then interpreted by CLR during execution.

Mapping

The act of creating a connection between an event and the event handler. For example, when a client makes a request, a handler mapping defines how to react to the request. A mapping normally includes the event to map, such as a request for a particular kind of file or a click of a button on a form, and the identification of the event handler, which is normally a piece of software.

MD5

See Message Digest 5

Media Player 3 (MP3)

A type of media encoding that relies on the Motion Picture Experts Group (MPEG) layer 3 standard. MPEG offers three encoding layer standards (layer 1 through layer 3). The layer 3 encoding removes all of the redundant portions of the sound signal that the human ear can't hear to provide compression. It also includes a MDCT (Modified Discrete Cosine Transform) filter that improves frequency resolution over that provided by layer 2.

Message Digest 5 (MD5)

The mathematical basis for creating a message digest (a value) based on the content of the message. The basis of this technology is that no two messages will produce the same message digest. Consequently, the recipient can validate the content of a message by performing the calculation and comparing it to the message digest value. MD5 is a one-way hash, which means that it isn't used for encrypting and decrypting the data. Professor Ronal Rivest created MD5 in 1991 to verify the authenticity of digital signatures.

Message Transfer Agent (MTA)

An X.400 standard term that refers to the part of a Message Transfer System (MTS) responsible for interacting with the client. For example, in an email system, the MTA delivers email to the individual users of that system. Microsoft Exchange Server is an example of an MTA.

Message Transfer System (MTS)

A method of transferring email from one location to another. In some cases, the transfer requires some form of encryption along with other transport-specific details. Most servers provide some type of MTS as part of their base services. However, the Internet requires special transport mechanisms. Several standards are available on the Internet for providing MTS as part of a Web site. The two most notable specifications are RFC 1421 from the Internet Engineering Task Force (IETF) and X.400 from the International Telecommunication Union (ITU).

Microsoft Intermediate Language (MSIL)

The tokenized output of all .NET language compilers. The Common Language Runtime (CLR) reads the MSIL output and uses the just-in-time (JIT) compiler to convert it to platform-specific code, which the platform then executes.

Microsoft Management Console (MMC)

An application that hosts specially constructed Component Object Model (COM) objects called snap-ins that help the user manage Windows, a device, or an application. MMC acts as an object container for Windows management objects such as Component Services and Computer Management. The management objects are actually special components that provide interfaces that allow the user to access them within MMC to maintain and control the operation of Windows. A developer can create special versions of these objects for application management or other tasks. Using a single application like MMC helps maintain the same user interface across all management applications. The combination of one or more snap-ins and the MMC host is called a console and the settings appear within Microsoft Console (MSC) files.

MIME

See Multipurpose Internet Mail Extensions

MMC

See Microsoft Management Console

Motion Picture Experts Group (MPEG)

A standards group that provides file formats and other specifications about full-motion video and other types of graphic displays.

MPEG2 Standard

Defines a method for transferring multimedia from a source to an application capable of displaying it on a device such as a monitor. The transfer can take place locally or over a network, including the Internet. This standard defines techniques for transferring 720×480 and 1280×720 resolution images at 60 frames per second (fps), with full CD-quality audio. The resulting data flow provides support for all of the major TV standards including National Television System Committee (NTSC) and High Definition Television (HDTV). (Originally, MPEG designed the MPEG3 standard for HDTV, but abandoned the effort.) In addition to the Internet, DVDs common rely on MPEG2 for data compression needs.

MP3

See Media Player 3

MPEG

See Motion Picture Experts Group

MSIL

See Microsoft Intermediate Language

MTA

See Message Transfer Agent

MTS

See Message Transfer System

Multipurpose Internet Mail Extensions (MIME)

The standard method for defining the content types of Internet messages. This standard allows computers to exchange objects, character sets, and multimedia using email without regard to the computer's underlying operating system. MIME is defined in the Internet Engineering Task Force (IETF) RFC 1521 standard.

N

Native Module

An older (unmanaged) DLL or other application element that lacks support for memory management and other features such as a garbage collector. These older modules normally support the Windows 32-bit Application Programming Interface (Win32 API) directly. The developer compiles the code directly into an executable file, rather than the Intermediate Language (IL) tokenized files that .NET modules use.

NCSA

National Center for Supercomputing Applications

O

ODBC

See Open Database Connectivity

Open Database Connectivity (ODBC)

One of several methods for exchanging data between database management systems (DBMSs).

In most cases, this involves three steps: installing an appropriate driver, adding a source to the Data Sources (ODBC) console in the Administrative Tools folder of the Control Panel, and using specialized statements, such as Structured Query Language (SQL), to access the database. The precise functionality and configuration requirements of ODBC depend on the ODBC driver used to create the connection.

P

PDF

See Portable Document Format

PEM

See Privacy Enhanced Mail

PERL

See Practical Extraction and Report Language

Permission

The level of access granted to an individual user, machine, process, or a Windows object to acquire and use resources controlled by the host machine or the server.

Personal Information Exchange File (PFX)

A technique for exporting a digital certificate from a memory or other data store to disk. This is one of several forms of X.509 certificate. In this case, the resulting file includes both the certificate and optionally, the private key associated with it. The PFX file relies on the Public Key Cryptography Standard #12 (PKCS #12) standard.

PFX

See Personal Information Exchange File

PHP

See PHP Hypertext Processor

PHP Hypertext Processor (PHP)

A scripting language used mainly for Web page design. The PHP language strength lies with its compatibility with a wide range of database management systems (DBMSs). As with ASP, the developer can switch easily between HTML and PHP, making it possible to create complex Web pages using script alone. Rasmus Lerdorf created PHP sometime in 1994. At this time, the original abbreviation meant Personal Home Page Hypertext Preprocessor, but it was later changed when the project became a public effort. Zeev Suraski and Andi Gutmans eventually rewrote the PHP parser from scratch to solve a number of issues in the PHP versions prior to PHP 3.

PID

See Process Identifier

PKCS

See Public Key Cryptographic System

Portable Document Format (PDF)

A formatted, book-like, document format originally created by Adobe. This document format initially captured the output of desktop publishing applications. Many other applications, especially graphics applications, now output to the PDF format. Users can view PDF files using the free Acrobat Reader utility or other applications.

Practical Extraction and Report Language (PERL)

Originally designed as a report generation language for the Internet, PERL has found other uses as well for more general Internet programming needs. PERL is normally an interpreted scripting language.

Privacy Enhanced Mail (PEM)

A multipart specification that defines how to maintain the privacy of email. It includes sections on email encryption, security key management, cryptography, and security key certification. The cryptography portion of the specification includes algorithms, usage modes, and identifiers specifically for PEM use.

Process Identifier (PID)

A numeric value associated with a process running on a specific machine. Every process has a unique PID, making it possible to locate a specific process, even if multiple copies of a single application are running on the machine. The PID is used by a wide variety of monitoring applications. It's also used to access an application or as a means of identification when terminating an errant application.

Provider (IIS)

The means of connecting a security database to an application or other Internet Information Server (IIS) feature. The two-part process of using a provider includes creating a connection string and then coupling the connection to the application. The provider acts as an intermediary between the IIS feature and the database. The connection doesn't provide database connectivity of the usual sort; the application won't use it for storing data. Instead, the IIS provider creates a connection to a source of users, roles, and profiles for an IIS feature.

Public Key Cryptographic System (PKCS)

A series of standards produced by RSA Laboratories to define the encryption and decryption of data using public key cryptography. You can learn more about these standards at `http://www.rsa.com/rsalabs/node.asp?id=2124`.

Q

Queue

A programming construct where new entities appear at the end of a memory area and old entities are removed from the beginning of a memory area. A queue is familiar to anyone who has ever stood in line for any type of service. The caller requests for computer services wait in line precisely the same way.

R

Realm

The means used to identify a particular server to a user when the server requests name and password. The realm uniquely identifies the server so that the user knows which name and password to provide as input when the user has connections to multiple servers.

Registry

A specialized hierarchical database used to hold settings, configuration, file associations, and other information for Windows. The registry is a hierarchy or tree consisting of keys and associated values. The operating system searches the registry tree for keys that it requires, then requests values for those keys in order to perform tasks such as configure an application. The registry is organized into hives. Each hive contains settings for a particular operating system element such as user information and hardware configuration. Users share common hives such as those used for hardware, but have separate hives for their information as long as Windows is configured to provide separate desktops for each user.

Response Module

The portion of the Internet Information Server (IIS) that formulates the method of handling caller requests. A response module creates output based on a particular kind of request. For example, when the caller requests a static Web page, the response module sends the requested HTML file.

Role-Based Security

A method for controlling access to an object based on the requestor's job function within an organization. In other words, if the requestor has a specific job function (or role), then they are allowed to access the object. This method of maintaining security is an extension of groups. However, unlike groups, a requestor must perform a specific job function before access is granted. This security methodology began with COM+ applications. It also appears as part of applications based on the .NET Framework.

S

SACL

See Security Access Control List

Script Map

The act of creating a connection between an event and script to handle it. In most cases, the hander is an EXE or DLL file. Script maps provide support for older native code handlers. For example, Internet Information Server (IIS) uses a script map to create a handler entry for ISAPI extensions.

Secure Socket Layer (SSL)

A digital signature technology used for exchanging information between a client and a server. An SSL compliant server will provide a digital certificate to the client machine as proof of the originating source of information. The server can also request that the client provide such a certificate. The certificates are used to encrypt data flowing through a network, such as the Internet, between the client and the server. Companies or individuals obtain these digital certificates from a third-party vendor like VeriSign or other trusted source that can vouch for the identity of both parties. It's also possible to implement SSL for testing or local purposes using a self-signed certificate.

Security Access Control List (SACL)

One of several specialized Access Control Lists (ACL) used to maintain object integrity. This list controls Windows' auditing feature. Every time a user or group accesses an object and the auditing feature for that object is turned on, Windows makes an entry in the audit log.

Security Descriptor

A reference to the level of security assigned to an object. This is the data structure that tells the security system what rights a requestor, such as a user, needs to access the object. The user's rights are contained with an access token. In short, the security descriptor is the lock and the access token is the key.

Server-Side Include (SSI)

A type of special tag added to Web pages that directs the Web server to generate special data, such as the server's date and time. The tag takes the form of a command that begins with a special symbol, the cross hatch (#) in most cases, within a comment, such as `<!--#command tag="value"...>`. Common keywords include #config, #echo, #exec, #flastmod, #fsize, and #include.

Session State

The data that defines a particular interaction between a client and server. The data includes a session identifier, the user's data, the application data, and any required server data. When used with a Web application, the session state must include a unique identifier and the application must provide a stable means of passing the data elements between client and server. One of the most common means of storing session state is cookies. However, the application can also rely on server-side database storage, the request header (POST method), or encoding within the URL (GET method).

SHTML/SHTM/STM File

A secure version of the standard HyperText Markup Language (HTML) file. It contains all of the same elements as an HTML file, with some additional security features.

Simple Mail Transfer Protocol (SMTP)

One of the most commonly used protocols to transfer text (commonly email) messages between clients and servers. This is a stream-based protocol designed to allow query, retrieval, posting, and distribution of email messages. Normally this protocol is used in conjunction with other email retrieval protocols such as point of presence (POP). However, not all uses of SMTP involve email data transfer. Some Simple Object Access Protocol (SOAP) applications have also relied on SMTP to transfer application data.

Simple Object Access Protocol (SOAP)

A protocol that provides the means for exchanging data between a requestor and a server. Originally, SOAP provided the means for binary technologies such as Component Object Model (COM) to exchange data with other binary technologies such as Common Object Request Broker Architecture (CORBA) using Extensible Markup Language (XML) as an intermediary. However, SOAP is often used as the basis for Web services communication today. A developer could also use SOAP on a local area network (LAN) or in any other environment that requires machine-to-machine communication and the two target machines provide the required infrastructure.

Single Threaded Apartment (STA)

A method of defining how object methods get executed. STAs include three restrictions not found in multi-threaded apartments (MTAs). The first is that an STA contains one, and only one, object. This ensures that once a component is instantiated, that the resulting object doesn't share memory space with any other object, which could result in corruption. The second restriction is that one, and only one, thread can enter the apartment to interact with the object inside. The reason for this restriction is obvious. A single threaded object can only handle the requests of one thread at a time, which means that COM must protect the object from access by more than one thread.

Ensuring that only one thread can enter the apartment at a time is the easiest way to accomplish this task. Finally, a thread can execute only one object method at a time. This restriction ensures that there won't be any data corruption due to shared variables within the object. As a result of these restrictions, a single process could contain multiple STAs; one for each STA object that the application instantiated.

SMPTE

See Society of Motion Picture and Television Engineers

SMTP

See Simple Mail Transfer Protocol

SOAP

See Simple Object Access Protocol

Society of Motion Picture and Television Engineers (SMPTE)

A standards group founded in 1916 to provide standards in full motion imaging technology.

SSI

See Server-Side Include

SSL

See Secure Socket Layer

STA

See Single Threaded Apartment

String

Two or more characters connected to form a word or other character-based information. Strings normally provide human-readable data, but you can find non-human-readable forms. For example, even though a path and filename normally appear in a string, you have to know how to read the string to interpret it correctly.

T

TCP/IP

See Transmission Control Protocol/Internet Protocol

Transaction Authority Markup Language (XAML)

A vendor-neutral technology for conducting multi-party business transactions within Web services. A transaction can't complete until all of the parties agree that it has completed. This technology appears as part of Microsoft's new Silverlight product (among other vendor offerings). Don't confuse this technology with Microsoft's similarly named eXtensible Application Markup Language (XAML) technology that provides user interface functionality. This form of XAML appears as part of the Windows Presentation Foundation (WPF) in the .NET Framework 3.0. (See `http://msdn2.microsoft.com/en-us/library/ms752059.aspx` for details on this second form of XAML.)

Transmission Control Protocol/Internet Protocol (TCP/IP)

A standard communication line protocol (set of rules) developed by the United States Department of Defense. The protocol defines how two devices talk to each other. TCP defines a communication methodology where it guarantees packet delivery and ensures the packets appear at the recipient in the same order they were sent. IP defines the packet characteristics.

Trust Level

A method for defining and managing the activities that code can perform on a system. The trust level defines how much trust the system can place in a particular piece of code. Restrictions ensure that the code can only perform safe tasks within its sphere of responsibility for processing data or achieving other goals.

U

UNC

See Universal Naming Convention

Unicode Transformation Format (UTF)

A standardized method of representing characters both printed and abstract using codes. Another term applied to this form of communication is encoding; assigning a numeric value to letters, characters, and symbols to define human-readable data in a form the computer can manipulate. Other forms of character representation include American Standard Code for Information Interchange (ASCII). Some sources also abbreviate this term as Universal Character Set (UCS) Transformation Format.

Uniform Resource Identifier (URI)

A generic term for all names and addresses that reference objects on the Internet. A URL is a specific type of URI. See Uniform Resource Locator (URL).

Uniform Resource Locator (URL)

A text representation of a specific location on the Internet. URLs normally include the protocol (http:// for example), the target location (World Wide Web or www), the domain or server name (mycompany), and a domain type (com for commercial). (Many URLs don't include the www portion of the address anymore.) It can also include a hierarchical location within that Web site. The URL usually specifies a particular file on the Web server, although there are some situations when a Web server will use a default filename. For example, asking the browser to find `http://www.mycompany.com`, would probably display the DEFAULT.HTM or INDEX.HTM file at that location. The actual default filename depends on the Web server used. In some cases, the default filename is configurable and could be any of a number of files. For example, Internet Information Server (IIS) offers this feature, so the developer can use anything from an HTM, to an ASP, to an XML file as the default.

Universal Naming Convention (UNC)

A method for identifying network resources without specifying a local resource such as a drive letter. In most cases, a user will employ this convention with drives and printers, but the user can also apply it to other types of resources. A UNC normally includes a server name followed by a device name in place of a local identifier. For example, a user might refer to a disk drive on a remote machine as `"\\AUX\DRIVE_C."` The advantage of using UNC is that the resource name won't change, even if the user's local device mappings do.

URI

See Uniform Resource Identifier

URL

See Uniform Resource Locator

UTF

See Unicode Transformation Format

V

Virtual Directory

A pointer to an actual directory on a hard drive. The virtual directory provides indirect access of the resources in the actual directory. It provides a convenient means of access from a central location, such as a Web site.

W

W3C

See World Wide Web Consortium

WAN

See Wide Area Network

Web Services Description Language (WSDL)

A method of describing a Web-based application (Web service) that's accessible through an Internet or intranet connection. The file associated with this description contains the service description, port type, interface description, individual method names, and parameter types. A WSDL file relies on namespace support to provide descriptions of common elements such as data types. Most WSDL files include references to two or more resources maintained by standards organizations to ensure compatibility across implementations.

Wide Area Network (WAN)

An extension of the local area network (LAN), a WAN connects two or more LANs together using a variety of methods. A WAN usually encompasses more than one physical site, such as a building. Most WANs rely on microwave communications, fiber optic connections, leased telephone lines, or virtual private network (VPN) to provide the internetwork connections to keep all nodes in the network talking with each other.

Wildcard Character

A special character used to represent one or more letters, numbers, punctuation characters, or other special characters. For example, the `Dir` (directory) command can use the asterisk (*) to represent any number of characters and the question mark (?) to represent a single character. Applications also use wildcard characters. For example, word processors often use wildcard characters to help you search for strings. Programming languages implement a complex wildcard character scenario called regular expressions used to match patterns in strings such as a telephone number.

Windows Media Audio (WMA)

Microsoft's media file format for streaming audio.

Windows Media Video (WMV)

Microsoft's media file format for streaming video.

WMA

See Windows Media Audio

WMV

See Windows Media Video

World Wide Web Consortium (W3C)

A standards organization devoted to Internet standards, especially security issues. This organization is also involved in other issues such as defining the special <OBJECT> tag used to implement ActiveX technology. The W3C also defines a wealth of other HTML and XML standards. The W3C first appeared in December 1994, when it endorsed the SSL (Secure Sockets Layer) standard. In February 1995, it also endorsed application-level security for the Internet.

WSDL

See Web Services Description Language

X

XAML

See Transaction Authority Markup Language

XML

See Extensible Markup Language

XML Schema Definition (XSD)

The portion of the Extensible Markup Language (XML) specification that defines data types and other data elements. Most browsers and other applications use XSD to verify the XML document. XSD is also related to a Web site containing such information by use of XML parsers. A designer can create a custom XSD for use with a particular application.

XSD

See XML Schema Definition

Index

Note to Reader: **Bolded** page numbers indicate main discussions and definitions. *Italicized* page numbers indicate illustrations.